C104 .T74 2006

ransnational identities
and practices in Canada
c2006.

Transnational Identities and Practices in Canada

Edited by Vic Satzewich and Lloyd Wong

Transnational Identities
and Practices in Canada

1 6 5 101

UBCPress · Vancouver · Toronto

15 14 13 12 11 10 09 08 07 06   5 4 3 2 1

Printed in Canada on ancient-forest-free paper (100% post-consumer recycled)
that is processed chlorine- and acid-free, with vegetable-based inks.

Library and Archives Canada Cataloguing in Publication

Transnational identities and practices in Canada / edited by Vic Satzewich and
Lloyd Wong.

Includes bibliographical references and index.
ISBN-13: 978-0-7748-1283-2
ISBN-10: 0-7748-1283-4

1. Transnationalism – Social aspects – Canada. 2. Transnationalism – Political
aspects – Canada. 3. Ethnicity – Canada. 4. Immigrants – Canada. 5. Ethnic groups
– Canada. 6. Multiculturalism – Canada. I. Satzewich, Vic, 1961- II. Wong, Lloyd
L. (Lloyd Lee), 1950-

FC104.T74 2006   305.8'00971   C2006-900497-8

Canadä

UBC Press gratefully acknowledges the financial support for our publishing
program of the Government of Canada through the Book Publishing Industry
Development Program (BPIDP), and of the Canada Council for the Arts, and
the British Columbia Arts Council.

This book has been published with the help of a grant from the Canadian
Federation for the Humanities and Social Sciences, through the Aid to Scholarly
Publications Programme, using funds provided by the Social Sciences and
Humanities Research Council of Canada.

UBC Press
The University of British Columbia
2029 West Mall
Vancouver, BC V6T 1Z2
604-822-5959 / Fax: 604-822-6083
www.ubcpress.ca

This book is dedicated to:

"The guys," again, Linda, Lucy, and Jack
– Vic Satzewich

Colleen, Leanne, Curtis, and Jasmine, and in memory
of my parents, Lee and Mavis Wong
– Lloyd Wong

Contents

Figures and Tables / ix

Preface and Acknowledgments / xi

Introduction: The Meaning and Significance of Transnationalism / 1
Lloyd Wong and Vic Satzewich

Part 1: Transnationalism in Historical and Political Perspective

1 The Politics of Transnationalism: Comparative Perspectives / 18
Sarah V. Wayland

2 Transnationalism and the Age of Mass Migration, 1880s to 1920s / 35
Christiane Harzig and Dirk Hoerder

3 Unmaking a Transnational Community: Japanese Canadian Families in
Wartime Canada / 52
Pamela Sugiman

Part 2: Contemporary Patterns

4 Characteristics of Immigrant Transnationalism in Vancouver / 71
Daniel Hiebert and David Ley

5 Transnational Urbanism: Toronto at a Crossroads / 91
Valerie Preston, Audrey Kobayashi, and Myer Siemiatycki

6 Contentious Politics and Transnationalism from Below:
The Case of Ethnic and Racialized Minorities in Quebec / 111
Micheline Labelle, François Rocher, and Ann-Marie Field

7 The Caribbean Community in Canada: Transnational Connections
and Transformations / 130
Alan B. Simmons and Dwaine E. Plaza

8 The Maple-Neem Nexus: Transnational Links of South Asian Canadians / 150
Dhiru Patel

9 The Invisible Transnationals? Americans in Canada / 164
Kim Matthews and Vic Satzewich

10 Latin American Transnationalism in Canada: Does It Exist, What Forms
Does It Take, and Where Is It Going? / 180
Luin Goldring

11 The New "In-Between" Peoples: Southern-European Transnationalism / 202
Luis L.M. Aguiar

12 Whose Transnationalism? Canada, "Clash of Civilizations" Discourse,
and Arab and Muslim Canadians / 216
Sedef Arat-Koc

13 Chinese Transnationalism: Class and Capital Flows / 241
Lloyd Wong and Connie Ho

14 Raising the Iron Curtain: Transnationalism and the Croatian Diaspora
since the Collapse of 1989 / 261
Daphne Winland

15 Canadian Jewry and Transnationalism: Israel, Anti-Semitism, and
the Jewish Diaspora / 278
Stuart Schoenfeld, William Shaffir, and Morton Weinfeld

Conclusion: Directions for Future Research / 296
Vic Satzewich and Lloyd Wong

References / 299

Contributors / 327

Index / 333

Figures and Tables

Figures

5.1 Immigrant arrivals from Hong Kong to Toronto / 95

8.1 Multidimensional transnational relationships / 153

8.2 South Asian Canadians' contact with family in Canada, countries of origin, and other countries / 155

Tables

4.1 Enumeration of transnational activities among Vancouver residents / 76

4.2 Respondents engaged in transnational activities by level of educational attainment / 79

4.3 Respondents engaged in transnational activities by 2001 household income / 79

4.4 Respondents engaged in transnational activities by period of landing / 81

4.5 Respondents engaged in transnational activities by selected immigration class / 81

4.6 Respondents engaged in transnational activities by ethnic origin / 83

4.7 Respondents engaged in transnational activities by interview language / 83

4.8 Respondents engaged in transnational activities by home language / 85

4.9 Respondents engaged in transnational activities by citizenship status / 85

4.10 Respondents engaged in transnational activities by identification as Canadian / 87

5.1 Hong Kong immigrants by location within the Toronto Census metropolitan area, 2001 / 98

5.2 Civic participation in Toronto by Hong Kong immigrants / 101

10.1 Frequency of contact with family in the country of origin or ancestry, for the population with such family, Canada, 2002 / 188

10.2 Period of entry to Canada by country of birth for Latin American immigrants (pre-1961 to 2001) and rate of change between 1981-90 and 1991-2001 / 196

13.1 Chinese immigrants to Canada: Sum and mean money in possession, 1986-2002 / 253

13.2 Chinese immigrants to Canada: Sum and mean money in possession by class, 1986-2002 / 255

13.3 Chinese immigrants: Source and sums of the flow of capital into Canada after arrival / 256

13.4 Chinese immigrants and business immigrants: Capital in flow, *in situ,* and elsewhere at time of arrival in Canada / 257

Preface and Acknowledgments

For much of the 1970s, '80s, and '90s in Canada, research in the area of immigrant and ethnic-group settlement focused on issues of economic integration, social inequality, language maintenance, ethnic-identity retention, maintenance and change, and racism, prejudice, and discrimination. If there was a gap in the literature on immigrant and "race"/ethnic relations, it was arguably most noticeable in the area of transnationalism. In other words, even though immigrant and ethnic relations were among the most researched areas of Canadian social life, there was a real silence within the academic literature both on the extent to which immigrants and members of ethnic groups maintain ties with their real and imagined homelands and on the personal, cultural, and institutional meanings and consequences associated with these ties.

This book answers a call made in the late 1990s by Daphne Winland in her article "'Our Home and Native Land'? Canadian Ethnic Scholarship and the Challenge of Transnationalism," in the *Canadian Review of Sociology and Anthropology* (1998). Canadian ethnic research and scholarship has traditionally analyzed groups, and intergroup relations, within the Canadian context and within the Canadian nation-state. This boundedness, as Winland pointed out, left little conceptual space for notions of transnationalism. She proposed a shift in analytical focus and discourse for Canadian ethnic studies that would put greater emphasis on transnationalism and its role in producing cultural practices and identities among immigrant and ethnic communities in Canada.

It has become clear that in a globalizing world individuals and institutions increasingly have multiple linkages and interactions that span the borders of nation-states. Although it is widely recognized that immigrants never completely sever ties with their families and homelands, the consensus among academic commentators is that the past twenty years have seen the emergence of quantitatively more and qualitatively different kinds of transnational linkages. At both the personal and institutional levels, these linkages are increasingly facilitated by advances in communications and transportation technology. Such changes in immigrants' lives have been met with a growing academic interest in the many facets of transnationalism, including transnational identities, social networks, family relationships, and migration as well as transnationalism within political, social-movement, religious, media, and economic institutional spheres.

This book analyzes existing transnational communities in Canada and the associated transnational identities and practices of individuals within these communities. It consists of an integrated collection of chapters on selected transnational communities written by some of Canada's most astute social scientists and historians. This is the first collection in Canada to present a comprehensive and interdisciplinary examination of transnationalism. We hope readers will enjoy the chapters as much as we have enjoyed working with the authors and bringing the collection together.

We are deeply indebted to the authors, who not only produced finely crafted pieces of work, but also graciously accepted editorial advice, met deadlines, and responded in a timely way to hurried e-mails. Emily Andrew, senior acquisitions editor at UBC Press, was enthusiastic about this project from the start. She helped us to stay on track, kept us well informed about the publication process, and was simply a pleasure to work with. As well, we would like to acknowledge Darcy Cullen, who oversaw the editing and production of the book, and Robert Lewis, who was responsible for copy editing the manuscript.

We also want to thank the anonymous referees who evaluated and commented on each of the chapters and on the manuscript as a whole. We appreciate their critical yet supportive and helpful comments. We also want to thank the departments of sociology at the University of Calgary and McMaster University for providing supportive environments in which to do research.

Vic Satzewich and Lloyd Wong

Transnational Identities and Practices in Canada

Introduction:
The Meaning and Significance
of Transnationalism
Lloyd Wong and Vic Satzewich

In a recent comparison with Britain, France, and Germany, the United States is described as "the foremost transnational nation" and as the country that "has gone the farthest in the development of a pluralistic community of citizens" (Munch 2001, 48, 57). If Canada were included in this comparison, there are reasons to expect that the ranking would change. On a yearly basis, the United States admits about four times as many immigrants as Canada, but few countries match Canada in the number of immigrants that they admit on a per capita basis. Further, Canada has displayed a long-lasting commitment to the principles of multiculturalism, which may have a role to play in fuelling transnationalism.

At the level of public policy, multiculturalism was institutionalized in Canada in 1971 as a form of corporate pluralism (Gordon 1981). Under this policy, cultural differences were encouraged and protected by the state, while ideologies of cultural assimilation and Anglo conformity for immigrants and ethnic minorities were officially rejected. Over the past three decades, as the Canadian policy on multiculturalism has evolved (Fleras and Elliott 2002, 62-68), there has been greater emphasis on encouraging immigrants to engage in transnational social practices and to develop transnational social identities. From one perspective, transnational practices and identities can be viewed as the logical extension of multiculturalism. However, transnationalism can also be viewed as challenging forms of multiculturalism that are bounded by the nation-state. For example, for the past ten years, the Canadian government has advanced the notion of "civic multiculturalism" with the goal of creating a sense of belonging and attachment to Canada among immigrants (68). Yet for some of these immigrants, transnational practices, like obtaining dual citizenship and becoming involved in the politics of their homelands, would suggest a sense of belonging and attachment that extends beyond Canadian borders and that thus poses a challenge to the present form of multicultural policy.

Given transnationalism's significance for the immigrant generation and given that its practices both extend and challenge multiculturalism, researchers in Canada have good cause to take transnationalism seriously.

Fortunately, they have done so. The aim of this book is to present the current state of research on transnationalism in Canada by bringing together a group of scholars working from a variety of perspectives. Canadian scholars have been at the forefront of research on immigrant settlement and community formation, and an ever-growing body of literature now frames issues in terms of the concept of transnationalism. A cross-section of this literature is brought together in this single volume.

The importance of this undertaking is underlined by four factors. First, transnational practices are an enduring aspect of the lives of immigrants and longer-settled members of ethnic communities. Although transnationalism is not a new phenomenon, modern communications and transportation technologies enable individuals and groups to engage in increasingly frequent and significant transnational practices.

Second, many different individuals, groups, practices, and identities have been described as transnational. Thus there is a need to establish the conceptual, theoretical, and empirical bases for the use of this concept in Canada. Like diaspora, transnationalism is an extraordinarily elastic concept that has been stretched to cover a range of activities and individuals. Sociologist Floya Anthias (1998) argues that the concept of diaspora is now so popular in academic circles that it is becoming a "mantra." Historian Donald Akenson (1995) also suggests that the concept of diaspora is akin to a massive linguistic weed that threatens to take over the discourse about migration and settlement in Canada. Both observations can arguably be applied to the concept of transnationalism.

Third, further debate and research about the meaning and significance of transnationalism are clearly warranted. Although the chapters in this volume are not "comparative" in the strict sense of the term, the diversity of groups, practices, and identities treated in the book may serve as a springboard for thinking more comparatively about transnationalism.

Fourth, transnationalism is a global phenomenon marked by local distinctions. Whether the transnational practices of immigrants and ethnic communities in Canada differ from those of immigrants in other countries is a question of interest. This volume makes comparisons of transnational experience possible by providing insights into the particulars of "Canadian-based" transnational practices and identities.

Conceptual Issues

Two recent developments attest to the growing importance of assessing the phenomenon of transnationalism. During the past decade, research funding has increasingly supported studies on transnationalism. At the same time, there has been a flourish of themed special issues on transnationalism in major academic journals, including "Transnational Migration: International Perspectives" (2003), in *International Migration Review;* "Transnational Communities" (1999) and "Transnational Edges" (2003), in *Ethnic and Racial Studies;* "New Research and Theory on Immigrant Transnationalism" (2001), in *Global Networks;* and "Transnationalism and Identity" (2001), in the *Journal of Ethnic and Migration Studies.*

Over the years, the transnational perspective has evolved conceptually both in Europe and the United States. The following discussion frames some of these developments in the context of the wider literature on immigration and ethnicity, lends weight to the transnational perspective, and assesses these developments vis-à-vis Canadian literature and research.

Conceptualizing the Transnational Perspective

In the early 1990s the work of cultural anthropologists Nina Glick Schiller, Linda Basch, and Christina Szanton Blanc set the stage for theorizing migration using a transnational perspective. This perspective conceptualized many contemporary immigrants not as "uprooted" or as having completely left behind their "old" countries but as maintaining multiple links and networks with their homelands (Glick Schiller, Basch, and Szanton Blanc 1995, 48).

Scholars in other fields also began arguing for a transnational perspective. The early 1990s saw the launch of *Diaspora: A Journal of Transnational Studies,* which features writings about diasporas, transnationalism, or both by scholars from a variety of disciplines. The transnational perspective emerged in the mid-1990s as a challenge to the more traditional understanding of immigration, which implicitly or explicitly assumes that immigrants leave behind their countries of origin upon entering a new country.

Canada has been slow to adopt a transnational perspective. Not until the late 1990s and early 2000s was transnationalism incorporated into analyzing ethnicity, international migration, and immigrant settlement (Winland 1998; Knight 2002). Only recently did Knight (2002) echo the call made a decade ago by American cultural anthropologists for a new theorization of international migration that considers transnational community formation. Although critics have pointed out that some of the early American proponents of transnationalism exaggerated its scope (Portes 2001, 182), they nevertheless recognize its importance to reformulating existing notions about migration and about how immigrants adapt to and are incorporated into their adopted country.

Transnationalism as a Mode of Adaptation

The conceptualization of transnationalism as a mode of adaptation is best exemplified by the work of Alejandro Portes and colleagues (1999, 221, 228), who identify three types of transnationalism (economic, political, and socio-cultural) along two levels of institutionalization (high and low). They argue that transnationalism is a form of immigrant adaptation that differs from assimilation. Transnationalism is one possible outcome grounded in the personal and family decisions made in a complicated process of adaptation, and it often depends on the availability of cultural resources (Portes 1999, 464-65).

Since transnationalism is associated with the processes of global capitalism, it is viewed by Portes and colleagues (1999, 227-28) as a potential form of individual and group resistance to dominant structures, which they term "transnationalism from below." An example is the adoption of transnational practices by immigrant entrepreneurs as an alternative to, or an escape from, low-wage labour, a choice that is perhaps also an expression of resistance and liberation. However, Portes (1999, 471) does not regard "transnationalism from below" as completely delinked from the process of assimilation but suggests that it "can act as an effective antidote to the tendency towards downward assimilation" and have positive effects on the second generation. Notably, discourse on transnationalism as a mode of adaptation has recently been extended to analyses of second-generation immigrants in the United States (Levitt and Waters 2002); immigrants' work and livelihoods (Sørensen and Olwig 2002); immigrants' religions, specifically Buddhism (McLellan 1999) and Islam (Mandaville 2001); and immigrants in the context of urbanism (Smith 2001).

Like transnationalism in the United States, transnationalism in Canada can arguably be perceived as a form of immigrant adaptation. However, the crucial difference may lie in the existence and prevalence of corporate pluralism in Canada and in Canada's official rejection of full assimilation. As mentioned earlier, transnationalism in Canada may be conceptualized as an extension of multiculturalism beyond national borders and thus as having a cross-border spatial dimension. Vertovec (2001a, 18) has suggested that multiculturalism depends on a public recognition of communal and cultural rights within a nation-state and that transnationalism extends this recognition to communal and cultural rights of affiliation outside of the nation-state. In legal terms, the logical outcome of this is dual or multiple nationality and citizenship. Canada has allowed immigrants to retain dual citizenship since 1977, but its implications are not entirely clear. One view suggests that multiple citizenship "devalues" Canadian citizenship and hinders immigrant adaptation. Conversely, another view suggests that it facilitates the incorporation of new immigrants who would otherwise fail to naturalize and who would thus remain socially marginalized.

Transnationalism as Social Space
The conceptualization of transnationalism as social space is partly a result of the contributions of geographers who have emphasized the importance

of socially constructed notions of time and space. For example, Pries (2001, 23) describes transnational social spaces as "pluri-local frames of reference which structure everyday practices, social positions, biographical employment projects and human identities, and simultaneously exist above and beyond the social contests of national societies." Perhaps a simpler description is offered by Faist (2000a, 2), who refers to the "ties and the unfolding strong and dense circular flows of persons, goods, ideas, and symbols within a migration system." For Faist (203) transnational social spaces take three basic forms: transnational kinship groups, transnational circuits, and transnational communities. These transnational social spaces are particular types of transnational morphologies that involve the notion of space. Geographically narrower variants of this notion of transnational social space include the terms "contact zones" and "borderland cultures" as well as Sassen's (2003, 265, 271) recent theorization of "analytic borderlands" and "cross-border spatialities." These are related to Bhabha's (1994) notion of "third space" as it applies to one's identity formation and consciousness.

The notion of transnational social space is also linked to immigrant and ethnic adaptation. In the case of Canada, this social space can also be thought of as an extension of ethnic pluralism beyond national borders.

Transnational Communities and Diasporas

Another important conceptual problem is how to distinguish between diasporas and transnational communities. While the term "diaspora" is more contested, the two terms are sometimes used interchangeably. However, they are not synonymous.

In the 1980s Connor (1986, 16) defined "diaspora" as "that segment of a people living outside the homeland." Since then, several more elaborate definitions have emerged. Cohen (1996, 1997) draws upon the classical tradition to expand the definition of diaspora to include not just people involuntarily dispersed from an original homeland, but also those displaced through community expansion due to trade, the search for work, and empire building. Although Cohen posits nine common features of a diaspora, he argues that no one diaspora will manifest all features (see also Satzewich 2002). Following Cohen's definition, Van Hear (1998, 6) conceptualizes diasporas as populations that satisfy three minimal criteria: (1) the population is dispersed from a homeland to two or more other territories; (2) the presence abroad is enduring, although exile is not necessarily permanent, with those in the diaspora possibly moving between homeland and new host; and (3) there is some kind of exchange – social, economic, political, or cultural – between or among spatially separated populations.

There is considerable overlap between the concepts of transnationalism and diaspora, with one often being used as an adjective to describe the other. Yet the concepts of transnationalism and transnational communities are broader and more inclusive than those of diaspora and diasporic communities. Diaspora may be appropriately conceptualized as a concomitant of transnationalism (Braziel and Mannur 2003, 7-8). Diaspora can also be conceptualized as a form of transnational organization related specifically to country of origin and society of settlement (Wahlbeck 2002, 221). Thus transnational communities encompass diasporas, but not all transnational communities are diasporas. This book utilizes the more general term "transnational communities," as not all of the cases examined fit the more narrow definitions of "diaspora."

Level of Analysis
The analysis of transnationalism is conducted at the middle range, or meso-level, of theory. Kivisto (2001, 560) notes that one advantage of this level of theory is that it is capable of shaping concrete research agendas. Vertovec's (1999, 448-55) effort to disentangle the concept of transnationalism may be useful as a basic framework for potential areas of research. He conceptualizes transnationalism as (1) a social morphology, (2) a type of consciousness, (3) a mode of cultural reproduction, (4) an avenue of capital, (5) a site of political engagement, and (6) a (re)construction of "place," or locality. Each chapter in this volume touches upon one or more of these conceptualizations.

Research Issues and Questions

Methodological Issues
The study of transnationalism raises questions about which methodologies best facilitate data gathering. From the previous discussion of the various conceptualizations of transnationalism, it is clear that theory determines the appropriate methods to be used by researchers. These methods, whether initially qualitative or quantitative, are likely to become increasingly more mixed and sophisticated. Distinctive methodological challenges face those seeking to operationalize and signify complex concepts such as transnational social fields and social spaces, avenues of capital, cross-border spatialities, transnational circuits, and multiple identities and citizenships.

Transnational ethnographies, which bring transnationalism alive by documenting the daily experiences of individuals and communities, have been prominent over the past decade and will probably continue to generate rich data. But ethnographic case studies are now slowly being supplemented by large-scale quantitative data sets generated from survey research. There are several recent examples. Portes and colleagues (2002) use a data set with a sample size of 1,200 respondents in order to assess transnational entrepreneurship among three immigrant groups. In searching for the correlates and predictors of transnationalism, both Rumbaut (2002) and Kasinitz and colleagues (2002) also use large-scale quantitative data sets to analyze transnationalism, language, identity, and notions of imagined communities among the children of immigrants. In Chapter 4 Hiebert and Ley base their assessment of transnationalism in Vancouver on data from a survey of hundreds of respondents. Although large-scale social surveys and quantitative data are not likely to increase understanding of the everyday lives of immigrants and others engaged in transnational practices, they will nevertheless help to answer fundamental questions about the extent of transnationalism, including its intensity, breadth, and spread.

Another methodological strategy that will engender more consideration is longitudinal research. The examination of the longevity of transnationalism over time and across generations is an important area of development, as pointed out by Portes and colleagues (2002, 294).

Global Perspectives

Nearly 20 percent of Canada's population is comprised of immigrants, and one of the defining features of the country is its policy of multiculturalism. These two factors identify Canada as a probable site of considerable transnational practices and perhaps even of qualitatively unique forms of transnationalism. At the same time, it is clear that immigrants and members of ethnic communities elsewhere manage to engage in transnational practices and to develop transnational identities even when they constitute relatively small proportions of the population and even without the encouragement of a policy of multiculturalism.

This raises questions about the role that host societies and larger global forces play in shaping transnational practices and identities. In other words, is transnationalism a "global" phenomenon that has emerged independently of specific local forces and circumstances? Or do national political cultures, traditions, and policies help to explain particular trajectories of transnational identities and practices?

Another factor in placing transnationalism in a global perspective is whether certain groups are more likely to engage in transnational practices than others. Much of the American literature on transnationalism focuses on individuals and groups from Latin America and the Caribbean. There are undoubtedly good reasons for this focus, but transnational practices and identities are not confined to immigrants and ethnic groups from these regions of the world. Arguably, a process of minoritization in the United States structures the transnational practices of the former groups. Yet groups that are comparatively privileged and that are not subject to racial or other forms of exclusion also engage in transnational practices. As a result, it is important to broaden the lens of transnationalism to include individuals and groups that are comparatively more privileged. This applies not just to class-related privileges, but also to privileges associated with ethnicity, gender, and skin colour.

Historical Perspective

Historians quite rightly relish pointing out that transnational practices are not a new phenomenon. Since the beginning of the latest phase of mass migration in the late nineteenth century, many individuals and groups have maintained political, social, and economic relationships with their homelands. Individuals and groups were engaged in transnational practices long before the rise of the World Bank, e-mail, and Air Canada. However, that immigrants have "always" engaged in transnational practices and developed transnational identities does not necessarily mean that there is nothing new about the phenomenon. Certainly, others have pointed out that new information and transportation technologies provide new opportunities for individuals and groups to engage in transnational practices. However, the new meanings imparted to transnational practices by these new technologies remain subject to empirical study and interpretation, making it necessary to put contemporary transnational practices into a broader historical and comparative perspective.

A historical perspective is also important because it takes into account changes in how countries like Canada have tolerated, promoted, and punished immigrants who maintain real and imagined transnational connections. It is necessary to determine how and why the concept of dual citizenship gained legitimacy as well as why some groups who maintained ties to their homelands – or who were believed to have maintained ties to their real or imagined homelands – were treated harshly by the Canadian state. Policies and practices designed to control enemy aliens during the First World War and efforts to deport Japanese Canadians after the Second World War can arguably be cast in terms of the attempted unmaking of transnational communities. Canadian officials were worried that some groups might use their real or imagined transnational identities to undermine national security. No doubt, racialization also played a role in efforts to unmake communities.

In the latter decades of the 1900s, many people believed that the "problem" of enemy aliens was a thing of the past, that national and international human-rights norms would prevent states from targeting groups with real or imagined transnational ties. Now, however, the situation is not so clear. The dramatic terrorist attacks of 11 September 2001 in New York and Washington, DC, launched in part by foreign nationals residing in the United States, changed the circumstances. The perception now is that certain individuals, particularly among certain immigrant groups, constitute "enemies within." Today certain groups who maintain multiple transnational ties and identities are subject to forms of surveillance and control that only a few years ago one might have reasonably thought to be part of distant Canadian history. Thus the question arises of the extent to which "race" feeds into social anxieties about enemies within and efforts to unmake transnational communities.

Transnational Social Fields and Social Spaces

As Portes and colleagues (1999) point out, the concept of transnationalism is elastic. Within scholarly research, it has been used to describe a wide range of practices, activities, and identities. Thus the authors of the chapters in this volume have been encouraged, if appropriate, to offer their own definitions of transnational social spaces and/or social fields. Some of the questions and issues in need of consideration include the following:

- Should individuals, immigrant and ethnic groups, or government policies be the focus of analysis?
- To what extent should transnationalism be defined as an "immigrant" phenomenon rather than as a phenomenon affecting a wider ethnic group?
- What criteria should be used to classify activities or identities as "transnational"?
- What are the categories of transnationalism?
- Do traditional categorizations of transnational activities (e.g., economic, political, socio-cultural) make sense in the Canadian context?

Although the term "social field" has been more popular in anthropological literature, the term "social space" has recently emerged to include not only geographical contexts, but also social-structural and institutional contexts.

Transnationalism and Gender

Even though gender is considered crucial to understanding transnationalism, many gender-related topics remain underresearched and undertheorized (Pessar and Mahler 2003, 812). Women account for approximately one-half of all immigrants to Canada and, in certain cases, are clustered in particular immigration programs or occupations. For example, Filipino women make up a large proportion of those in the Live-In Care Giver Program and of those who come to Canada as mail-order brides. These cases raise the possibility that the national identities of both young and old Canadian citizens will be transformed by the transnational practices of these immigrant women.

In many cases, women's relationships to their cultures of origin are often stronger than those of men, particularly when they leave children or aging parents with the intention to support them from abroad. In the case of female domestics in Britain, the flow of remittances has been along gendered networks (mothers, sisters, daughters) with little involvement of men (Vertovec 2000).

As Pessar and Mahler (2003, 818) suggest, women's practices across transnational spaces can be usefully analyzed within a framework of gendered geographies of power. Thus understanding how gendered relationships of work are negotiated is of particular importance in the transnational context. Furthermore, where the state entails a hegemonic gender regime, gender and the state need to be analyzed simultaneously. Goldring's (2001) work on gender in US-Mexican transnational spaces is one of the few studies that accomplishes this kind of analysis, but more research is needed.

Transnationalism "from Above" and "from Below": Issues of Class, Hegemony, Resistance, and Mobility

Class differences are implied in the terms "transnationalism from above" and "transnationalism from below." Transnationalism from above involves the capitalist class and international elites, whose activities are mediated at the macrolevel by multinational corporations and other supranational organizations (Sklair 2001). Transnationalism from below involves non-elites, or ordinary people, whose macro- and microlevel activities generate multiple and counterhegemonic forces. Their activities are micro in the sense that they are grounded in daily life and practice and include the development of cultural hybridity, multipositional identities, and the transnational business practices of migrant entrepreneurs (Mahler 1998, 67; Guarnizo and Smith 1998, 5).

In some respects, economic transnationalism may provide an alternative to stagnant, low-wage, menial labour. One practical significance of this type of economic transnationalism is that it can also be a form of resistance and liberation. Another example of transnationalism from below, which also constitutes a form of resistance, is the involvement of nongovernmental organizations (NGOs) in transnational advocacy networks (Appadurai 2003, 16-17). Guarnizo and Smith (1998, 5) point out that the political influence of working-class movements has waned as a result of advances in global capitalism. In this context, the conduct of new social actors, such as transnational immigrant entrepreneurs who are neither self-consciously resistant nor very political, becomes invested with oppositional possibilities. Their entrepreneurship may amount to an expression of popular resistance. These transnational actors may try to recapture a lost sense of belonging by recreating imagined communities and engaging in a process of subaltern identity formation that produces narratives of belonging, struggle, resistance, or escape. This grass-roots economic transnationalism relies on the skills and social capital of individuals. Portes and colleagues (1999, 230) speculate that in time transnational activities may become the normative path of adaptation chosen by groups seeking to escape the fate of cheap labour.

Casting transnationalism in a dichotomous framework based on a distinction between practices from above and practices from below may be problematic because there is always ambiguity. For example, are the practices of modestly middle-class Chinese immigrant entrepreneurs from Hong Kong who established small transnational businesses in Canada in the mid-1990s examples of transnationalism from above or from below? Their practices are certainly not generated from below in the same sense as those of NGOs engaged in transnational advocacy networks, nor are they generated from above in the same sense as those of a hypermobile transnational capitalist class. Further, while the conduct of a transnational capitalist class is clearly consistent with the notion of transnationalism from above, the practices of other kinds of international migrants who may be considered part of a transnational working class (such as agricultural workers, domestics, and information-technology workers) do not fit easily into a framework based on a dichotomy between transnationalism from above and from below.

Class inflects, if not haunts, the formation of the categories of nationality, diaspora, race, gender, and sexuality (Braziel and Mannur 2003, 5). As a result, it also complicates, perhaps in constructive ways, the intersections of other axes of power in transnational communities, suggesting the importance of the political economies of the regions in which transnational communities are anchored. This gives rise to the question of whether transnational activities and transnational social spaces reproduce or transform established relationships of power and privilege. One part of the answer lies in the literature on transnationalism as a site of political engagement (Vertovec 1999; Sheffer 2003; Østergaard-Nielsen 2003).

Hybrid Identities, Citizenship, and the Role of the State

Through their transnational practices, transmigrants are likely to experience both economic and ethnic stratification. This raises the issue of the impact of transnationalism on ethnic identities, an area in which, as Anderson (2001) suggests, postmodernist conceptualizations are particularly useful. Transnational and diasporic subjects experience dual or multiple identities characterized by hybridity. These hybrid identities are grouped with other identity categories and severed from essentialized, nativist identities associated with constructions of the nation, or homeland (Braziel and Mannur 2003, 5). Given that transnationalism involves deterritorialized networks connecting several societies, there are differences in the terms and the intensity of transmigrants' identification with their homelands as well as in the degree of hybridity found among transmigrants.

Regardless of these differences, the transmigrant is subject to a deterritorialization of social identity. This delinking of identity from place (in favour of space) creates possibilities for new theoretical developments. At the same time, there must be continued recognition of the importance of place, or at least geographic contextualization in transnational discourse (Mitchell 1997).

The notion of deterritorialization can relativize or decentre a local "place" or territory rather than exclude or negate it. The terms "translocalities" and "multilocationality" have emerged to indicate the local embeddedness, or "rootedness," of transnational processes; in other words, they refer to culturally heterogeneous places that are largely divorced from their national contexts and that straddle formal political borders (Hyndman 1997, 153). Thus transnational identity formation shows that identity is not singular but plural and always evolving. Although deterritorialized and hybrid social identities provide a challenge for nation-states, this challenge is usually confronted via policies of state citizenship that attempt to forge the identities of a state's members. Of most interest are research questions that concern the kinds of identities that emerge when subnational, hybrid social identities are confronted by what may be two or more hegemonic state-sanctioned constructions of identity. Are governments' attempts to shape the identities of transmigrant populations succeeding? Or will transnationalism lead to more encompassing postnational forms of identification?

Multiple citizenship is really the institutionalization of people's already existent transnational ties. In the mid-1990s the Standing Committee on Citizenship and Immigration Canada recommended that Canadians who hold dual citizenship should accord precedence to their Canadian citizenship. Moreover, it also recommended that a condition of obtaining Canadian citizenship should be the acknowledgment of this principle by immigrants who seek citizenship via naturalization (Labelle and Midy 1999, 219).

The Canadian state reluctantly continues to allow for dual and multiple citizenship. Why is there reluctance, and does dual citizenship present a challenge to the state? The assumption is that dual citizenship means greater ambivalence, divergence, and perhaps opposition to Canada and that it encumbers immigrant adaptation and integration. Although it is counterintuitive to think that multiple citizenship actually enhances integration, recent work in the United States suggests this possibility. Spiro (1999, 7) maintains that dual nationality may help to facilitate the cultural and political incorporation of new immigrants who would otherwise fail to naturalize and who would remain politically and culturally isolated.

The debate on the effects of hybrid identities and multiple citizenship gives rise to many research questions, including the following: (1) How does Canadian citizenship policy influence transnational hybrid identities? (2) Do transnational hybrid identities translate into citizenship building and more civic participation? (3) Is there a move toward more global forms of citizenship within transnational communities?

Outline of the Book
The chapters in this book address many of the conceptual and research

issues noted above. Sarah V. Wayland begins with a well-theorized analysis of transnationalism's political dimensions and the practices of transnational actors in the context of the changing role of states in an era of globalization. By examining cases from a number of countries, she demonstrates the fluidity of national political cultures, traditions, and policies as well as their importance in shaping transnational identities and practices. She also suggests, albeit tentatively (because there is little available data), that participation in transnational political networks may in fact facilitate social incorporation and political participation in Canada.

In Chapter 2 Christiane Harzig and Dirk Hoerder provide a historical and comparative perspective that questions the newness of transnationalism while also providing a critical analysis of the historical development of the concept. Focusing on the period from the 1880s to the 1920s, they examine the transnational experiences of new Canadians and compare these to the experiences of American immigrants. They argue that although there are similarities between immigrants in the United States and Canada, a number of factors make Canada unique. The absence of a specifically "Canadian" citizenship until 1947, the existence of the French-English divide, and the provision of few social services in Canada before the Second World War afforded immigrants the opportunity and space to develop and maintain transnational identities.

Chapter 3, by Pamela Sugiman, examines a little-studied nuance of transnationalism. She illustrates how the Canadian state's racist perception of imagined transnationalism among Japanese Canadians led to the attempted unmaking of the Japanese Canadian transnational community during and after the Second World War. She also examines how state efforts to unmake this particular transnational community through a policy of repatriation and deportation were understood, negotiated, and contested within families.

The next three chapters cover transnationalism in Canada's largest cities, where the majority of immigrants have settled. Chapter 4, by Daniel Hiebert and David Ley, provides an overview of language, transmigration, socioeconomic status, and citizenship among immigrants in Vancouver. Based on empirical survey data, their analysis shows that transnationalism among immigrants may be an alternative to social and economic integration rather than a mode of economic integration. That is, their evidence suggests that immigrants' transnational practices tend to be associated with "weak" connections to Canada. Valerie Preston, Audrey Kobayashi, and Myer Siemiatycki take a different tack in their analysis of Toronto in Chapter 5. Using the case of immigrants from Hong Kong, they examine how the social geography and transnational landscape of the city is associated with, and consequently shapes, contemporary transnational migration. They argue that even though individuals in the Chinese Canadian community maintain a variety of transnational connections with China, they are "integrated" into Toronto in a number of important ways. Nevertheless, their efforts to transform the city's built landscape as a means of claiming their rights to city space have met with difficulties. In Chapter 6 Micheline Labelle, François Rocher, and Ann-Marie Field focus on the Province of Quebec and, more specifically, on Montreal to explore the transnational politics of ethnic and racialized minorities in terms of "transnationalism from below." Utilizing data derived from interviews with ethnic leaders, this chapter documents these leaders' claims, their "repertoire of actions," and their transnational practices, participation in transnational networks, and understanding of "transnational citizenship."

The remaining chapters are case studies of transnational communities or transregionalism. In Chapter 7 Alan B. Simmons and Dwaine E. Plaza examine the transnational connections and transformations of the Caribbean community using a structural social-inequality framework. They show that members of the Caribbean community in Canada maintain relatively deep relationships with their respective homelands. They also argue that issues of power and inequality are crucial to understanding the complex relationships that are maintained with the Caribbean; though immigration policy provides opportunities for immigrants to maintain transnational ties with the Caribbean, an "outward gaze" is also promoted by racism and discrimination. Further, they note the importance of examining differences in transnational identities and practices within ethnic communities and the tensions to which these differences give rise. In Chapter 8, on South Asian transnational links, Dhiru Patel examines global networks within sociocultural contexts, such as the family. He ends his chapter by noting several key policy questions that pertain not only to South Asian transnationalism, but also to transnational communities more generally. Chapter 9, by Kim Matthews and Vic Satzewich, analyzes the presence of Americans in Canada in terms of whether they are "invisible transnationals." By examining three issues within this generally understudied group – American dual citizenship, Democrats abroad and Republicans abroad, and Americans in Canada avoiding military service in US-led wars – they suggest that a transnational perspective is in fact highly relevant to an analysis of this relatively privileged, yet socially invisible, immigrant population.

In Chapter 10 Luin Goldring poses several questions about Latin Americans' transnationalism in Canada in light of their growing numbers and the relative recentness of their immigration to the country. Her analysis looks at the ample research on Latin American transnationalism in the United States to theorize possible trajectories in Canada while at the same time providing some preliminary secondary Canadian data. Chapter 11, by Luis L.M. Aguiar, provides a critical analysis of the transnational perspective and its applicability to southern Europeans (Italians, Greeks, and Portuguese) in

Canada. Their cases are interesting because there is now very little new migration to Canada from these three countries and because emigration from some of the communities was so extensive in the 1950s and 1960s that there are few relatives left with whom to maintain transnational ties and relationships. He also argues that although forms of transnationalism are encouraged at the political level by the three countries of origin, immigrants from these countries display ambivalence and uncertainty about the wisdom of becoming too involved in "homeland" politics.

In Chapter 12 Sedef Arat-Koc's assessment of Arab and Muslim Canadians also offers a critical take on transnationalism. Arat-Koc examines how the transnationalism of these communities has come under siege since the terrorist attacks on the United States of 11 September 2001 and how this process has been furthered by the dominant transnationalisms of the Canadian state and "ordinary Canadians." She ends her chapter with suggestions for alternative transnationalisms. Chapter 13, by Lloyd Wong and Connie Ho, conceptualizes Chinese transnationalism as an avenue of capital and shows that it is associated not only with capitalists, but also with working and middle classes. Using secondary data, they demonstrate the extent of the flow of capital from China to Canada between the late 1800s and the present and discuss its implications for popular perceptions of Chinese commitment and allegiance to Canada.

In Chapter 14 Daphne Winland examines the Croatian diaspora in Canada since the collapse of the Yugoslav federation and its members' complex relationships to the homeland. Her chapter highlights the conceptualization of transnationalism as a site of political engagement and as the reconstruction of "place." She examines the various factors, strategies, and negotiations affecting Croats' identity formation and how this relates to the politics of visibility and representation. The final chapter, by Stuart Schoenfeld, William Shaffir, and Morton Weinfeld, examines Canadian Jewry and transnationalism. The authors show that Canadian Jews are a modern diaspora by providing case studies of (1) those who leave for Israel but eventually return to Canada, (2) Israelis in Toronto, and (3) South African Jews in Toronto. They argue that Jews have had to deal with allegations of transnational, dual loyalties for some time. They also argue that though many traditional anti-Semitic measures are declining in Canada, there are reasons to be concerned about a new wave of transnational, globalized anti-Semitism that mixes anti-Israeli and anti-Jewish sentiment.

Part 1
Transnationalism in Historical and Political Perspective

1
The Politics of Transnationalism: Comparative Perspectives
Sarah V. Wayland

As addressed in this volume, transnationalism usually refers to the experiences of individuals whose identities and relations span national borders. Researchers focus on persons, mostly migrants, whose lives subsume two or more languages and cultures and who have frequent contact with ethnic kindred ("coethnics") in other locations. Transnationalism involves the creation of new identities that incorporate cultural references from both the place of origin and the place of residence. Political scientists, however, define "transnationalism" differently: they use the term in reference to the practices of organizations or institutions that operate below the level of the state but whose activities transcend national borders. In the 1970s transnationalism was associated mostly with economic relations, especially between transnational corporations (e.g., Keohane and Nye 1971). By the late 1990s the concept had been extended to the practices of nongovernmental organizations and "transnational advocacy networks" united by shared values, a common discourse, and extensive information exchange among like-minded activist organizations (Keck and Sikkink 1998).

In this chapter, I focus on the political dimensions of transnationalism, particularly as exercised by transnational ethnic actors. Transnational ethnic actors are transnational in both senses of the word outlined above: (1) they have a common identity that spans state borders, and (2) they engage in substate relations by forming political networks across state boundaries to influence policies. The term "political" usually describes matters that concern the state or its government, government policies, or public affairs generally. In the context of immigration, where persons may not have formal citizenship, "political" must be broadly defined. It refers not only to party politics and policy making, but also to informal dimensions of politics, such as fundraising, organizing, and lobbying efforts around political causes. Political transnationalism, then, consists of various types of "direct cross-border participation in the politics of their country of origin by both migrants and refugees" as well as their indirect involvement via either political institutions of the receiving state or international organizations (Østergaard-Nielsen 2003, 762). Thus political transnationalism involves an interchange of ideas, issues, and conflicts between individuals, groups, and political entities in two or more countries.

Involvement in homeland politics is often referred to as diaspora politics. "Diaspora" refers to a particular type of transnational political community that has been dispersed from its homeland and whose members permanently reside in one or more "host" countries as well as possess a collective, sometimes idealized, myth of the homeland and a will to return (Sheffer 2003). Not all transnational political actors constitute diasporas, but I do refer to diasporas in this chapter where appropriate.

The chapter is constructed as follows. First, I situate contemporary interest in political transnationalism and diaspora politics within the context of globalization and the changing role that it entails for states. Second, I present a conceptual overview of the three principal sets of factors that influence the levels and characteristics of political transnationalism: policies and practices in immigrant and refugee receiving states, policies and practices in sending states, and characteristics of migrants, refugees, and ethnic communities themselves. I show how different variables within these three areas interact to produce specific forms of political transnationalism. Next, I briefly highlight research results on the prevalence of transnationalism among immigrant and ethnic communities. In the concluding section, I look at the relationship between political transnationalism and the political socialization of immigrants and refugees, including implications for social cohesion in receiving states. Throughout the chapter, I emphasize that political transnationalism is shaped by context-specific variables and that empirical research on this phenomenon is still in its infancy. As a result, it is particularly difficult to make generalizations about political transnationalism.

Transnationalism, Globalization, and States

The rise of scholarly interest in transnationalism has accompanied growing attention to globalization. Both phenomena illustrate the declining importance of territory as a source of identity and power. And both point to the importance of social networks. Under conditions of globalization, persons are said to experience "complex connectivity ... the rapidly developing and ever-densening network of interconnections and interdependences that characterize modern social life" (Tomlinson 1999, 2). Globalization theorists such as Castells (1996, 359) argue that as territories become less important and networks become more salient, power is no longer concentrated in institutions, organizations, and mass media but "is diffused in global networks of wealth, power, information, and images, which circulate and transmute in a system of variable geometry and dematerialized geography."

Some researchers of transnationalism have argued that social relations are being transformed by globalization to such an extent that the nation-state is becoming an outmoded political formation (Appadurai 1996; Sassen 1998). Scholars of this postnationalist vein argue that territorial sovereignty is declining and that nations are no longer confined by spatial boundaries (Appadurai 1996, 160-61). Waters (1995, 136) asserts that the possibility may arise that "ethnicities are not tied to any specific territory or polity." Nations are said to be "unbound," and they now operate with fewer constraints than ever before (Basch, Glick Schiller, and Szanton Blanc 1994). Postnationalist approaches emphasize the rise of transnationalism concurrent with the decline of states.

However, most scholarship in this area recognizes the continuing importance of states: people are not deterritorialized but live their lives on earth, in states, and in communities. A growing interdisciplinary literature situates transnationalism within states and localities (e.g., Smith and Guarnizo 1998; Koopmans and Statham 2000, 2003). In this view, sending and receiving states, regions, and localities influence the creation and perpetuation of transnational social spaces. Grass-roots activities are influenced by and carried out within larger policy contexts at the supranational, national, and subnational levels. Within these contexts, persons and groups become transnational political actors. This interplay between state and nonstate actors occurs in a number of ways: when migrants are influenced by policies and practices of the receiving states, when migrants are influenced by policies and practices of the sending states, and when migrants' contexts and circumstances influence their transnational practices. These are elaborated upon in the following sections.

Receiving States

Policies and practices of receiving states (sometimes referred to as "host states" or "host countries") influence the nature and extent of mobilization by migrants, refugees, and the ethnic minority groups formed by their descendants. States play a key role in regulating access to national territories and shaping regulations that affect immigrants and refugees. Ethnic identity is mediated through host-state institutions, practices, and traditions. Opportunities in liberal democracies are different from those in other types of states, and there are even differences between liberal democracies, which have various conceptions of citizenship and ethnic belonging. Answers to the following types of questions help to elucidate the contexts in which political transnationalism exists: Is the state a democracy? To what extent are human rights and civil liberties upheld? Does the electoral system make any provisions for ethnic minority parties, such as reserving seats in the legislature for ethnic minorities? Other factors include the citizenship and incorporation policies and models of the receiving state. Is citizenship difficult to obtain? Is the state highly assimilationist, or does it make provisions for cultural pluralism? The answers to these questions comprise the state's political-opportunity structure – that is, the context that either encourages or discourages groups to make demands on the state (Tarrow 1998; McAdam, McCarthy, and Zald 1996). Several variables that potentially impact the nature and extent of political transnationalism are discussed below.

Political Systems

Political systems in the country of origin can impact transnationalism in several ways. Authoritarian states in general prohibit freedom of expression and suppress the identities of ethnic minorities. As a result, ethnic minorities of immigrant origin may lack the means to be involved in homeland politics. Over time, they may be unable to retain their ethnic identities. On the other hand, living under conditions of repression may heighten the sense of group identity and keep the ideal of the homeland alive. Such a transnational orientation passed down through the generations is in keeping with the traditional understanding of a diaspora. The prototypical diaspora, the Jews, kept Jewish identity alive for centuries even in the absence of a homeland to which they could return. Other examples include Kurds and Armenians.

Conversely, democratic states are characterized by openness. The presence of civil rights in receiving states, such as freedom of assembly and freedom of expression, facilitates the maintenance of ethnic identities and transnational ties. Even in states that do not institutionally support cultural pluralism (discussed below), ethnic groups are guaranteed a minimal level of freedoms. Immigrants and refugees and their descendants can meet regularly, educate the broader public about their place of origin, and lobby politicians around various issues of concern. Moreover, living in a democratic space allows groups to accumulate the resources necessary for mobilization, including financial resources. Yet it may also be hypothesized that in democracies, transnational political ties will eventually decline. If ethnic minorities have access to the political system and do not suffer discrimination in their new place of residence, they may embrace the host country wholeheartedly – at the expense of any transnational sentiments. This may especially be true if they come to rely on the welfare state for resources more than than they do on their own ethnic communities.

Within democratic systems, different electoral systems may also impact the maintenance of ethnic identities over time. Proportional representation and mixed electoral systems tend to have a stronger presence of smaller political parties, including ethnic parties (Tossutti 2002). Ethnic representation may alleviate the impetus for transnational politics, although little research on this relationship exists.

Citizenship Policies

Another set of policies and practices relevant to transnational ties is that of citizenship. Via citizenship policies, states control who becomes a member of the polity. States use diverse criteria to control membership, but generally the differences between states' policies are based on the ways that jus soli and jus sanguinis principles are combined to determine the transmission, attribution, and acquisition of citizenship (Brubaker 1992; Aleinikoff and Klusmeyer 2001). According to a strict definition, jus soli grants citizenship to all persons born in the national territory. Thus the children of immigrants have an automatic right to citizenship. Jus sanguinis, on the other hand, restricts citizenship to those descended from earlier citizens. Thus the descendants of immigrants would have no claim to citizenship. Most citizenship regimes fall somewhere between these two extremes but favour one model more than the other. Among the democracies of western Europe and North America, citizenship favouring jus soli models is found in the traditional immigrant-receiving states of Canada, the United States, Great Britain, France, the Netherlands, and Belgium. Jus sanguinis is predominant in Germany, Switzerland, Sweden, and Japan.

States also control access to citizenship through application procedures such as residency requirements, necessary paperwork, and the application fees involved. In Canada, for example, one can apply for citizenship after only three years as a permanent resident ("landed immigrant"). The citizenship process costs only $100, but the previous step of obtaining permanent residency status includes a fee of at least $475 for the principal applicant. On top of this, since 1995 every adult immigrant accepted as a permanent resident has been required to pay a $975 "right of permanent residence" fee. In this way, Canada's fee structure discourages applications for permanent residency while at the same time encouraging permanent residents to apply for citizenship.

Although citizenship regimes determine who has access to the polity, their impact on transnational relations is less clear. Some scholars have hypothesized that exclusion from the polity of residence will spur the maintenance of a transnational orientation and that easy acquisition of citizenship will reduce transnationalism. However, a recent survey of political transnationalism among Latin American immigrants to the United States found that acquiring American citizenship did not affect transnationalism (Guarnizo, Portes, and Haller 2003, 1229). Indeed, the authors argued, possessing an American passport enabled former migrants to travel back and forth to their homelands more easily, thereby facilitating the maintenance of transnational linkages.

A related factor is the rise of dual citizenship, as more and more receiving states allow new citizens to retain their existing nationalities as well. An analysis of Canadian Census samples from the period 1981 to 1996 revealed that levels of dual citizenship increased rapidly (Bloemraad 2004). Bloemraad showed that dual citizenship is more likely to be acquired by persons with higher mobility and higher education levels, but she noted that only 16 percent of adult immigrants identified as dual citizens. This study supports the view that transnationalism in the form of dual citizenship is on the rise but remains largely limited to an educated elite. However, dual citizenship is an incomplete indicator of transnationalism: its acquisition points to identities that span borders, but it does not imply the existence of any actual transnational networks.

Models of Minority Incorporation

As with formal citizenship, preferences vary from state to state concerning the extent to which newcomers and ethnic minorities should conform to the dominant culture. These preferences influence migrants' perceptions of belonging within a state and may influence transnational orientation as well. Models of minority incorporation may be divided into three ideal types (Castles and Miller 1998, 244-50; Castles 2002, 1154-57). *Assimilationist* societies encourage minorities to subordinate or abandon communal identities in favour of adopting the language, values, and behaviours of the dominant group. Until at least the 1960s, assimilationism was prevalent in the "classic" immigrant-receiving states of Australia, Canada, and the United States. France is another example of an assimilationist state. France has liberal access to citizenship by European standards but recognizes persons only as individuals, not as members of cultural groups. In a *differential exclusion,* or segregation, model, society is segmented according to skin colour, language, religion, or national origin. Migrants are integrated into certain parts of society, such as the labour market and the welfare system, but they are excluded from others, namely, political forums. European countries that recruited "guest workers" but offered them little possibility of obtaining citizenship were considered exclusionist. Germany, especially, received much international criticism in this regard, although it did liberalize access to citizenship somewhat in 2000. Today, exclusionary models can be found in Japan and the Persian Gulf states.

Under both assimilation and differential exclusion models, immigration does not significantly change the dominant culture of the receiving society. Advocates of *cultural pluralism,* on the other hand, view heterogeneity and the expression of different cultures as compatible with national unity and identity. In this spirit (or having recognized that assimilation was becoming less prevalent), countries such as Australia, Canada, and Sweden have introduced official policies of multiculturalism. In some cases, such as Canada and the Netherlands, states may even stimulate cultural pluralism through the funding of ethnic organizations or ethnic or religious media. Individuals are allowed to retain their group identities in the public sphere, including in schools, the military, and the media. This may extend to special rights and exemptions for members of some cultural groups. In some receiving states, for example, Muslim girls are excused from participation in coeducational physical-education classes. In Britain, turbaned Sikhs are exempt from laws requiring the use of motorcycle helmets.

These models of incorporation influence the claims that ethnic minorities make on their state of residence. How these models impact transnational mobilization is, however, not clear. Some scholars have hypothesized that a more negative context of reception facilitates the maintenance of strong transnational ties (Smith 1998; Portes 1999). Downward occupational mobility and expectations of return to the sending state have also been posited as factors increasing political transnationalism (Guarnizo, Portes, and Haller 2003, 1217-18). However, in this volume Wong and Satzewich hypothesize that multiculturalism can be conducive to the formation of transnational social spaces insofar as ethnic and religious organizations are supported by the state. Faist (2000b, 199-200) and Castles (2002, 1161) assert that both discrimination and multiculturalism can contribute to the formation of transnational communities. Other research in this area has argued that modes of minority incorporation may not impact transnational politics to the same extent that they impact immigrants' domestic political activity. According to Østergaard-Nielsen (2001, 264), inclusive and exclusive states alike view political transnationalism as impeding political incorporation. Few states favour any transnational political practices by their residents. Moreover, she points out, homeland-oriented political organizations are not solely dependent on the receiving state: they can draw resources from outside the receiving state, such as from sister organizations in other states.

One of the few comparative studies in this area was conducted by European scholars Koopmans and Statham (2003). In their research on Britain, Germany, and the Netherlands, they asked how forms of transnational political activism were influenced by the specific citizenship and integration regimes of the receiving states. Based on a content analysis of major newspapers in their three case-study states, they found that the public mobilization of migrants and ethnic minorities was much more likely to include a transnational dimension in Germany than in Britain or the Netherlands. In the latter two countries, the authors reasoned, ethnic organizations are better incorporated into the policy process, so migrants focus more on issues of integration. In Germany, on the other hand, migrants may focus more on homeland politics because they have no input on policy decisions in the host state (224-29).

The work of Koopmans and Statham provides evidence that citizenship laws and models of minority incorporation do influence transnationalism. Their research provides support for the hypothesis that, even in an era of globalization, states continue to shape the issues around which their residents mobilize. However, a comprehensive understanding of the claims that migrants make about experiences in their homelands and in receiving states cannot focus on the latter alone. The authors themselves recognize the potential importance both of homeland influences and of migrant groups' own characteristics. It is to these other sets of factors that I now turn.

Sending States

The second major set of factors influencing migrants' mobilization relates to the sending state, or "home state." The policies and practices of sending states that are important in this regard roughly parallel those that matter in the receiving states, namely, political systems and citizenship laws. In addition, "outreach" by states to citizens and ethnic kindred living abroad, including electoral provisions and the practices of political parties, may be important. Each of these is examined below.

Political Systems

As above, these include whether the regime is democratic or authoritarian and the extent of democratic freedoms. The level of civil conflict may also be an important factor. If a state has significant ethnic and religious cleavages, these often contribute to the formation of transnational social spaces because minorities in the diaspora are eager to keep tabs on homeland politics. This is especially true when states are young and in the process of nation building (Faist 2000b, 199).

Citizenship Laws

As discussed above, citizenship regimes determine who is a member of the polity and who is not. Some states seek to retain ties to their expatriates by allowing for dual citizenship and by conferring citizenship on the descendants of citizens living abroad. Historically, countries of emigration tended to base nationality primarily on ancestral lineage (jus sanguinis). This understanding of citizenship encouraged emigrants to retain their nationality and to transmit it to their children, thereby facilitating closer ties with their homeland. This can also become the basis for a "law of return" aimed at reintegrating former emigrants. For example, Germany's ethnic conception of citizenship meant that "ethnic Germans," or *Ausseidler,* could apply for German citizenship even if they could not speak German and had never visited Germany. The 3.5 million Ausseidler who are living in Germany come from eastern central Europe, namely, Poland, Romania, and the former Soviet Union. Since the end of the Cold War, however, the Ausseidler policy has become increasingly restrictive, requiring applicants to pass a language test and to prove that they face discrimination as Germans in their homeland (Klekowski and Ohliger 1997). Israel has an even more extensive citizenship policy. The 1951 Israeli Law of Return grants every Jew in the world an automatic right to citizenship. This law is the concrete expression of the Zionist vision of the "ingathering of exiles." Thus, in addition to the estimated 10 to 15 percent of Israelis who live abroad – mainly in the United States – millions of other persons around the world have a claim to Israeli citizenship. That there are more Jews in the United States than in Israel has a potential bearing on Israeli politics. In brief, by granting citizenship to persons living abroad, citizenship laws may encourage transnational politics.

About half the countries in the world now recognize dual citizenship (Vertovec 1999, 455). From the sending country's perspective, dual citizenship is good for business: it keeps remittances flowing in, increases interest in development projects, and is thought to foster investment from citizens who have accumulated wealth overseas. The extent to which dual citizenship provisions are related to financial considerations is revealed upon closer examination of India's policy on dual citizenship. Enacted in 2003, India's policy is limited to Indians living in the world's wealthiest places: the United States, Canada, Australia, New Zealand, eleven western-European countries, and Singapore! Dual citizens can own real estate and engage in business transactions without special permits, but they cannot vote in India or run for public office (Lakshmi 2003).

The number of dual and multiple citizens in the world is not known. Although such citizens no doubt comprise a small minority, their numbers are growing, suggesting their potential significance to future political relations (Castles 2002, 1162). Dual and multiple citizens are the most visible sign that political communities can have overlapping memberships.

Electoral Provisions
Some countries, such as the United States, allow overseas citizens to vote in elections by absentee ballot. In its first postcommunist election in November 1990, Poland allowed citizens abroad to vote at Polish embassies and consulates (Koslowski 2005, 13). In Croatia ethnic Croats were allowed to vote in the 1990 and 1992 Croatian elections from abroad even if they did not hold citizenship in Yugoslavia (1990) or Croatia (1992) (Wayland 2003, 8). Since 1995 in Croatia 10 percent of the seats in Parliament have been reserved for the diaspora. Attempts to eliminate this representation, including a review by the centre-left government elected in 2000, caused an outcry from expatriate Croatians (Winland 2002, 699). In Israel, on the other hand, voting can occur only on Israeli soil (with the exception of voting by Israeli diplomats and members of the merchant marines). Most Israelis believe that expatriates, who do not experience the security risks of living in contested lands, should not play a crucial role in elections. Thus the estimated 300,000 to 500,000 Israeli citizens who live in the United States are

hindered from participating in Israeli politics. However, the diaspora is not without resources. Every time there is a national election, charter planes bring thousands of Israeli citizens back to Israel to vote. In a country where a party can be given a seat in the Legislature with only 1.5 percent of the vote, it is possible that the diaspora can impact election outcomes.

Political Parties

Political parties provide another avenue for transnational participation. Sometimes expatriates return to stand as candidates for election. This was particularly prevalent after the fall of communism in central and eastern Europe. For example, Polish-born Canadian Stanislaw Tyminski ran for the presidency of Poland in 1990 and actually received more votes than the sitting prime minister, thereby prompting his resignation. (Lech Walesa, however, won the election.) In July 1992 Serbian-born American citizen Milan Panic was elected prime minister of Yugoslavia (Koslowski 2005, 13). Lithuanian president Valdus Adamkus lived most of his life in the United States before returning to run for office in 1998. In 1999 retired University of Montreal professor Vaira Vike-Freiberga became president of Latvia. In addition, people also make campaign contributions to political parties in their homelands. In Croatia newly formed political parties sent emissaries to the United States, Canada, and Australia to raise funds from the diaspora – even before noncommunist political parties were legalized. The Croatian Democratic Union (HDZ) raised the vast majority of its funds, at least US$4 million, primarily in Canada. Ottawa businessman Gojko Susak was a major fundraiser and was rewarded for his efforts by being appointed defence minister after Croatia achieved independence in 1991 (Wayland 2003, 68).

The increased interest among sending states in maintaining transnational identities indicates the extent to which states continue to define identity and pursue their own interests, even beyond their borders. Some states send money, teachers, and clergy abroad to work with their expatriate citizens. Or they sponsor visits so that migrant youth can return "home" for summer camps. Likewise, political parties and ethnic and religious organizations in the sending states have various means of reaching out to citizens and coethnics overseas. These variables in the sending states – political system, citizenship laws, electoral provisions, and political parties – influence the next important variable in political transnationalism: the set of factors shaped by the migrants themselves.

Context and Circumstances of Migrants

This final contributor to political transnationalism relates to the particulars of migrants and refugees themselves. Of primary interest are the conditions of departure, the context of arrival, and characteristics of the individuals and the ethnic community. Did a person migrate to escape conditions of persecution or ethnic war? Is he or she a skilled worker, a dependant, a refugee, or an undocumented migrant? Is the migrant male or female, old or young, well educated or not? Is there a concentration of migrants within a particular city or neighbourhood, or are they widely dispersed? Is the immigrant population new or well established?

Conditions of Departure

Certain conditions of departure, such as repression of an ethnic or political group, can contribute to strong transnational political orientation, particularly if family members are left behind. Some studies of Latin Americans in the United States have found that political refugees have taken a more active stance on issues affecting their home country than have economic migrants (Landolt, Autler, and Baires 1999; Portes 1999, 465). Landolt (forthcoming) found that strong support for the partisan left in El Salvador helped to unite the Salvadoran population in Toronto during the 1980s. In the wake of the 1992 peace accord that ended the civil war, Salvadoran organizations and political mobilizing by Salvadorans in Toronto declined dramatically.

There are also cases where conditions in the sending state are such that expatriates seek independence for their ethnic kindred in the homeland or the overthrow of the current regime. Some of the most politicized migrant groups worldwide have suffered some degree of repression in their homelands. Diasporic communities advocating self-determination in the homeland include Kashmiris, Sikhs, and Sri Lankan Tamils (Ellis and Khan 1998; Tatla 1999; Wayland 2004).

Context of Arrival

As a result of institutional and contextual differences across settlement locations, immigrant populations from the same sending country may experience different processes of incorporation and thus develop different transnational orientations. In one of the few comparative studies in this area, Landolt (forthcoming) compared Salvadorans in Toronto and Los Angeles. She found a "distinct institutional landscape" in each locale "that facilitates some and hinders other modes of transnational and incorporationist practices." These distinct landscapes were the product of each city's respective labour-market conditions, political culture, and immigration history.

Other factors that might be important, and that beg for more empirical research, include the geographical concentration of the immigrant community, the chronology of arrival, and how long the ethnic community has had a presence in the receiving state. Did members arrive in quick succession, or did migration occur over the span of several decades? Did they settle in proximity to one another? Has the community had enough time to get established in the receiving state by sending children through the school system and establishing businesses and media outlets?

Individual and Group Characteristics
These include the status of the immigrants and refugees, their age, sex, race, and level of education. Does the community have its own organizations and places of worship? How strong are social networks within the immigrant community?

How these factors combine to influence mobilization by migrants and their descendants is addressed in several recent empirical studies. Cheran (forthcoming) points to networks of more than three hundred voluntary associations of Tamils in Canada, formed on the basis of people's home villages in the northern and eastern parts of Sri Lanka or on the basis of the high schools that they attended in the region. These networks have been mobilized to aid in relief, reconstruction, and development efforts in the conflict zones of Sri Lanka. Moreover, they act almost completely independently from any state structures. In their study of Salvadorans, Colombians, and Dominicans living in the United States, Guarnizo and colleagues (2003, 1232) found that the presence of social networks facilitated transnational ties.

They also found that involvement in transnational politics increased significantly during adulthood and then declined as persons became elderly (Guarnizo, Portes, and Haller 2003, 1229). Their survey data indicated that the transnational activists were predominantly married men and that one's likelihood to engage in transnational politics increased with education level. In brief, Guarnizo and his collaborators found that the profile of persons most likely to engage in political transnationalism is associated with being well connected, well established, educated, and male. Although based on a limited sample, this finding contradicts earlier speculation that persons resort to transnational activism as a reaction to marginalization in the receiving state.

In sum, migrants to a particular country generally face the same set of institutions in the receiving society. Yet the extent and characteristics of domestic and transnational political activism vary widely among ethnic communities. These differences are rooted in factors pertaining to the particular circumstances of each community. The studies cited above give us glimpses into why these circumstances matter, but these findings hold true only for limited samples. Obviously, more comparative research in this area is needed before further conclusions can be drawn.

Putting the Pieces Together: Toward a Conceptual Framework
Above I presented three sets of factors that may influence the types, directions, and extent of political transnationalism: policies and practices in receiving states, policies and practices in sending states, and the context and

circumstances of migrants themselves. Any comprehensive analysis of political transnationalism must recognize the interplay between these sets of factors. No single factor in the sending or receiving state produces transnationalism. Moreover, some combinations seem more conducive to transnationalism than others. A particular combination that is seen in much of the literature on diaspora politics and political transnationalism involves migrants who leave a situation of persecution for a democratic state that guarantees civil liberties. In such situations, migrants have strong grievances and are able to take advantage of newfound freedoms to publish, organize, and accumulate financial resources to an extent that was impossible in the homeland. In some countries of settlement, public funding even supports various forms of ethnic media and organization. As a result, "migrants and their descendants can then mobilize in the host country to publicize their cause as well as to lobby decision-makers to obtain additional political rights for their co-ethnics in the sending country" (Wayland 2004, 417).

Take the case of the Sri Lankan Tamil diaspora. In the wake of anti-Tamil riots in 1983, many Tamils were accepted as political refugees in Britain, Canada, Australia, and other states. Since then, they have become a very mobilized diasporic community, lobbying for an independent homeland, sending relief aid to their homeland, and sending financial contributions to the separatist Liberation Tigers of Tamil Eelam (LTTE) (Wayland 2004). A Tamil refugee from Sri Lanka expressed the following sentiments about living in Canada: "Here you could practise democracy [more] than [in] our country. You could raise your voice according to whatever you think. You could tell your opinion whatever good for the community or the country. You don't need to be scared to tell your opinion even though the government ruling party doesn't like your idea" (personal interview 2000).

Another example is Germany, home to an estimated half-million Kurds who hold Turkish passports (Lyon and Uçarer 2001). Many Kurds in Turkey would like their own separate state, but they are constrained from mobilizing in Turkey. The Kurdistan Workers' Party (PKK), which was formed in 1978 in Turkey, used acts of violence against Turkish authorities to draw attention to its separatist claims. In Germany, by comparison, it was able to operate in the open and to mobilize within the Kurdish community, which had already been there for three decades. The PKK organized large public demonstrations, disrupted traffic, and attacked and vandalized Turkish businesses and associations in Germany to draw attention to the Kurdish cause.

These diasporic communities can better mobilize in the receiving states than in their homelands, yet their actions are constrained by policies of the receiving states. In the most extreme case, states may ban certain ethnic organizations deemed to be a security threat or to be affiliated with terrorist activity, thereby prohibiting them from organizing or fundraising in that state. In the United States, there is a ban on the Liberation Tigers of Tamil Eelam, which has spearheaded the insurgency for a separate Tamil state on the island of Sri Lanka. Canada has imposed a partial ban on LTTE-related activity. Between 1993 and 1998, Germany banned the PKK and its affiliate organizations under provisions used to restrict terrorist organizations.

Another way that various sets of factors combine to produce specific configurations of transnationalism concerns the foreign policies of the receiving state concerning its dealings with the sending state. National interests in the receiving state can influence transnationalism. During the Cold War, the United States encouraged anticommunist mobilization among its immigrants from eastern Europe, the Soviet Union, and Cuba. More recently, Cuban American lobbyists were important players in the passage of the Helms Burton law that sought to increase Cuba's economic isolation (Shain 1999, 73-77). Sometimes a receiving state's priorities put a damper on transnationalism. The United States has discouraged Arab Americans from supporting the Palestinian cause within Israel and the occupied territories because such activities conflict with American foreign policy goals in the Middle East (92-131). These examples highlight how ethnic minority policies can become intertwined with foreign-policy considerations. Domestic politics become globalized, while at the same time global politics may influence domestic policies.

The foregoing illustrates how differences in the political systems of sending and receiving states affect the political opportunities open to migrant communities. It also shows that foreign policy interests of receiving states can influence the extent to which migrants and ethnic communities are able to mobilize around transnational concerns. These are just two examples of how different sets of factors interact to produce various types of political transnationalism. Other influences not addressed here include the role of civil-society organizations in sending and receiving states and the importance of locality and translocal experiences.

How Widespread Is Transnational Political Activity, and Is It Limited to the "First Generation"?

A major criticism of scholarship on transnationalism is that most research has been based on case studies of those who engage in transnational activities. By failing to study those who do not participate in transnational affairs, researchers may give the impression that transnationalism is more widespread than it really is. What proportion of an immigrant community is involved in transnational politics, and how much does this vary according to ethnicity, place of origin, and country or community of residence? What motivates political transmigrants, and what characteristics do they share in common?

Just as many citizens do not engage in domestic politics or consider them-selves politically active, so, too, is it probable that only a minority of mi-grants and their descendants engage in transnational politics. The little empirical research that has been conducted in this area suggests that much depends on the definition of political transnationalism. A smaller percent-age is involved in electoral politics, whereas more people are active around issues that can loosely be construed as political. In their survey of more than a thousand adult Dominicans, Colombians, and Salvadorans living in the United States, Guarnizo and colleagues (2003, 1227) found that as many as one-third of the sample engaged in transnational politics when the defi-nition was extended to include membership in hometown civic associa-tions, financial contributions to civic projects in the homeland, and regular membership in charity organizations aimed at the homeland.

Smaller groups of hardcore transnationals may be supplemented by larger contingencies of "softer" transnationalists during certain situations, such as a crucial election or a national disaster in the homeland. This may unite some immigrant communities, but others experience internal cleavages in response to developments in the homeland. Kelly's (forthcoming) research on Filipinos living in Canada found that they were deeply divided over the dictatorial rule of Ferdinand Marcos during the 1970s and '80s. Some re-mained loyal to Marcos to the end, while a broad range of other Filipinos formed an anti-Marcos coalition. In the early 1980s, with tensions high between the anti-Marcos activists and the Philippine consulate in Toronto, each organized rival events for the annual Philippine Independence Day celebrations.

Can transnational identities be passed down over generations, or do they decline among those who never lived in the "homeland"? People probably feel their primary allegiance to the society in which they are socialized. But some studies have documented transnational political activism among the descendants of immigrants, although it is likely to be "less frequent and more selective in scope" (Levitt 2003, 184). One need only look to the nu-merous ethno-national student associations present on Canadian univer-sity campuses for evidence of persistent transnational identities. Some of these associations are directly engaged in homeland issues.

Other persons "rediscover" their ethnic identities as they get older. In her interviews with migrants and their descendants in the Boston area, Levitt (2003) found some Irish Americans who did not become transnational ac-tivists until they reached middle age. Once again, there is no single answer to the question of who engages in transnational politics and when. What we can say is that interest in transnationalism can wax and wane over the course of one's life and that patterns may differ among ethnic groups as well as among individuals within the same ethnic group. There is not necessarily any linear path that transnationalism follows. According to Levitt (2003, 184), "migrants put together a constellation of strategies at different stages of their lives and combine these with host-country integration strategies. The resulting configurations produce different mixes of upward and downward mobility in both contexts."

Conclusion: Domestic Implications of Transnational Politics

Linear assimilation theory predicts that, over time, migrants assimilate into the society of the receiving state (Gordon 1964). In doing so, they cease to identify with their society of origin and to be involved in homeland politics. Recent research on transnationalism challenges this perspective and points in a different direction. Political transnationalism does not occur at the expense of mobilization around domestic political issues. Domestic and transnational activism are not mutually exclusive.

In fact, there is some evidence that – far from destroying social cohesion in receiving states – interest in homeland issues can actually positively contribute to one's integration into the receiving society. This was the conclusion reached by Karpathakis (1999) in her study of Greek immigrants in New York City. She found that their mobilization over Turkey's invasion of Cyprus in 1974 actually facilitated their incorporation into the American political system. Similarly, in a challenge to the view that American foreign policy has been damaged by ethnic lobbying, Shain (1999) argues that ethnic groups are in fact good for democracy. First, he says, they can influence American policies toward their homelands only if they demonstrate how the policies will disseminate American values and ideals abroad, namely, democracy, pluralism, and respect for human rights. Second, he argues, ethnic mobilization around foreign policy benefits American civic culture because it reinforces values of democracy and pluralism among ethnic groups in the United States.

In general, transnational ethnic actors who wish to influence the foreign policies of the countries in which they live must learn how to negotiate the political landscapes of their countries, cities, or communities of residence. This includes learning how to lobby elected officials through telephoning and letter-writing campaigns, how to frame their demands in the language of human rights and democratic ideals, how to obtain permits for marches, and how to form associations to send relief aid and initiate development projects. So, even while ethnic actors may be focused on the homeland, they are building social and political capital that they can use in the long term to become active participants in their host societies.

This chapter has provided an overview of our knowledge of political transnationalism, adressing the sets of factors that contribute to its forms and prevalence, how these factors interact with each other and with other variables, and how widespread transnationalism is. This overview has been supported by a discussion of various research results, some of which contradict each other. Almost all the research, however, shows that transnationalism is clearly influenced by specific national contexts and circumstances. In the introductory chapter, the editors of this volume ask: "Do national political cultures, traditions, and policies help to explain particular trajectories of transnational identities and practices?" After reading this chapter, the answer should be clear.

Canada is home to millions of persons with ties to other parts of the world. Many of them engage in some aspect of political transnationalism, including assistance with relief and rehabilitation efforts in war-torn areas, contributions to political campaigns in other countries, and support for independence movements in the homeland. In its most extreme mode, transnationalism assumes the form of terrorist activity, such as the 1985 bombing of Air India flight 182 allegedly by Sikhs demanding the creation of a separate state in India's Punjab region. Examples of political transnationalism abound in Canada, but social-scientific research lags behind. If, as stated above, national contexts and cultures influence the extent and nature of transnationalism, it is imperative to go beyond the existing body of research that focuses predominantly on the United States and – to a lesser extent – the European context. As shown in this chapter, scholars have an excellent base of hypotheses on which to build Canadian, and ultimately comparative, research.

2
Transnationalism and the Age of Mass Migration, 1880s to 1920s
Christiane Harzig and Dirk Hoerder

When the concept of transnationalism emerged in the early 1990s, it quickly achieved widespread recognition. The discursive context was favourable: not only had the critique of nationalism and nation-centred scholarship begun to counter traditional, bounded approaches, but since the early 1960s, migration had changed societies. Although many social scientists specializing in post-1965 migrations considered the concept a breakthrough, historians of migration had recognized earlier that the concepts of boundary-enclosed nations and bounded ethnic groups had little validity. Historians, situated between the literary narratives of the humanities and the analytical approaches of the social sciences, had begun to question the traditional nation-centred master narratives as well as the (hi)stories of particular ethnic groups. Essentialist concepts of nationality and ethnicity lost their hold over minds and theories, while historians' diachronic perspective revealed changing national and societal contexts over time. In this chapter, we discuss the emergence of these new approaches and historicize the concept of transnationalism. We also provide examples of transnational experiences in Canadian society and compare these experiences to those of migrants in the United States and to those of individuals in migrants' cultures of origin. The examples are situated in the period of mass migration from the mid-1880s to the 1920s in the United States and from the early 1900s to 1930 in Canada, the latter period being marked by the war-mandated interruption of transatlantic migration between 1914 and 1918. In a concluding section, we discuss the relevance of transnational attitudes among individual migrants and newcomer communities to processes of insertion into the receiving society.

The Historical Dimension of the Concept of Transnationalism
The study of migration, which until the 1950s was called immigration history in North America and emigration history in Europe, and the study of migrant insertion into receiving societies, then called "assimilation," have undergone vast changes. Conceptually, two US-based schools determined

approaches in the first half of the twentieth century. Up to the 1920s, the Chicago School of Sociology took the lead in investigating immigrant as-similation. Scholars such as Robert E. Park, William I. Thomas, and Florian Znaniecki did so in a climate of resentment toward new immigrants: while fewer farmers and skilled urban migrants came from western- and northern-European societies, the number of migrants from eastern Europe (said to be of dark complexion) and from southern Europe (said to be of olive-coloured skin) increased rapidly. Whether these immigrants were considered "white" was highly contested (Jacobson 1998). Further, they were ranked low re-garding their contribution to the "American nation" since they had grown up under "despotic regimes" and were "unskilled" in terms of industrial labour. That economic conditions in Europe had prevented them from learn-ing a trade and earning a living did not enter the ascriptions of economists and sociologists. Although the (male) scholars of the University of Chicago could rely on sophisticated data collection by (female, academically trained) social workers in immigrant neighbourhoods, such as Jane Addams, Edith Abbott, and Sophonisba P. Breckenridge, their interpretations remained tied to a notion of the "dislocation" and personal and social "disorganization" of newcomers (Matthews 1977; Persons 1987; Lissak 1989). The second "school" emerged from Oscar Handlin's (1951) study of the Irish in Boston, whom he labelled "the uprooted." In this approach, immigrants were de-scribed as torn out of their societies of origin, bewildered, and in need of guidance. A decade and a half later, Rudolph J. Vecoli (1964) began to em-phasize cultural transfer and continuities in the process of men's migration. Feminist scholars would later add women's migrations and their transcultural mediation to the picture (Gabaccia 1994).

In Canada and Cuba, two societies hidden by the global impact of Ameri-can research, scholars had already questioned the paradigm of bounded ethnic groups and of assimilation to a single national culture. Approaches not recognized internationally emerged in bicultural Montreal and in Spanish-African-Anglo Havana. To explain the practices of 1940s Cuban society, Fernando Ortiz (1940) developed a concept of transculturalization, and at McGill University, Everett Hughes and Helen M. Hughes (1952) ar-gued that Canada's French-Anglo dualism precluded emergence of a single national model of acculturation. However, American scholar Milton Gordon's (1964) much narrower, national concept of assimilation became the stan-dard reference for scholarship in the United States and in Europe. From the 1960s, long before American scholars left the *e pluribus unum* mould, Cana-dian scholars recognized the importance of interethnic relations and gave increasing attention to multiple narratives (Juteau-Lee 1983; Burnet et al. 1992; Isajiw 1999; Li 2003b).

Traditional scholars, socialized into particular nation-state discourses, pursued the "nation to ethnic enclave" paradigm, which argued that migrants left nations and arrived in an ethnic enclave in another nation. This paradigm could not accommodate more than one culture: immigrants were said to be "in between," "in limbo," "suspended between" cultures. Salvation might come through a "melting pot," or unconditional assimilation. Often scholars in North America lacked the original languages of the migrants whom they studied and thus were unable to include cultures of origin in their research. Rather, they took recourse to a "cultural baggage" approach, supplemented in the United States by an "Ellis Island–Statue of Liberty" approach. The latter had no equivalent in Canada, where immigration facilities at Montreal's Grosse Isle and at Halifax's Pier 21 did not lend themselves to the creation of a national myth. Scholars from ethno-cultural communities who knew the language of origin and who had knowledge of the cultural background often wrote contributions history of the "we were there, too" variety because hegemonic academics from the national culture overlooked the immigrants' share in creating societies.

In the 1970s and 1980s it was accepted that migrants, unless departing in infancy, had been socialized in their respective cultures of origin and, after arriving at their destination, had to adapt or transform aspects of their everyday culture in order to function in the new society. They began a process of conscious or unconscious negotiations between old and new customs and norms that transposed the culture in which they had been socialized to the one in which they lived (Hoerder 1996; Kazal 1995). Parallel to this new understanding of acculturation, or insertion, other tenets of the master narrative of migration collapsed: the seemingly one-directional trajectory was far more complex: migrants might move in stages, perhaps first to a city in their culture of origin or within a traditional diaspora, such as the Chinese or Jewish one, then to a port town, and finally across the ocean; migrants might be highly mobile workers, such as the Italians in Montreal or the Chinese in Vancouver, who went back and forth; migrants might have planned to return "home" but stayed in the new society until death. Thus the movement between cultures involved a capability to at least function in two or more cultures. Migrants, neither uprooted nor "transplanted" by some mysterious force, negotiated their own positions. They were agents in their own lives (Jackson and Moch 1989).

Migrants' socialization in the society of origin, their accommodation, and their intermediary steps of actual movement across space need to be analyzed in terms of microlevel local conditions within a mesolevel regional culture and economy and within a macrolevel frame of statewide regulations and laws (Green 1997; Hoerder 1997). Eastern-Ukrainian migrants had acquired everyday practices different from those of their western-Ukrainian counterparts, just as men and women from the many regions of South Asia had undergone different socializations. Migrants transferred local and regional patterns and created translocal or transregional cultures (Harzig 1997).

In their life-writings – autobiographies, letters, diaries – migrants arriving in pre–First World War Canada hardly ever mentioned Canada as a whole or as a national state, nor did they refer to a British or French Canadian hegemonic culture (Hoerder 1999). Most of them, in fact, did not originate in nation-states but in empires of many peoples: the Hohenzollern, Hapsburg, Romanov, and Hanoverian realms in Europe, the Chinese Empire, or the British Empire in South Asia. Only from the mid-1880s on did nation-state governments begin to regulate departure or entry – or, in many German regions, for example, both departure *and* entry. Although migrants came with local belongings, neither the immigration officials at the point of arrival nor their neighbours in the social space of settlement were able to differentiate between the many origins and thus, for need of cognitive simplification, called the newcomers Germans, Chinese, or Ukrainians. The migrants, in turn, realizing that in democratic processes there is strength in numbers, came to call themselves by generic rather than differentiated local terms. Migration thus involved a process of "becoming ethnic," whereas postmodern hybridization theories assume that previous "givens" are merged.

Recent studies of Europe's nations reveal how cultural entities were constructed and whose interests were incorporated into the constructions. They also show that people who lived in cultures other than the one declared "national" were excluded from political processes and that even within the culture called "national," women and working-class men were relegated to inferior positions (Harzig, Hoerder, and Shubert 2000; Hoerder, Harzig, and Shubert 2003). Consequently, common people of a particular nation-state often found it difficult to express a "national" belonging. The borderlines drawn by gatekeepers cut through cultural borderlands. As a result, unless people were barred from crossing by fences or guards, boundary constructions often had little impact on their everyday lives; as a British scholar put it, dividing lines were "fuzzy" (Cohen 1995), and scholars in the social sciences came to talk about flexible identities rather than about uniform national identities.

This also applies to ethno-cultural groups and enclaves, as was demonstrated by research on ethnic-settlement patterns in Chicago as early as 1895 (Hull House Residents 1895). It took a century for scholars to accept the concept of flexible identities into their theorizations and to understand that ethnic identity was a construction, or as some called it, an "invention of ethnicity" (Sollors 1989; Conzen et al. 1992). Since the 1950s the essentialist *cultural descent* characteristic had been downgraded in favour of a concept of civic society that included social-security networks and frameworks of human (or basic) rights. However, naming groups in terms of "nations" or "ethno-culture" still serves as everyday shorthand for complex cultural belongings. Whereas Canadian scholarship had been at the vanguard of reconceptualizing the "nation to ethnic enclave" approach, the emphasis on the "contribution" of "ethnics," or "allophones," remained. Robert Harney and colleagues (1985), for example, narrated the stories of Toronto's ethnic groups rather than engage in a sociological study of newcomer interaction. The concept of "transnationalism" was first introduced by American cultural anthropologists Glick Schiller and colleagues (1992). While they argued for a scholarship "unbound" from the nation-centred paradigms when considering late-twentieth-century migrants, they adhered to the paradigm of uprootedness when they argued that pre-1965 migrants broke off all social relations to the "homeland" (Kivisto 2001). Although their approach seemed new, it in fact duplicated the results of historians' research on migration across the ages, which had revealed networks, economies, and relationships spanning continents. For example, Canada's North was part of a global fur economy that induced hunters and traders from both local and distant cultures to migrate. America's southern slave economy equally had been part of a global plantation belt. Such economic relations have been captured by Wallerstein's (1974-88) world-systems approach, which, however, privileges Europe over other parts of the world and short-changes migrants and human agency in general (Abu-Lughod 1989; Hoerder 2002). The concept of transnationalism was adopted by American sociologist Alejandro Portes and his collaborators (1999), who emphasized new, faster modes of transportation of people and of messages (communication) as well as the role of second-generation migrants. Within the historical context, slower communication (letters) and transportation (multiple crossings) networks had never prevented migrants from living transnational lives.

The concept of transnationalism, as developed by the German political scientist Thomas Faist (2000b), is, as of now, the most historically grounded and theoretically advanced. Building on previous models of migration and centre-periphery models, he argues that border-crossing migrants create integrated social spaces that follow a logic other than that of nation-states. Historians had already pointed to the mental maps that compress or enlarge "distance" and "time" while migrants move from one stage of economic development to another in a different society. Faist (2000b, 197-210) deals with the levels of individuals and families, of groups and classes, and of state structures and civic societies; he differentiates between social and symbolic ties; and he emphasizes positions in networks and relationships between networks of kinship groups, transnational circuits, and transnational communities. Following Salman Rushdie, he calls migrants "translated" rather than "transplanted" people. Societies ascribe cultures to migrants, and migrants engage in a continuous process of translating patterns of everyday life, whether material or spiritual, normative or ephemeral, intellectual or emotional, social or symbolic. Other scholars have used concepts of negotiating between societies or of brokering different patterns. As in the concept of diaspora, the continued linkages to the society of origin and to other destinations of coethnics, as well as, perhaps, intermediate stopovers, are central to the concept of transnationality (Cohen 1997; Walaszek 2003; Li 2003; Gabaccia and Ottanelli 2001).

Throughout the nineteenth and twentieth centuries, the self-defined nation-states and the empires – in which one group (Russian, German Austrian, German, English, Chinese, or other) designated itself a hegemonic nation – lost those inhabitants who preferred the economic options and political frame of one of the several migrant-admitting societies. In the present, states may have to compete for citizens, who select between cultures rather than defining themselves by one particular essentialist belonging. Citizenship regimes will determine attractiveness of a society for life projects (Wong 2002a).

Living in a Transnational World
Although everyday transnational life cannot be compartmentalized, we deal with the aspects of communication and economic insertion first, before turning to the social spaces of individuals, families, and friends. We adopt an intergenerational perspective in discussing transnationality and include transnational ethno-cultural communities in the analysis. Finally, we turn to the level of whole societies and states.

Information Networks, Economic Insertion, and Emotional Ties
In the past, communication with the society of origin was time-consuming; speed grew with the coming of steamships and expansion of railways. Nineteenth-century migrants crossing the Atlantic or Pacific had access to hemispheric information networks. Italians looking for a job in Montreal, Chinese in search of a job in the New Westminster boom region, and Ukrainians planning to homestead in the Prairies made decisions based on information provided by letters from friends and relatives, by returning migrants, by emigration agents, or, less often, by newspaper reports. The accuracy of newspapers could not be verified, but the flows of transnational information between people who knew (and believed that they could trust) each other involved safeguards against misinformation. Upon arrival at their destinations, migrants expected kin and friends to provide temporary accommodation and support in finding a job. Success stories would bring friends and kin to the doorsteps of the writer. Thus migrants were careful about what to report. They sometimes advised prospective migrants to postpone departure because of economic conditions or demanded speedy arrival because their labour was needed. Young women in particular (i.e., fiancées or sisters) were often asked to follow since their household labour

skills were always in demand, as domestics, as wives, and/or as farm workers. Analyses of migrant letters indicate that news about an economic recession in North America led to a reduction of departures from Europe within a year. The information network worked well, and the time lag may be explained by the interval needed to restructure migration plans.

As to transatlantic networks, the United States Congress's (1911) Immigration Commission provided a wealth of information: throughout the voyage – from departure somewhere in Europe to embarkation in a port city, travel in North America, and arrival at the final destination – individuals were under the care of hemispheric travel organizations run by the large shipping companies. Further, they moved among men and women who shared expectations and experiences, and they found knowledgeable guides among those who crossed the Atlantic or Pacific repeatedly; 12 percent of all Europeans – every eighth traveller – arriving in the United States between 1899 and 1910 had been in North America before. The Atlantic world was transnational and transfamilial: between 1908 and 1910, 94 of every 100 persons arriving at US ports declared that they were going to relatives (79 percent) or to friends (15 percent). Canadian immigrant life-writings confirm this exchange of information and the existence of similar transnational networks (Hoerder 1999, 27-35). After arrival, the newcomers' first moves depended on their "starting capital." Between 1899 and 1910, when labour migrants to the United States brought an average of US$21.50 per person, they had to be certain that their networks would provide them with an income-generating job within days. Transnational mobility between labour-market segments did not allow for much room to manoeuvre at the beginning (US Congress 1911, vol. 3, 349-54). The need of individuals and families to earn a living, combined with the labour-force needs of particular Atlantic economies, intensified migration. Transnational labour markets emerged that were accessible to men and women who did not yet speak the language of the receiving society. And workers communicated about their prospects regarding these transnational labour markets. In publications by German trade unions and the Social Democratic Party, for example, workers published farewell notes before their departure to "America." In the English-language realm, because of the miserable standard of living in Ireland and England in the 1870s, the National Agricultural Labourers' Union sent a "scout" to Canadian and American cities to investigate job options and working conditions before organizing emigrations intended to lower the supply of labour in the British Isles. These economic aspects and labour-market theory have been neglected both in the interstate approach to migration and in the cultural approach to migrant insertion (Hoerder 1996, 226-31; 1999, 66-68). However, Donald Avery's (1983) sensitive labour-history approach to insertion of working men and women, which addresses Canadian society's

reluctance to host them, does justice to the complex processes of acculturation and rejection in labour markets.

Next to economic factors, emotional factors were part of transnational
lives. In fact, the two were inextricably entwined. Upon departure not only
did migrants look forward to new options, but they were also aware that
they had obligations to those left behind and that they would probably
never see the social space of their childhood again. This separation needed
to be mitigated, and once again communication, usually by letter, was important. Relationships could be reaffirmed, feelings expressed, sequential
migration arranged. Any information about the new society had to be translated into terms that could be decoded in the receiving society (Kamphoefner,
Helbich, and Sommer 1991). How this was achieved is shown by the correspondence of the Leveridge family, which migrated from eastern England
to Hastings County, Ontario, in the early 1880s (Leveridge 1972). The emigrants had to explain to their kin at home that their lives were not "primi-
tive" and that "unusual" behaviour was economically rational. A study of
1970s newcomers in Toronto shows comparable communication networks
but new media: telephone and Internet (Opitz-Black 2002). Similar patterns
emerge from migrant letters to and from many parts of the world (Baily and
Ramella 1988). The theoretical frame of family economies, developed by
Louise Tilly and Joan Scott (1978) for early modern Europe, may well be
applied to families spread over different societies.

The migrants' transnational social space included economic exchange
across continents inside and outside of families. First, remittances of savings by migrants to their families in the culture of origin and the impact of
such foreign exchange on the economic development of "old world" societies, whether in Europe or in Asia, have been studied. However, the assumption that the North American receiving societies provided the means
of survival for families left behind overlooks a generational aspect: after
their parents' death in the culture of origin, emigrant children were entitled
to their share of the inheritance. As a result, up to the early 1870s, more
funds were sent from – mostly peasant – families in Europe to migrant kin
in the United States than were sent from the United States to families that
stayed behind. Second, small businesspeople in the immigrant community
imported goods from the society of origin to ensure some measure of continuity in food and clothing habits. In the opposite direction, material gifts
brought from North America by returning migrants introduced family and
friends to new devices. These transnational exchanges are particularly well
studied for Italy (Foerster 1919; Bezza 1983; Baily 1992). And third, individual migrants in rural regions asked people "at home" to send seeds so
that migrants could feed families with customary vegetables and re-create
blossoming farm gardens remembered from childhood. Such gardenscapes
impacted on neighbours in their new locality.

Symbolic and Generational Communications

Changes in symbolic communication are a further intergenerational aspect of transnational lives. Life-writings from an Icelandic immigrant family in Winnipeg and a Russian-Jewish one in the Prairies indicate that religious stories, historic myths, and fairytales passed on to children born in Canada by parents socialized in Europe lacked context: as the children no longer shared the memory of a local culture, the tales became decontextualized. In addition, the parents' symbols stood in contrast to the children's lives among their receiving society's schools and peers. However, Canadian teachers' stories, in the minds of immigrant children, also lacked context. In the mixed classrooms, they had to form their own views of their life-worlds. Multiple frames of reference were the rule, particularly since English-speaking Canadian teachers often did not relate a Canadian narrative but a British (imperial) one (Salverson 1939; Maynard 1964; Petrone 1995; Rosenberg 1981). Attention to the second generation adds a timeline, a processural aspect to the concept of transnationality: if children stay in the receiving society, the transcultural aspect of their life-worlds recedes in favour of a predominance of the receiving society's culture or one of its components. Since, both for internal reasons and through the input of immigrants, the receiving society is constantly in motion, the children of newcomers do not simply become members of *the* new nation; the society does not provide one fixed frame. Transnationality, or in older terms multiethnic cultural input, involves the transformation of the receiving nation-state and its civic society (Hutchinson 1950; Rumbaut and Portes 2001; Portes and Rumbaut 2001).

The emergence of ethno-cultural transnational communities within receiving societies indicates that people from particular regions of origin share ways of life and structure their new social spaces, neighbourhoods, and local communities in a manner that accommodates both old and new. Old and new mentalities and practices overlap in a single space, and through migrants' linkages both worlds overlap in communities of origin, too. Such community formation, in addition to permitting the sharing of premigration customs and the language of childhood, allows for the establishment of institutions deemed necessary for adjustment and backward linkages. However, informally lived structures linked to old life-world practices and values may also function as constraining factors in the new social environment. Formal institutions such as mutual-aid societies, banks, travel agencies, and parishes provide transnational links to the society of origin: pastors or priests are requested from the Church of origin, funds are transferred in both directions, and aid is provided through association when kin networks remain in the old life-world. The stability of such institutions over time depends on backward and diasporic linkages. Slovak immigrants, for political-cultural reasons, kept intense ties to Slovakia since in North America they had the liberty to counter the Magyar nationalism that threatened their culture at home. In response to persecutions, Jews, in many instances, formed lasting diasporas, or interlinked settlements, in many parts of the world. High rates of return and of multiple migration among Italians and Croats furthered continued linkage. Situations of crises, whether a local fire or a continent-wide war, intensified institutional links since aid was channelled back to the homeland. Wars, however, could also reduce emotional ties because the exchange of letters and travel were interrupted or because networks and even whole communities of origin were annihilated. The constant need for formal and informal adaptation was, however, detrimental to some groups in the immigrant community. Clerics, journalists, bankers, or teachers, functioning as gatekeepers, sometimes attempt to draw boundaries inclusive both of other groups and of the host society since their positions and incomes depend on a viable ethno-cultural community that does not adopt the language of the host society or mix with neighbouring parishes. In contrast, young people passing through multiethnic classrooms and peer groups tend to dissolve boundaries (Kuropas 1991; Cleveland Project 1986-91).

Local communities were marked by various transnational aspects: personal, institutional, emotional, intellectual, spiritual. A young Finnish woman, migrating with her parents to Timmins, Ontario, found the community wanting, as she remembered their Helsinki apartment with central heating and her highly regarded school (Schneider 1986). A German family in a small Prairie town pointedly informed family members and neighbours remaining in Germany that, in Canada, they elected local officials themselves. No God- or state-given hierarchy of officials was imposed; rather, civil society constituted itself. Such bits of information provided the recipients with mental options that would not have been available otherwise. Social reform projects, or utopias, were aimed at – distant – larger societies (the macrolevel). Local elections opened perspectives for change in the immediate life-world (the microlevel). However, migrant transnationalism had only a limited impact on local old-world communities. Italian immigrant women, on return visits, dared talk back to haughty officials. But most return migrants were marginalized by members of the local establishment, who feared for their position if social institutions were re-formed. Nevertheless, knowledge of the practicability of different institutions permitted a political discourse that referred to "America" as the better society – an "America" that was neither the United States nor Canada but a transnational image of potentialities. This process involved a secularization of hope: a better life in a society in this world, albeit on the other side of an ocean, replaced the assumedly better world after death (Hoerder 1992). Migrants, contrary to received language, did not create little Italies, Germanys, or Irelands in most Canadian cities; they had left their old life-worlds because they found them wanting and intended to create new life-worlds for themselves that combined whatever seemed viable and desirable from new and old. Certain norms, however, could centre life projects on the old community. Belief systems that mandated the authority of older generations over younger ones in transnational extensions of norms to North America, such as Confucianism, imposed the return of sons to the homeland for the spiritual welfare of the parents.

In the late nineteenth and early twentieth centuries, Canada – the country, the society, the polity – was more or less absent from immigrant communications, as were particular laws or institutions, although it was present implicitly in descriptions of urban job options and rural life-ways. Nevertheless, the macrolevel provided the frame for local potentialities. References to the larger context sometimes involved irony, particularly when options did not match hopes: the sods with which Prairie settlers built their first huts were called "government brick" (the government did provide easy access to land, but the accommodation was less than satisfactory). Politicians or statesmen in Ottawa or in provincial capitals were never mentioned, but helpful local immigration officials received praise. Conversely, when immigration policy became more restrictive in the 1920s and when aid-requesting immigrants became liable for deportation during the Great Depression, government officials were seen as a threat. The one national institution mentioned again and again, Canada Mail, was referred to only in its local form, the post office. Without it and its worldwide extension through other national postal services, no communication and transnational exchange would have been possible except for among those who had time and money for a return visit (Hoerder 1999, 151-75, 190-204, 239-77).

On occasion, Canada's government, too, chose transnational rather than international approaches. When "movement into the West" pretty much come to a halt in the United States in the 1880s and when the frontier officially closed in 1893 according to a pronouncement from the Census Bureau, Canada was still in need of people to settle the Prairies and to complete its national project. A policy to promote "the last best West" was formulated, and Mennonites and Jews were able to find a new homestead under the group-settlement plan. However, the results were meagre, and when it became obvious that the preferred immigrants of British or other northern- and western-European origin would no longer be coming in sufficient numbers, no intergovernmental accord with a sending state was negotiated. Rather, the secretary of the interior, Clifford Sifton, issued his oft-cited but usually masculinized call for "men in sheepskin coats." Sifton, who knew that family labour was needed to establish a farm, said "I think a stalwart peasant in a sheep-skin coat, born on the soil, whose forefathers have been farmers for ten generations, with a stout wife and a half-dozen children, is good quality." Through this careful phrasing, he skirted the issue of racial origin, high on the agenda of public opinion in the Atlantic world. If he had called for peasants from Ukraine, he would have raised the issue of "dark" eastern-European people coming to a "white" Dominion. He might also have antagonized the tsarist government. Instead, he invoked the imagery of soil-rooted (British) yeomen farmers. By referring to sheepskin coats, he indicated self-sufficiency. He thus carefully changed a racialized image to permit the development of a transnational community of farmers in the interests of the Canadian state and society. However, like his colleagues in the government, he overlooked the fact that Canada's economy was industrializing and that urban workers were needed. Although farmers did come, far more migrants went to the cities. The government's intervention was helpful to one group of migrants, but its hostility to the working classes, unions, and single working men (said to be unruly) would have slowed down Canada's industrialization if migrants hadn't come to their own conclusions and, regardless of governmental position, moved to urban labour markets and communities (Sifton, quoted in Dafoe 1931, 142). That Sifton's words are hardly known to younger Canadians in the present indicates another shift in transnationalism: the linkage to Europe has been replaced by globalized linkages, particularly to societies in Asia and in the Caribbean.

Transnationality is a highly dynamic process; its cultural content changes depending on historical context and on migrants' cultures of origin and regions of settlement. The cultural content of relations between social spaces in Canada and the several cultures of the British Isles – English, Scottish, Welsh, Irish – is, of course, different from that of relations to spaces in Ukraine or in France since the first male migrants in Canada established the institutions and, jointly with women, the socio-cultural patterns. Migrants from France and later from Ukraine, again in contrast to smaller groups, did establish regional patterns in Quebec and parts of the Prairies. A decline in the volume of migration from particular regions or a severance of connections with some regions, as was pursued by Quebec's elites under the theory of the two Frances in the late nineteenth century, reduces the intensity of transcultural life-ways. New relations to other regions of origin transform the inputs and outputs of transculturalisms as well as the social-geographic spaces involved. From 1914 to 1918 the war in Europe severed relations between families and ethno-cultural communities, as did anti-Asian policies that excluded Japanese, Punjabi, or southern Chinese families. In contrast to the United States, which restricted immigration after the First World War, Canada remained an immigrant-receiving country until the worldwide Depression of the 1930s curtailed migration. Notwithstanding a brief resumption of migration from Europe in the late 1940s and the 1950s, processes of transculturalization from the mid-1960s on became increasingly the experience of migrants from the Pacific and the Caribbean.

The Politics of Transnationalism and the Process of Insertion
Governments may provide a broadly conceived frame for migration and

transcultural life-ways, they may react to what bureaucrats perceive as specific problems, or they may attempt to regulate all details of immigrant arrival and insertion. Frames set by society and government should take migrant agency into account. Men and women who determine their migration themselves develop their own networks. Refugees, in contrast, depart involuntarily; thus their networks, if any, and acculturation processes are different. Persons displaced by wars, after years of internment in camps, often need support to overcome the consequences of having been torn out of their networks. For voluntary as well as involuntary migrants, coming to terms with the new society, both statewide and local, depends on their capabilities to achieve negotiated compromises between their and the receiving society's value systems and life-ways; it also depends on the society's ability to provide for a balance between continuities and changes. Emotional ties and societal belongings, particularly customs and values rooted in childhood socialization, cannot be easily discarded. Such continuities provide the basis from which to explore new options and fashion new life-worlds. Migrants need a strategic competence if they are to turn life projects into actual trajectories in environments that they may influence but that they cannot change altogether. However, their premigration desire to change their circumstances permits them to critically assess shortcomings of the society of origin and to free themselves from what they dislike. Thus migrants negotiate a social space for themselves in their own minds and with their families in the context of receiving communities and in the framework of the receiving society's political and legal institutions.

Depending on the historical period and on receiving countries' concepts of state, nation, and society, migrants either have been offered culturally and economically determined options or have had their self-agency limited by constraints. A historical perspective encompassing prenational dynastic societies indicates that newcomers could negotiate special status for their customs, values, and religious practices. For centuries, merchants trading within different cultural frameworks across the world were accorded special status and often housed in separate quarters (Hoerder 2002, 30-38, 75-86). Fleeing and being expelled from seventeenth-century Catholic France, the Huguenots, whose human and social capital was valued by rulers across Europe and in the British North American colonies, were effectively inserted into society by state policy, their temporary impoverishment notwithstanding. Huguenots negotiated entry: as a group, they agreed to be loyal subjects of the respective ruler and in return received freedom to use their own language, follow their own religious precepts, and practise their own ways of life. To avoid lasting poverty among migrants, many rulers provided refugee newcomers with an initial grant-in-aid and a period of tax exemption. Reestablished in their crafts, they would and did contribute to the principality's economy and revenues. In contrast, the treatment of Polish minorities

under the Second German Reich around 1900, when the concept of a domi-
nating German nation within the polity had gained predominance, exem-
plifies exclusion. Since the division of the Polish state between the three
neighbouring monarchies in the 1790s, Polish-cultured people had lived in
Prussia. Many were bilingual, hundreds of thousands migrated to the industrial cities of the Ruhr District in pursuit of work, and all had adjusted to
the political structures. However, fearing a nationalist agenda and the Poles'
Catholicism, Prussia's Protestant authorities prohibited use of the Polish
language in public and placed all ethno-cultural organizations under police
surveillance. In protest, a large segment of the empire's Polish population
began to reaffirm its own cultural values. This has been called an imposed
process of "secondary minority formation": minorities in the midst of leaving their assigned social slot to enter the majority society are forced back
into a separate-enclave status through discrimination and governmental
repression (Hoerder 2002, 105-7, 348-49; Kleßmann 1985). More often than
not, dynastic states embraced populations of many cultures, economic pursuits, and social strata. State authorities negotiated a particular legal status
with each group; the one shared status was that of subject of the respective
ruler.

   With the emerging discourses about nation-states, the frame for incor-
porating resident minorities and immigrant newcomers changed fundamentally. According to the Enlightenment's concept of human rights and
republican governments, people were to be equal before a state's laws.
According to Romanticism's recasting of the dichotomy between trans-
European noble and folk cultures to arrive at a concept of peoples in particular regions with particular cultures, all peoples were expected to live in the
traditions of their ancestors and to develop their cultural expressiveness.
However, these two *concepts* were then combined into the fundamentalist
or essentialist *ideology* of nation-states. This introduced a power hierarchy:
first, some people were elevated to majority status within the cultural nation, and others were downgraded to cultural minorities; second, equality
before the laws was turned into homogeneity of culture, and assimilation
by the hegemonic national culture was imposed on the multiple other cultures. For historically resident groups, now labelled minorities, the resulting
cultural oppression often motivated them to depart for immigrant-receiving
societies that provided better economic as well as cultural options. Under
the new ideology of national identity, migrants already present could no
longer negotiate their status; rather, they were expected either to assimilate
into the hegemonic nation, or, if this nation was built on the myth of a
homogenous origin, to retain their inferior legal status, or, if designated
permanently alien, to become a rotating labour force required to depart
after a specified period of time.

Although migrations occurred on all continents, those in Asian and African societies were intra-imperial and intercolonial or interregional rather than international. Their legal frames differed from those affecting migration across borders of nation-states. Given the historic patterns of mainly transatlantic migration toward the Americas, the two North American immigration states and civic societies became the point of reference in public discourse. To 1914 both democratic federal states retained particular aspects of dynastic states' flexibility in order to attract newcomers. In the United States the (regionally varying) practice of granting voting rights in municipal elections to immigrants without citizenship was based on the concept that by forswearing allegiance to a foreign monarch – but not to their everyday culture – newcomers could legally be regarded as belonging to their new local societies. In Canada the federal government's decision to incorporate cultural groups under special status – Icelanders in Manitoba, Mennonites in several Prairie locations, Doukhobors on small reserves – followed dynastic states' practices of incorporation. Such special status contradicted the principle of equality before the law for all inhabitants of a polity, but it respected cultural specifics.

In the late nineteenth century, the Canadian state imposed few regulations on migrants, provided many regional options for arrivals, and collected few taxes but also delivered few services. This provided newcomers with manoeuvring space. In rural regions, provisions for homesteading permitted establishment of an economic base from which migrants could then contribute to the polity's revenues. Provision was even made for newcomers yet unable to pay taxes. They could work off their taxes by accepting some kind of public employment. In urban regions, access to segments of the labour market was afforded newcomers who sought jobs commensurate with their professional, linguistic, and social skills. Since neither craft organizations nor municipal regulations for the food and service sectors existed, anyone could open shop as an artisan or commence work in services. Although the absence of regulations permitted easy entry, it precluded consumer protection. Communities had to devise their own control mechanisms to ensure the quality of goods produced, groceries sold, and services provided.

As regards national identity, an intensive Americanization drive in the United States around 1910 rigorously demanded loyalty to the nation. In contrast, the "Canada First" movement of the same period had difficulties in postulating loyalty to "the nation" because the anglophone elites remained in limbo between nationhood and either dependency on Britain or adherence to British imperial belonging. Furthermore, the French-British dichotomy precluded imposition of a single concept of nationhood. This prenational status was reflected in the fact that no distinct Canadian citizenship, different from the British one, existed before 1947. Immigrants applying for citizenship, having completed their trajectory to the many-cultured life-world in their adopted country, had to accept British citizenship rather than the Canadian one that they expected and desired. Migrants in Canada had more leeway in charting a course for themselves than they would have had in any self-declared and allegedly monocultural nation-state with an institutional apparatus to enforce loyalty and homogeneity. Most migants became imbued with a cultural and social Canadianness without being able to express this by a conscious adoption of *Canadian* citizenship (Hoerder 1999, 281-91).

Since migrants seek change but also attempt to avoid a disruption of their cultural identifications, they adjust the speed of their acculturation to their capabilities and desires; since they aim at economic security, they negotiate cultural change in order to settle a farm, find a job, or establish a business within the legal frame and customary practices of Canada's regional societies. Thus a legal frame that permits the establishment of distinctive ethno-cultural clubs and culture-based mutual-aid associations prevents disruptions of individual and family lives as well as of cultural practices shared by people of similar regional origin. Identifications emerge not through concepts of descent from some ancestral group, such as Anglo-Saxonism or *pure laine* Franco-Canadianism, but through the option for self-determined life projects within the societal structures. Such transnationalism continues across time: Ukrainian and Mennonite settlers on the Prairies pursued their particular goals, whereas Italians in Montreal had different ones, and Jews in Toronto or the Chinese in British Columbia had still others. They did so within a frame of laws and gradually emerging concepts of common belonging. Many, however, had to do so under the weight of ethnic labelling and racialization. For a century and a half, governmental institutions, under the sway of the two ethno-national groups that came to style themselves as founding nations, made no effort to remove these obstacles.

Since changes to the immigration regulations in 1962 and afterward, newcomers from South Asia, from Caribbean and Latin American societies, and from the three Chinas (mainland, Taiwan, and Hong Kong), with their many regional variants, have come to pursue similar goals. However, changes in people's transcultural lives have occurred more gradually. The demand for political recognition was expressed in the fourth volume of findings published by the Bilingualism and Biculturalism Royal Commission in Canada in the 1960s. Today speed and the low cost of travel, a change in telecommunications, and since the 1970s a policy change from biculturalism to multiculturalism have changed experiences of transnational belonging.

It is no paradox that the stability of Canada's polity and society emerged from its flexibility and adaptability. The repressive imposition of a monocultural national identity requires costly institutions and creates friction. Newcomers' ability to create stable and acceptable living conditions is also based on their flexibility in adjusting their premigration cultural practices and value systems. The decision to depart their homelands severs allegiances to other economic and political *systems* but not to the positive aspects of *everyday cultures*. Upon entering a new socio-cultural environment, they develop, either intentionally or unconsciously, translocal, transregional, transcultural, and transnational ways of life. Such communities are always in transition. Migrants move toward a new society, while adding their particular cultural and economic input, in a transformative process that is furthered by their involvement in additional transnational circuits. The Canadian state's structural flexibility toward cultural distinctiveness permitted incorporation even of groups who pursued fundamentalist – but not missionary – positions. Mennonites and other Anabaptist groups could practise their ways of life and accept the costs, whether technological backwardness or doctrinal splits. Refugees from US-supported Latin American dictatorships, arriving from camps after long periods of dislocation, could reestablish identities and life-ways without immediate pressure to Canadianize. Vancouver's and other cities' "Chinatowns," which are in fact multiple differentiated neighbourhoods, provide Canadian settings for cultures in change. The frame called "Canada" changes in the process. In contrast to those of the period before the 1960s, polity and civic society consciously accept (or at least debate) change rather than attempt to impose (bi)cultural uniformity. As can be historically shown, such impositions were never successful but proved a hindrance to societal development in the past.

Thus the concept of transnationalism, or transculturalism, is vastly more appropriate to understanding migration and societal developments than the old "nation to ethnic enclave" paradigm. It emerged from interdisciplinary cooperation in migration and acculturation research as well as from political theorists' reconceptualization of nations and nation-states. Just as inter- or transdisciplinarity frees scholars from limiting boundaries between disciplines, transnationalism frees societies and policy makers from the boundaries of nations and their exclusionist myths and from the dead weight of historical constructions.

3
Unmaking a Transnational Community: Japanese Canadian Families in Wartime Canada
Pamela Sugiman

In 1877 the first Japanese immigrant to Canada landed on the shores of British Columbia. The welcome of the many immigrants from Japan in the years to follow was contingent largely on capital's need for cheap labour to work on railroads and in the mines. Enticed by the promise of "easy wealth" in these developing industries and pushed by the prospect of starvation on tiny rice farms in Japan, thousands of Japanese men settled on Canada's West Coast. After the men, women arrived. Many entered the country as "picture brides," their qualifications being a hardy constitution and a willingness to endure taxing labour in a strange land (Kitagawa 1985, 218).

Together, women and men built up communities that dotted the Fraser Valley and the British Columbia coast, and in Vancouver a Japanese business, cultural, and social community flourished. This first generation of Japanese in Canada were known as the *issei*. Over time, issei women gave birth to the next generation, the *nisei*. The birth of the nisei brought forth a new relationship to the nation, a new (Canadian) citizenship, and a strengthened commitment to the dominant cultural, social, and political ideals of Canadian society. The early experiences of issei parents largely revolved around building a better life for their children, for whom Canada was home (Kitagawa 1985, 219).

With the outbreak of the Second World War, however, many families were displaced from home. All were unsettled. From the time of their arrival, Japanese immigrants in Canada had suffered intense racism. Both institutional discrimination and ostracism from the Anglo-Celtic population restricted Japanese Canadians to specific jobs and neighbourhoods while barring them from most institutions of higher learning, from holding public office, and from voting in an election (see Roy 2003; Ward 1978). But the events of the war, almost surreal in quality, had an unprecedented impact. The war, writes Kitagawa (1985, 220), "came to tear out the roots of our lives." During these years, Canada's federal government uprooted, interned, and dispossessed all persons of Japanese descent. Just after Japan's bombing of Pearl Harbor in 1941, government agents confiscated the fishing boats, cars, stores, and farms of Japanese residents. With little notice, families were forced from their homes and had to abandon most of their personal possessions to looters. Some people were temporarily deposited in the former horse stables of the Pacific National Exhibition grounds in Vancouver. Others were directly dispersed to various sites of internment. Women, children, and some men were placed in ghost towns located throughout the interior of British Columbia. Men who displayed resistance of any form or degree were incarcerated in prisoner-of-war "camps" in Ontario (Miki and Kobayashi 1991, 30-31, 41). Many males were also sent to perform arduous labour on roads or in lumber camps. A minority of families who possessed sufficient financial resources were moved to so-called self-supporting camps in British Columbia. Other family units performed gruelling labour on the sugar-beet farms of Alberta and Manitoba.

In this chapter, I explore the links between these acts of racism, perceived transnational identities, and the attempt to unmake a transnational community. As noted by Satzewich and Wong in the Introduction, there is at times a celebratory tone to some of the literature on transnationalism. Yet less often recounted is its more menacing side, which may surface as perceived transnationalism feeds into racist stereotypes about who does and does not constitute a loyal citizen. In the case of Japanese Canadians, the combination of racism and assumptions about their transnational identities resulted in a process of forced "repatriation" and exile. This is arguably a sinister dimension of transnational movement and the politics surrounding it.

Although the nisei and many issei in fact did little border crossing, racist government actions during the 1940s, fuelled by the imagined transnational identities and allegiances of people of Japanese ancestry, took on enormous meaning. Government wartime policy was legitimated by the belief that, despite time spent in this country, those of the "Japanese race" were fundamentally loyal to the emperor of Japan and, by virtue of their phenotypical traits and kinship ties, disloyal to Canada. Most of the measures directed at Japanese Canadians during these years were guided by the notion that transnational loyalties cross generations, override current citizenship, and eclipse fluid perceptions of homeland.

Further, the wartime experiences of Japanese Canadians highlight the family as an important site of transnational movement (see Levitt 2000; Parrenas 2001). In much scholarly writing, state policy tends to assume an impersonal form, seeming to be external to, or above, personal lives and intimate relationships. But focusing on the family underscores the link between public (state) policies and the people who form the nation. The family bridges the public and private components of transnationalism, thereby revealing the artificiality of dichotomizing these social spaces or prioritizing one over the other. Moreover, mapping the lives of various family members, old and young, highlights the different generational experiences of transnationalism, prompting consideration of questions relating to the "persistence of trans-national ties" (Itzigsohn 2001) over time, across generations, and in rela-tion to citizenship status.

"Repatriation" Policy and the Illusion of Choice

During the war, the federal government's control of the Japanese Canadian community was all-encompassing. In this chapter, I focus on one dimen-sion of the larger internment narrative: government "repatriation" policy and the community's response to this measure. By the mid-1940s, as the war was coming to an end, Japanese Canadians had spent roughly four years at the sites of internment. Many women and children remained sepa-rated from their husbands, grown sons, and brothers. For four years, some men had endured severely curtailed rights and freedoms in austere prisoner-of-war camps. These years were marked by disillusionment and demoraliza-tion, deepening over time. Some people complained primarily of boredom and aimlessness; others lamented lost gains, limited opportunities, and stunted aspirations. Still others suffered from exhausting agricultural labour. All were aware of the violation of their rights. Communities were marked by intense feelings of despair and a strong sense of injustice.

At this juncture, the Canadian government forced all people of Japanese origin, regardless of citizenship or birthplace, to make a decision: 22,000 persons, 75 percent of whom were naturalized or Canadian-born citizens, were ordered to "choose" either "repatriation" in Japan or relocation east of the Rockies in Ontario or Quebec, far from the site of their former West Coast homes. The goals behind this policy were clear: wholesale elimina-tion of the "Japanese race" from the Province of British Columbia (as well as from the country more generally) and insurance that a concentration of such people would not resurface in any other part of Canada (Miki and Kobayashi 1991, 46, 50, 52).

In an effort to prompt people to move from British Columbia, Prime Min-ister Mackenzie King's government introduced what has come to be known as the "repatriation survey." This survey was administered by T.B. Pickersgill, commissioner of Japanese placement for the federal Department of Labour. Beginning on 13 April 1945 in Tashme, a detachment of Royal Canadian Mounted Police (RCMP), under Pickersgill's authority, canvassed all Japa-nese and Japanese Canadians over the age of sixteen. Before asking people to sign the repatriation forms, RCMP officers posted two notices at each internment site. The first notice stated that anyone who sought repatria-tion would receive free passage to Japan. In addition, it explained that upon signing, Canadian citizens were expected to declare a desire to relinquish their "British nationality and to assume the status of a national of Japan"

(Adachi 1991, 298). The second notice also offered (limited) financial support to those who agreed to move east of the Rockies. This support, however, was contingent on one's willingness to accept whatever employment the government deemed appropriate. Failure to do so would be regarded as evidence of "disloyalty" to the nation.

The RCMP completed the repatriation survey of the internment sites in just one month, thereby leaving people with little time to make decisions that would potentially shape the rest of their lives. This situation was made even more untenable because many families were living apart at the time. Individuals were therefore forced to sign or not sign independent of one another. Although many people communicated to friends and relatives by mail, such correspondence was most often partial. As well, it was written with an awareness that government officials would be reading and censoring the contents of their letters.

Not surprisingly, the repatriation survey put many families in a state of crisis. According to writer Ken Adachi (1991, 300), "the interior camps were thrown into an acute state of tension and turmoil, stirred up by a series of rumors about impending government action." In April 1945 a nisei woman in Slocan wrote to a friend in Vernon: "We are really stuck with this 'voluntary' business. We want to move east but do not wish to say we did it voluntarily when it's really forced. 'Do this or that!!!' with a threat implied. I'll be glad when we sign though. This suspense and uncertainty is a torture. We sleep eat and move – always speaking or thinking of our signatures on a form which determines our whole future" (Intercepted Letters, 23 April 1945).

Such anguish was aggravated by the inefficiency and ineptness of the government officials who were administering the survey. For example, without clear information, many people mistakenly believed that by agreeing to move eastward, they would have the right to remain in Canada without qualification. On the incorrect assumption that those who signed for repatriation would not lose their Canadian nationality unless they were actually deported, Pickersgill himself informed the residents of Tashme that signing would in no way reflect disloyalty (Sunahara 1981, 121).

People signed for repatriation also in response to the intense racial hostility that they had thus far encountered in Canada. Such racism produced anger, worry, and a sense of futility among Japanese Canadians. In a letter to a friend in British Columbia, a nisei man from Lethbridge, Alberta, wrote,

Just as bad as the Jews without a country. Canada won't have anything to do with us, except to push us around where ever there's a shortage of labour, and when that's finished, they're planning to ship us to Japan. When we get there, we're not Japs, so we'll be pushed around. I wonder if we really are to be sent back to Japan, if it would be advisable to denounce our Canadian citizenship, whatever the hell that's worth, and become a Jap, even if our ideals etc., aren't Jap? What a wonderful country this democracy of Canada must be: being pushed around, kicked around, discriminated against, and even made to think that we'll be repatriated. (Intercepted Letters, 7 November 1943)

Through the community newspaper, the *New Canadian,* by word of mouth, or in correspondence with family and friends who had already ventured east, people also received warnings about the harsh treatment that they would face in Ontario and Quebec.

People were further guided by a host of practical concerns about the preservation of "home" and the maintenance of kin relations. Although they had been uprooted and divided and had lost property and savings, many had invested what little they had left in an effort to make their ghost-town homes more habitable, however ramshackle. In addition, they had cultivated subsistence gardens and had built latrines and communal bath houses, and some had opened small stores that supplied Japanese groceries. Moving east would once again force them to leave "home" and start over. After years of dislocation, many people simply wanted to stay in one place. Although families that "chose" to repatriate could temporarily remain in British Columbia, those who opted to stay in Canada would immediately be moved to Kaslo and subsequently shipped east of the Rockies. Insofar as repatriation to Japan would occur at an unspecified future date, repatriates could at least forestall yet another dislocation.

In addition, as mentioned, people who moved east were expected to accept whatever work government officials offered. Refusal of such employment would be recorded on file as evidence of disloyalty. Importantly, refusal to take a job offer would also result in disqualification for both individual and family relief benefits. Families that signed for repatriation, in comparison, would be given some financial relief, although meagre.

Under these circumstances, over ten thousand Japanese Canadians signed up for "expulsion to Japan" (Miki and Kobayashi 1991, 52). This figure constituted nearly half the "Japanese" population in Canada. Then the war ended with a suddenness. Immediately after Japan's unconditional surrender on 2 September 1945, a great many people, now facing exile, desperately attempted to revoke their requests for repatriation. By October the commissioner of Japanese placement had received 2,056 requests for revocation of applications. Of these, 467 were from Japanese nationals, 236 from naturalized Canadians, 543 from Canadian-born over the age of sixteen, and 810 from Canadian-born dependants ("Voluntary Repatriation"). By April 1946, 4,527 (including dependants) of the 6,844 adults who had signed the forms officially wished to cancel (Sunahara 1981, 124).

As time passed, it became increasingly clear that the repatriation survey had been coercive. Although government officials had presented the survey as voluntary, thousands claimed that they had in effect signed "under duress." In presenting an either-or proposition, the very language of the notices was indicative of its restrictive nature (Adachi 1991, 302). Nevertheless, some politicians remained intent on making the signatures binding. At a meeting of the Special Cabinet Committee on Repatriation and Relocation, Humphrey Mitchell planned to follow through on the repatriation survey with a repressive program of deportation (Sunahara 1981, 124). His plan called for the deportation of four classes of people:

1 all Japanese aliens who had signed for repatriation (with the exception of a few who would be permitted to stay in Canada on compassionate grounds) or who had been interned as prisoners of war
2 all naturalized Japanese Canadians who had signed repatriation requests and had not revoked their requests before Japan's unconditional surrender on 2 September 1945
3 all nisei who had not revoked their repatriation requests before Japan's unconditional surrender; Canadian-born citizens who tried to revoke their signatures after Japan's surrender would be assessed insofar as their loyalty was in question, and any cancellation of requests by Japanese nationals would not be considered (Adachi 1991, 303)
4 the wives and minor children of the above classes (Sunahara 1981, 127).

In order to implement this program, Mitchell needed the Special Committee to support three orders in council under the War Measures Act. The first declared the repatriation requests binding on the persons who had signed (and their dependants). The second would strip the deported naturalized Japanese Canadians of Canadian citizenship. And the third would establish a body called a Loyalty Tribunal, a quasi-judicial commission that would determine which cases were to be heard on "compassionate grounds," investigate the background and attitudes of "persons of the Japanese race" (Miki and Kobayashi 1991, 50; Sunahara 1981, 124), and, more generally, evaluate the loyalty of any Japanese Canadian referred by the minister of labour. The government passed the deportation orders in council in December 1945.

Negotiating "Repatriation" and Deportation
Although a long-standing view has been that Japanese Canadians were passive and accepting of their wartime treatment, the community in fact made concerted appeals to revoke their signatures on the repatriation forms. As individuals, as members of families, and as part of a larger collectivity represented by organizations such as the Co-operative Committee on Japanese Canadians (CCJC) and the Japanese Canadian Committee for Democracy (JCCD), "persons of the Japanese race" fought to continue to live in Canada.[1]

The negotiation of national status and homeland throughout the mid- to late 1940s tells us much about Japanese Canadian families and the government's understanding of these families, especially in relation to nationalist sentiment and transnational ties. In the following section, I highlight three themes that emerge in discussions surrounding the attempt to unmake the Japanese Canadian transnational community at the war's end. First, central to such protests were concerns about the (re)unification of families and the weight of familial bonds. In their correspondence with the government, Japanese Canadians repeatedly underscored the importance of family as both an emotional and economic resource. Second, at the same time, repatriation narratives reveal the family as a site of conflict and contestation. Although government policy largely regarded Japanese Canadian families as homogeneous units that fell under the authority of the issei father, they were marked by divisions that promoted often tense, as well as powerfully loving, relations. These familial differences were based on generation, citizenship, and gender. Paradoxically, such differences were exacerbated as a result of state wartime policies. Third, much of the discourse revolves around individuals' relationships to the nation. Although government leaders presented the repatriation survey as a necessary act of "nation building," Japanese Canadians themselves viewed the racialized policy as a violation of the nation's principles and an affront to their citizenship. Resonant in their protests against the repatriation measure was an almost compulsory assertion of their goodness as citizens, their national loyalty, and their contributions to building Canada.

Families Together

In August 1945 a Japanese Canadian family wrote to Humphrey Mitchell. The family's eldest son was enlisted in the Canadian army. When surveyed, the rest of the family, unaware of the son's intentions, signed for repatriation. They later regretted this decision and wished to withdraw their signatures and retain their Canadian citizenship. The family's overriding concern was to be together. Faced with the threat of deportation, four members of the household explained to Mitchell: "On the event that we must return to Japan, this inevitably would mean the breakup of our family. It is the ardent desire of our son that we remain in Canada and be united together" (Correspondence, 18 August 1945).

This letter echoes the sentiments articulated in many others. Family unification was among the most commonly cited reasons that people gave for wishing to revoke their repatriation requests. When the government uprooted Japanese Canadians at the outset of war, families were distraught, and the community cried out in protest. At the war's end, they again faced separation, but this time it was of a different nature. If the government were to uphold the repatriation claims, the result would be a transnational separation of families. And most people recognized that at a time when spatial distances were not easily or quickly traversed, an uprooting across nations would effectively result in the severing of personal ties – in some cases, for life.

In a dramatic effort to keep families intact, the nisei often took responsibility for communicating with government officials on behalf of younger siblings and issei parents. Their educational background and generational status rendered the nisei more effective spokespersons. In December 1945 a nisei daughter wrote to Mackenzie King urging that her father, mother, and four siblings be permitted to remain in Canada. In highly emotional language, this young woman explained, "when the war broke out with Japan, like a tornado, fear swept over us all ... Because I was the eldest of the five children, responsibility fell on my shoulder." While a student worker in St. Thomas, Ontario, she learned that her parents had signed for repatriation:

The sorrow in my heart was too too great. However, my parents and on behalf of my young brothers had requested for cancellation of their signatures in June and July 1945, before the cessation of war. My parents being unnaturalized are pressed with tremendous fear whether their cancellation ... would be realized ... Our whole family yearns to be integrated into the Canadian community and putting forth the energy for Canada. Every day and every night I am praying to God and to you, Mr. King that you will save my parents from this doom. My mother had long been suffering from heart trouble and I cannot bear to watch her being taken away. (Correspondence, 27 December 1945)

Especially compelling are the pleas of the very young Canadian-born children for their immigrant parents to remain in the country. As dependants under the age of sixteen, these children knew that despite their own nativity and citizenship, they would be deported along with their parents. Such fears prompted a ten-year-old girl to write a government official:

My parents signed for repatriation because they did not want to go East. Now I hear that they may have to go back to Japan. That means that I have to go back with them since I am under age. I really do not want to go to Japan. I have never seen the place and I do not want to either. I was born in B.C. and I like my country very much. I know I can't get along in Japan. My parents have done nothing bad that they have to be departed [sic]. Please let my parents stay here so that I, a Canadian-born may remain also. (Correspondence, 21 March 1946)

Yet even when there was no apparent reason for not granting an individual (in some cases aging and/or ill) permission to remain with her or his family in Canada, Pickersgill, Mitchell, and Deputy Minister of Labour Arthur MacNamara exercised striking caution in their judgments, a caution rooted in suspicion of the Japanese as a devious and deceitful people. In private correspondence with one another, these men referred to various discoveries that they had made in their investigations of the applicants for revocation. A widowed mother of Canadian-born children had a living relative in Japan. A couple who planned to marry may not have had "genuine intentions." An applicant was a prisoner of war who had once expressed "pro-Japanese sentiments" in correspondence with a friend (Correspondence, MacNamara to Pickersgill, 29 November 1945). Assessing case after case, these three men were arbitrary in patrolling the nation's borders. At their discretion, people would either be allowed to remain within the nation or exiled overseas. When they did permit an applicant to stay in the country, this was done with paternalistic authority and a seemingly benign racial superiority.

At the same time, however, politicians did recognize the Japanese Canadian family as a viable *economic unit,* particularly when it became desirable to hold the younger nisei responsible for shouldering the financial burden of supporting dependent children and aging, sick, or otherwise unemployable kin. Although government policy was to separate many families, it also dictated that these families remain economically interdependent. In other words, although people were not permitted to live together, they were expected to maintain one another, albeit from a distance. For example, a memorandum issued by the federal government in 1945 stated that "the family head should contribute to the support of the family whether actually residing in the settlement or engaged in private employment in B.C." It further stipulated that "if the family head is engaged in private employment outside of B.C. when the family continues to reside in the settlement, he should be urged to contribute what he can to [its] support" (Memorandum, 1).

And though primary responsibility for the economic support of families fell to the issei father, the fact was that aging, ill, incarcerated, and otherwise unemployable men could not necessarily assume the breadwinner function. Thus the government also outlined the economic obligations of other family members. Cognizant of the government's interest in minimizing state responsibility for maintenance of the interned, many nisei highlighted their own economic viability in their requests to save their parents from exile. In February 1946 a nisei man in Toronto wrote on behalf of his mother and seven siblings requesting that the family be permitted to stay together in Canada by joining him in Toronto, where he and one sister were currently employed. He was most worried about their recently widowed mother, a woman in poor health who was on the deportation list (Correspondence, Trueman to MacNamara, 27 February 1946). To government leaders, this young man made a plea:

You told me that she [mother] did not cancelled [sic] it early enough. That was when my father was living. Now my father is dead so she has nobody to depend on except myself and my sisters. If she has to go back she has to take my 4 youngest brothers and sisters the youngest being only 6 yrs. She is not a very well woman. She'll be really lost when she goes over. Couldn't you make just an exception in this case and let her stay. We promise to take care of her if you only let her stay. I loved my mother tremendously and she really took my fathers death hard. All she does now is worry about deportation. (Correspondence, Nisei Man to Minister of Justice, January 1946)

Pickersgill was not moved by this request. He replied with bureaucratic authority: "As your mother is a naturalized Canadian and did not request cancellation until after midnight, September 1st, 1945, according to present policy she is eligible for deportation" (Correspondence, 29 January 1946). In private correspondence with Arthur MacNamara, he further remarked: "While it is true that the two children sixteen years of age and over who signed have since revoked, and such revocations will be granted, there is nothing to prevent them from accompanying the mother to Japan so that she will have somebody to depend upon ... I am afraid that if we start making known now exceptions, that we would be just inundated with requests for exceptions on compassionate grounds" (Correspondence, 20 February 1946). Significantly, to MacNamara, Pickersgill noted two additional considerations. First, the son had been interned as a prisoner of war in Angler. This indicated that he had at some point, in some fashion, resisted the authority of the Canadian government. Second, this man and his sister had recently spent all of their savings on their father's funeral. Given this recent expenditure, which was appreciable, the ability of the son and daughter to provide for their aging (unemployable) mother was in question. Better, then, that she be deported to Japan.

Families Apart
Although many families struggled to stay together, family unification was not always possible. In some cases, the obstacles were directly mounted by men such as Pickersgill and MacNamara. In others, the matter was more complicated, as family members were not in consensus about which path to take out of British Columbia. Political leaders of the day had not anticipated the latter. Repatriation policy, after all, was based on the assumption of a unified, male-breadwinner family. The General Japanese Repatriation Notice, for example, stipulated that if a husband was a repatriate, then his wife and minor children also had to be repatriated. In practice, however, there were significant social differences within families. And in their failure to recognize these differences, government officials were unprepared for

the contestation of the issei father's authority (and the government ruling itself) by both wives and Canadian-born children. These intrafamilial divisions and the more general unsettling of traditional patriarchal relations were developments that political leaders were uncomfortable with but ultimately had to negotiate. Further, such developments placed some Japanese Canadians themselves in a vexatious position, forcing them to choose between family and nation.

Daughters and Sons

Even before the war's end, family decision making around repatriation was fraught with disagreement. A significant basis for such disagreement was generational. For the nisei in particular, the very idea of repatriation made no sense. According to Miki and Kobayashi (1991, 49), the government's term was a misnomer. "Repatriation," they explain, was a "euphemism for what was in actuality, a forced exile: the 'patria' or country of birth for the majority of these citizens was Canada, so they could not, in this sense, be 'repatriated' to Japan." This critical point is expressed in much of the private correspondence of nisei during these years of indecision. A nisei woman, for instance, wrote to her sister in Bay Farm, British Columbia, "there should be no doubt as to your all staying in Canada. It's your home the only home you all know and worth fighting for! The Japan that all the Issei remember is a dream Japan – one they have visualized as when they left it! ... Of course the government would like to get rid of an unpleasant issue by deporting us – it is deportation and you don't 'repatriate' people born here!" (Intercepted Letters, 2 May 1945).

Any transnational ties that existed for the nisei were only symbolic and indirectly transmitted via their parents in Canada. The nisei, most of whom were teenagers or young adults at the time of war, had limited, if any, links or loyalties to a country other than Canada. Their social and cultural resources were solidly rooted in the West. Many had never even visited Japan. Despite their parents' direction over such matters as weddings, births, religion, and attendance of Japanese-language school, nisei children had become more Canadian than Japanese (Kitagawa 1985, 219).

Given this, many nisei felt compelled to remain in their country of birth, despite mother's and father's will. Forced to decide between family and nation, some people chose to remain in the *territory* of home. Personal identity was so strongly embedded in Canada that they saw no other choice. In addition, some Canadian-born citizens steadfastly believed that they must remain in the country on principle, as an assertion of their political rights. In doing so, however, they were forced to abandon the family home, the home of emotional intimacy. A nisei woman in Hamilton, Ontario, suffered such a loss. She wrote to a friend in Tashme, "I left home because [my] parents were making me sign up to go to Japan. I wouldn't sign up cause I'm Canadian and I've got rights to stay in Canada" (Intercepted Letters, 15 July 1945).

Wives and Citizens

Although economic dependency on husbands or grown children circumscribed the choices of most wives and mothers, some of these women, too, articulated strong and independent views on repatriation. Although they were most likely a minority, notable are the wives who openly opposed their husband's decisions about relocation. For instance, a woman in Popoff, British Columbia, wrote to her husband in Angler, "No sir, I won't go out of here even if you divorced me or they kill me ... No one in the families will move out of here so don't forget that. You think I am selfish and mean but what can I do ... All this time I thought my husband was a man but not anymore. If you don't do or listen [to] what I say well, do anything you like but don't forget I'll never forgive you, never" (Intercepted Letters, May 1945).

Such resistance must have perplexed government officials. As noted, government policy initially stipulated that as economic dependants, wives must follow their husbands. However, complications arose in those cases where a woman held a different citizenship from that of her spouse. Early in 1946, Arthur MacNamara received a number of letters from women in such circumstances. Some of these women had signed for repatriation and were now wishing to revoke. Others had never signed (Correspondence, Pickersgill to MacNamara, 18 and 20 February 1946). In February 1946, one nisei woman raised forthright questions about the patriarchal underpinnings of repatriation policy. Why, she asked, should her marital status eclipse her citizenship status? As a Canadian, she wished to remain in Canada, notwithstanding her husband's fate. She wrote,

Why should I lead a life as an enemy alien just because I married a Japanese National? I was born at Vancouver, B.C. on March 28th, 1918, and have never immigrated or set foot upon the earth of Japan. I've had all my education here, and was leading a happy normal life as a Canadian citizen till I became married, which changed my name, and also my status. I already know that if a girl marries, it is her duty to become whatever status her husband is, and follow wherever he goes as his wife, and do what she should as his partner. I think a wife should be as his partner in name only, and not change her status from a Canadian-born to her husband's status ... I think a wife should serve her country, her native land, in the status she was, at the date of her birth ... I have no intention or do not wish to repatriate to Japan on any terms as I do not know Japan. (Correspondence, Nisei Woman to District Registrar, Births, Deaths and Marriages, 22 February 1946)

After one month of stalling and indecision, MacNamara informed this woman that as she was born in Canada, although her husband was a Japanese national, she would be permitted to remain in the country and should therefore resettle in the East (Correspondence, 2 April 1946). MacNamara's decision reflected a change in government policy, one that was made in response to the collective protests of the Japanese Canadian community. After the government had passed the deportation orders in council at the end of 1945, the Co-operative Committee on Japanese Canadians challenged the minister of justice, Louis St. Laurent, to refer the matter to the Supreme Court of Canada. In 1946 the Supreme Court ruled that under the War Measures Act, the government did have legal authority to deport Japanese Canadians. However, the court made one exception: the wives and dependent children who did not sign for repatriation (Correspondence, Pickersgill to MacNamara, 18 February 1946). With this change, the government would be deporting fathers and husbands, while leaving in Canada their wives and children, thereby separating families in a different way from previously. Not only would this measure challenge the patriarchal family model, but it would also mean that mothers and minor children in Canada would have to find some means of economic support in the absence of a husband/father. In light of this dilemma, and in the context of growing public sympathy for the plight of Japanese Canadians, Mackenzie King called off the deportation orders (Miki and Kobayashi 1991, 55).

Family Ties or National Ties? A Question of Loyalty
As the repatriation debate suggests, throughout the war and postwar years, the Canadian government failed to recognize the flexible and complex nature of national allegiance as well as the fluidity of cultural identity. Political leaders were blinded by the belief that national loyalty must be exclusive, is dictated by "racial origin," and is therefore unchanging over the course of a lifetime. Guided by these essentialist ideas, they regarded every person of Japanese ancestry as suspect. Suspicion of loyalty served as the basis for the establishment of a Loyalty Tribunal. Although the government abandoned its restrictive deportation policies before the tribunal took form, its proposal had been seriously regarded. Indeed, a number of leading citizens had put forward their names for appointment to this body. In some ways, the very idea of a commission to judge the loyalty or disloyalty of Japanese Canadians served as a threat – an effective one (Adachi 1991, 302).

Faced with this threat, and in light of the allegations made against them over the years since the bombing of Pearl Harbor, Japanese Canadians repeatedly asserted their allegiance to Canada and their contribution to nation building, both politically and economically. For instance, in petitioning Humphrey Mitchell to revoke their repatriation forms, internees in Greenwood, British Columbia, asked that he take into account the record of their "loyalty, obedience and readiness to cooperate with the Dominion regulations during the national emergency," and they reminded him that "there has not been a single act of sabotage on record against us" (Correspondence, 12 December 1945). Further asserting a static view of national allegiance, as well as an imagined and unmediated link between race and nation, some politicians believed that the issei in particular would forever maintain a primary tie to Japan. Distrust of the first generation was heightened by the fact that many issei appeared to be "unassimilable." Although they had lived in Canada for decades, many were not fluent in the English language, spoke only Japanese at home, and ate meals of rice and salty pickles; some followed Buddhist religious practice. Importantly, they had either retained a dual citizenship or remained Japanese nationals. A significant number of issei did express a devotion to Japan, the "motherland," and like many other first-generation immigrants, some also intended to one day return permanently to their country of birth. However, it is important to remember that during these years, time and space held very different meanings from those held in the current period of global border crossing. Lacking time and money, many issei had never taken the long steamship voyage back and forth across the Pacific Ocean. Busy raising children and providing for their families in Canada, they had limited contact with Japan in the absence of quick high-tech modes of communication. In short, many people were "spatially immobile" (Yeoh et al. 2003, 209). Thus, when faced with deportation, a number of issei parents came to realize that Canada was now home. One issei woman poignantly stated: "Having left Japan nigh fifty years ago I have no place nor immediate kin to go back to. Being now seventy years I would rather be buried where I have lived most of my life and where my husband lies buried" (Correspondence, Issei Women to Prime Minister and Minister of External Affairs, 12 December 1945).

Further, the issei reminded government leaders that, in part, they had not become citizens of Canada because they were not permitted to do so. It was not a straightforward matter of choice. On the issue of citizenship, a group of internees at Greenwood explained that the state had constructed for them another boundary of exclusion. They declared,

It is alleged that we nationals have, as it were, created for ourselves the convenient situation of a dual allegiance. Under such coverage we were accused of seeking naturalization rights. This, we assert, is only another of the many complications which, it seems, developed as a logical sequence to the Dominion Act of 1923, which denied us the right to seek citizenship. Satisfactory reasons for the passage of this act were never proffered us on the Coast. We would like to make clear that on our part we have consistently sought after and were eager of acquiring these coveted rights so that we might have a common economic assurance of laboring side by side with other working class immigrants of Canada. (Correspondence, Petition from Greenwood to Humphrey Mitchell, 12 December 1945)

Accused of being "of two countries" (see Murphy, cited in Yeoh et al. 2003, 213), legal citizenship and selective cultural retention notwithstanding, many issei had become bound to "one" country: Canada. In the context of racist assault during the war years, the nisei in comparison frequently described themselves as being trapped between two nations, dedicated to one but rendered marginal to each. An awareness of the nisei's displacement prompted many issei parents to declare Canada home. Just as some nisei left for Japan out of a sense of obligation to their mothers and fathers, a number of issei in turn felt a commitment to their youthful offspring. For these parents, national fidelity was inspired by their Canadian-born children. Canada became home to them because Canada was home to their kin.

In seeking to revoke their applications, 287 residents of Lemon Creek, British Columbia, stated their reasons for wishing to remain in Canada. Among this group, the Japanese nationals asserted,

> We ... firmly believed that we were being permitted to enter Canada as permanent residents. It was our aim to bring up our children as good Canadian citizens ... Our children, naturally feel that Canada is their country, and wish to remain here. What will happen to these children if their parents are deported? They will have no alternative but to go with their parents. It is very disconcerting to see the future of these children completely overturned by their parents' repatriation ... If we are deported leaving grown-up sons or daughters in Canada, our families will be split up forever, a condition which would be unbearable to us. (Correspondence, Petition by Lemon Creek Internees to L.S. St. Laurent, 28 November 1945)

Conclusion: The Attempt to Unmake a Community

As noted by Nicholas Van Hear (1998, 42), when speaking of transmigration and diasporic communities, the categories "voluntary" and "involuntary" are seldom satisfactory, never discrete, and often misleading. Migration entails "choice," but it also involves "compulsion." Questions of force and compulsion prompt us to explore the attempted "unmaking" of transnational communities and to look at how groups have tried to resist their dispersal in an effort to preserve home. During the Second World War, racism and prevailing perceptions about loyalties to another nation-state placed Japanese Canadians in jeopardy and resulted in government efforts to dismantle and disorganize their British Columbia community. On much the same premise – perceived national identities – the Canadian government likewise made decisions about Italian Canadians and Ukrainian Canadians during years of war (see Iacovetta, Perin, and Principe 2000). Although the treatment of Japanese Canadians was significantly distinct from that of the latter groups, each of these historical episodes underscores a crucial question for modern liberal democracies: how to achieve a balance between the civil liberties of some and the needs of many. The ability to maintain the essence of such a balance, although imperfect, is "tested to the breaking point" by crises such as war and by economic, social, or political breakdown (3).

During the summer of 1946, 4,700 people of Japanese descent moved east from the British Columbia internment sites, and hundreds of others left Alberta. Some settled in Quebec and others in Manitoba. The majority located in southern Ontario. "While the resettlers moved through the hostels into new jobs and communities, five ships left for Japan. The 3,965 people on those ships ostensibly went voluntarily. In fact, most went because they felt they had no alternative" (Sunahara 1981, 143-44). Repatriation to a war-torn foreign country resulted in extreme hardship for most and death for some. By December 1946 the internment sites had been left empty. Only the sick and elderly and their families continued to live in New Denver. Over thirteen thousand Japanese Canadians had moved east of British Columbia. By January 1947 there remained a mere 6,776 Japanese Canadians in the Province of British Columbia, less than one-third of the 1942 population (145).

Also, by December 1946 the Privy Council had declared the deportation orders in council legally binding. However, by this time, the government had lost interest in enforcing them. The policies were no longer necessary, nor were they politically wise. Unrelenting, in January 1947 Justice Minister Louis St. Laurent again urged that the orders in council be implemented. St. Laurent's reasoning was that if such measures were not taken, Japanese Canadians "would increase the population, and demands would be made later when Japan was a settled country to have the Japanese in Canada given the same rights as the white population." To this, Mackenzie King responded that the deportation issue should be dropped. But restrictions on Japanese Canadians would be maintained for an additional two years to ensure that they were permanently resettled (Sunahara 1981, 145).

Remaking home in various parts of Canada, years after the war, many nisei made concerted efforts to integrate themselves into the dominant society, largely by trying not to draw too much attention to themselves. The lessons of war had taught them the merits of invisibility in shielding themselves and their children against racist assault. Few nisei parents encouraged their *sansei* (third-generation) children to speak the Japanese language. The rate of interethnic marriage within the community now hovers at close to 100 percent. Most sansei have grown up without a cultural community. The government's wartime measures have been aptly described as an act of "cultural genocide" (Miki and Kobayashi 1991, 52). The resulting assimilation was punitive. Racist perceptions of transnational allegiances and ties have had a profound impact on the postwar community.

The boundaries drawn by the Canadian state in this "era of nationalism" were both physical and symbolic (see Gellner 1983). The costs of these boundaries of inclusion and exclusion were territorial, material, and emotional. Moreover, the transnational ties upon which the government's construction of boundaries was based were for the most part imagined. For persons of Japanese descent, Japan became a spectre during the years of war: they were haunted by their Japanese blood, Canadians trapped in "Japanese bodies." Japanese Canadians' limited imaginings of transnational community reflect their general tendency to homogenize their lives. The government's racialized policy of repatriation and its unmaking of this community both rested upon and reinforced a belief in the sameness of all persons "of the Japanese race."

Importantly, these border politics were negotiated largely around the family. A focus on the family underscores the need to understand how public transnational politics shape the private, intimate lives of people within the nation-state. The family, argues Levin (2002, 9), is the "transnational link." Decisions about whether or not to sign were negotiated within family households. Moreover, people shifted allegiances and negotiated conceptions of home partly through family relations. As noted by Yeoh and colleagues (2003, 211), transnationalism is a "dynamic social process." The family is a social space in which many oppressed groups have found a voice and agency to resist the boundaries imposed upon them. For Japanese Canadians, the fragments of community have recently been reconstructed and revitalized, and fractured cultural identity is being slowly restored precisely because of family memory transmitted over time and across generations.

Acknowledgments

This project was funded by the Social Sciences and Humanities Research Council of Canada and the National Association of Japanese Canadians. For their helpful suggestions and support, I wish to thank Robert Storey, Vic Satzewich, Lloyd Wong, Gillian Anderson, and of course Tamura Sugiman-Storey.

Note

1   The Co-operative Committee was established in June 1945 in support of Japanese Canadians facing deportation and all those facing other violations of their rights as citizens in Canada. In close collaboration with the also recently formed nisei group (the Japanese Canadian Committee for Democracy), the Co-operative Committee soon emerged as a broad-based national coalition composed of over thirty organizations, including church and labour groups as well as civil-liberties and professional associations, all of whom were critical of the government's treatment of Japanese Canadians (Miki and Kobayashi 1991, 53-54).

Part 2
Contemporary Patterns

4
Characteristics of Immigrant Transnationalism in Vancouver
Daniel Hiebert and David Ley

Transnationalism is one of a series of supranational processes discussed within the theoretical context of globalization. If globalization represents a larger "space of flows" said to overrun national borders, thereby shaping more expansive regional and global geographies, then transnational migration is one of these flows; it is the movement of labour that accompanies the reconfiguration of national economies and societies. Like the movement of capital, labour has now liberated itself from containment within national borders to engage in continuing movement and communication between countries of origin and destination as well as to establish a status of flexible identification in terms of national citizenship.

It is no surprise that transnational migrants touch down at precisely the sites that John Friedmann (1986, 71) first identified as the "basing point" of the new globalizing economy: the global cities that act as gateways between national societies and the world system (see also Sassen 2001). In Canada, Toronto and Vancouver have emerged as the nation's two primary windows on the world, and both, if not yet global cities, are in the process of gaining this stature. In 2001 these cities had some of the highest proportions of foreign-born residents among advanced societies: 43% in the Toronto Census metropolitan area (CMA) and 37% in the Vancouver CMA. These ratios are much higher than those found in Los Angeles, New York, London, and Tokyo, the quintessential global cities of our era. Moreover, a substantial proportion of the foreign-born in Toronto and Vancouver are newcomers, having landed between 1991 and 2001, amounting to 39% of the immigrant population in Toronto and 44% of this population in Vancouver. These percentages translate into large numbers: 792,000 landings in Toronto and 325,000 in Vancouver in the period 1991-2001. Among this recently arrived cohort in particular we might expect to see considerable transnational activity.

The landscapes and social geographies of both cities have undergone significant restructuring in the past decade. An important development has been the suburbanization of the immigrant population, which is no longer confined to older inner-city reception areas but now includes substantial concentrations in inner suburbs, where proportions in 2001 ran as high as 54% in Richmond and 47% in Burnaby, compared with a City of Vancouver share of 46% (Hiebert 1999; Rose 2001). Moreover, the composition of immigrant cohorts in Vancouver has strongly favoured the economic classes of independent and business migrants, more so than in any other Canadian urban centre. The high human capital and substantial financial assets of members of these groups have permitted residential selection in the region's high-status districts (Ley 1995). Impacts on the Vancouver housing market more generally have been appreciable: between 1986 and 2001, immigration dominated population growth, and a very high correlation existed between annual immigration landings and changes in metropolitan house prices (Ley and Tutchener 2001).

A gateway city whose existing coethnic communities have been enlarged by a sizable, newly landed population provides a fertile laboratory for transnational behaviour. This behaviour has been examined among members of the largest immigrant communities, notably those from Hong Kong and Taiwan (Waters 2002; Ley and Waters 2004) and from India, particularly the Punjab (Walton-Roberts 2003). In this chapter we make use of a large metropolitan survey of 1,479 immigrants conducted in 2001 to assess the intensity of transnationalism along a number of dimensions and to establish relationships between transnational practices and socio-economic and ethno-cultural characteristics of the population. To this end, we pose several key questions: How significant are transnational activities among Vancouver's immigrant communities? Are there systematic differences between ethno-cultural groups in terms of their transnational behaviour? How is transnationalism related to socio-economic achievement? And how is transnationalism related to identity?

Transnationalism: The Story So Far
Soon after Friedmann's (1986) pioneering discussion of global cities, the early literature on transnationalism followed. Anthropologists noted a high density of transactions between immigrants to the United States and relatively proximate home countries such as Haiti, the Dominican Republic (Glick Schiller, Basch, and Szanton Blanc 1992), and Mexico (Rouse 1992). This early work on nearby sending nations has continued (Mountz and Wright 1996; Guarnizo 1998; Glick Schiller and Fouron 1999; Levitt 2001b; Pries 2001) and also been expanded to include examinations of transnational flows in many other regional settings, such as between East Asia and North America (Mitchell 1997; Ong and Nonini 1997b; Ong 1999; Ley 2003), among countries in Asia (Yeoh et al. 2003), and between Africa and Europe (Al-Ali, Black, and Koser 2001).

In the past, transnational ties have been obscured in the Canadian literature on ethnicity, which has been based largely on assimilationist or multicultural frameworks, both of which presuppose a model of immigrant containment within national borders (Winland 1998). Recently, however, considerable work, particularly in the Vancouver region, has examined transnational ties among members of the Chinese diaspora, which has been the leading immigrant group for the past twenty years (Mitchell 1997; Wong 1997; Wong and Ng 2002; Ley 2003; Waters 2002, 2003; Ley and Waters 2004). Other contributions have demonstrated the diverse linkages between Greater Vancouver (particularly suburban Surrey) and the Punjab (Walton-Roberts 2003) as well as the transnational fields of much smaller groups, such as the Burmese (Hyndman and Walton-Roberts 2000). One of the few Canadian studies with a large sample considered the overseas linkages of more than four hundred immigrants to Quebec, including the scale of home-country travel, remittances, and property ownership, ten years after landing (Renaud et al. 2002). Several of the questions in the Quebec study are repeated in our Vancouver survey, and comparative results are noted below.

As the literature has proliferated, several attempts have been made to take stock of the field and to shape its often unruly growth (Kearney 1995; Vertovec 1999; Levitt 2001b). The interdisciplinary nature of research has led to methodological debates as sociologists and geographers have entered the discussion. The early ethnographic work has been challenged, particularly by Portes and his colleagues in a series of papers arguing that anthropologists' ethnographic approach has tended to exaggerate the incidence of transnational behaviour because it has selected only those cases where transnational practices have been observed, neglecting all others (Portes, Guarnizo, and Landolt 1999; Portes 2001; Portes, Haller, and Guarnizo 2002). Rather than examining only those cases where transnationalism may be discerned, researchers should provide broader coverage of an entire community to include observations of instances where such activity is lacking. There is growing recognition that earlier work tended to overlook the considerable variation both within and between immigrant groups of a common nationality, particularly as concerns their migration strategies on the spectrum from assimilation to multiculturalism and transnationalism (Al-Ali, Black, and Koser 2001; Wimmer and Glick Schiller 2002). In this respect Itzigsohn and Saucedo (2002) conclude from a comparative study of Latin American groups in the United States that while participation in a particular transnational activity may be limited in an immigrant population, there is broad participation across the whole range of socio-cultural activities.

Portes and his colleagues have also expressed suspicion that earlier anthropological studies overemphasized the novelty of transnationalism, although unlike stronger critics (e.g., Mintz 1998) they have not dismissed its conceptual utility as a result. But they do urge a more rigorous approach that seeks measurable, rather than anecdotal, evidence.

Although there is agreement that under transnationalism the relationships between society and space have been reconfigured (Pries 2001), some authors have gone further to suggest a deterritorialization of immigrant social fields, the outcome being a footloose mobility that has replaced the importance of grounded spatial experience (Ong and Nonini 1997b; Winland 1998). The mobility of transnational migrants is acknowledged (Waters 2002), but this does not mean that space has been eroded as a significant factor. Following a conceptual challenge by Mitchell (1997), other geographers have shown how space matters, both in the effects of distance upon family relations and in terms of the discernments that transnational migrants from East Asia make in differentiating between the opportunity structures of nation-states (Ley and Waters 2004). In addition, transnational behaviour is strongly grounded in distinctive spatial clusters of ethnic services that facilitate the hypermobility of astronauts moving on the "Pacific shuttle" between East Asia and the West Coast of North America (Zhou and Tseng 2001).

Survey data with medium to large samples are required to establish the more discriminating relationships called for by recent criticisms. Although there are relatively few precedents at present, an important exception is the Comparative Immigrant Entrepreneurship Project (CIEP) directed by Portes and Guarnizo, which has undertaken several phases of data collection among Colombian, Dominican, and Salvadoran immigrants in four American cities. Their research shows that transnational entrepreneurs are of higher socio-economic status and more likely to be American citizens than foreign-born wage earners and entrepreneurs with only domestic linkages (Portes 2001; Landolt 2001). Transnational entrepreneurs are, in general, more satisfied with life in the United States, and the duration of their residence exceeds the immigrant mean. Moreover, immigrants engaged in political transactions with their home countries fit a similar socio-economic profile. In this research, transnationalism, defined by economic and political transactions, emerges as a means of successful economic integration in the United States. Although these relationships establish some empirical expectations for our Vancouver survey, the definition of transnationalism posited by the CIEP would seem to identify the process theoretically, not as an alternative to assimilation but as a subset of assimilation processes (Kivisto 2001).

Methodology

Our results come from a large survey of Vancouver residents conducted in 2001.[1] The goal of the survey was to gather information on the experiences of immigrants and the attitudes of the general population toward immigration and immigrant settlement. The survey included 2,000 respondents, but we concentrate in this study on the 1,479 who were immigrants (immigrants were oversampled in the survey; see Hiebert 2003). Given the uneven settlement pattern of immigrants in the Vancouver metropolitan area, we opted for a cluster design, with random sampling within five target areas selected for their distinct socio-economic profiles (see Hiebert et al. 1998; Hiebert 1999). A telephone survey was conducted by a specialized marketing company employing interviewers able to work in English as well as Cantonese, Mandarin, Punjabi, Hindi, and Tagolog. Most recent immigrants chose to be interviewed in their native language, while the opposite was true of those who had been settled for at least ten years. Interviews were conducted with an adult family member who received the call. Consequently, interviews included family dependants as well as the principal wage earner. Among the sample of 1,479, a total of 944 were in the labour force.

The survey was extensive and covered a variety of topics, including household and family structure, employment, income, immigration history, demographic characteristics of the respondent (age, gender, ethnicity, and place of birth), quality of neighbourhood life, perceived discrimination, attitudes toward immigration and multiculturalism, citizenship, satisfaction with Canada, and transnational activities. In this chapter we concentrate on the transnational module of the survey and cross-tabulate results for this dimension with the socio-economic, demographic, and immigrant status of respondents. Our questions broadly explore several of the facets of transnationalism discussed by Vertovec (1999).[2] We asked respondents about the presence of family and friendship networks overseas, the degree of interaction across these networks (communication and travel in both directions), the frequency and methods of interaction, and the extent of economic linkages (property ownership, work-related travel, and transnational business practices). In doing so, we revealed some of the contours of transnationalism as a social morphology and – indirectly – as a type of consciousness. We also enumerated some of the ways that transnationalism facilitated capital accumulation but found that the extent of this form of transnationalism was rather limited in the Vancouver context. Further, our questions touched on the issue of commitment, or allegiance, raised by Van Hear (1998) in his seminal study of transnationalism and diaspora. In particular, respondents were asked to reveal their citizenship status and, more important, their degree of identification with Canada. We found that, in general, transnational practices were inversely related to the degree of affiliation with Canada but that there were important exceptions to this pattern.

Transnational Activities
We begin with a brief enumeration of the answers to eight questions about transnational behaviour (see Table 4.1). As might be expected, a large proportion of our respondents have friends and relatives who remain in their

Table 4.1

Enumeration of transnational activities among Vancouver residents

Question	Yes #	Yes %	No #	No %	Refused	Total
(1) Family or friends in premigration country?	1,332	90.1	143	9.7	4	1,479
(2) Do you keep in touch with them?	1,271	95.4	60	4.5	1	1,332
How often?						
Daily	87	6.8				
Weekly	486	38.2				
Monthly	524	41.2				
Yearly	139	10.9				
Less than once a year	23	1.8				
Don't know/Refused	12	0.9				
(Total: 1,271)						
How do you keep in touch?[a]						
E-mail	652	51.3				
Telephone	1,167	91.8				
Postal mail	253	19.9				
Visits	302	23.8				
Refused	3	0.2				
(Total: 1,271)						
(3) Do you travel to that country?	1,008	68.2	468	31.6	3	1,479
How often?						
More than once a year	201	19.9				
Once a year or so	238	23.6				
Less than once a year	550	54.6				
Don't know/Refused	19	1.9				
(Total: 1,008)						
(4) Does your job require travel to that country?[b]	48	5.8	781	93.9	2	831
(5) Do you own property or have a home there?	329	22.2	1,123	75.9	27	1,479
(6) Do you run a business there?	47	3.2	1,411	95.4	21	1,479
(7) Do you financially assist people there?	212	14.3	1,247	84.3	20	1,479
(8) Do you receive visitors from that country?	903	61.1	567	38.3	9	1,479
How often?						
More than once a year	123	13.6				
Once a year or so	237	26.2				
Less than once a year	514	56.9				
Don't know/Refused	29	3.2				
(Total: 903)						

a   Respondents were allowed two answers to this question; percentage figures therefore exceed 100.

b   Of the 1,479 immigrant respondents, 831 are currently employed. Of these, 155 are self-employed.

countries of origin, and nearly all keep in touch with them. Contact in most cases takes place either weekly or monthly, although a small number maintain daily communication. The vast majority utilize electronic means of communication, especially the telephone, although a high number also use e-mail. It appears that the postal system has receded in significance, with only one in five immigrants mentioning this form of communication (multiple responses were allowed, so percentages sum to more than 100). Approximately two-thirds of those who answered our survey travel to their premigration countries. Of those, the majority do so irregularly, less than once a year. However, one-quarter travel once a year or so, and one in five make this journey on a more frequent basis. There is also considerable interaction in the opposite direction: over 60 percent host visitors from their home countries. As before, this travel occurs regularly (at least once per year) for about half of the respondents and more occasionally for the others.

We also asked about economic links that facilitate or require transnational connections. Of the 831 respondents in the labour market (155 of whom are self-employed), only 48 are involved in work-related travel to their countries of origin. We were surprised, given the literature on transnationalism, by this low figure. The same trend was repeated for transnational business ownership: again just under fifty respondents operate businesses in their home countries.[3] A much larger proportion, nearly one-quarter, own property abroad. Finally, on the economic front, around one in seven respondents send money to family and friends in their premigration countries.

These basic data on transnationalism reveal a clear pattern already well established in the literature: there is much variation in the extent and intensity of transnational activity. Some immigrants presumably do not participate in these sorts of interactions at all, as they have no family or friends left in their premigration countries. Also, small numbers of our sample have friends and relatives in the home country but make no effort to stay in touch with them. There is also what we could call a middle level of transnationalism, with occasional visits to and fro mixed with regular electronic contact and, perhaps, some financial interests that stretch across the vast distances separating pre- and postmigration contexts. There are also those who no doubt answered all, or nearly all, of our questions affirmatively – those who fit the description usually offered of cosmopolitan transnationals, whose lives are characterized by geographical fluidity and who identify themselves with at least two places. The interesting question, of course, is what distinguishes those who maintain extensive transnational links from those who do not?

In the remainder of this chapter's tables, we cross-tabulate a socio-economic or demographic feature of our sample with eight indicators of transnationalism. Cells in each table refer to the percentage of respondents in a particular category who answered the question positively. As we constructed these tables, we conducted chi-squared tests to identify statistically significant relationships. Note that these tests should be seen as instructive, rather than definitive, in several cases where the sample size is quite small. This is particularly the case when dealing with the questions about job-related transnational travel and transnational business ownership. Also, readers should be alert to the cases where socio-economic and demographic categories are small and should treat them with caution.

Socio-economic Variations in Transnationalism
The first and perhaps most important finding of our study is that the relationship between transnational activity and socio-economic status is relatively weak.[4] Education is largely unrelated to the presence or absence of family and friends in the premigration country and also unrelated to the propensity to stay in touch and send them money (see Table 4.2). Surprisingly, education and the tendency to travel to the home country were also unrelated. There was a significant relationship between educational attainment and the tendency to hold property in the premigration country, but it was not linear; that is, those at both the higher and lower ends of the educational scale are more likely than those in the middle to hold property – a difficult pattern to explain. The only two predictable associations were between education and the likelihood of holding a business in the premigration country and the likelihood of hosting visitors from the premigration country: in both cases, those with university degrees and other forms of postsecondary education engaged in more transnational activity.

As with education, household income does not appear to be strongly linked to the level of transnational activity (see Table 4.3). Not surprisingly, households across the income spectrum are about equally likely to have family and friends in their home countries. However, that there is little differentiation between high- and low-income households when it comes to maintaining social contact *as well as* economic relationships is surely more unexpected.

Around 3 percent of our respondents in every income category, for example, operate businesses overseas. Clearly, however, income is associated with increased travel in both directions between Canada and the premigration country. The level of household income is also associated with the propensity to retain property in the home country, although not in the manner that many would expect. Households with the lowest incomes in Canada are most likely to hold property abroad, while those with higher incomes in Canada tend to give up their overseas land. There are several plausible explanations for this pattern. For example, those who have not yet found their economic footing in Canada may be hedging their bets by maintaining the ability to return, while those who have "made it" in Canada might have shifted their economic activities to this country. Alternatively,

Table 4.2

Respondents engaged in transnational activities by level of educational attainment (%)

	Number of respondents[a]	Family in home country	Keep in touch	Travel to home country	Job requires travel	Property in home country	Business in home country	Send $ to home country	Visits from home country
Less than high school	46	87.0	92.5	73.9	0.0	28.3	0.0	10.9	34.8
Some high school	101	86.1	96.6	63.4	5.6	34.0	2.0	14.0	36.6
High school	308	91.5	95.7	70.8	3.7	19.0	3.0	17.3	61.0
Some postsecondary	185	89.7	91.6	67.0	6.7	14.7	2.2	11.9	63.8
Postsecondary diploma	228	89.9	96.1	67.0	7.9	16.6	3.6	16.0	67.8
University degree	606	91.1	96.4	68.3	10.2	26.9	3.8	13.8	64.6
Probability		*0.646*	*0.213*	*0.798*	*0.354*	0.000	0.007	*0.630*	0.000

Note: Figures in italics indicate nonsignificant results in chi-squared tests.
a The total number of respondents in the survey is 1,479; the number of respondents answering each question is different and less than the total indicated here.

Table 4.3

Respondents engaged in transnational activities by 2001 household income (%)

	Number of respondents[a]	Family in home country	Keep in touch	Travel to home country	Job requires travel	Property in home country	Business in home country	Send $ to home country	Visits from home country
Less than $25,000	246	91.9	94.2	57.7	11.1	33.9	2.9	16.3	46.1
$25,000 to $49,999	328	91.5	96.7	70.7	6.3	21.7	2.7	17.1	59.0
$50,000 to $74,999	218	91.7	92.0	70.6	5.5	19.7	2.3	16.1	66.1
More than $75,000	223	91.0	97.0	71.7	11.5	14.9	3.2	9.9	77.1
Probability		*0.987*	*0.052*	0.002	*0.482*	0.000	*0.958*	*0.101*	0.000

Note: Figures in italics indicate nonsignificant results in chi-squared tests.
a The total number of respondents in the survey is 1,479; the number of respondents answering each question is different and less than the total indicated here.

perhaps we are seeing the effects of "cash rich, income poor" individuals who live comfortably in Canada while earning little income – in this case, property overseas may provide a source of income that is unreported or underreported by respondents.

Immigration Status, Ethnic Origin, and Variations in Transnationalism

Statistical relationships were more readily discernible between transnationalism and other variables. The duration of settlement in Canada plays a strong role, with significant effects upon each of the indicators (see Table 4.4). Recent immigrants, defined in our study as those who landed between 1991 and 2001, tended to keep more contact with family and relatives overseas and were much more apt to retain economic linkages between Canada and their premigration countries. However, those who were longer settled travelled more and acted as host to more guests from their home countries. This stands to reason, as they were likely to have the financial resources required for transcontinental travel.

The Canadian immigrant-selection system also plays an important role in transnational activities (see Table 4.5). A small number of our respondents were admitted under a special program designed to bring domestic servants and caregivers to Canada. Although our results for this group are not definitive, they suggest that live-in caregivers maintain extensive social and economic linkages with family and friends in their premigration countries: they have the highest rates of regular communication, remittances home, and property ownership. However, respondents in this category do not operate businesses overseas, and they receive few visitors from their home countries (although they travel home relatively often). Business immigrants also exhibit a distinct profile. As might be expected, they have the highest tendency to operate a business in their home countries, and one in three engage in job-related transcontinental travel. In general, this group has the means to travel and host visitors, and most do so. Nearly all have family and friends overseas and maintain regular contact with them. More than one-third maintains property overseas. In contrast to live-in caregivers, however, business immigrants are very unlikely to send money home – perhaps because it is not needed given the high socio-economic status of this group.

Refugees (again, a small subgroup in our survey) exhibit the opposite profile. Given their flight from dangerous circumstances, refugees have the lowest level of contact with family and friends in their home countries and are least likely to travel there. They also receive few visitors from their home countries. However, a fairly high proportion send money to overseas friends and family.

The largest groups included in our survey – independent immigrants, their spouses and dependants, and family-sponsored immigrants – are fairly similar

Table 4.4

Respondents engaged in transnational activities by period of landing (%)

	Number of respondents[a]	Family in home country	Keep in touch	Travel to home country	Job requires travel	Property in home country	Business in home country	Send $ to home country	Visits from home country
Since 1991	703	95.4	98.8	64.3	10.9	32.3	5.4	17.2	57.1
Before 1991	773	85.7	92.1	71.9	6.0	13.8	1.2	12.2	65.4
Probability		0.000	0.000	0.002	0.004	0.000	0.000	0.007	0.001

a The total number of respondents in the survey is 1,479; the number of respondents answering each question is different and less than the total indicated here.

Table 4.5

Respondents engaged in transnational activities by selected immigration class (%)

	Number of respondents[a]	Family in home country	Keep in touch	Travel to home country	Job requires travel	Property in home country	Business in home country	Send $ to home country	Visits from home country
Spouse and dependants	543	89.5	95.2	67.8	*5.0*	17.9	*2.3*	8.4	63.3
Family	292	*92.8*	95.9	69.9	*5.5*	29.0	*2.4*	21.4	48.6
Refugee	41	78.0	81.3	46.3	*7.7*	22.0	*4.9*	24.4	41.5
Independent	416	*91.5*	96.3	67.8	*13.5*	21.3	*3.9*	16.9	69.7
Business	55	*94.5*	100.0	81.8	*33.3*	38.9	*11.1*	1.9	80.0
Caregiver	22	*85.7*	100.0	72.7	*0.0*	52.4	*0.0*	33.3	28.6
Other	78	*84.6*	93.9	65.4	*3.8*	23.1	*3.8*	19.2	52.6
Probability		*0.063*	0.002	0.020	*0.080*	0.000	*0.070*	0.000	0.000

Notes: Classes with fewer than twenty respondents have been omitted. Figures in italics indicate nonsignificant results in chi-squared tests.
a The total number of respondents in the survey is 1,479; the number of respondents answering each question is different and less than the total indicated here.

in terms of their transnational activities, which tend to range from the extremes set by refugees on the one hand and by business immigrants on the other. A couple of distinguishing features are evident when we look more closely at differences between these groups: independent immigrants, as might be expected, are more likely to engage in work-related travel and to operate a business overseas.

There are also profound differences in transnational activities related to ethnic origin (see Table 4.6). Those who identified themselves under the general category of East Asian in origin – including Chinese, Korean, and Japanese Canadians – are, by far, the most transnational of our survey participants. Individuals from these backgrounds maintain the strongest links with family and friends, travel the most in both directions, have the highest tendency to maintain business interests in their home countries, and engage in the most job-related travel (see Ong 1999). Of course, it is worth noting that most of the business immigrants in our survey were Chinese Canadians. The contrast between those with East Asian backgrounds and those from Latin America and the Caribbean is particularly sharp. The latter group of respondents is small, but its members appear to have relatively modest links with home countries (except for remittances). Those of European origin are also less transnational than average, especially when we look at their relative lack of economic connections (property and remittances). This probably reflects several factors: European immigrants in our survey tend to have been in Canada longer; they come from more affluent countries where remittances are less needed; and, possibly, they make more of a clear break with their previous economic activities when migrating to Canada. Two other groups are distinctive in specific ways: South Asians are, by a large measure, most likely to own property in their home countries (in almost all cases this is India),[5] and those declaring Southeast Asian origins are most likely to send remittances home (this is related to the high number of Filipinas who entered Canada as live-in caregivers).

Language and Transnationalism

We can learn more about the Chinese-origin subgroup by turning to the language in which the interview took place. Our survey reveals strong differences between immigrants from the Cantonese-speaking regions of southern China and Hong Kong on the one hand and those from Taiwan and Mandarin-speaking parts of China on the other (see Table 4.7). Excepting travel, the latter maintain more social and economic ties with their premigration countries. Remarkably, every one of our 164 Mandarin-speaking respondents has friends and family in their home countries, and virtually all keep in regular contact with those overseas. They are also far more likely to be involved in transpacific work-related travel and to own property and businesses abroad. Cantonese speakers, by comparison, travel more regularly

Table 4.6

Respondents engaged in transnational activities by ethnic origin (%)

	Number of respondents[a]	Family in home country	Keep in touch	Travel to home country	Job requires travel	Property in home country	Business in home country	Send $ to home country	Visits from home country
European/Canadian	421	87.4	93.4	67.4	7.7	10.8	1.7	8.6	70.7
Arab/West Asian	36	88.9	90.6	52.8	0.0	27.8	0.0	19.4	44.4
South Asian	255	85.9	96.8	61.6	1.8	41.2	1.6	16.9	32.5
East Asian	614	93.8	97.0	76.0	13.1	23.9	5.5	12.7	72.7
Southeast Asian	93	92.5	95.3	54.8	4.8	21.7	3.2	35.9	34.4
Latin American/Caribbean	30	90.0	88.9	50.0	0.0	10.0	0.0	30.0	63.3
Probability		0.002	0.020	0.000	0.099	0.000	0.006	0.000	0.000

Notes: Figures in italics indicate nonsignificant results in chi-squared tests.
a The total number of respondents in the survey is 1,479; the number of respondents answering each question is different and less than the total indicated here.

Table 4.7

Respondents engaged in transnational activities by interview language (%)

	Number of respondents[a]	Family in home country	Keep in touch	Travel to home country	Job requires travel	Property in home country	Business in home country	Send $ to home country	Visits from home country
English	933	87.2	93.5	63.9	6.1	15.8	1.8	14.0	63.1
Cantonese	263	96.2	98.4	84.4	9.7	21.0	3.2	15.7	73.1
Mandarin	164	100.0	99.4	72.0	27.9	41.7	12.6	13.2	66.0
Punjabi	109	89.0	99.0	64.2	2.0	57.8	0.9	17.4	15.6
Probability		0.000	0.000	0.000	0.000	0.000	0.000	0.798	0.000

Notes: Language categories with fewer than twenty respondents have been omitted. Figures in italics indicate nonsignificant results in chi-squared tests.
a The total number of respondents in the survey is 1,479; the number of respondents answering each question is different and less than the total indicated here.

across the Pacific. Punjabi speakers tend to hold overseas property, while the fact that they receive few visitors probably reflects their recent settlement in Vancouver and their modest economic means. We also found that respondents who felt most comfortable participating in our survey in English tended to be the least transnational.

Does this mean that there is an acculturation effect visible in our results? We have already seen that more settled immigrants participate in fewer forms of transnationalism (although travel is an exception). Table 4.8, which divides respondents by their language use in the home, offers some evidence on this point (up to three languages were coded to yield the categories used in the table). Those respondents who speak only a non-English language at home engage in more intensive transnationalism in terms of several of the activities explored in our survey: they keep more regular contact with family and friends, and they are more apt to own property and businesses in their premigration country. Similarly, those who speak only English at home are the least transnational (although a high proportion receive visitors from abroad). However, a careful look at the data demonstrates that the relationship between home language and transnationalism is far from perfect. There is in fact no statistically significant difference between language groups and their propensity to travel to home countries either generally or for work. The question on remittances also yielded ambiguous results. Rather than showing a straightforward acculturation effect, the language data may reflect the distinction between European immigrants (who have tended to embrace English as their home language) and immigrants from other parts of the world.

Citizenship and Transnationalism

The argument that transnationalism may dissipate over time, or as circumstances change, is more apparent when we shift our attention to citizenship status (see Table 4.9). Here the general pattern is clearer: those who have taken up Canadian citizenship and revoked their original citizenship tend to maintain fewer transnational ties, whether social or economic. Conversely, those who have not acquired Canadian citizenship tend to have the strongest overseas links, especially economic ones; this group comprises a mix of those who have been in Canada fewer than four years, those who want to retain their original citizenship but who would become Canadian citizens if their countries of origin allowed dual citizenship, and those who do not wish to become Canadian citizens. We see the same results when examining the relationship between national identity and transnationalism (see Table 4.10). Respondents who say that they *always* "feel Canadian" are less attached to friends and family in the premigration country and maintain fewer economic linkages. Those who only *occasionally* or *never* feel a Canadian identity are engaged in more transnational lifestyles; for example, they

Table 4.8

Respondents engaged in transnational activities by language use in the home (%)

	Number of respondents[a]	Family in home country	Keep in touch	Travel to home country	Job requires travel	Property in home country	Business in home country	Send $ to home country	Visits from home country
English only	330	83.0	92.3	66.0	9.2	9.2	1.2	9.1	69.6
English and other	579	91.2	94.5	67.0	7.5	21.3	3.1	17.4	63.7
Non-English	567	93.6	98.1	71.1	7.6	32.0	4.5	14.8	54.5
Probability		0.000	0.000	*0.189*	*0.167*	0.000	0.027	0.003	0.000

Note: Figures in italics indicate nonsignificant results in chi-squared tests.
a The total number of respondents in the survey is 1,479; the number of respondents answering each question is different and less than the total indicated here.

Table 4.9

Respondents engaged in transnational activities by citizenship status (%)

	Number of respondents[a]	Family in home country	Keep in touch	Travel to home country	Job requires travel	Property in home country	Business in home country	Send $ to home country	Visits from home country
Canadian only	696	86.5	92.2	69.3	4.5	16.2	1.0	14.5	60.2
Canadian and other	339	93.5	98.1	81.4	8.7	15.5	2.4	10.4	77.0
Other only	441	93.7	98.3	56.5	14.2	38.6	7.4	17.8	51.4
Probability		0.000	0.000	0.000	0.007	0.000	0.000	0.015	0.000

a The total number of respondents in the survey is 1,479; the number of respondents answering each question is different and less than the total indicated here.

are six times more likely to operate a business in their home country, three times more likely to own overseas property, and between 1.5 and two times more likely to send remittance payments. However, again the travel variables are outliers to this pattern: the more that respondents feel attached to Canada, the more they travel to their premigration countries and the more they host reciprocal visits.

Discussion: Vancouver in Comparative Context

We would not expect transnational practices to be the same in any two places. Much of the American research has been undertaken in southern California and the cities of the East Coast, whose migrants are typically of modest means and travel between their homes in the United States and relatively close origins in Central America and the Caribbean. In Vancouver, in contrast, recent immigration is dominated by arrivals from points in East Asia, principally China, Hong Kong, Taiwan, and Korea, in Southeast Asia, notably the Philippines and Vietnam, and in South Asia, principally India. Older migration is from Europe. Movement between Vancouver and these origins is of long duration and can be undertaken only by air, an expensive means of transport. Distance and cost are bound to affect the easy movement of transnational migrants.

It is instructive to compare the incidence of transnational activities in Vancouver with those documented in a longitudinal panel survey undertaken in Montreal (Renaud et al. 2002). In the fourth round of interviews with some three hundred immigrants ten years after arrival, 96% of respondents had family in their home countries, compared with 90% in Vancouver who specified that they had friends or family in their home countries. Among the Vancouver sample, 68% had travelled to their home countries at least once, approaching the Montreal figure of 72%. There were also surprisingly similar likelihoods of owning property in a country of origin (22% in Vancouver, 24% in Montreal) and of owning a business there (3.2% in Vancouver, 2.3% in Montreal). In contrast, remittances were sent by far fewer Vancouver immigrants (only 14%), compared with figures between 28% and 67% in the four rounds of the Montreal panel (Renaud et al. 2002).

Given that more than half of the Vancouver respondents had landed in Canada more than ten years before the interview, compared with none of the Montreal group, the samples are not comparable in length of residence, a variable highly associated with the incidence of transnational activity. Nor, indeed, are the samples comparable in terms of immigrant countries of origin. Consequently, despite similar profiles on several items, it is difficult to know how to interpret the Vancouver-Montreal comparisons, aside from a few observations. Not surprisingly, the different indicators of transnationalism reveal marked variations in incidence. With Itzigsohn and Saucedo (2002) we find that there is broad participation in transnational

Table 4.10

Respondents engaged in transnational activities by identification as Canadian (%)

	Number of respondents[a]	Family in home country	Keep in touch	Travel to home country	Job requires travel	Property in home country	Business in home country	Send $ to home country	Visits from home country
Always	462	85.4	93.6	71.3	6.8	18.3	1.8	11.2	60.3
Most of the time	399	91.2	93.4	70.6	7.3	17.0	1.5	13.4	68.1
Sometimes	309	93.2	97.9	70.9	3.8	20.0	2.9	18.3	59.2
Occasionally	110	93.6	97.1	60.0	20.0	32.7	3.7	21.3	56.9
Never	160	95.0	98.7	59.4	16.7	45.9	10.8	15.8	53.5
Probability		0.001	0.011	0.001	0.030	0.000	0.000	0.044	0.008

Note: Categories with fewer than twenty respondents have been omitted.
a The total number of respondents in the survey is 1,479; the number of respondents answering each question is different and less than the total indicated here.

linkages among the immigrant population, although some specific activities, notably economic transactions, are limited to relatively few. The restriction of transnational entrepreneurship to a small group was also noted in the CIEP's assessment of Latin American immigrants in four American cities (Portes 2001; Landolt 2001). Travel seems quite different from other indicators and increases in incidence in both directions with increasing length of residence. The distance from Vancouver to immigrant origins is probably a factor here, for cross-tabulations reveal that higher income respondents are more likely to visit their home countries and to host reciprocal visits.

In general, socio-economic status emerges as a weak predictor. In contrast, the CIEP's results showed much stronger positive associations between transnationalism, socio-economic status, and length of residence. Our results are different. Length of residence is significantly associated with all of our indicators, but aside from the two travel measures, all other indicators show some weakening with the passage of time. Vancouver immigrants arriving since 1991 are more than four times as likely to engage in transnational business ownership as earlier arrivals, whereas the CIEP's findings showed a greater probability of transnational entrepreneurship with *increasing* length of residence. Moreover, though education is positively associated with entrepreneurship, it is seemingly randomly distributed across different income bands of immigrants in Vancouver.

In contrast to socio-economic status, with its weak showing, immigration class and cultural variables show strong associations with transnational activity. Business-class immigrants expressed the strongest transnational behaviour, with high proclivities to maintain contact and strong tendencies to engage in economic-related travel to their home countries, reflecting the familiar profile of the East Asian astronaut household (Ong 1999; Waters 2002). Although immigrants who were live-in caregivers had minimal business connections with their home countries, they, too, kept in close contact (although not through personal travel), were the most consistent in sending remittances home, and had the highest proportion owning property in their countries of origin. Refugees were the second most likely to send remittances but otherwise had moderate or low linkages. The remaining classes, those landing through family sponsorship or as independents (skilled workers) had intermediate positions, with skilled workers predictably expressing greater job-related connections but lower levels of remittances and less property ownership.

The role of immigration status, largely independent of socio-economic status, is an important finding, but no less relevant were a series of ethnocultural variables, reinforcing the view in the literature of substantial intergroup (as well as intragroup) variation in transnational activity. The strongest tendency in the data was for immigrants from East Asia (China, Hong Kong,

Taiwan, and Korea) to exhibit the highest level of homeland contact in most categories aside from remittances, which was led by Southeast Asia (particularly the Philippines). The data on mother tongues showed that Mandarin-speaking regions (China and Taiwan) were the most transnational. In contrast, English-speaking groups and those with national origins in Europe and (surprisingly) Latin America and the Caribbean had considerably more limited homeland contact. Due to these relationships, groups self-identifying as nonwhite (or as visible minorities) were more likely to live in a transnational field, although these differentials were not generally as great as those associated with language use in the home.

A final area of interest is the relationship between transnational behaviour and a sense of Canadian identity. Again our results counter those of the CIEP's data but are perhaps closer to the expectations outlined by Van Hear (1998). Respondents who always identified as Canadian showed low levels of transnationalism, other than visits to their homelands and receiving visitors from those countries. But all economic linkages (including remittances) were very low. These relationships were significant across all of our transnational indicators – suggesting that none of them is trivial in differentiating a sense of belonging (although the direction of the relationship is reversed for the two travel items). Relationships between transnationalism and citizenship status – where the options were Canadian only, dual citizenship, and non-Canadian status – were even stronger. Indeed, among all our variables, citizenship status was the best predictor of transnational activity. Aside, once again, from the two non-economic travel indicators, all the indicators showed (unlike the CIEP's results) that heightened membership in a transnational field limited the probability of Canadian citizenship by a marked degree. For example, only 1% of immigrants with Canadian citizenship ran a business in their home countries, compared with 7.4% of those without Canadian citizenship; 4.5% of the former group engaged in job-related travel to their countries of origin, compared with 14.2% of the latter.

This leads to our principal conclusion: whereas the American research identifies transnationalism as a form of integration, if not assimilation (Portes 2001; Kivisto 2001; Itzigsohn and Saucedo 2002; Portes, Haller, and Guarnizo 2002), our Vancouver results locate membership in a transnational field among immigrants who are weakly connected to the Canadian nation-state. For this group, at least at present, transnationalism is not a subset of integration but an alternative to it. Their place of origin remains more central than their place of residence to their sense of self.

Conclusion

In light of the few large surveys of transnational behaviour in Canada, it would be unwise to press a Canada-America contrast too far. From our analysis, we would concur with the American research that transnational practices are widely shared in such routine events as maintaining social contact but are far more restricted when it comes to entrepreneurial transactions. So, too, is there evidently considerable variation among national-origin groups in their scale of activity, to which we would also add the distinctive effects of class of immigrant landing.

But our indicators of transnationalism also diverge from the CIEP's influential study in important respects. Our findings indicate that transnational entrepreneurs are far more likely to be recent immigrants and not to hold Canadian citizenship. So, too, are they not well specified by socio-economic status. Our profile is closer to the original anthropological representation of transnationalism as an alternative to social and economic integration – a view reinforced in Vancouver by more focused qualitative studies (Waters 2002; Ley and Waters 2004) – than to the position that transnational behaviour is an aid to economic integration (indeed, to assimilation) in the United States for well-settled immigrants (Portes 2001; Kivisto 2001; Portes, Haller, and Guarnizo 2002).

Notes

1 We thank the Vancouver Centre of Excellence for Research on Immigration and Integration in the Metropolis (RIIM) for the funding that enabled this project. The survey results reported here are part of a larger study designed to investigate the relationship between global and local processes in five subregions of the Vancouver metropolitan area. The research team includes Gillian Creese, Isabel Lowe Dyck, Daniel Hiebert, David Ley, Arlene Tigar McLaren, and Geraldine Pratt.
2 Our survey was designed to explore transnational linkages only between source and host country and did not pose questions about more complex forms of international linkage, such as economic transactions between migrants in several host countries. The overall effect of our methodology would be to underestimate the total scale of transnationalism.
3 Of course, this figure must be an underestimate, as most migrants with transnational business activities are overseas for most of the year and would therefore not be at home for a telephone interview.
4 Unfortunately, only 1,015 of the 1,479 immigrants in our survey provided an answer to our question on household income. Around one-third of those who didn't answer the question explained that they did not know their household income, while two-thirds simply refused to specify it.
5 It is notable that most of the migrants who have moved from India to Vancouver have come from the Punjab region and that many were engaged in agriculture (Walton-Roberts 2003), which may help to explain their effort to retain property in India.

5
Transnational Urbanism: Toronto at a Crossroads

Valerie Preston, Audrey Kobayashi, and Myer Siemiatycki

The effects of transnationalism on the messy politics of place making (Smith 2000, 5) are readily apparent in the Toronto metropolitan area, which is home to more than 2 million immigrants drawn from every region of the world (Statistics Canada 2003a). Scholars have recognized for some time that, as transnationals, recent immigrants transform the urban landscape with their efforts to maintain social links and social identities at their places of origin and destination (Basch, Glick Schiller, and Szanton Blanc 1994; Rouse 1991). Settlement itself affects the extent and nature of transnational activities and the transnational social fields that result. Discussions of this dialectical relationship often emphasize the significance of the local, however, without specifying its effects (Foner 2001b). In this study, we examine changes in the built form and social environment of metropolitan Toronto associated with recent transnational migration to discern some of the ways that local circumstances shape transnational activities and their impacts.

Our analysis begins from the premise that technological, political, economic, and social changes in the last half of the twentieth century have facilitated and encouraged transnational behaviours. We explore the social and political processes by which transnational migrants claim and transform urban spaces in the Toronto metropolitan area. The analysis reveals how transnationalism is affecting urban places and migrants' citizenship claims, their rights to the city (Isin and Siemiatycki 2002), and the reciprocal ways that an urban place shapes transnational behaviours. Our empirical findings reveal data lacunae that must be addressed before a full understanding of the impacts of transnationalism on Toronto and other urban places is possible.

For three reasons, our analysis draws mainly on information about recent immigrants from Hong Kong who settled in the Toronto metropolitan area. First, Hong Kong migrants are pioneering transnationals (Skeldon 1994). After Great Britain agreed to return the colony to China, reluctant exiles drew on their long history of migration, leaving Hong Kong to seek opportunities and political stability elsewhere (Skeldon 1994). Many headed for Canada, where immigration and citizenship policies encouraged a transnational lifestyle (Waters 2003; Siemiatycki and Preston 2004). In Canada, Hong Kong immigrants[1] became concentrated in a few major cities, where their large numbers, affluence, and educational attainments supported the media outlets and specialized services that underpin transnational lifestyles.

Second, Hong Kong immigrants have had tremendous influence in Toronto because of their numbers and their immigration history. In 2001, more than 110,000 people born in Hong Kong were living in Toronto (Statistics Canada 2003a).[2] The recent influx of Hong Kong immigrants was rapid, occurring between 1987 and 1997, a period that coincides with the end of an economic boom and a deep recession from which the local economy recovered slowly. Hong Kong immigrants were an important consumer market for Toronto's developers and retailers, who were struggling to survive the worst economic downturn since the Great Depression.

Third, Toronto merits attention as a site of transnationalism. With a large and diverse immigrant population that accounted for 43.7% of the total population in 2001, the metropolitan area is the preeminent destination for immigrants settling in Canada. In recognition of their importance, the City of Toronto, home to approximately half the metropolitan population, has adopted the slogan "Diversity our Strength." The commitment to multiculturalism and equitable treatment of diverse individuals and groups has led to a well-developed infrastructure of settlement services and ethnocultural organizations that helps to sustain transnational ties. Our analysis indicates that even a metropolis officially committed to valuing newcomers and their diversity may struggle with transnationalism.

We begin our discussion of the effects of transnational migration with a brief review of contemporary literature that explores how migrants create transnational social fields. A description of Hong Kong immigrants in Toronto follows. The third section draws on questionnaires completed by Hong Kong immigrants living in Toronto. Selected landscape changes associated with the transnational behaviours of Hong Kong immigrants in Canada are discussed in the fourth section. We conclude with a brief summary of the implications of our findings both for understanding transnationalism and for future research.

Transnational Migrants, Transnational Spaces
The burgeoning literature about contemporary transnational migration examines how improvements in communications and transportation technology, combined with globalization of economic activities and recent political events, have encouraged the maintenance of diverse social relationships and social identities across the boundaries of nation-states (Kelly

2003; Kivisto 2001; Vertovec 1999). Transnational activities that range from economic to cultural and political ties take various forms and occur with varying intensity. They may involve people acting on behalf of nation-states, multinational corporations, and international organizations in cross-border activities as well as those acting on behalf of themselves, their families, and their communities (Portes, Guarnizo, and Landolt 1999). Transnational ties are diverse and are influenced by migrants' own social characteristics, such as gender, social class, and migration history; state policies and actions at migrants' places of origin and destination; and the local urban context in which migrants settle (Levitt 2000). We can distinguish between *narrow* transnational practices, which are institutionalized, involve constant participation, and occur regularly, and *broad* transnational practices, which are associated with more loosely defined identities (Itzigsohn et al. 1999). Transnational ties shape social and symbolic connections and position people in networks and organizations that link two or more geographically distinct places in different nation-states (Faist 1999; Levitt 2000). Transnational social fields are highly differentiated, ranging from the weak connections and short-lived ties of transnational groups that have assimilated and dispersed to the dense and persistent social networks in places of origin and destination that characterize transnational communities and that extend beyond the first generation of immigrants to second- and third-generation citizens (Faist 1999, 44; Fouron and Glick Schiller 2002).

The form, intensity, and impact of transnational social fields reflect processes operating at various spatial scales. The policies and practices of nation-states frame transnational ties and the social fields that result, just as the experiences of daily life at the destination inevitably influence the actions of transnational migrants (Yeoh et al. 2003). The destinations of contemporary migrants are increasingly large cities, these being the focal points of international migration (Ray 2003). A city's immigration history, patterns of residential segregation, labour-market segmentation, local political structures, local social institutions, and even predominant urban values – as we show in the case of Toronto – influence settlement and the transnational social fields that result (Foner 2001b).

Cities are also transformed by the transnational social fields of contemporary migrants in distinct ways. Affluent transnationals seeking political stability and economic security often invest locally, purchasing real estate, developing small retail and service establishments that largely serve their own communities, buying local firms, and establishing branches of international conglomerates based in their home countries (Mitchell 1995; Olds 2001; Li 1998). Although some arrive as sojourners determined to accumulate the capital that will enable them to return home better able to support themselves and their families (Wong 2003; Owusu 1998), newcomers also create new social organizations that link their places of origin with the destinations where they have settled (Levitt 2000). At the same time, they transform existing organizations with demands for new social services and the implementation of new ideas and ideologies transplanted from their societies of origin (Mitchell 2001). At a political level, newcomers struggle to exercise their citizenship rights by participating fully in civil society while still maintaining links to politics in their countries of origin (Itzigsohn 2000; Preston, Kobayashi, and Man forthcoming). Such transformations are often evident both in the built environments where residential concentrations of migrants appear and in the commercial and social activities that these environments generate.

In the case of Toronto, relatively little is documented about the ways that transnational migrants have transformed the urban area. The major sources of information about transnational migrants in Toronto are case studies of migrants from countries such as Ghana, South Korea, Hong Kong, and the Philippines (Bakan and Stasiulis 1997; Kwak 2002; Lam 1994; Man 1997; Wong 2003). Each study emphasizes a different aspect of transnationalism. For example, recent studies of Ghanaians in metropolitan Toronto underscore the importance of remittances to family and friends in Ghana and the overwhelming desire to invest in Ghanaian real estate and businesses (Owusu 1998; Wong 2003). Apart from Menyah's study of businesses owned and operated by Ghanaian immigrants (Menyah 2002), little work has been done regarding the impacts of the transnational social fields constructed by Ghanaians on the city itself. Studies of Filipinas, who often migrate alone and enter Canada as domestic workers, have emphasized their political involvement in organizations dedicated to improving the working conditions and immigration policies affecting foreign domestic workers (Bakan and Stasiulis 1997). We also know how the transnational ties of Korean immigrants influence their economic activities in Toronto, which in turn alter gender roles within their households (Kwak 2002). Among Hong Kong immigrants, astronaut households, in which one partner, usually the man, returns to Hong Kong and leaves the rest of the family in Canada, often experience profound changes in gender relations and gender roles (Lam 1994; Man 1997). Despite their important contributions, none of these case studies provides a comprehensive and comparative analysis of transnational activities in Toronto or of their impact on the urban environment. We have only partial descriptions of transnational activities and the social fields constructed by transnational migrants, and little information about how their social fields overlap and intersect, either with one another or with the larger society.

In the remainder of this chapter, we detail the transnational social fields constructed by recent Hong Kong immigrants in metropolitan Toronto and their implications for the social and built environment. Our focus on Hong Kong immigrants reflects their status as pioneering transnational migrants, their significant impact on the Toronto metropolitan area, and the avail-

ability of information. The empirical analysis draws on information provided by participants in focus groups that were organized to discuss Hong
Kong immigrants' settlement experiences in Canada, their ties to Hong Kong,
and their views concerning citizenship. Focus-group participants completed
questionnaires soliciting detailed information about transnational behaviours, information not readily available for other immigrant groups in
Toronto. We also draw on the findings from case studies of the residential
and employment experiences of women who immigrated from Hong Kong
to Toronto after 1985 (Chiu 1998; Preston 2003). These sources of information are diverse, but they allow us to explore the extent and nature of Hong
Kong immigrants' transnational activities and the potential impacts of
transnational activities on metropolitan Toronto.

Hong Kong Canadians in Toronto
Hong Kong has been a steady source of immigrants ever since Canada liber-
alized its immigration policies in the 1960s. The number of Hong Kong
immigrants increased dramatically after 1984, when the government of Great
Britain announced that the colony would be returned to China in 1997 at
the end of Great Britain's lease (Skeldon 1994). By 1996, Hong Kong was the
largest single source of recent immigrants, those who settled in Canada between 1991 and 1996 (see Figure 5.1). Immigrants from Hong Kong entered

Figure 5.1

**Immigrant arrivals from Hong Kong to Toronto and Canada
by destination, 1980-2002**

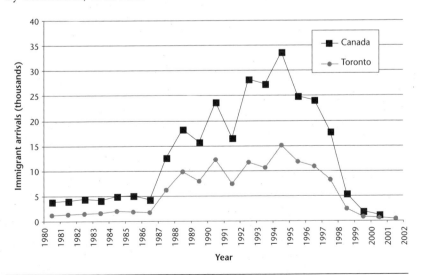

Source: Citizenship and Immigration Canada (CIC 2003a), LIDS, Landed Immigrant Database
System.

Canada mainly under two immigration programs: one for skilled workers and the other for the business class. As skilled workers, applicants were admitted on the basis of their education, years of work experience, and occupation. Business-class immigrants were admitted as investors with sufficient financial assets, specifically entrepreneurs whose experience was deemed useful for the Canadian economy and self-employed migrants whose skills and experience would enable them to be self-employed in Canada.

Although Hong Kong immigrants were the single largest group of immigrants to settle in the Toronto census metropolitan area (CMA) between 1991 and 1996, they were still only one of a large number of different immigrant streams.[3] The preponderance of Hong Kong immigrants who were admitted as skilled workers is evident in their high levels of education. Hong Kong immigrants are better educated than the average adult living in the Toronto metropolitan area. Twenty-nine percent of Hong Kong immigrants in Toronto, compared to only 24.9% of the total adult population, have at least one university degree.

The Hong Kong immigrants who participated in our focus groups share many of these characteristics.[4] The majority immigrated after 1985.[5] They are well educated and most are either in their early twenties or middle-aged. More than 30% (17 of 53) have a university degree. Consistent with the entire Hong Kong immigrant population in the Toronto metropolitan area, the largest group, 37% of the participants, immigrated as skilled workers. Family sponsorship was almost equally important as an avenue for admission to Canada, mentioned by approximately one-third of the participants.

The reasons mentioned for immigrating to Canada underscore the role of family considerations in the migration decisions of Hong Kong immigrants (Ong 1999; Waters 2003). Among these participants, the fact that other family members had decided to move to Canada was the most frequently mentioned reason for migrating, listed by almost two-thirds as an important factor. Educational concerns that are intimately linked with family considerations were also mentioned by approximately 38% of participants. Political issues such as Hong Kong's imminent return to China and the events of Tianamen Square were cited as reasons for immigrating by less than 16% of participants. While the findings may reflect some retrospective rationalization, they indicate that chain migration and educational opportunities were important reasons for immigrating to Canada, just as Waters (2003) has reported for Hong Kong immigrants in Vancouver. This finding is consistent not only with the value placed on education within this community, but also with the fact that Canada had provided education for many Hong Kong residents for at least two decades prior to the major immigration that occurred in the 1990s.

While the high levels of educational attainment among Hong Kong immigrants in Toronto contribute to high rates of labour-force participation, the participants in our focus groups were less likely than the average immigrant to be working. Approximately 45% of focus-group participants reported being unemployed and not seeking work. Our information does not indicate the reasons for this high unemployment rate, but it may reflect the preponderance of recent immigrants in the focus groups and local economic conditions. In the 1990s improvements in immigrants' economic status were slow and hard-won in Toronto (Preston, Lo, and Wang 2003). The economic difficulties of the participants are reflected in their low household incomes, with only 30% reporting an annual household income of at least $50,000 at a time when the median household income in metropolitan Toronto was $59,502.

Unlike earlier immigrant groups, recent Hong Kong immigrants have settled directly in suburban Toronto, where the concentrations evident in 1991 (Lo and Wang 1997) have strengthened. The largest concentration, located northeast of downtown Toronto, extends from Scarborough into Markham and Richmond Hill to the north and into North York to the west (see Table 5.1). There is a second concentration in the western suburb of Mississauga. Hong Kong immigrants have avoided the traditional pattern of immigrant settlement that begins with a residential concentration near the city core and disperses or relocates to the suburbs (Murdie and Teixeira 2003). As we shall see, suburban settlement has important implications for the integration of Hong Kong immigrants into Toronto.

Transnationalism in Everyday Lives

Our analysis concentrates on transnational activities that may be expected of well-educated, middle-class migrants. In terms of informal measures of attachment to Hong Kong, we assessed immigrants' ties to Hong Kong, their efforts to stay informed about Hong Kong, and their civic participation in Canada and Hong Kong. Formal attachment was evaluated in terms of citizenship, specifically naturalization as Canadian citizens. Transnational ties among Hong Kong immigrants are rooted in family relations and friendships, as reported elsewhere (Waters 2001). Almost every respondent has one or more family members still living in Hong Kong. Of the fifty-five people who participated in the focus groups, 69% had immediate family members living in Hong Kong. Many are members of astronaut families. An even higher percentage, more than 78%, reported that they had extended family members in Hong Kong. Friendship is a second basis of important social ties to Hong Kong, where 89% of respondents reported that they had friends. By any measure, the focus-group participants are transnationals with extensive and intense social ties to Hong Kong.

Economic ties that involve ownership of business assets are much less frequent, being reported by only about one-quarter of participants. Contrary to previous commentary about the Chinese family that emphasizes how family members are dispersed as part of a family strategy of capital

Table 5.1

Hong Kong immigrants by location within the Toronto Census metropolitan area, 2001

Category	Municipality	Total immigrants	Hong Kong immigrants	Total recent immigrants	Recent Hong Kong immigrants	% recent Hong Kong immigrants	
						Among all Hong Kong immigrants	Among all recent immigrants
Centre		**396,795**	**6,505**	**85,885**	**450**	**6.9**	**0.5**
	East York	51,580	805	16,810	0	0	0
	Toronto, City of	269,045	5,410	55,530	420	7.8	0.8
	York	76,170	290	13,545	30	10.3	0.2
Inner suburbs		**811,210**	**49,010**	**192,745**	**7,690**	**15.7**	**4.0**
	Etobicoke	149,925	1,295	31,410	50	3.9	0.2
	North York	337,785	17,865	88,950	3,425	19.2	3.9
	Scarborough	323,500	29,850	72,385	4,215	14.1	5.8
Outer suburbs		**748,620**	**54,450**	**130,430**	**9,925**	**18.2**	**7.6**
	Aurora	7,195	145	905	10	6.9	1.1
	Brampton	129,285	695	20,795	45	6.5	0.2
	Markham	109,930	27,780	19,715	5,730	20.6	29.1
	Mississauga	285,650	9,565	60,125	1,440	15.1	2.4
	Newmarket	12,200	375	1,000	60	16.0	6.0
	Oakville	39,610	675	5,045	85	12.6	1.7
	Pickering	25,115	410	1,915	25	6.1	1.3
	Richmond Hill	63,615	12,940	12,980	2,360	18.2	18.2
	Vaughan	76,020	1,865	7,950	170	9.1	2.1

Exurbs	69,730	680	4,425	60	8.8	1.4
Ajax	18,500	355	1,415	10	2.8	0.7
Bradford & West Gwillimbury	4,595	10	305	10	100	3.3
Caledon	9,890	30	340	0	0	0
East Gwillimbury	2,790	15	145	0	0	0
Georginas	4,435	25	330	0	0	0
Halton Hills	7,405	105	475	20	19.0	4.2
King	3,955	10	105	0	0	0
Milton	4,945	10	290	0	0	0
Mono	1,050	0	100	0	0	0
New Tecumseth	3,250	10	220	0	0	0
Orangeville	3,090	10	290	0	0	0
Uxbridge	2,170	20	130	10	50.0	7.7
Whitchurch & Stouffville	3,655	80	280	10	12.5	3.6

Source: Statistics Canada (2003d).

accumulation (Ong 1999; Waters 2003), the majority of focus-group participants had no economic links to Hong Kong. Only 40% owned property there, and only 25% were running businesses in Hong Kong. The relatively low frequency of economic ties probably reflects the preponderance of participants who entered Canada under the skilled-workers and family-sponsorship programs. Only 25% of the participants in our study came to Canada through the business-class program. Other types of economic links were infrequent. Only one person sent financial assistance to family members in Hong Kong. The low rate of remittances probably reflects the economic wealth of Hong Kong, which, unlike many countries of origin, is highly developed and fairly affluent. These immigrants maintain few active social and political links to Hong Kong. Slightly more than one-quarter of focus-group participants were still members of Hong Kong organizations, and only four still voted in Hong Kong elections. In comparison, the vast majority stayed in touch with family, friends, and popular culture in Hong Kong. More than 90% of participants watched television or listened to radio that originated in Hong Kong. An almost equal number of participants, 87%, read Hong Kong newspapers, typically the local edition of *Ming Pao* (Szonyi 2002). The large population of Hong Kong immigrants in Toronto supports Cantonese-language television and radio programming and three Chinese-language daily newspapers.

Participants' social contacts with Hong Kong underscore the importance of family. Although participants were asked about many different types of social contacts, they had regular contact only with family members living in Hong Kong. Eighty-nine percent telephoned family members monthly, and about one-third contacted family members through e-mail each month. The majority of participants returned to Hong Kong less than once a year and 13 of the 54 participants who answered this question had never returned to Hong Kong after migrating to Canada.

For these newcomers, civic participation patterns reveal stronger ties to Hong Kong and to community organizations in Canada that are linked to their Hong Kong identities. Many immigrants were involved in voluntary organizations that originate in Hong Kong (see Table 5.2). Approximately half of all participants reported that they volunteered for a Hong Kong association, and an even larger number were members of sports, religious, cultural, and social associations that originate in Hong Kong. In contrast, none of the participants belonged to a Canadian social organization, but almost 30% had donated to Canadian charities. Involvement within one's immigrant community is the norm for newcomers (Breton 1997; Frideres 1997), but it is noteworthy for this group of well-educated and English-speaking immigrants who are settling in Canada's most multicultural metropolitan area, since they were not expected to face linguistic and economic barriers that would encourage participation in ethno-specific organizations.

Table 5.2

Civic participation in Toronto by Hong Kong immigrants

	Total	
	N	%
Vote in Canadian elections	12	22
Belong to political parties	0	0
Donate to political party	0	0
Donate to Canadian charities	16	29
Donate to Hong Kong associations	2	4
Volunteer for Hong Kong associations	27	49
Member of Hong Kong organization	36	65
Belong to Hong Kong political party	0	0

Levels of formal participation in Canadian society are low, but they exceed those in Hong Kong. None of the focus-group participants was a member of a Hong Kong political party, and few had voted in Hong Kong elections, only 4 of 55. In Canada, none of the participants belonged to a political party, nor had anyone donated to a Canadian political party. Hong Kong immigrants were more likely to vote, however, with about one-fifth of focus-group participants already having voted in a Canadian election (Table 5.2). More significantly, perhaps, Hong Kong immigrants are also making their mark as elected politicians. Although visible minorities remain massively underrepresented in Toronto electoral politics (Siemiatycki and Saloojee 2002), Chinese Canadians have fared better than other visible minorities. The Toronto area presently has five elected politicians (4 municipal and 1 provincial) of Chinese origin. Three were born in Hong Kong, an indication of their rapid political integration into Canadian civic life. The electoral success of Hong Kong immigrants represents a departure from past patterns, when the children of immigrants were the first representatives of their communities to be elected (Chui, Curtis, and Lambert 1991).

Naturalization is often viewed as the ultimate indication that international migrants are committed to their countries of destination (Foner 2001a). Among the participants in our focus groups, more than three-quarters had Canadian citizenship, indicating their commitment to Canada. Migrants' willingness to become naturalized citizens also depends on the citizenship policies of their countries of origin. There is a low rate of dual citizenship among the participants in focus groups: only 22.6% of participants reported that they combined Canadian citizenship with another citizenship. The low rate of dual citizenship may reflect the distinct status of Hong Kong residents, very few of whom possessed a British or Chinese passport prior to Hong Kong's return to China. Under these circumstances, the acquisition of a Canadian passport, which is widely recognized and which facilitates return to Canada at any time, has particular significance.

The transnational behaviours of recent Hong Kong immigrants in Toronto underscore their social connections to Hong Kong and their avid interest in Hong Kong affairs. Among the newcomers in our focus groups, there is limited support for the image of Hong Kong immigrants as hypermobile migrants seeking citizenship arrangements that will facilitate transnational family strategies for capital accumulation. The men and women who participated in the Toronto focus groups are settlers interested in acquiring Canadian citizenship while still maintaining kinship and friendship ties to Hong Kong and staying in touch with Hong Kong politics and popular culture through the media.

A lack of comprehensive studies of transnationalism in Toronto makes it difficult to assess whether the transnational ties of Hong Kong immigrants in Toronto are typical of other transnational migrants in Toronto; however, we can compare them with Hong Kong migrants in Vancouver, where, just like those in Toronto, the vast majority of Cantonese-speaking migrants maintain ties to family and friends in Hong Kong (Hiebert and Ley, Chapter 4, this volume). In both urban areas, few Hong Kong immigrants maintain economic ties to Hong Kong or send remittances. However, far fewer of the immigrants in our focus groups than the Cantonese-speaking immigrants in Vancouver regularly travel across the Pacific, perhaps because of the additional distance, cost, and time involved in travelling from Toronto rather than from Vancouver. The differences in travel patterns may also reflect the large number of business-class immigrants who have settled in Vancouver and who continue to operate their businesses in Hong Kong while establishing residence in Canada (Ley 2003).

Transnational Landscapes in Toronto

Hong Kong immigrants' transnational ties are not as frequent or as intense as we had expected, if measured in terms of frequency of contact. But we define the transnational social field as a much wider set of spatial relationships that involves the circulation and concentration of human connections, cultural practices, and consumable goods as well as bodies moving to and fro. Transnationalism encompasses the complex set of social practices through which places are created and given meaning and through which people situate themselves within the social field circumscribed by these places. In this case, the process involves the continuous placement and replacement of social selves within a set of relationships that defines both Toronto and Hong Kong, with important consequences for the urban environment. Three of the most significant forms of place construction within the transnational field are residential choices, employment decisions, and investments in commercial enterprises. An examination of each activity reveals how transnational links alter the urban landscape in Toronto.

Residential Choices

Recent immigrants settle in Toronto primarily to join family and friends (Statistics Canada 2003f). Kinship and friendship networks also play an important role in the decision to live in specific neighbourhoods upon arrival in the metropolitan area (Chiu 1998). In-depth interviews with thirteen women who immigrated from Hong Kong to Canada after 1985 revealed that the most important reason for moving to the northern suburbs of Markham and Richmond Hill, the heart of the residential concentration of Hong Kong immigrants, was the presence of family and friends from Hong Kong. Transnational ties, then, include relationships that connect one place to another, in the process redefining both places. Chiu notes that Ada's story is typical: "They all moved up here already ... We were looking for houses together. Together, we bought here. My sister-in-law ... every Saturday and Sunday, she came over to look for houses" (80).

Ada describes moving to Toronto, where she stayed temporarily with her sister-in-law, who then helped her look for housing. The two eventually bought houses near one another. Other women talked about relying on a friend or relative to recommend a location in Toronto even before they had left Hong Kong (Chiu 1998). Transnational social ties, which were the main source of information about residential alternatives in Toronto, encouraged Hong Kong immigrants to locate near other members of the community. Chiu found that proximity to family members was very important to working women, who often rely on their relatives to assist with childcare and household chores. Astronaut household arrangements may also reinforce the tendency toward residential concentration (Man 1997). The family obligations and responsibilities are reciprocal. Parents assist their adult children, and their adult children assist them. Several women described selecting a residential location close to aging parents who needed their attention.

Others moved into neighbourhoods where there are Cantonese services for parents who speak little English. The specialized retail and service outlets located near existing concentrations of Chinese Canadians also appeal to recently arrived Hong Kong immigrants (Chiu 1998). Lily's comments, reported by Chiu, underscore the attraction of living near stores that provide a range of familiar goods and services at good prices: "Wanting to eat anything, it is here. Although not as good as Hong Kong, but superb in cheapness, these places are clean and tidy ... Here, going out in the night, we can have something to eat, we can buy any medicine such as white flower oil and tiger balm. It is very convenient" (90). The stories told by

Chiu indicate how transnational social ties may influence individual residential decisions that, in aggregate, contribute to the residential concentration of Hong Kong Chinese immigrants in the northeast sector of the metropolitan area. The migration experience, as a result, is not simply one of leaving one place for another or even of maintaining ties between one place and another. It is the extension of a social field, the enfolding of one place and another into a web of relationships that depends as much upon interpersonal ties as it does upon any abstract notion of a place or destination. Hong Kong and Canada are thus brought closer together in ways that transcend distance measured in kilometres. More important than distance is the meaning invested in the new urban environment as a place of support and familiarity.

Employment Decisions

Transnational social ties also influence immigrants' employment experiences in Toronto by providing a major source of information about job vacancies and referrals to employers (Preston 2003). Interviews with a second group of women who had immigrated to Canada after 1985 indicated that information from social contacts located originally in Hong Kong is used in three ways. First, some women accept job offers from friends and family who have migrated earlier. Carla is typical of this group. She arrived in Canada knowing that she had a job in her friend's store: "Yes, she was my ex-school-mate in high school. We were good friends in high school ... She was very happy and excited when I told her that I was moving to Canada and she asked me to work for her" (Carla, in Preston 2003, 15).

A few women were referred to potential employers in Canada by their previous employers and friends in Hong Kong. Susan describes her work history in Canada as a series of referrals from previous employers: "I got my first job successfully because my previous boss in Hong Kong recommended me to the owner of the computer wholesale company. Then, one of my colleagues from the wholesale company introduced me to my current boss, and that was how I got my second job" (Susan, in Preston 2003, 16).

The largest group of women drew on their transnational social networks for employment information and referrals after failed efforts to find jobs by submitting applications and responding to advertised job vacancies. When discussing her job search, Margaret described the experiences of many of her compatriots: "I found it very difficult to get my first job when I came here, because I knew nothing about the job market or the social structure of Canada. I was lucky that my friend helped me to find this job" (Margaret, in Preston 2003, 17).

Unable to obtain remunerative employment commensurate with their qualifications through formal channels, women took advantage of social capital in their transnational social fields. Transnational social ties were crucial in helping the women to find paid employment, but transnational ties did not lead to appropriate or desirable jobs. None of the women had a job equivalent to her previous job in Hong Kong. For example, a woman who had been a hotel manager was now a café owner. She opened a café as a way of escaping her first job in Toronto as a sales clerk. Another woman was a sales representative for a small company, a job that was less well paid and less prestigious than her job as a sales assistant in Hong Kong. Nevertheless, the job as a sales representative was better than her first job in the garment industry. The difficulties that nearly all of the participants found in obtaining employment underscore the widely held belief that racial discrimination operates sufficiently in the Canadian labour market to push individuals into ethno-cultural enclaves, where there is both security and – at least to some extent – opportunity.

These women's stories reveal two related aspects of place making that create conditions within their new society. As transnational (and increasingly translocal) social ties reinforce social relations within the Hong Kong community in Toronto, at the same time, structural discrimination encourages residential concentration and labour-market segregation. Although some women arrived in Canada with job offers obtained through their transnational connections, others who were unable to find jobs through formal channels turned to friends, family, and other social contacts from Hong Kong to learn about job opportunities, many in businesses owned by other Chinese Canadians who valued the women's Hong Kong work experience and their fluency in Cantonese. Our analysis does not indicate how working in businesses that are part of an ethno-cultural economy affects women's settlement over time, although other research about Chinese immigrants in Toronto suggests that, initially, participation in an ethnic economy reduces opportunities for economic mobility (Liu 1996). Workers in the ethno-cultural economy have fewer opportunities to practise English, and their work experience is not valued by many employers outside the ethno-cultural economy. The result may be both a downward economic spiral from which it is difficult for immigrants to escape and an increase in social distance from dominant Canadian society.

Employment experiences, in turn, alter transnational social fields, although the effects are difficult to predict. For some transnational migrants, economic difficulties during settlement reinforce transnational ties that enable immigrants to maintain and retain their former social status (Goldring 1998; Levitt 2000). Other migrants find that economic difficulties impede their efforts to maintain links with their places of origin. They cannot afford to travel home or to purchase the gifts that are expected of returning migrants (Wong 2003). The transnational connections of other migrants are strengthened when they invest resources obtained through employment in Canada in their countries of origin (Owusu 1998; Wong 2003). Transnational ties are often strengthened by those who abandon the paid-labour market for business ownership, an undertaking in which transnational links are often an important commercial advantage (Faist 1999).

Commercial Investments
The commercial landscape illustrates the contradictions of place making even more strikingly, as disputes over the creation of shopping areas that cater to a community of Hong Kong origin have reinforced the distance between the immigrant and the dominant society at the same time that they have facilitated the enfolding of Hong Kong and Canadian places into a setting of familiarity and comfort, reinforcing immigrants' links to their place of origin and to one another. Responding to the growing consumer market represented by Hong Kong immigrants, developers built "Asian" malls, which are distinguished from other shopping malls by their enclosed design, the large proportion of floor space devoted to restaurants and eating establishments, often twice the proportion of other shopping malls, numerous small retail units, and condominium ownership of the retail units (Wang 1999; Preston and Lo 2000). Asian malls imitate the built form and retail mix of many commercial developments in Hong Kong in an attempt to attract recent Hong Kong immigrants (Preston and Lo 2000). The Asian-mall format could also help Hong Kong immigrants to meet the business-class program's investment criteria by establishing new businesses, while it catered to a familiar consumer market in which immigrants' knowledge of Hong Kong consumer tastes and suppliers creates a competitive advantage. At least in one case, the proposed mall was said to be marketed extensively to potential emigrants in Hong Kong prior to obtaining necessary approvals from the municipal government (Preston and Lo 2000).

The response to the growing number of Asian malls in metropolitan Toronto reveals the highly differentiated geography of transnational social fields. By 1994 there were fifty-two plazas and enclosed malls with another twenty-two proposed or under construction (Wang 1999). Some were renovated and redesigned strip malls, but others were purpose-built. In many cases, particularly in the former municipality of Scarborough, Asian malls appeared with minimal public comment, in part because planners revised parking standards to accommodate the new types of retail development (Qadeer 1997).

In the nearby municipalities of Richmond Hill and Markham, Asian malls were more controversial. In Richmond Hill, disputes about one proposed mall led the municipality to change its official plan and several bylaws governing the size and retail mix of commercial developments. Most of the changes in municipal regulation were subsequently overturned at a hearing before the Ontario Municipal Board (OMB), the provincial tribunal responsible for resolving land-use disputes. Nevertheless, the untoward speed with which the municipal government responded to complaints about the proposed mall reflects the intensity of the complaints and their impact on municipal politicians, who took them very seriously (Preston and Lo 2000). Complaints centred on each novel aspect of the Asian mall. The large number of stores in the proposed mall and its enclosed design would act as a regional magnet for shoppers rather than serving the local neighbourhood. The high proportion of floor space devoted to restaurants and eating establishments would increase parking needs while creating additional activity and noise at night. The condominium form of ownership would preclude effective management to maintain and renovate the mall as it aged. The OMB adjudicator, who reduced drastically the number of retail outlets in the proposed mall, wrote that he was influenced by the views of Chinese Canadian residents in the neighbourhood who opposed the mall. Yet it is unclear whom these witnesses represented. In the transcripts of the hearing, there is little heard from recent Hong Kong immigrants, other than the representatives of the developer, who viewed them as his target market (Ontario Municipal Board 1996).

In Markham the proposed development of Asian malls led to infamous comments by the deputy mayor, Carole Bell, who suggested that many residents of Markham did not welcome the growing number of immigrants in their midst. She is reported to have commented that Chinese stores and restaurants often lacked English signs. Moreover, in her opinion, plans to develop "more than 2 million square feet of what appears to be Chinese theme malls in application form" were excessive (Krivel 1995b). The controversy centred on the emergence of residential concentrations rendered visible by changes in the built environment. It was similar to the controversy that occurred when Muslim Canadians sought permission to build a mosque in East York (Isin and Siemiatycki 2002). Both groups of immigrants wanted to signal their presence in Canadian society and their rights to full participation in the society by building facilities that would reinforce their identities as Chinese Canadians and Muslims respectively.

The deputy mayor's reported comments caused a political uproar (Dexter 1995; Krivel 1995b). At a public meeting of more than four hundred concerned citizens held on 21 August 1995, some residents expressed support for Deputy Mayor Bell's purported statements, while representatives of the Chinese Canadian community and twelve mayors from the Greater Toronto area demanded a public apology (Krivel 1995a).

Press coverage of the Markham controversy emphasized its impact on Markham residents' sense of belonging, an important aspect of citizenship (Bloemraad 2000). Those who approved of Chinese Canadians' efforts to claim their rights to the city emphasized that living in residential concentrations where they were served by Asian malls helped Chinese Canadians to feel at home. These residents strongly opposed the deputy mayor's comments, arguing that immigrants from Hong Kong "try our best to mix" (Gionas 1995, NY1). Other residents were much more concerned about the perceived adverse consequences of residential concentration and the overt presence of Asian malls. Their views were summarized by the comment that "the heavy concentration of Chinese residents in one community isn't a good thing" (NY1). The differences in opinion were not necessarily related to place of birth. Some Hong Kong immigrants were as opposed to the growing residential and commercial concentration in Markham and Richmond Hill as Canadian-born residents from other ethnic and racial backgrounds (Spears 1995).

The deputy mayor never made a public apology. The mayor of Markham did respond, creating an advisory committee chosen from 110 applicants (Murray 1995). In June 1996 the advisory committee recommended several actions, including measures to increase sensitivity to race issues among all Markham residents, particularly town officials, and cooperation between town officials and the business community to develop guidelines concerning English on all signs (Krivel 1996). The town was also asked to promote intercultural activities, to work closely with provincial and federal officials to develop a municipal approach to immigration, and to create race-relations awareness programs for staff, politicians, and community groups (Town of Markham 1996).

The controversy in Markham was reported across Canada, particularly in Vancouver. The Hong Kong newspapers that publish in Vancouver and Toronto also reported the story in their Hong Kong editions. The transnational links that had prompted migration and encouraged residential concentration in the northeastern suburbs of the metropolitan area were also the channels by which news of the Markham controversy was transmitted to Hong Kong. At least one newspaper editorial expressed concern that the controversy might adversely affect the reputation of Markham and Toronto as welcoming communities (Editorial 1995).

Conclusion

Toronto has been remade by contemporary immigration. We have tried to illustrate some of the ways that transnational activities of contemporary migrants are involved in the "messy politics of place-making" (Smith 2000). The Hong Kong immigrants at the centre of our story settled rapidly in Toronto, where they engage in numerous transnational activities. Those activities do not constitute simply a reconstruction of Hong Kong in Canada. Nor, however, do they denote a group of hypermobile migrants motivated primarily by economic interests, as we might have expected based on the literature (Ong 1999). Rather, we found a complex process of place making in which flows of bodies, information, foods, and social practices connect people across a social field that needs to be understood in terms of family, friendship, allegiance, comfort, and memory. The transnational social field can be seen in the creation of large residential concentrations of Hong Kong immigrants and striking commercial landscapes that in turn affect the economic integration of these immigrants and their efforts to claim rights to the city by transforming its built landscape. Their stories underline the challenges of transnational migration both for migrants and the societies in which they are newcomers. Even in Toronto, a metropolitan area that prides itself on its multiculturalism and where the foreign-born comprise almost half the population, there remains residual suspicion about the willingness of transnational migrants to root themselves in the local place. Our findings that demonstrate the roles of family and friends in transnational connections and the importance that voting holds for recent Hong Kong immigrants suggest that these fears are groundless; the commitment to place is strong. There is an important role for strong leadership on the part of public officials, such as that recommended by the advisory committee in Markham, to dispel the fears that underpinned recent controversies. But our analysis also shows a need for fluidity in the ways that we define citizenship, particularly in the ways that the most publicly visible practices – such as housing, employment, and consumption choices – are designated as normative. A multicultural city is not only one that accepts immigrants in its midst, but also one that accepts changes that produce a transformation, rather than a segmentation, of the urban landscape.

Our analysis of Hong Kong immigrants' transnational activities is partial and incomplete in two important respects. We have not addressed how residential concentration, employment difficulties, and land-use disputes have affected the identities of Hong Kong immigrants as Canadians. Public accounts emphasize the possible detrimental impacts of the disputes in Markham and Richmond Hill on immigrants' sense of belonging in Canadian society, but little attention has been paid to the effects of either residential concentration or immigrants' economic experiences. In addition, we know little about transnational aspects of Hong Kong immigrants' entrepreneurial activities. The suburbanization and economic diversification of businesses owned by Chinese Canadians in the Toronto metropolitan area is well documented, but the analysis does not distinguish between immigrant and Canadian-born business owners, so we know little as yet about how the transnational field changes over time and through generations.

Although Hong Kong immigrants have a presence in Toronto, they account for approximately 5 percent of all immigrants in the metropolitan area. Other immigrant groups are likely to engage in different transnational activities, constructing transnational social fields different from those maintained by Hong Kong immigrants and with very different implications for Toronto's social, economic, political, and cultural landscapes (Faist 1999). To understand fully how transnational migration is transforming Toronto and how the transformation of Toronto is influencing immigrants' transnational activities, we need information about the transnational activities of other immigrant groups.

The need for more research is clear, but it can be achieved only with additional information about immigrants' transnational activities and about the various ways that immigrants construct transnational social fields. In contrast to American and European research, where comparative studies are well advanced, Canadian research still draws mainly on isolated case studies. Case studies provide information about a number of immigrant groups that fall into different categories in Faist's typology (Faist 1999). It is time to build upon the case studies by means of a comparative analysis of the different groups. Comparative research will lead to a fuller understanding of Toronto as a site of transnational urbanism, a place where transnational circuits come together with local and translocal practices. We also need to understand these processes not as occurring in separate spheres, one for each identifiable group, but simultaneously as a transformation of the cosmopolitan city. We need to understand Toronto as a trans- (or multi-) national place, not just as a collection of transnationalisms. Much more work is needed if we are to understand how transnational fields overlap and intersect as well as how they are pushed apart by forces of discrimination and social distance in the messy politics of place making and the social construction of identities and power relations.

Acknowledgments

We are grateful for helpful comments from two reviewers and the editors as well as for the superb research assistance of Bjorn Surborg, Kitty Li, Kareem Sadiq, and Ann Marie Murnaghan. Statistical information was provided by Statistics Canada through the Data Liberation Initiative. This research was funded by the Social Science and Humanities Research Council of Canada, grant no. 829-99-1012 to Dr. David Ley, Dr. Guida Man, and ourselves. Any errors or omissions remain our responsibility alone. All correspondence should be addressed to the first author at Geography Department, York University, 4700 Keele Street, Toronto, ON, M3J 1P3.

Notes

1 In recognition of immigration and settlement policies premised on the assumption that migrants will become permanent residents of Canada, we follow everyday usage in Canada by referring to Hong Kong migrants to Canada as immigrants.
2 These numbers underestimate the number of immigrants arriving from Hong Kong since some were born in China, relocated to Hong Kong, and migrated subsequently to Canada.
3 Hong Kong was the birthplace of 5.4% of all immigrants living in the Toronto metropolitan area in 2001 and of 6.9% of recent immigrants who arrived between 1991 and 2001.
4 Participants in focus groups were recruited by reputational sampling. Initial seeds were drawn from university alumni groups, Hong Kong service organizations, and personal contacts. We sought participants who had immigrated to Canada since 1985.
5 The number of respondents for each question differs depending upon the number who did not answer a question.

6
Contentious Politics and Transnationalism from Below: The Case of Ethnic and Racialized Minorities in Quebec

Micheline Labelle, François Rocher, and Ann-Marie Field

Historically, citizenship has presupposed a set of rights and duties, shared identity, and membership in a particular political and national community. The multinational and multiethnic framework of Canadian and Quebec society makes this type of membership and the political construction of identity even more complex. Moreover, we must also consider what belonging means when immigrants and minorities draw on multiple identities and citizenship, particularly when these multiple affiliations are reinforced by spokespersons and intellectuals who advocate transnationalism and defend the well-known fact that immigrants and minorities often establish close, long-term links with their countries of origin or with global community and diasporic flows.

The international ties of solidarity emerging from the fight against racism and discrimination are not new phenomena in Canada and Quebec. The ethno-history and social history of numerous minority groups in Canada provide a vast field for research into the forms and sources of transnational protest politics that oppose racism, sexism, and systemic discrimination.

Engagement in transnational activities by different types of social and political actors is not a new phenomenon. However, given the revolution in transport and communication media, as well as the intensity of global, human, cultural, and political flows, the present approach of transnationalism provides an interesting perspective from which to study minority protest politics. This approach allows us to rediscover a segment of a *counterpublic* whose transborder activities aim at a *global reach* (Drache 2004) and have grass-roots origins (Portes 2003, 874-76). It is important to note that not all migrant groups or all minorities are in a position to practice transnationalism.

The first section of this chapter presents the theoretical approaches that inspire our interpretation of transnational practices of ethnic and racialized minorities within the Quebec context. The second section presents our methodology and provides an overview of our fieldwork. We conducted interviews during the period 2001-02 with social actors who are activists within associations that defend the rights of ethnic and racialized minorities. The following sections outline the claims put forward by these actors, their "repertoire of actions" (McAdam, Tarrow, and Tilly 2001), and their transnational practices as well as their understanding of "transnational citizenship."

Minorities, Transnationalism, and Citizenship

During the last decade, theorists who focus on postnational citizenship and globalization have stressed the impact of the international human-rights regime on social and associative movements, documenting increased integration of legal arguments in claims and the broadened scope of democracy (Sommier 2001, 87; Lochak 2002). Given the impact of the norms upheld by this international regime, some have concluded (too quickly, in our opinion) that there has been a significant erosion of national citizenship linked to the nation-state. They base their observations on the fact that citizenship acquisition, political participation, and integration in the "host society" are no longer prerequisites for the protection and integration of noncitizen residents (Schmitter-Heisler 2000). This thesis lacks nuance. It will be discussed in the last section of the chapter.

Transnational protests by migrants and minorities can be interpreted either as an expression of their resistance to assimilation, as one of the perverse effects of neocolonialism and globalization on their country of origin, or as a conseqence of their fragmented incorporation into the workplace and the institutions of the "host society." Thus Michel Laguerre (1999) claims that "diasporic citizenship" represents a protest position against the social spaces where the racialized minorities of Western societies are confined. Constructed and controlled by the dominant system, these minority spaces help to maintain and reproduce a subaltern minority identity. In contrast, Thomas Faist (2000b) suggests that transnational social spaces are a survival strategy, and Vertovec (1999, 453-55) describes them as sites of political engagement.

Others (ourselves included) question the characterization of transnational practices of migrants and minorities as necessarily liberating. In all Western countries, minorities are organized into hierarchies, with some groups being better off in economic, political, and cultural terms. They are not homogeneous. Furthermore, internally, some elements promote reactionary or conservative positions or are based on essentialist identities (Castells 1999; Guarnizo and Smith 1998). Thus, as Guarnizo and Smith conclude, "the liminal sites of transnational practices and discourses can be used for the purposes of capital accumulation quite as effectively as for the purpose of contesting hegemonic narratives of race, ethnicity, class, and nation" (6).

The elements of contemporary transnational practices strengthen the networking strategies of groups involved in protest actions as well as the role played by international institutions in the construction of a transnational space as a locus for political mobilization. However, since the terrorist attacks of 11 September 2001 in New York and Washington, DC, which were launched in part by foreign nationals residing in the United States, it has become vital to stress that activist mobilization has come in response to the progression of conservative and right-wing ideologies, racism, an obsession with security, and the infringement of civil rights in several countries.

In fact, the increasing visibility of transnational activities by minorities (national, racialized, religious, immigration-related, diasporic, etc.) has become a priority on the list of concerns for both internal and foreign policies of North American and European societies. In the current international context, the security measures to control transborder activities (Drache 2004) come together with the ideological dominance of the "clash of civilizations" thesis (Huntington 1996) to portray immigration and minorities in extremely politicized terms. The fear that "ethnic communities" become the driving force of foreign interests working within Western political groups is not new (Portes, Guarnizo, and Landolt 1999). This concern arose in 1994 when members of the Standing Committee on Citizenship were consulted on the revision of the Canadian Citizenship Act. They said that they agreed with a number of witnesses who deplored the presence of those who import and perpetuate, in Canada, their ethnic and nationalist interests, arguing that those who choose to come to live in Canada should demonstrate allegiance to Canadian standards, values, and principles (Comité 1994, 15; see also Labelle and Salée 1999). This perception lies in a socio-political and ideological context characterized by the increasing regulatory constraints imposed on societal actors, particularly those affected by security measures that limit migratory flows. The concept of security has also served as a moralizing leitmotiv, articulated around the idea of anomie, or the loss of national values (Bigo 1998, 2002). Although present before, the obsession with security was greatly reinforced following 11 September 2001.

Amid this obsession with security, the one point that we must stress in particular is the transformation of racism and discrimination in this new context. Rodolfo Stavenhagen has distinguished various stages in the analysis of racism since the founding of the United Nations. In the first stage, racism is primarily identified with the Nazi ideology. During that time, the United Nations' response in the fight against racism was embodied in the Universal Declaration of Human Rights, 1948 (Article 2). A second stage derives from the struggles against colonialism or apartheid and from the civil-rights movement in the United States. At that time, the United Nations proclaimed the Declaration on the Granting of Independence to Colonial Countries and Peoples, 1960, incorporated in the International Covenant of Civil and Political Rights, 1966 (paragraph 2). Throughout the 1970s and 1980s, various analyses pointed to a neoracism targeting migrant workers, refugees, former colonial subjects, and their descendants (Stavenhagen 2002; Wieviorka 1998).

Currently, most analyses focus on structural and economic racism resulting from increasing inequalities worldwide. This racism must be seen as "a system of power relations between racialized actors, including not only individuals, but also institutions, the state and the global economy" (Stavenhagen 2002, 43). Poverty in the South, compared to a fortress of prosperity in the North, is a major indicator of these disparities. This form of racism thrives in highly industrialized societies, as shown in negative changes to immigration policies and in restructured workplaces. Moreover, the period since 11 September 2001 has seen the stigmatization of Arabs and Muslims (Antonius 2002).

The current struggles against racism are characterized by claims that require us to develop new understandings of justice and of recognition. As Rodolpho Stavenhagen (2002, 43) remarks: "Identity and identification, dignity and diversity, power and politics, rights and resources: these are some of the contested spaces in the struggle against discrimination and racism in our post-colonial, globalized world."

Interpreting the Positions of Leaders of Ethnic and Racialized Minorities

For decades the Quebec government has contributed to the struggle against racism through public policies and the implementation of special job-creation and employment-equity programs, by financing community groups, and by supporting awareness campaigns against racism and discrimination, among other initiatives. Despite these state actions, studies conclude that racialized minorities are underemployed in the workplace and that they face disparities in salaries, professional segregation, and underrepresentation in public institutions (McAndrew and Potvin 1996; Conseil des relations interculturelles 1999; Torczyner 1997; Icart 2001; Labelle and Lévy 1995; Labelle and Midy 1999; Jedwab 2001).

The actors to whom we refer in this text take part in social movements associated with ethnic, racialized, and immigrant identity groups that join forces in Quebec society. Our goal is to make known their claims as well as their repertoire of actions, their transnational practices, and the networks linked to international institutions and transnational nongovernmental organizations (NGOs). It will become clear that the main objective of these transnational activities is to promote various causes on the local and national fronts in order to generate changes in institutions and in Quebec and Canadian politics, although pushing for changes worldwide is at times also an objective.

Following the example of Aboriginal peoples' defence groups, the movement associated with ethnic, racialized, and immigrant identity uses transnational activist networks that include actors working on an international scale who are linked by shared values, a common discourse, and dense exchanges of information and services (Tarrow 2000, 209). These networks vary in size and structure based on the place, time, and level of institutionalization as influenced by the state and public policies (Pal 1993; Soysal 1994). They put forward claims for an alternative to neoliberal globalization (Sommier 2001, 69). Often, but not always, their leaders act according to resistance identities, which Manuel Castells (1999, 8) defines as follows: "resistance identity is generated by those actors that are in positions/conditions devalued and/or stigmatised by a logic of domination, thus building trenches of resistance and survival, on the basis of principles different, or opposed to, those permeating the institutions of society." In contrast to Aboriginal peoples, ethnic and racialized minorities do not aspire to governmental autonomy or self-determination, which Natives may seek based on the past occupation of a given territory, on issues of nondominance, and/or on identity claims (Schulte-Tenckhoff 1997, 9-10).

Minority defence groups are part of a body of "new protest movements." These movements bring together three types of groups: (1) people who experience absolute or relative suffering; (2) politicized and competent militants and association leaders; (3) experts and resource persons needed at a given time, such as intellectuals, jurists, civil servants, and consultants on international institutions (Sommier 2001, 49-53).

Our analysis is based on twenty-one in-depth interviews with activists or spokespersons belonging to one of twenty associations or NGOs chosen according to three selection criteria: the associations had to be (1) pressure groups, not just simple service or cultural organizations; (2) based in the Montreal area; and (3) participants to varying degrees in pan-Canadian networks.[1]

Five of the twenty associations that we investigated are umbrella organizations. Either they have an antiracism action committee (e.g., Ligue des droits et libertés, LDL) or antiracism subgroup (e.g., Alternatives), or they target various types of discrimination (e.g., Centre for Research-Action on Race Relations, Canadian Council for Refugees).

Each of the other fifteen associations represents a specific group within Quebec society. These associations are mobilized according to a particular identity marker: religion, nationality, or colour (e.g., Jews, blacks, Muslims, Latin Americans, Chinese, etc.). The majority of these work to protect racialized minorities in Canadian and Quebec society (e.g., Black Coalition of Quebec, Canadian Arab Federation, Communauté vietnamienne au Canada). The interviews were carried out between August 2001 and June 2002, most of them after the events of 11 September 2001.

Claims and Repertoire of Action of Ethnic and Racialized Minorities

Although there is not necessarily complete agreement among spokespersons, they share numerous concerns that lead to similar claims. A first group of claims touches upon human rights and the protection of vulnerable social categories, including migrants and refugees, women, children born or socialized in Canada (e.g., fighting against the expulsion of immigrants who are minors but have committed crimes in Canada or who are not Canadian citizens but have been socialized in Canada), sexual minorities, and Native peoples.

Some claims target economic integration, eradication of poverty, economic inequalities, and work conditions for certain immigrant categories (e.g., domestic workers are not protected by labour standards in Quebec), or they question Canadian citizenship as an employment criterion for some positions – a measure that is seen as obsolete in a knowledge-based economy requiring international mobility for work, according to a spokesperson for the Centre for Research-Action on Race Relations (CRARR). Other claims focus on social insertion and social and political participation. They question both the effectiveness of pursuing legal recourse for victims of racism and these victims' representation within public institutions, the political arena, and the media of the racialized or ethnic groups that the interviewees' associations defend.

Claims that have an international reach include questions raised about continental integration and regional commercial agreements, the effects of neoliberal globalization, and the potential for an alternative model to the current one of neoliberal globalization in the name of a "common humanity." Issues that focus on the country of origin are pushed forward by the diaspora, including democracy, cooperation, development aid, and Canada's foreign policy.

Fights against sexism, racism, Arabophobia, Islamophobia, and anti-Semitism constitute a priority. Central to certain groups' actions are cultural rights regarding, for example, language, religion, access to public funds to maintain a particular heritage, and different forms of recognition in civil society. Also among the most important issues for certain groups is the state's duty to redress past wrongs, such as those suffered by victims of slavery in America or by those subjected to discriminatory immigration policies (e.g., the Chinese head tax). Many NGOs are also interested in the problems linked to "intersectionality," "a term introduced by legal theorists to refer to the specific conditions that exist when one holds two or more social statuses and the results that arise from that combination" (Jedwab 2004, 2).

Identity markers can work as obstacles to attempts to come together against some form of oppression. Spokespersons have explained the difficulties of mobilizing minorities based on assigned or "designated" identities (e.g., black community, Latin Americans, visible minorities). One spokesperson mentioned that Canadians and Quebeckers tend to perceive Latin Americans as forming a monolithic and homogeneous community. Not only are there profound differences between Argentines, Chileans, and Salvadorans, but differences based on social class within a national group can also be an important determining factor. Regardless, because Latin Americans are defined as one homogeneous group, they must take advantage of the opportunity offered by this false assumption and organize themselves in pressure groups, speaking as one voice in order to have a greater influence on the municipal, provincial, and federal political scenes.

People of African descent and those belonging to the Jewish and Arabic communities in Quebec also face tensions attributable to their historic, national, linguistic, religious, and class differences. Historically, Quebec's language and national questions have contributed to the political construction of these tensions (Labelle and Lévy 1995). The generational card is also at play. One young leader sees a need to recognize "a shared black Quebec experience." He attributes the divisions within black communities to the fact that middle-class, older, first-generation people monopolize community-leadership positions.

As for strategies used to influence outcomes, these are multiple and varied. They include evaluating public policies, lobbying state authorities and leaders in the Quebec, Canadian, and foreign governments, dealing with leaders in workers' unions and the like, and evaluating major economic and political issues linked to globalization. Professionnal expertise is at times necessary to facilitate these tasks. For example, the Ligue des droits et libertés counts on its relationship with the International Federation for Human Rights in order to evaluate the impact of continental integration in the Americas on human rights.

The judicial dispute mechanism used by CRARR, the Conseil national des citoyens et citoyennes d'origine haïtienne (CONACOH), Black Youth in Action (BYIA), and B'nai B'rith is inspired by the American model. It rests on legal expertise. For example, CRARR has launched legal proceedings against various government authorities for problems relating to systemic discrimination. CRARR also looks at laws and public policies to verify their compliance with the equality clauses in the Canadian Charter of Rights and Freedoms and with other international conventions in terms of human rights. CRARR admits that Canada is perceived as a progressive country on issues of diversity, equality, and human rights. Yet it still wants to see the concepts of equality and discrimination modified so that they are consistent with progressive jurisprudence in the area of equality rights. This understanding draws from two American theoretical strands: critical race theory and legal feminism.

Other mechanisms used to influence outcomes include the organization of public-opinion campaigns; training and awareness programs using forums, newsletters, and conferences; and consultations with various grass-roots organizations, Canadian and international NGOs, and supranational institutions. The wide use of the Internet allows for the disclosure of information and the organization of awareness and information campaigns. This practice, adopted by minority defence organizations in many countries, promotes information exchange for on-line diasporas and constitutes a battleground for political opponents in exile (Dewitte 2002). In Quebec, Jews, Chileans, Haitians, Africans, Asians, and other ethnic minorities also use this method. For example, the Canadian Togolese Community (CTC) uses the Internet to disclose information and to press for democracy in Togo (see http://www.diastode.org/ausujet.html). Indeed, new technologies favour transnationalism from below, globalization, and the internationalization of "know how." Thus Haitians are linked through haitipressnetwork.com, metropolehaiti.com, and sakapfet.com.

Some organizations prefer observation missions or economic and political cooperation abroad. The CTC, the Association of Islamic Charitable Projects, the Arab Canadian Human Rights Organization, the Communauté vietnamienne au Canada, and B'nai B'rith lobby members of Parliament, ambassadors, and international organizations, targeting foreign policy and international relations. Some associations present reports to various committees and tribunals of the United Nations. Alternatives, a human-rights organization, is part of international networks, including the World Social Forum of Porto Allegre, the Quebec Network on Continental Integration, and the Canadian Council for International Cooperation.

Associations that are better off financially participate in national and international conferences in collaboration with Canadian and foreign government organizations (e.g., "World Conference against Racism, Racialized Discrimination, and Xenophobia and Related Intolerance" in Durban). Some organize meetings for youth and their communities (e.g., Association of Islamic Charitable Projects, B'nai B'rith). Finally, others seek reparations for historic wrongdoing (e.g., Chinese Canadian National Council).

In preparing for the Third People's Summit, the LDL, a member of the Quebec Network on Continental Integration, collaborated with the Canadian organization Common Frontiers under the aegis of the Continental Social Alliance, which comprises national coalitions, regional organizations – such as the Interamerican Workers Regional Organization and Coordinadora Latinoamericana de Organizasiones del Campo (CLOC) – and other associations from Latin America. According to an LDL representative, use of the Internet has facilitated the success of their operations. He is aware, however, that not all NGOs have the expertise and technical equipment for projects of this magnitude or the financial resources to send participants abroad. The magnitude of this project prevented the LDL from participating in the United Nations' "World Conference against Racism" in Durban in 2001, a forum that it also considered important.

Associations with limited means keep their participation in networks to a minimum (e.g., being on a listserver or exchanging e-mails) or associate themselves with umbrella organizations that can promote their views in different forums. For example, the Congress of Black Women works in association with the Fédération des femmes du Québec to foster progress on issues on its agenda.

Participation in Transnational Networks and Embedded Citizenship
All NGOs chosen for our study engage in either formal or informal international activities, with eight of the twenty associations being part of structured networks and the others participating in less formal ones. In the category of structured networks, we can distinguish two types: diasporic networks targeting specific communities or groups (e.g., Chinese, Togolese, Haitian, Vietnamese, Arab, Jewish, etc.) and those with a more general aim (e.g., the LDL and the Canadian Council for Refugees), which focus on issues such as immigration, right of asylum, human rights, and the impact of neoliberal globalization on freedom and rights.

With respect to diasporic networks, several associations advocate developing and maintaining political ties with compatriots dispersed abroad. The Association des Chiliens du Québec maintains links with Chile through its participation in the Fourteenth Region, or, as it is called, the Dirección de las Comunidades Chilenas en el Exterior, which comprises Chilean citizens living abroad. This is a government initiative overseen by the Ministry of Foreign Relations, an agency mandated specifically to bring diasporic Chileans together. In the case of the Canadian Togolese Community, this diasporic network aims essentially to coordinate political action, influence the political life in the country of origin, and promote democracy. In a similar way, members of the Communauté vietnamienne au Canada work to promote Vietnamese culture in Canada and Quebec and to combat communism in their home country. These activities by diasporic networks remind us of the Haitian associations in Quebec that have long advocated the recognition of the Haitian diaspora as the Tenth Haitian Department (Labelle and Midy 1999). This recognition has, in fact, been achieved through the Alliance of Haitians Overseas, "designed to represent the interests of the Haitian communities overseas within Haiti ... and to articulate the Diaspora's vision of a national social and political space that accounts for them as potentially important actors in the nation's development" (http://www.representaction.net). Similarly, a Congrès mondial haïtien, inspired by the World Jewish Congress, is in the making in Montreal.

The Centre d'études arabes pour le développement (CEAD) has been part of the NGO Network on the Question of Palestine within the United Nations (UN). This network was established under the umbrella of the Committee on the Exercise of the Inalienable Rights of the Palestinian People of the UN General Assembly. It includes representatives from North America, Europe, and the Middle East.

The B'nai B'rith in Quebec represents a section of B'nai B'rith International, whose head office is in Washington and which mounts efforts in fifty-six countries. This international organization's main concerns are Jewish communities around the world and in Israel. For example, given the critical economic situation in Argentina, B'nai B'rith is actively committed to helping the Jewish community there. B'nai B'rith International is one of the rare, if not the only, NGOs to have a regular office at the United Nations, according to their spokesperson. The Quebec branch also networks with other Jewish NGOs in Quebec, elsewhere in Canada, and throughout the world.

The Arab Canadian Human Rights Organization is a section of the Arab Organization for Human Rights based in Cairo. It defends individuals of all origins whose human rights are not respected in Arab countries. It networks with Amnesty International.

One of BYIA's leaders maintains relations with the Global Afrikan Congress, an international NGO created at the time of the "Afrikans and Afrikan Descendants World Conference against Racism," held in Bridgetown, Barbados, in October 2002. This organization comprises people of African descent from the continent and the diaspora who join forces to demand compensation from companies or states that took advantage of slavery.

As for to the networks with a more general function, a number of these associations integrate formal international networks. For example, the Canadian Council for Refugees (CCR) is a member of the International Council of Voluntary Agencies, which intervenes with the UN High Commissioner for Refugees. The CCR has also participated in the Puebla Process (or the Regional Conference on Migration), a group established by governments in the Americas that includes NGOs. The LDL is a member of the International Federation for Human Rights, and one of its representatives sits on the federation's board of administration. This federation comprises 142 organizations from around the world that advocate human rights.

Some NGOs have links with United Nations organizations, such as the UN High Commissioner for Refugees, the Special Rapporteur on Migrant Workers, the UN Development Programme, the UN Educational, Scientific, and Cultural Organization (UNESCO), and the Special Rapporteur of the Committee on Human Rights, which addresses contemporary forms of racism, among other things. Some have even acquired their status as intervenors before the UN Economic and Social Council. In the Americas, although only the Canadian Council for Refugees has developed formal relations with the Inter-American Commission on Human Rights, other organizations have shown an increasing interest in the Organization of American States (OAS).

The amount of time devoted to transnational activities by NGOs is dependent on their material resources and can vary considerably, ranging from 10 to more than 50 percent of all activities. Since 2001 the Arab Canadian Federation has placed increasing emphasis on transnational activities. Today, it regards civil and political freedom as the target of unprecedented attacks within Canada and around the world. None of the associations in our study is active solely on the international scene, even though overall there is an awareness of the interdependence between social problems and the growing influence of international standards on lobbying activities in Canada and Quebec.

Heterogeneous Motivations for Transnational Activism

As shown in the previous section, the ways of participating in transnational networks are far from uniform. Similarly, organizations' motives for engaging in such activities are many. They follow, in great part, from the mission specific to each group. When the raison d'être of some, such as Alternatives, is to act on the international scene, networking gains a particular importance.

Overall, the reasons put forward to justify transnational action relate to its role in promoting national heritages, international solidarity, activist visibility, and minority rights; its influence on decisions that establish international standards, such as those made by the UN High Commissioner for Refugees; and its effectiveness in pressuring states to respect international standards, in helping to define the political and social stakes that result from globalization, and in implementing political action networks in countries of origin. Transnational activism also aims to draw lessons from experiments carried out elsewhere in order to widen the range of local actions.

The cases defended by some associations unavoidably lead them to the international scene. For example, both the CCR and the LDL are concerned with refugee and immigrant rights and have no other choice but to be present on the international scene. In the same vein, a BYIA representative, who is concerned with the rights of people of African descent, offers the following argument: "What we are looking at is really to put pressure on different parties, governmental, financial organizations or corporations ... like the Inter-American Commission on Human Rights, to make sure that their actions take into account the needs and interests of the black populations across the Americas."

The goal of some organizations is to influence the politics in their countries of origin. The CTC is a good example of this dynamic. The group has sent missions to observe the elections in Togo and has participated in an activity called "Meeting on the conditions of a pacifist and responsible political changeover," a political activity that focused on democracy and human rights in Togo. Moreover, the group has directly supported some NGOs working on site, such as the Togolese League for Human Rights or other national organizations dedicated to training and awareness through workers' unions. This same group also supports Togolese diasporic networks.

Finally, for other associations, the sense of belonging to the country of origin is central to their commitment at the international level. As a representative from the Canadian Arab Federation explains,

> the Arab community in Canada is experiencing a dilemma, or at least a particular situation, because it is diversified. People come from different Arab countries and immigrate to Canada for social, economic, political, and security reasons, etc., to start their life all over again. But they are always confronted with the reactions to the situations that prevail in their country of origin. For example, a Palestinian who comes to Canada to study and raise a family cannot disconnect from what is happening in his country when people there are slaughtered ... That is where the dilemma arises of having to look at the situation as a Canadian. That is the message we are trying to promote, to be respectful of our Constitution here, our values here, our Charter of Rights whether at the provincial, federal level, etc. We must not be indifferent when situations relating to abuses of human rights take place in our country of origin. (Our translation)

Clearly, the reasons that transnational networks put forward to justify their participation depend largely on the raison d'être of each association.

Network building also takes place at the local level to ensure that governments or political authorities address claims likely to be influenced by international norms and standards. For example, the Table de concertation des organismes au service des personnes immigrantes et des réfugiés brings together NGOs and representatives both of Citizenship and Immigration Canada and of the ministère des Relations avec les citoyens et de l'Immigration du Québec. These associations often rely on international texts to formulate their demands. Through their participation, they come together to present a shared position to governments (who participate as observers), giving more weight to their claims than if each association pressed for its own position alone. In short, the main reason mentioned for networking is that it offers a more solid position for claims presented by associations, often allowing for easier gains.

Instrumentalizing Transnationalism

Transnational activism does not change the nature of the claims advanced; rather, it changes the way things are done and the discourses used to support claims. International standards and rights are put forward – for example, by CONACOH, BYIA, and the LDL – to gauge the actions of public authorities and to pressure them to pursue their commitments. Some NGOs have willingly appealed to international forums to embarrass the Canadian government. During their Head Tax Redress campaign, organizations representing Canadian citizens of Chinese origin have used these forums to force the government to adopt a reparation policy. Thus the Chinese Canadian National Council went to Durban with the goal of putting pressure on the Canadian government (Li 2004).

The existence of international standards, and more widely of international law, is a source of inspiration for action and contributes to enrolment in transnational networks. When putting forward claims, the majority of leaders refer to international texts or to instruments dealing with human rights, migrant or refugee rights, and racism, such as charters, conventions, covenants, United Nations documents, and documents prepared by the Quebec or Canadian governments for their participation in conferences at the United Nations (e.g., Durban). CONACOH, CRARR, and BYIA refer to international standards to push their claims forward, either by appealing to tribunals or by pressuring Canadian political authorities. A CONACOH representative specifically mentioned using texts by the Council of Europe, referring to the standards set out in the jurisprudence. A spokesperson for CRARR gave the example of migrant workers' rights, particularly the rights of female domestics coming from Southern countries:

> According to labour standards in Quebec, temporary workers, those who are referred to as *migrant workers* in international law, are not protected ... We will launch a constitutional court challenge against this restriction because certain classes of professionals are allowed to travel between the United States and Canada, but certain classes of workers are restricted from travelling. We will add the "race" dimension to demonstrate that this type of restriction has a discriminatory impact on certain classes or racialized minorities. If we look at who forms domestic personnel, mainly black and Asian women, it has a discriminatory impact; it is a form of indirect racism, if not direct, depending on the explicit or implicit nature of this type of exclusion. (Our translation)

The CCR turns to international standards to ensure that refugees' rights are respected: "We studied all relevant texts to try to see which international standards in terms of detention could or should be applied in cases where people are detained according to immigration law" (our translation).

Many spokespersons claimed that the globalization process has encouraged recognition of the interdependence of social problems and the law. Associations also recognized the importance of international law, using it as leverage and to establish the perimeter of their domestic action. Their initiatives are partially conditioned by standards developed within international organizations and by the necessity to promote them within their own national spaces. The transnationalization of activities is partly determined by the extent to which states respect these standards, which emanate from the UN and the OAS, among other organizations. In short, claims are now evaluated according to international law and conventions. As the leader of BYIA noted,

> Just the document coming out of the World Conference, because Canada was a signatory and participating in the deliberations, we are definitely going to use that to advance our claims and put pressure [on the government]. We will say: "Listen. These are what you agreed to do." And also, the Canadian preparations for the World Conference, which were signed by Canada ... some of these documents formulated certain position statements. We will remind them: "This is what you said! So these are the types of commitment that you have to respect." So in that sense it is really the World Conference in itself that is really going to help us move to get us a greater credibility to our actions.

Some NGOs provide each other support and form ad hoc coalitions. For example, the Congress of Black Women has seen its claims taken up by the Fédération des femmes du Québec at the World March of Women (De Sève and Maillé 2004). B'nai B'rith has had various meetings with a coalition of black communities in Quebec and, during the Gulf War, with Muslim associations. A spokesperson for B'nai B'rith says: "The next question could be why we don't have one [a coalition with Muslim associations] now, and that's an important question ... And the answer to the question is that when we're satisfied that Muslim leadership is speaking out against anti-Semitic outrages and that they will denounce terrorism, especially here in Canada, that will be the time that we would be prepared to meet again."

The impact of NGOs on Canadian public policies is extremely uneven. The minority-community structure is very hierarchical and, in some cases, conflicting, and it is dependent on a range of interests. Strong differences exist between community associations in terms of their financial resources and their power to lobby the Quebec and Canadian governments. Yet the influence of some Quebec NGOs on the international scene must be mentioned. For example, the LDL has played a prominent role in Quebec in the case of Native people's rights. The work it does has been taken up by the International Federation of Human Rights and other transnational NGOs. Their spokesperson explains:

> Historically, the LDL has played a pioneering role in regards to the recognition of Native rights ... It has become involved several times over almost twenty years on the Native rights question and has added to the agenda the fight against racism toward Natives. The league has also played a key role in

raising awareness within the International Federation of the importance of the Native problem. In fact, in the past ten years, each time the International Federation has intervened [e.g., in the UN's Draft Declaration on the Rights of Indigenous Peoples], it has always asked the LDL to be its representative at the working committee on this issue. Moreover, a few years ago, the International Federation created a Native Affairs Delegate position, and a former president of the Ligue des droits et libertés du Québec is filling it. (Our translation)

The Arab Canadian Human Rights Organization feels that it has contributed to raising awareness within Amnesty International and various Arab governments regarding political prisoners. Even though CONACOH is only at the beginning of its international commitment, its representative mentioned the organization's contribution to the "World Conference against Racism" in Durban. He noted that its lobbying efforts in collaboration with the Association multiethnique pour l'intégration des personnes handicapées du Québec contributed to the inclusion of people with a handicap in the preamble of the document adopted by the UN during the conference. A BYIA representative stated that organizations like his, which have been active for a longer time, have had important successes on the question of racism particular to black communities, a theme that inspires the activist discourse of this association: "Black organizations in America have been quite successful influencing the Inter-American Human Rights Commission and the Inter-American Development Bank ... both have incorporated antiblack racism into its discourse and created specific programs just to deal with that. In that sense ... it has been effective."

If the proliferation of international law since the end of the Second World War has appreciably modified the range of action of certain groups, the political situation in the country of origin has greatly influenced others. It is important to stress that the deepening of racist attitudes and practices toward Arab populations since 11 September 2001 has strongly driven them to reinforce or develop their links with similar organizations in North America and Europe.

We must recall that international action can target goals that are specifically national. Governments do not like to project a negative image abroad. International instruments, which must be respected by signatory countries, are an important tool in the action strategies adopted by NGOs. Not only are they used to influence Quebec and Canadian public policies, but they also shape and define transnational networks. Overall, the developmental scope of these networks is difficult to measure. However, their impact takes various forms, such as increased information sharing, the fine-tuning and harmonization of claims, changes in terminology, and contributions to some texts that define international standards.

In short, international commitment helps to modify both the mobilization strategies and the discourses used to advance claims at the local and national levels. In this sense, the inclusion of international standards via transnational practices represents an additional tool in the arsenal to which groups have access.

Conclusion: Toward Transnational, Postnational, or Global Citizenship?
Colonialism, conquest, slavery, sexism, and racism are the outcomes of a universalist ideology that has governed the formation of the world system since the sixteenth century (Wallerstein 1990). These historical phenomena, linked to international economic and state division, have generated systematic inequality and discrimination that endures in contemporary economic structures and public spaces. Inequality and discrimination remain the real reasons for international action by Aboriginal peoples, women, and racialized minorities and the organizations that represent them in Quebec and Canada, the Caribbean, the Americas, and elsewhere.

At the same time, associations and NGOs are seeking to deepen their understanding of how neoliberal globalization affects the social groups that they defend. Of particular interest is the impact of supranational institutions such as the World Bank and the World Trade Organization and the consequences of regional and international trade agreements. Many associations are concerned with negotiations related to the Free Trade Area of the Americas (FTAA), which provide significant opportunities for mobilization as well as for collaboration between various organizations.

How does transnational activity change the parameters of citizenship in Quebec and Canada? Questioned on the relevance of transnational, postnational, or global citizenship and on the establishment of a "global civil society," leaders adopted a clearly critical position. In fact, not one spokesperson was inclined to endorse these, and none saw them as being adequate or significant.

The idea of civil society itself is questioned, as seen in the testimony of a spokesperson for the Centre d'études arabes pour le développement (CEAD): "Civil society – what is it exactly? Chambers of Commerce and universities are included in it. It dilutes the notions of popular movements, of community movements, of citizen action movements ... What is the common denominator; what is the common project? Is there a civil-society movement? So why trouble myself with a nonoperative concept when people who have the same preoccupation as me, the concern of citizenship, equality, social justice, the rights of the person ... can be found under another name?" (our translation).

A widely shared perspective suggests that it is impossible to talk about "global citizenship" if "local" problems are not taken into consideration. It is argued that "global citizenship is a vague concept. It cannot apply until we have addressed disparities between states" (Chinese Family Services of Greater Montreal, interview). Further, it has been said: "International citizenship, talk about that to a guy from Burkina Faso [or any other Third World country] ... He'll tell you: give me food first, it isn't time to talk about that" (Association of Islamic Charitable Projects, interview). The leader of BYIA similarly commented:

> People in the West may feel as global citizens, but this is not a reality for most individuals around the world ... Because of our location within the process of globalization, because of the amount of resources that are available to us, because of the facility we have of travelling ... we can feel we are global citizens. But for the average person, say living in downtown Port-au-Prince, where there are hardly no resources for them ... a sense of being part of the citizens of the world is not really relevant. So ... I think that [the concept of global citizenship] is really kind of parochial, almost ethnocentric.

A spokesperson for Carrefour de liaison et d'aide multiethnique reacted very strongly when the idea of planetary, or world, citizenship was brought up:

> Are we Canadian citizens? Are we Quebec citizens? This already is an obstacle for thinking beyond here. We are Canadian citizens because we have a Canadian passport ... but in Quebec ... we sort of have a different identity because of language, culture, or different ways of seeing things. We are different. When I talk about difference, we can feel it when we meet Ontarians: we face two different worlds, and that's where we discover our difference. Ontario is an hour and a half from here, and it makes us wonder how we will position ourselves on the international level talking about nationality or citizenship ... Let's fix our problems here first, and then we can see. (Our translation)

Our study demonstrates that the approach to implementing transnational networks is both pragmatic and instrumental, the aim being, first and foremost, to modify public policies of the Canadian and Quebec governments. By turning to international rights and standards, NGOs seek to put pressure on various government bodies in Canada and Quebec. In this sense, their participation in transnational networks does not imply a focus essentially on international actions; rather, their core purpose remains national.

From this perspective, discussions about transnational, postnational, or global citizenship are regarded as "vague," "utopic," or "ambiguous" by the association leaders whom we interviewed. We can certainly present ourselves as "world citizens" on the basis that transnational networks produce a planetary conscience regarding shared stakes and the necessity to act globally. Yet, for most of the leaders interviewed, the concept of transnational, postnational, or global citizenship does not correspond to reality and thus remains superfluous.

As far as identity is concerned, according to the leaders with whom we spoke, the notion of citizenship is always bounded by one or several defined territories. Moreover, from the perspective of a racialized and ethnic group, belonging becomes possible when obstacles to integration are removed. From this perspective, the importance of developing a sense of belonging to Canada and/or Quebec is given precedence over the vague notion of global citizenship. In fact, several associations work closely with the Canadian government on questions related to citizenship and immigration. After all, the general meaning of citizenship still refers to the rights that are supposed to be included in citizenship and to the exercise of these rights in a defined political community.

The concept of citizenship, even when referring to a set of rights, is quite broadly defined, inasmuch as it is not limited to the status of "Canadian citizen." It goes beyond legal and administrative issues, as it also refers to one's ability to participate in Quebec society (Labelle and Salée 1999; Labelle 2005) and to take part in social movements that defend the rights of minorities. In short, citizenship involves the recognition of everyone's contribution to society. Not being endowed with the legal status provided by Canadian citizenship should not prevent citizen participation in the political community.

As far as community intervention is concerned, we stress the importance of resolving problems that appear on the local and national scene. This focus probably results from the fact that the social actors whom we met initiate actions against multiple types of discrimination that affect racialized minorities in Quebec and Canada. In this respect, the use of transnational networks is undeniably filtered by their immediate concerns. Moreover, the concept of citizenship is problematic at the national level. Feelings of exclusion, rampant racism, systemic discrimination, and the problem of uneven social mobility indicate that the conditions for living together have not yet been met within the national context, making talk of broadening citizenship even more utopic. As the spokesperson for the Table de concertation des organismes latino-américains du Québec remarked: "We have to understand that not everybody is a citizen, even in their own country" (our translation).

Combined with the question of democratic practices, citizenship takes on a different meaning. Because more and more structural decisions are made within international organizations, the political processes lack transparency, treaties are written in a language that is understood by only a few experts, and the capacity to influence various states is asymmetric. Many representatives have stressed the importance both of a greater mobilization of actors and social movements within national spaces and of a better understanding of the stakes raised by neoliberal globalization. Moreover, the dominance of the United States on the world scene becomes a problem in the establishment of a "world citizenship" that transcends national spaces. In sum, the announcement of the death of the nation-state is somewhat premature. Even though the capacity of states to intervene has been eroded by the implementation of supranational political structures, even though state sovereignty is not absolute because of the application of international legal standards, and even though the logic of the market seems to have been forcefully imposed to the detriment of political concerns, the nation-state is still the first area of identification and intervention for social movements. Far from claiming that a new identity has emerged based on postnational belonging, we emphasize the importance among social actors of focusing on practices that are national in aim, as has traditionally been done. Of course, the globalization phenomenon is real, but it does not undermine the fact that the nation-state and local spaces remain an important focus for these groups. Globalization adds real constraints, but it also generates new courses of action.

Acknowledgments
This text is an abridged version of a chapter from Labelle and Rocher (2004). We wish to thank the Presses de l'Université du Québec for authorizing the chapter's translation and republication as well as Wayne Saunders for translating the original.

Note
1 These are the associations from which interview subjects were drawn:

Alternatives
Arab Canadian Human Rights Organization
Association des Chiliens du Québec
Association of Islamic Charitable Projects (AICP)
Black Coalition of Quebec
Black Youth in Action (BYIA)
B'nai B'rith
Canadian Arab Federation
Canadian Council for Refugees (CCR)
Canadian Hispanic Congress
Canadian Togolese Community (CTC)
Carrefour de liaison et d'aide multiethnique (CLAM)
Centre d'études arabes pour le développement (CEAD)
Centre for Research-Action on Race Relations (CRARR)
Chinese Canadian National Council
Chinese Family Services of Greater Montreal
Communauté vietnamienne au Canada
Congress of Black Women
Conseil national des citoyens et citoyennes d'origine haïtienne (CONACOH)
Ligue des droits et libertés (LDL)
Table de concertation des organismes latino-américains du Québec

7
The Caribbean Community in Canada: Transnational Connections and Transformations
Alan B. Simmons and Dwaine E. Plaza

More than a half-million people living in Canada trace their origins to the Caribbean.[1] Many were born in the Caribbean and migrated to Canada in the period from the mid-1960s to the present following fundamental changes to Canadian immigration rules. Others are children and some are grandchildren of these immigrants. The Caribbean immigrants and their descendants live overwhelmingly in Canada's largest cities. More than half of them live in the Greater Toronto area, a quarter live in Montreal, and the rest are scattered throughout Canada in major cities such as Vancouver, Calgary, and Winnipeg.

Canadians of Caribbean background are quite diverse – after all, they originate from different islands, ethnic groups, and cultures within the Caribbean region, and many are now part of a second if not a third generation in Canada. Despite this diversity, they form a cultural and social community based on their identification with the music, history, traditions, and achievements of people from the region and their participation in Caribbean community organizations, cultural events, churches, and temples.

The Caribbean community in Canada is clearly transnational, drawing on strong links to Caribbean communities in other countries. Some Canadians of Caribbean origin take annual trips to the Caribbean for vacation and to see friends and kin. They receive visits from relatives living in the Caribbean, the United Kingdom, and the United States. Family members in Canada send large amounts of cash and gifts (often in the form of "barrels" of clothing and household items) to support relatives in home countries. When a sufficiently authentic ethnic food or ambience cannot be found in Toronto or Montreal, an easy solution is at hand: members of the community organize weekend bus tours for shopping and entertainment in the very large Caribbean settlements in New York City. The Caribbean community in Canada has access to several newspapers published in Canada by its own members, which cover local news, upcoming festivals, visiting music bands, speakers, and international events of interest to people of Caribbean background. The annual Caribana parade and cultural festival in downtown Toronto brings together many Canadians of Caribbean origin, along with tens of thousands of other local participants and thousands of visitors of Caribbean origin from Boston, Baltimore, Florida, and New York as well as from the Caribbean. In sum, the Caribbean community in Canada takes on the full scope of what we understand a transnational community to be: it is widely and deeply linked to Caribbean communities elsewhere and feels part of them; it is established and connected in Canada; and it is one of the many immigrant and cultural communities in Canada that constitute and transform this multicultural nation.[2]

In this chapter we focus on how the Caribbean community emerged in Canada and why its transnational links are so strong. We also examine the challenges faced by this community and how it has transformed over time. The chapter begins with a brief review of previous research and the main issues that other studies raise for our analysis. This is followed by sections covering the historical roots of contemporary Caribbean transnational communities, the role of Canadian immigration and settlement policies in shaping the Caribbean community in Canada, and important transformations taking place in this community today. A short concluding section draws attention to the main contributions of the chapter and to issues for future research.

Throughout the analysis, we focus on the anglophone (or Commonwealth) Caribbean transnational community. This is the largest Caribbean community in Canada, and it has distinctive characteristics. Our analysis does not include the French- and Creole-speaking immigrant community of Haitian origin that has settled primarily in Quebec. The arrival of the first Haitian immigrants as political refugees and their particular settlement experiences would require a separate analysis.

Research Issues and Approach

Between 1950 and 1980 some 4.2 million people left the Caribbean for other countries, principally the United States, Canada, and the United Kingdom (Simmons and Guengant 1992, 98). Movement from the English-speaking countries was particularly large in proportion to the population in the origin nations: for example, during every decade between 1950 and 1980, Jamaica lost an additional 12 to 18 percent of its population to emigration. This truly massive exodus led to a significant "contemporary diaspora" (Clifford 1994) of Caribbean peoples spread across major receiving countries. The strong links that the migrants have retained to the home region and to people of Caribbean origin wherever they live have played a central role in informing research and theory on transnational communities (Vertovec 2001a). The relevant research literature covers the black diaspora in the North Atlantic (Gilroy 1993) and its cultural politics in Britain (Gilroy

1991, 2000), Caribbean transnational politics in the United States (Basch, Glick Schiller, and Szanton Blanc 1994), and transnational family structures and processes in Britain and Canada (Plaza 2000; Turner and Simmons 1993). Studies in Canada point to the important role of Christian churches (Duncan 2003), Hindu temples (Singh 1997), and annual cultural festivals (Foster 1995; Nurse 1999) in regenerating and transforming Caribbean identities and transnational connections.

Previous research informs three major questions for the present analysis. First, the literature shows a deep awareness of the importance of discrimination, marginalization, and antiracist action in the development of community solidarity within particular migrant communities of Caribbean origin (Henry 1994, 1999). In the present chapter we extend the analysis to examine how racism and antiracist action have shaped transnational links and identities for the Caribbean community in Canada. Second, previous studies have generated a great deal of knowledge about the nature of Caribbean transnational communities. However, less is known about how these communities are transforming over time, a matter that we address in this chapter. Finally, the literature largely regards transnational social networks, community linkages, and outcomes as positive for the communities concerned, yet there is a small but important body of more cautionary and critical research findings that should be kept in mind. Mills (1989) argues that transnational networks and information flows in St. Kitts have deeply distorted the local culture and promoted negative social and economic outcomes. Youth tend to think only of following the example of uncles, aunts, and others by moving away as soon as they can to unskilled jobs in North America. Examining US-Mexico transnational community linkages, Goldring (2001) observes that the roles played by migrant women are quite different from those played by migrant men and that women's roles tend to reinforce existing gender stereotypes and inequalities. Mankekar (1994) argues that expatriate elites can influence home-country politics in ways that are not necessarily progressive. In this chapter we seek to examine Caribbean transnationalism in terms of its potentially mixed positive and negative outcomes.

We begin our analysis by examining how imperial power and colonial history laid the foundations for the emergence of a Caribbean transnational community. We then examine how Canada, as a powerful contemporary nation-state, has shaped the settlement of Caribbean immigrants through its immigration and settlement policies. Finally, we examine how struggles within the Caribbean community (across differences of ethnicity, gender, generation, sexual orientation, and social class) tend to increase, reduce, or transform solidarity and common identity.

Each step in our analysis builds on the work of previous researchers. Gilroy's (1993, 2000) analysis of the black diaspora, its origins in colonial slavery, and its diffusion to Europe and North America in the postcolonial era provides insights on which we base our analysis of the role of colonial history in the formation of the Caribbean transnational community in Canada. Vertovec's (1999) analysis of transformations in transnational communities arising from contemporary economic globalization, refugee movements, migrant trafficking, and proactive state immigration policies provides perspectives that guided our analysis of Canadian state policies. The work of various authors (Basch, Glick Schiller, and Szanton Blanc 1994; Fouron and Glick Schiller 2001; Goldring 1996; Portes, Guarnizo, and Landolt 1999) provided us with ideas about the ways that the Caribbean community in Canada has developed its unique character and identity – for instance, by generating its own geographic markers (e.g., stores and neighbourhoods), staging cultural events (e.g., parades and music festivals), and founding institutions (e.g., churches, newspapers, and community organizations).

In sum, our analysis pursues two main arguments. One argument emphasizes the ability of colonial systems and powerful nation-states to shape the conditions under which transnational communities emerge. The other argument stresses the efforts within the communities to control their own destinies by continually rebuilding bonds and reaffirming common goals in the face of forces that tend to fragment the community. The framework emphasizes the tensions that exist between nation-states and transnational cultural communities. It also draws attention to tensions within transnational communities arising from the different worldviews, opportunities, and migration/settlement experiences of community members, who vary in terms of social class, ethnic background, gender, generation, sexual orientation, and other important characteristics. Finally, our perspective highlights the ways that outcomes for the community and for the nation-state are mutually interdependent. As transnational communities change, so do the nation-states where they are located.

Colonial Power

In the period of European colonialism, Canada and the Caribbean were linked indirectly through transnational commercial and political systems because both were colonized outposts of powerful European nations, particularly Britain. The historical legacy of colonial power is evident in the origins and nature of the contemporary Caribbean transnational community in Canada.

Racism in Canada has its roots in the colonial system and in nation building in postcolonial Canada prior to the 1960s. During the colonial period, European settlers in Canada were linked closely to their home countries. British immigrants were particularly linked to Britain. In consequence, the favoured status of European immigrants until the 1960s was part of Canada's image as a European nation in the New World. Racism associated with this perspective lingers in certain communities in Canada even today, becoming part of a matrix of circumstances that shape the extent to which Caribbeans feel that they do or do not belong in Canada.

As regards the Caribbean side, the Africans brought as slaves to the Caribbean did not entirely lose their links to home. Part of the quest of Afro-Caribbean people has been to constitute themselves as a community linked to their African roots. At the same time, they have found themselves constituting a black community of distinctively Caribbean origin spread across their home region and the nations to which they have moved. They are both African and Caribbean, and they live in many countries.

Also on the Caribbean side, migrants from India came to the Caribbean as indentured workers and thus had the prospect of working themselves out of debt, of saving and sending remittances to their families, and of eventually returning home. Most settled where they originally went to work, namely, in Trinidad and Tobago and in Guyana. The historical roots and conditions of the Afro and Indo ethnic communities in these nations were different, leading to a subsequent history of competition and political conflict between these two ethnic groups.

Unfortunately, the above historical outline is far too brief to capture either Caribbean transnationalism's rich and varied textures in the colonial past or its present legacy. It omits Caribbean peoples of European origin as well as the Chinese, Lebanese, and other settlers in the region. It also omits the fact that intermarriage in the Caribbean has created many people with multiple ethnic origins. In some countries, such as Jamaica, the middle class and political elites are relatively light in complexion and are less subject to racialization when they emigrate to Europe or North America.

The central legacy of the colonial period for contemporary Caribbean transnational communities is a set of enduring values and social relationships referred to as a "culture of migration." The Caribbean culture of migration emerged as a survival strategy in the context of a long and continuous historical decline in sugar production and plantation agriculture starting in the early 1800s. Circulation to neighbouring islands and countries for work became part of the culture of Caribbean peoples (Marshall 1982; Simmons and Guengant 1992).

Over time, circulation within the Caribbean region further expanded to include longer-distance movement to the United States from 1900 to 1930, before the McLaren Act essentially shut down immigration to the US during the Great Depression. Caribbeans also moved to Britain in the 1950s for jobs arising from the postwar reconstruction effort. The longer-distance moves were associated with longer-term residence abroad and in some cases led to permanent settlement.

During this period and until the 1960s, one can see the genesis of a Caribbean diaspora in some major cities in the eastern United States (e.g., New

York, Boston, and Baltimore) and in the United Kingdom (e.g., London, Manchester, and Birmingham). The formation of large migrant communities of Caribbean origin in these cities and the resources that such immigrant communities provided to new migrants strengthened and transformed the Caribbean culture of migration. Caribbean peoples began to see themselves as both "here" and "there," with the "here" being wherever they were living (for instance, in the Caribbean, Britain, Canada, or the United States) and the "there" being any of the Caribbean communities in another country to which they were connected through family ties, friendships, and community linkages. "Home" began to be viewed not just as the place where one was born or where one lived, but more generally as all places where friends, relatives, and members of the cultural community were to be found. In effect, what began as a Caribbean culture of migration expanded over time to become a Caribbean transnational cultural community.

Canadian Policy
Canadian immigration and multiculturalism policies played a central role in determining the size, geographical concentration, and leadership potential of the Caribbean community in Canada, thereby reinforcing the transnational linkages and identities of immigrants of Caribbean origin and their children.

The large size of the community. Dramatic changes in Canadian immigration policy in the mid- to late 1960s led to the formation of a large Caribbean community in Canada. Prior to the 1960s, Canada had selected immigrants through a nation-of-origin preference system that favoured Europeans and virtually excluded immigration from other regions of the world, including the Caribbean. After 1967 immigrant selection came to be based on individual attributes – such as occupational skills, schooling, language skills, and age. Country of origin (as an indirect indicator of ethnicity and race) was no longer relevant for immigrant selection. As a result of this policy shift, from the late 1960s through the mid-1970s, some eight to twelve thousand immigrants arrived in Canada from the Caribbean each year (Plaza 2001). Various forces contributed to the size of this flow, including high unemployment and low wages in the Caribbean relative to Canada and the preexisting culture of migration in the Caribbean. Also important was that many individuals in the Commonwealth Caribbean had skills and attributes that met Canadian immigration-selection criteria, such as an ability to speak English and/or French and possession of at least middle levels of schooling and occupational skills.

Concentration in large Canadian cities. As noted, Canadian policy since the late 1960s has favoured immigrants with trade and professional skills and with middle or higher levels of schooling. Canadian economic policy from the 1950s through to the 1980s favoured national industrial production (in order to reduce imports of industrial products from other countries). These policies had the complementary effects of drawing in workers from three large urban centres in the Caribbean: Kingston (Jamaica), Port-of-Spain (Trinidad), and Georgetown (Guyana). These large Caribbean cities are places where schooling and job skills suited for the Canadian urban economy were and are more common.[3] Given their urban background and occupational skills, it is not surprising that the Caribbean immigrants settled in large urban centres in Canada. From the beginning, Toronto was a more favoured destination because it was English-speaking and offered considerable employment opportunity. By the 1970s the textile and other manufacturing sectors in Montreal had begun to experience significant downsizing, and Toronto's position as the main destination for anglophone Caribbean immigrants was consolidated.

Leadership potential. A significant proportion (around 8 percent of all immigrants) had university-level schooling prior to arrival. These highly educated and socially networked migrants subsequently played a strong role in community leadership. The selection of these better-educated and more affluent Caribbean immigrants in line with Canadian immigration policy strengthened the community's collective identity, social capital, and leadership potential. Many professional immigrants knew one another directly and had common friends or school affiliations prior to emigration. Some had gone to the same elite high schools in the Caribbean, while others had completed studies at the University of the West Indies prior to their arrival in Canada.

Canadian state policy contributed in other ways to the identity and transnational character of the Caribbean community in Canada. With the passing of the Canadian Multiculturalism Act, 1988, state settlement policy become officially more proactive and antiracist. Unfortunately, these official steps did not mean that racism was immediately or completely removed from the application and outcomes of immigration or settlement policies (Simmons 1998). There is evidence of continuing nonofficial yet institutionalized racism in Canadian immigration policy in the years immediately following introduction of the 1967 points system (Satzewich 1988, 1989) as well as beyond that time both in policy and in Canadian society (Simmons 1997, 1998). Although citizens of Caribbean origin have been centrally involved in the antiracist movement in Canada from the time of their arrival, the passage of the Multiculturalism Act encouraged their efforts and promoted antiracism as one source of community solidarity.

In sum, the large number, high level of concentration in a few cities, and leadership potential of Caribbean immigrants in Canada provided the structural foundation for the development of a robust Caribbean Canadian community.

Difference, Power, and Transformation within the Community

The Caribbean transnational community in Toronto faces several major challenges that will in all likelihood eventually lead to important transformations in its size and character. Some of the challenges come from outside the Canadian community. Others are based on differences and tensions within the community. The external and internal forces interact with one another over time as the community changes.

Reduced Immigration Levels

The number of Caribbean-born immigrants arriving in Canada has varied over time. Numbers of Caribbean immigrants virtually exploded in the first few years after Canadian immigration policy changed in 1967. Starting with flows measured in the hundreds per year, the inflow peaked at more than 28,000 immigrants in 1974. Subsequently, numbers of arrivals declined through the 1970s, then began to rise again in the 1980s, broadly following general trends in overall Canadian immigration patterns (Immigration Statistics, 1966-96, http://www.cic.gc.ca/english/research/index.html). Total numbers reached a new peak level in 1993, when somewhat more than twenty thousand Caribbean-born individuals arrived in a single year. Subsequently, however, the Caribbean-born inflow dropped dramatically. Over the period 1998-2001, approximately eight to ten thousand Caribbean-born immigrants arrived each year (Government of Canada 2001c). These numbers – half or less of those in the peak year – are similar to those observed twenty years earlier, in around 1980.

There are three broad reasons why Caribbean immigration to Canada has declined since 1993. To begin with, changes to immigration policy introduced in the early to mid-1990s had a negative impact on Caribbean immigration. Canada increased the educational and occupational-skill requirements for individuals entering Canada within the "independent class" of immigrants (see Simmons 1999), making it more difficult for individuals from the Caribbean to be selected. In addition, Canada has increased the wealth requirements of "sponsors" of family-class immigrants, so fewer Caribbean families resident in Canada were subsequently able to sponsor relatives. Increased financial requirements for sponsoring immigration by relatives are particularly difficult for migrant families in Canada facing job discrimination and wages that are below average relative to the wages paid to others with similar levels of schooling. A second but related reason for the decline in Caribbean immigration to Canada is that the Caribbean communities in the United States are larger, closer, and often easier for immigrants to join because American immigration policies have more open family-reunification features. A third reason, more general and more difficult to assess, concerns the end of high fertility and rapid population growth in the Caribbean region in the late 1970s, the effect of which is that the absolute number of young adults in the Caribbean who might constitute the next wave of immigrants is no longer growing as rapidly as previously.

The Shifting Centre

In the post–Second World War period, various international linkages played a powerful role in the spread of Caribbean culture. These included tourism, trade, development assistance, the commercialization of Caribbean music, and the presence of Caribbean nations in the United Nations and in the Organization of American States. Initially, when Caribbean people abroad and foreigners sought to find a reference point for Caribbean culture, social life, and politics, the place of reference was naturally the Caribbean region itself. The most dynamic cultural centres were understood to be Kingston, Port-of-Spain, and Georgetown. These urban centres were not only the repositories of "original cultural roots," but also places that drew upon migrant and expatriate experiences to transform and regenerate Caribbean culture. In other words, they were the core of the emerging transnational Caribbean community.

Over time, the Caribbean communities in London, New York, Miami, and Toronto have grown larger and become more important reference points for Caribbean culture. They are becoming the main places in which Caribbean culture is transformed and to which people of Caribbean origin look for their own authenticity, inspiration, and relevance in the political sphere. In some cases the communities in these cities have displaced the capital cities in their home countries as the centres of culture, social life, and politics.

Georgetown, Guyana, is perhaps the extreme case of a city that has been displaced. Once a significant cultural centre (with a major university) and an important political centre (as a capital city and the home town of well-known regional political leaders), Georgetown is now increasingly marginal in the Caribbean transnational system. A high proportion of the younger generation and many in the older generation of the urban skilled, professional, and commercial classes of Guyana, nearly all of whom lived in Georgetown, have emigrated. The Indo-Guyanese community, once a dynamic cultural enclave and the main commercial group, has been particularly affected. The country has gone from one economic crisis to another and now has few resources to restore the level of development that it experienced during the late 1950s and early 1960s. The reasons that émigrés might have had for wishing to return to Guyana for visits or to retire have now disappeared. Unfortunately, life in Guyana has become very difficult and culturally less dynamic. A wry joke in the expatriate Guyanese community states that if you want a really good Guyanese meal, the best place to find it today is in New York! In sum, Guyana as a physical place is no longer very relevant to the future plans of the Guyanese transnational community. It is now a memory and reference point for a community that is still transnational but based primarily outside the region. Guyanese living abroad do not necessarily or frequently dream of going back to an ancestral home. Their future home is part of a transnational network and is located where they make it.

What is true in an extreme form for Guyana is becoming true to a lesser but important extent for those in the Caribbean transnational community who have origins in Jamaica, Trinidad and Tobago, Barbados, and other Caribbean countries. More of them still view the Caribbean as a place to which they would like to return and as a geographical region to which they belong. Yet they increasingly see the Caribbean parades in cities such as New York and Toronto as authentic spaces for the development and expression of Caribbean culture and identity. If they return "home," more often it is for a brief visit rather than for long-term residence. They are equally, if not more, likely to visit relatives outside the Caribbean than in the Caribbean itself.

Confronting Racism and Discrimination

If there is a "core" issue that focuses the collective and political actions of the Caribbean transnational community, it is surely racism in its multiple linked forms, which include underdevelopment in the Caribbean as a legacy of colonialism, slavery, and indentured labour; the mobility "ceilings" faced by members of the community in jobs and careers; and the failure of Canadian schools to encourage youth of Afro-Caribbean origin and to ensure that their levels of school achievement and graduation rates are as good as the average for all students. To this list one must add the targeting of non-white youth by police profiling practices and the deportation of individuals born in the Caribbean when they have committed crimes in Canada. These are deeply troubling issues that profoundly concern the Afro-Caribbean community in particular. Yet they are also issues that pull the whole Caribbean community together, regardless of their ethnic background. People of Caribbean origin join together in a concerted effort with people from many other communities in antiracist action. As racism and discrimination are common to Caribbean communities in Europe and North America (and also within the Caribbean itself) they are fundamental concerns that bond Caribbean peoples across the different nations where they live.

The challenge for the community is what to do next in the antiracist fight, given the long history of effort and a core of racism that seems not to disappear. Solidarity and initiative thrive on hope and a plan of action. For many within the community, the only way forward is to continue along established lines, which means joining with other concerned groups to confront the school system, state officials, the police, and court systems by tabling evidence of bias and seeking redress. However, for the Caribbean community and for the antiracist movement more broadly, the issues that they need to address are shifting.

Recent immigrants of nearly all backgrounds are finding it more difficult in the years following their arrival to achieve levels of employment and incomes commensurate with their years of schooling (Statistics Canada 2003b). Since this trend affects so many groups from so many regions and includes South Asian and Chinese immigrants with relatively high levels of schooling, there is a growing realization that the problem of discrimination is based on a number of overlapping factors, such as nonwhite skin colour, evidence of a non-European cultural background, a foreign accent, schooling credentials from a less developed country, and lack of Canadian work experience. One interpretation (Reitz 2002) of these trends is that, in addition, the new immigrants are now competing in the Canadian job market with the highly educated children of previous immigrants in their own ethnic communities and in Canada as a whole, such that differences in the perception of the quality of job credentials are an increasing source of discrimination against immigrants. The "credentials" of the Canadian-trained youth include not only what they have studied, but also where they have studied and the known sources of their reference letters. Added to this is that they are native-born Canadians who speak, dress, and act in a way that makes employers feel connected and comfortable with them. In other words, in the eyes of employers, they have cultural and social capital that surpasses that of their more recently arrived ethnic kin. From the perspective of qualified immigrants, employers are unfairly biased against them.

How the Caribbean transnational community will react and refocus its antiracist efforts over the future is not known. The new environment suggests that the focus on discrimination against blacks may become an even greater priority than in the past and may with the passage of time lead to a further drift toward the separation of Afro- and Indo-Caribbeans. This matter raises more general concerns about the ability of the Caribbean community to retain solidarity among its current members. We turn next to this large issue.

Maintaining Solidarity

The political logic of a transnational community rests on its overall resources: size of membership, sum of all human skills, and the financial capital and leadership capacity of its most active participants. Size of membership depends on many factors, including the ability to involve individuals who have different backgrounds and goals within the same community. Given the huge diversity among peoples of Caribbean origin, the extent to which they have been able to generate solidarity is impressive. At the same time, the outward image of solidarity has always been something of a fiction. Much of the real effort to construct a community with transnational linkages has been done by subgroups for their own interests. Thus there is a structure of subgroup solidarities and tensions between subgroups within the Caribbean community. These are structured along many dimensions, including ethnicity/race, gender, generation, sexual orientation, and social class.

Ethnicity/Race

The long-standing tension between the two largest ethnic groups in the Caribbean – the Afro- and Indo-Caribbeans – emerged long ago when the Indo-Caribbeans originally arrived in the region in the late 1800s, having been brought in voluntarily as part of a system of indentured labour in order to undermine the newly freed African-peasant labour force and thus maintain low-cost sugar production. In the postcolonial period, from the early 1960s onward, these old ethnic tensions have grown and become part of an antagonistic political divide, particularly in Guyana and more recently in Trinidad and Tobago.

The Caribbean community outside the region often feels awkward about this old ethnic conflict based in the home region. Many who have left the region would like to forget these divisions and to establish a new pan-Caribbean solidarity abroad. The circumstances that led to the earlier conflicts are more distant, and the challenges faced by people of Caribbean background who live abroad are now different. Working together on common causes and to regenerate a new pluralist, antiracist transnational community, enriched by Caribbean music and traditions, is an attractive vision. Within the Caribbean community broadly, this kind of sentiment promotes, for example, the Caribana festival in Toronto. However, there is ample evidence that past differences cannot be easily forgotten and that the pan-Caribbean solidarity envisaged by some is largely a rhetorical reality with less and less substance in the daily life of the community. That the two major ethnicities within the Caribbean community are drifting apart reflects not so much the region's past conflicts as it does the different roots, identities, and contemporary interests of the two ethnic groups.

Afro-Caribbeans, regardless of their countries of origin, have deeper Caribbean roots and a stronger sense of regional belonging. This is reinforced by the greater racial discrimination they have faced abroad. Furthermore, Afro-Caribbeans form by far the largest group in the Canadian black community – in fact, this group has become a principal reference point for what the Canadian public at large visualizes when it thinks of a black Canadian. In addition, most Afro-Caribbeans do not identify with blacks in the United States and do not seek to link up with them; rather, they view their own histories and circumstances as completely different. Unlike Indo-Caribbeans, who benefit from the size and vigour of the very large Asian Indian community in Canada and in North America more broadly, Afro-Caribbeans in Canada are much more likely to see the Caribbean as their ancestral home and the Afro-Caribbean community elsewhere as their second or potential future home.

Gender

The very different experiences of men and women of Caribbean origin in Canada with respect to migration, economic opportunity upon arrival, and connection to kin at home create separate gendered transnational spaces. These in turn generate the potential for tensions, misunderstandings, and even conflict between male and female Caribbean immigrants. Caribbean immigration to Canada was in large part led by women motivated by the prospect of jobs in Canada for female immigrants, for whom immigration was made easier by the culture and the strong social and economic roles of women in the Caribbean. Various studies have pointed to the fact that Caribbean immigrant women were able to find work in Canada after arrival more easily than were the men who came with them or who followed later (Turner and Simmons 1993; Richmond 1993; Henry 1994). They, like the men, faced many racist barriers, but over time they achieved or exceeded the income levels that one might have expected for female workers with their education. Unfortunately, this has not been true for men. Among youths between twenty and twenty-four years of age and most likely to be studying in postsecondary institutions, the same gender patterns are being reproduced: young Afro-Caribbean women have far higher levels of university participation than do young Afro-Caribbean men (Simmons and Plaza 1998). While the females now outnumber males among university and college students in Canada, this pattern is exaggerated among those students of Afro-Caribbean background. In sum, gender differences in schooling and job achievements are now increasingly becoming a concern broadly in Canadian society. That these are exaggerated in the Afro-Caribbean community creates a particular concern for the community but also an opportunity to address the issue more broadly in ways that will shape their coalitions with others in Canadian society.

Generation

To a large extent, those born in Canada to parents of Caribbean origin (the second generation) and those born in the Caribbean but schooled in Canada find themselves in a "marginal" position as neither fully Caribbean nor fully Canadian. (For original statements of the "marginal man" hypotheses, see Park 1950 and Stonequist 1961.) Growing up in Canada, they fall between mainstream Canadian culture and the transnational Caribbean culture of their parents and other family members. Struggles to overcome this marginal status tend to take various forms. By late adolescence some second-generation youth follow an assimilation path and seek to identify themselves entirely with the host culture. In this choice, they risk facing rejection in Canadian society without a strong support group. Others, however, have begun to reestablish a strong coethnic transnational identity, drawing upon traditional Caribbean cultural ideologies and practices in their everyday lives with family and friends as well as in the community. These practices include an engagement with Caribbean art, music, food, dress, religion, social norms, myths, customs, and "language" (i.e., accents and sayings). Such a return to their parents' culture provides them with community support in their efforts to overcome marginalization in Canadian society.

Still others have identified with the dominant African American hip-hop culture, which has diffused from places like New York City and become part of the culture for many marginalized, underclass groups living in ghetto-like conditions. In this case, there is a transition to another transnational community, one that is youth-oriented and that cuts across various racialized groups.

Adolescents and youth in the community of Caribbean origin often develop segmented identities. Segmented identities are commonly manifested in language-code switching, which is conversing in proper English when talking to teachers and authority figures, then slipping into patois or some other Caribbean dialect when among kin or close friends. Code switching is an integral part of hybrid identity and transnational social incorporation. One code facilitates better incorporation in mainstream Canadian institutions, jobs, and lifestyles, while the other code facilitates the development of networks of friendship and support within the community.

For young Indo-Caribbeans, the path to acculturation and transnational identity formation in Canada has been different. Some Indo-Caribbean youth have chosen to identify with a pan-Indian subcontinental community. This identity seems to be based primarily on their religious connection to Hinduism or Islam. It may be reinforced by their East Indian physical appearance and by stereotypes in society that tend to racialize people into major groups, some of them identified pejoratively by terms such as "Paki" (used by racists as a label for all people who appear to be of South Asian background). Yet these youth often remain somewhat marginal in the pan-Indian community because their religious practices and culture are seen either as fixed in a previous era (e.g., when their grandparents left India) or as no longer entirely East Indian, having drifted away from their original roots. Others have found themselves straddling two different worlds. They are at the margins within the West Indian community, where they were never fully "black" because the Indo-Caribbean history of voluntary indentured labour is not always perceived by Afro-Caribbeans as having been sufficiently brutal to permit these youth to be considered true "West Indians." For young

Indo-Caribbeans growing up in Canada, identity formation has been confusing and troubling: they are Caribbean but perhaps less so than others; they are Canadian but sometimes marginalized and othered as "Pakis"; and they are South Asians but not necessarily authentically so.

The experience of transnational ethnic-identity formation for youth in the Caribbean community in Canada involves a fluid and complex interplay of culture and identity. A range of different ethnic identities and identity combinations are found within this youth community. Many youth and young adults have dual and even multiple identities. This situation may be understood as a stage in the life cycle, one characterized by a constant shifting and assembling of identity. It may also be understood as an aspect of transnational communities that reflects the global reorganization of peoples and cultures and the insecurities of minority communities in the era of contemporary globalization. Dual and even multiple identities may also be viewed as adaptive for members of minority communities who seek to build their security through multiple attachments in a shifting world.

Sexual Orientation
The Caribbean broadly and some places in particular, such as Jamaica, have a long and deeply established homophobic cultural tradition promoted by a literal interpretation of Christian texts. Male homosexuals in Jamaica, for example, face constant threat from organized homophobic gangs. They risk physical harm and even death if they publicly reveal their sexual orientation. Lesbians are frowned upon but not subject to the same violent repression. In contrast, over time the main migrant destinations – in Canada, the United States, and the United Kingdom – have all moved toward greater cultural acceptance of homosexuality. Gays and lesbians within the Caribbean transnational community are therefore often caught between two very different cultural traditions. Those within the community who "come out" and declare their sexual orientation have tended to mobilize around a combined antiracist and antihomophobic agenda, seeking to build bridges with broader like-minded movements in the larger society. They have made some progress in gaining greater tolerance for homosexuality within the Caribbean diaspora. Although the transnational Caribbean community in Canada is perhaps less violent in its stand against homosexuality, it has not for the most part abandoned its opposition. Attitudes within the Caribbean are shifting slowly, putting a constant brake on efforts to change views within the transnational community. Some major exceptions need to be noted. In both Barbados and Trinidad and Tobago, but not visibly elsewhere to our knowledge, the gay and lesbian movement has been active and has created a space for public gatherings, dances, and cultural events for its members and supporters. The organization Barbados Gays and Lesbians Against Discrimination (BGLAD) keeps track of current gay-rights and other

gay-related issues in Barbados, elsewhere in the Caribbean, and internationally (http://bglad2000.tripod.com). Its website posts local and international newspaper articles that discuss gay rights and issues. An attempt is made by BGLAD to raise the consciousness of the public about the overt and covert discrimination faced by the gay and lesbian community in Barbados and elsewhere in the Caribbean. Developments such as this over the past ten years suggest room for future changes in the region and in the Canadian Caribbean community.

Social Class
In both the Caribbean and Canada, there is a popular denial of the importance of social class. Most people within the Caribbean community like to see themselves as middle class, although they recognize that some people have more money than others. The failure to see class as important stems from a lack of day-to-day acknowledgment of how property ownership and wealth in previous generations tend to be perpetuated over time. But there are occasions when awareness is heightened and people are suddenly struck with large social-class differences within their own communities. In the case of the Caribbean community in Toronto, the awareness of social-class differences emerges in relation to social clubs, voluntary organizations, and cultural events, such as Caribana (the annual Caribbean parade and festival, usually held during the first week of August).

The Caribana parade is organized into bands of participants ranging in size from the largest, with 700 members, to the smallest, with 100 members. Within each band, members are stratified by wealth, and overall some bands have many more wealthy people within them. Wealthy individuals are identifiable because they buy expensive premade costumes and display them with pride. When one examines the backgrounds of the wealthier masqueraders, one sees that they are typically professional men and women of generally lighter skin colour within the Caribbean "rainbow," which includes individuals of African, Chinese, European, Indian, Lebanese, and other backgrounds as well as all possible mixings of these backgrounds through intermarriage. The boat cruises that leave from the harbour front on Lake Ontario contain revellers who typically share both privileged socio-economic status and ethnic or professional backgrounds. Such clustering of privileged people within the community is maintained by restricting advertising of the boat cruises and by exclusive parties and social gatherings. Invitation is by word of mouth or by limited ticket sales to members of a closed fraternity of friends and acquaintances.

The telephone area codes within the Greater Toronto area have more recently become a marker of social class within the Caribbean community, as they distinguish those who live in the "416" central city area from those who live in the "905" suburban area. Members of the Caribbean community who are more recent arrivals or from poorer social classes often find themselves living in low-income government-assisted housing in places such as Regent Park, the Jane and Finch area, and Bathurst Heights (all in the 416 area). These housing projects are well known to police and social workers as hotbeds of criminal activity. Families living in these housing areas are often caught in a deep cycle of poverty and are disproportionately single-parent (mother and children) households. In contrast, members living in the 905 area tend to be more affluent and to be single-family homeowners. The families in the 905 area tend to have been in Canada the longest and are likely to have transferred some social and material capital from their "home" countries to Canada. With these advantages, they are able to obtain better jobs or to start their own businesses in Canada, which ultimately enables them to afford homes in suburban communities in places such as Brampton, Oakville, and Pickering.

The social-class differences between these two segments of the Caribbean Canadian community can lead to strain and tension. The more affluent members of the community express some shame when its less wealthy members are stereotyped negatively in the Canadian media with regard to matters such as poverty and criminal activity. Conversely, the less affluent often see the wealthier community members as "sellouts" who are trying to climb ahead socially while conveniently forgetting about where they came from and about their part in a racialized community with a common cultural background.

Conclusion

Transnational minority communities cannot be understood without reference to the powerful historical and contemporary forces that gave rise to them. Nor can the contemporary transformations of these communities be understood without examining the interplay of "external" and "internal" forces challenging the community's solidarity and its ability to generate new social capital in order to transform and survive (or not). In sum, the analysis of transnational communities becomes more informative when issues of difference, power, and inequality are examined at various levels and across time. Our analysis of the anglophone Caribbean community in Canada from this perspective leads to the following three conclusions.

First, we conclude that it is very important to analyze the historical roots of transnational community culture. The "culture of migration" that has been so central in the development of Caribbean transnational communities emerged as part of a historical process of adaptive accommodation to restricted and unstable social and economic opportunity in the colonial period. This culture of migration carries on because it is reinforced by a continuing lack of opportunity in home countries and by a mix of racism and restricted opportunity in countries outside the Caribbean where the migrants and their families have settled. The individuals and families within the multiethnic Caribbean community who are most racialized and marginalized continue to have a strong "outward" interest in the transnational communities of which they are part.

Links and mutual support across families within the transnational system are important for day-to-day emotional and material security. The transnational links and support may also be relevant to future moves of those in the diaspora. For some, the future move of interest is not back to the Caribbean, since the home country has so few opportunities, but to the transnational community located elsewhere. For peoples of Caribbean origin in Canada, the potentially attractive destination is typically the United States. But the United States also exhibits widespread problems of racial discrimination. Thus most Canadians of Caribbean origin are inclined to renew their efforts to improve circumstances and feel more "at home" in Toronto, Montreal, or elsewhere in Canada where they reside while staying closely in touch with relatives and friends who live in other countries.

Second, our analysis makes clear that contemporary policies of powerful nation-states play an important role in forming and transforming transnational minority communities. Canadian immigration and settlement policies have provided an important "door of opportunity" for Caribbean immigrants and for the emergence of a transnational community of Canadian citizens of Caribbean origin. If Canada has opportunity "doors," it also has racial and ethnic "ceilings" that constrain schooling, job, and income opportunities for entrants of minority status. Although Canada's immigration policies are formally and officially nonracist, they may still include informal racist elements, rendering them ineffective in overcoming the broader social and cultural racism that affects the immigration and settlement of minority peoples (Simmons 1998). The result is frustrating for the Caribbean community in Canada: despite its major antiracist efforts, racism continues in hidden forms and is difficult to end. This reality supports the "outward" international gaze and interest of many members of the Caribbean community, who know that if opportunities cannot be improved in Canada, one should be ready to move someplace else where greater opportunities exist or may emerge. Conversely, there is always the threat that racism elsewhere will flow more forcefully into Canada unless everyone is vigilant.

Third, our analysis of the Caribbean Canadian community points to the important influence of differences and inequalities within communities on how they build social capital, retain solidarity (or not), and transform themselves (or disintegrate) over time. We gave particular attention in our analysis to the tensions that arise from very different ethnic histories and contemporary experiences, social-class divisions, gendered settlement experiences, generational differences, and debates over values (such as those concerning sexual orientation). The different histories of Afro- and Indo-Caribbean peoples before arrival in Canada are compounded by different settlement experiences in Canada and elsewhere, with the Indo-Caribbean immigrant community in Canada, for example, benefiting from the size, institutional complexity, and leadership of the larger Indo–North American community in ways that have no parallel for Afro-Caribbean immigrants. Despite these differences, their shared history, culture, and antiracist sentiments continue to generate bonds between the Indo- and Afro-Caribbean communities, at least among members of the first generation of immigrants from the Caribbean.

In a nonracist and more equal world, transnationalism would be sustained primarily, and perhaps even only, by positive affect for culture and language and by a positive memory of shared history. In an unfortunately still-racist world, transnationalism is sustained by the need for solidarity in a common antiracist cause, as has clearly been the case for the Caribbean community in Canada. Will desired progress in the antiracist struggle paradoxically weaken the community or at least transform it into one that has largely cultural objectives and few social or political goals? How will the apparent trend toward a wider geographical spread of the Caribbean community in Canada to the suburbs of Canadian cities and to communities with faster rates of economic growth in North America affect the Caribbean transnational community? Although our analysis identifies these and other sources of potential transformation of the Caribbean Canadian transnational community, it cannot foretell what will happen next. We leave these and other questions to future studies.

Acknowledgments
The authors wish to thank Cheran Rudhrmoorthy and Jean Turner for valuable comments on the draft version of this chapter. We also thank two anonymous UBC Press readers for their encouragement.

Notes
1 The 2001 Census of Canada registered 493,000 individuals born in the Caribbean, which comprises the countries of the Greater Antilles, the Lesser Antilles, and Guyana (Statistics Canada 2003f). Of these, about eight thousand were nonpermanent residents (i.e., visitors, visa workers, and so on). All others were permanent residents of Canada (i.e., landed immigrants). Extrapolation from previous trends indicates that some eight to ten thousand Caribbean-born immigrants have arrived each year since the 2001 Census. In addition, a significant number of children born in Canada to Caribbean immigrants identify with the Caribbean and may be considered part of the Caribbean Canadian community. Somewhat more than 80 percent of all Caribbean immigrants in Canada are from the Commonwealth, or anglophone, Caribbean, the community examined in the present chapter. The others come primarily from Haiti, although small numbers come from the other non-English-speaking countries: Cuba, the Dominican Republic, Guadeloupe, Martinique, and the Netherlands Antilles.
2 Due to the limited length of this chapter, we cannot provide as many examples as we would like of the institutions and practices that shape the Caribbean transnational com-

munity in Canada. Readers who wish to find such examples can do so by following the many leads in stories and advertisements in Caribbean Canadian newspapers, such as the three published in Toronto: *Caribbean Camera; Share;* and *Pride.* They can also examine the websites for major community cultural events like Caribana and major music festivals. See, for example, http://www.Caribana.com and http://www.iriemusicfestival.com or take one of the buses organized by community members for weekend shopping and family visiting in New Jersey and New York; such buses leave every Friday night from the Scarborough Town Centre in Metro Toronto.

3   Of all Commonwealth Caribbean immigrants to Canada, approximately 45% originated in Jamaica, 24% in Trinidad and Tobago, and 21% in Guyana, the three most urbanized and developed large nations of the Commonwealth Caribbean. Only 8% came from the small islands of the Eastern Caribbean, where populations are smaller, schooling levels are on the whole lower, and the population is more dependent on agriculture.

8
The Maple-Neem Nexus: Transnational Links of South Asian Canadians
Dhiru Patel

This chapter deals with the over 1 million Canadians who are variously referred to as "East Indian," "Indo-Canadian," or "South Asian" (Statistics Canada 2001).[1] It should be noted that such broad labels mask the reality of vast, complex ethno-cultural, religious, socio-economic, and other differences both within and between the countries of South Asia, their peoples, and their descendants, some of whom live beyond South Asia. Although members of the major regional, ethno-cultural, and religious groupings found on the subcontinent are present in Canada, some have a greater presence here than do others.

Some scholars and community members have rightly questioned or resisted the application of the term "South Asian," which they see as an imposition by the larger North American society and which leaves these diverse communities little choice but to forsake their respective regional or ethno-specific attachments. Aside from the fact that such forsaking is almost inevitable, over time young people confront their common challenges in North America (and Europe) under the larger "South Asian" banner. Van der Veer's (1995, 7) observation that "those who do not think of themselves as Indians before migration become Indians in the diaspora" can be applied more widely to South Asians in general.[2] The term "South Asian Canadians" is used here to refer to Canadians who, in the latest Census, claimed *origin* in the *geographic* area called South Asia, which includes India, Pakistan, Sri Lanka, Bangladesh, and Nepal. However, much of the existing literature, and this chapter in particular, deals primarily with those whose origins are in present-day India; they constitute about two-thirds of the total. In the absence of a more acceptable alternative, this term is used for convenience to discuss broad issues shared by South Asian Canadians. As space and data limitations preclude discussion of differences between specific subgroups or their transnational and other links, some generalizations may of course not apply to all.

As discussed in the Introduction to this book, the terms "diaspora" and "transnationalism" are elastic concepts and need to be refined; they are used here virtually interchangeably since much of the literature uses both terms. As Vertovec (1999, 447) notes, "to the extent that any single '-ism' might arguably exist, most social scientists working in the field may agree that 'transnationalism' broadly refers to multiple ties and interactions linking people and institutions across borders of nation-states."

Vertovec's (1999) review of recent research suggests at least six clusters or themes that help to disentangle the term: "transnationalism as a social morphology, as a type of consciousness, as a mode of cultural production, as an avenue of capital, as a site of political engagement, and as a reconstruction of place" (447). These clusters, of course, are not mutually exclusive. "Transnational communities" are social formations spanning borders, sustained by "a range of modes of social organizations, mobility and communication" (449). Transnational consciousness is usually marked by more than one identity and by simultaneous links to more than one nation. Often, it is maintained through cultural artefacts and a shared imagination and is "associated with a fluidity of constructed styles, social institutions and everyday practices" (457) – for example, in fashion, music, film, and visual arts – and with the production of hybrid cultural phenomena, especially among transnational youth, that flow from global media and communications. Then there is the "transnational capitalist class" (452), consisting of not only the big players within transnational corporations, professionals, and the like, but also the little players – small traders and entrepreneurs – whose impact is ever increasing and whose pursuits also include political, cultural, and social activities. Transnationalism as a site of political engagement encompasses local and global issues that can be addressed only in transnational public space; it primarily involves international nongovernmental organizations and ethnic diasporas. Lastly, transnationalism as a (re)construction of "place," or locality, involves the transference and regrounding of practices and meanings "derived from specific geographical and historical points of origin" (455); modern mobility and technology have contributed to the creation of "translocal understandings" that are nevertheless anchored in places that emerge as new "translocalities" (456).

To varying degrees, all of these apply directly to South Asian Canadians (as discussed in the following two sections), most of whom could be more accurately described as "immigrant transnationals" since they arrived recently (about 83 percent are foreign-born) and maintain strong transnational links. For them, transnationalism involves a kind of social morphology, a type of consciousness, and an avenue of capital. It also entails a mode of cultural (re)production and transformation with plurilocal (i.e., cross-national) frames of reference of family, kinship group, and community. The transnational activities of South Asian Canadians create sites for political engagement and for the (re)construction of "place," or locality, discussed mainly in the section on the role of families and communities in transnational links.

Multidimensional Transnational Relationships

The modern global flow and resettlement of people, particularly of non-European immigrants across national borders, together with revolutions in transportation and communications technologies, have raised basic questions about the significance of national identity, allegiances and loyalties, attachments, citizenship, and the very notion of the "nation-state." Rapidly growing communities such as those of Chinese and South Asian origins are becoming established in Europe and North America, but thanks to modern technologies, unlike their predecessors, they are not as isolated from their countries and cultures of origin. Indeed, they maintain significantly greater, more intense, and much stronger social, cultural, psychological, and economic ties not only with their home countries, but also with other parts of the world, creating a new set of dynamics both within and beyond national borders (Vertovec and Cohen 1999).

One such group, South Asians, has established itself in various parts of the globe, albeit in different eras and under widely varying circumstances. The more recent migrants maintain fairly close ties not only with their home countries, but also with other places where their relatives and friends have settled. Earlier migrants, such as those in the Caribbean, attempt to reconnect in myriad ways with their ancestral homeland (Patel 2000b). Any discussion, therefore, of South Asians must include this important transnational context, which plays a significant role in their lives. As Figure 8.1 shows,[3] South Asian Canadians operate through often overlapping individual and collective transnational networks and with a transnational consciousness that varies not only from one subgroup/situation to another, but also within the same subgroup/situation; these variations emerge as a result of differences of ethnicity, language, caste, socio-economic class, and the like. Given the absence of systematic studies on transnationalism among South Asian Canadians, this chapter draws on sources and studies treating non-Canadian situations. However, since there are significant parallels in these situations across national borders, especially in North America, these studies are suggestive of what may be happening in Canada. Perhaps the most important characteristic shared by South Asians (discussed more fully later) is the central role that community bonds of kin play in their lives and the great efforts that they make to maintain these over time and space. Thus, while they may live and work in different societal contexts, their behaviour generally follows a common pattern that transcends national borders, albeit adapted to particular circumstances. In any case, these differences between

Figure 8.1

Multidimensional transnational relationships

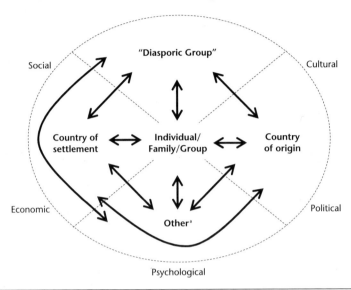

a Fellow "diasporic groups" in other societies.

the countries of South Asian settlement in the West are not such as to have a major differential short-term impact on these patterns. Furthermore, because the bulk of the migrations to Europe and North America are recent, it is too early for significantly new or divergent patterns to have emerged among the first or possibly even the second generation.

In North America, especially in the United States, there are the transnational Indian immigrant multibillionaires of the high-tech revolution, such as Wipro CEO Aziz Premji, the world's third-richest person according to *Fortune*; the multibillionaire founder of Sycamore Networks, Desh Deshpande; and a cocreator of Hotmail, Sabeer Bhatia.[4] They have joined the transnational capitalist class, with its transnational social networks and consciousness. Such immigrants are a vital part of the growth of the knowledge-based sector that is fast surpassing many of the traditional sectors of the North American economy. In her study of California's Silicon Valley, Saxenian (1999) estimated that as of 1998 Chinese and Indian immigrants had started over a quarter of the technology businesses (about 3,000), generating 60,000 jobs, exports, and wealth for the region. Their activities have simultaneously accelerated the integration of California into the global economy by forging mutually beneficial long-distance social and economic ties with other countries. There are similar trends in other parts of the United States and in nonhigh-tech sectors (Penta 2000).

Of course, these skilled immigrants represent a small fraction of immigrants from these regions, most of whom still occupy, according to Lessinger (2000), the traditional middle to lower parts of the socio-economic spectrum. However, Saxenian observes that their increasingly important contributions to North America's (and their home countries') economies is still largely unrecognized. This is at least partly due to the persistence, contrary to all the historical evidence, of the negative stereotypes of Asians (as unsophisticated, backward, tradition-bound) developed during the colonial era (discussed below). As Kotkin (1993, 210) argues, the "emergence of the Indians as a sophisticated global tribe contradicts many stereotypes developed in the West, yet the roots of this international success lie deep in history."

For some professionals and entrepreneurs, transnational business networks have two noteworthy features: (1) international commuting by some entrepreneurs who live and work for part of the year in one country and for part in another (Dugger 2000; Wilhelm and Biers 2000) and (2) the overlap of business and family networks. Kotkin and others have underlined, for example, how much the model of the "joint family company," whose origins lie in India's earliest history, is successfully followed at home and internationally by Indian businesses with well-developed, family-based global networks. In many cases, according to Kotkin (1993) and Jacob (1993) the joint family activity is not limited to business aspects but can extend to living in the same house and sharing a common kitchen and family worship. Frauenheim (1999, 2) quotes R. Motwani of Stanford, who suggests that Indian culture tends to be a web of interrelationships among family and neighbours and that this "culture of connectedness" may be "one reason why Indians have shown a knack for Internet firms." Of course, there are also nonfamily-based business networks, such as those of Indian executives who played a role in American corporate investment in India and those of the heads of Indian subsidiaries of Du Pont, Hewlett-Packard, and Pepsi, all of whom worked for their parent companies at one time or another.[5]

Kotkin's point that such networks and success have a long history in South Asia helps to explain why so many South Asians in the diaspora, especially in North America, are major players in modern transnationalism. In this context, "they seek to *create* identities because they have been cast into a new world bereft of any sense of place" (Jacob 1993, 172, emphasis in the original). Furthermore, they have not only learned to handle the turmoil of their uprooting over the past 150 years, but have also enriched themselves by what Lal terms *"a selective engagement* with other cultures" (n.d., 1, emphasis added). Perhaps the very diverse social, cultural, religious, and ethnic environments of their original homelands in South Asia better prepared them to thrive in their "new worlds" and in the "global cosmopolitan society." Thus a transnational consciousness, with its *multi*national identities, comes more easily to them. Perhaps this helps to explain Kotkin's (1993) view that overseas Indians are "the supreme cosmopolitans" and more likely to successfully navigate their way through the changes that the world is undergoing by adopting a modern form of the traditional "selective engagement" developed by their ancestors.

More broadly, the active transnational networks of South Asian Canadians generally appear to be quite extensive, often spanning several countries on different continents, and their contacts are usually regular and close, particularly among (often extended) family members and kinfolk. Figure 8.2 shows that 89% maintain at least monthly contact with family in Canada (compared to 34% of the general population), 58% with family in countries of origin, and 53% with family in other countries; very few seem to have no contact. Contact often consists of weekly or fortnightly phone calls, voice-mail, and e-mail as well as regular travel for a wide variety of reasons, such as simply visiting family and friends, exposing the young to their relatives and heritage, attending to family matters, and arranging or participating in important social events, whether births, (often transnational) marriages, deaths, or religious activities. Even those of modest means can and do make trips regularly and operate within their own networks (Patel 2000a; Buchignani, Indra, and Srivastava 1985; Ballard 1994; Rex 1996). Furthermore, modern media, particularly those targeted at "ethnic" audiences – such as the transnational Asian Television Network, the weekly newspaper *India Abroad*, the Canadian television station CFMT, and various radio stations and other newspapers (especially ethnic-specific ones) – increasingly

Figure 8.2

South Asian Canadians' contact with family in Canada, countries of origin, and other countries (%)

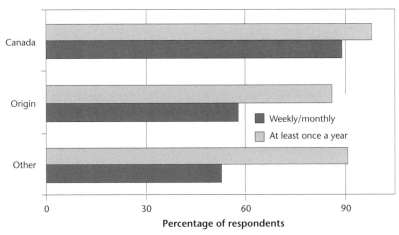

Percentage of respondents

Source: Statistics Canada (2003c).

supply a daily or weekly diet of news, information, and entertainment that includes content from and about South Asia (Karim 2003).

South Asian Canadians also engage in transnational political activities that range from simply following political and other developments, as well as lobbying for various benefits and rights in more than one country, all the way to engaging in separatist or revolutionary movements such as those for Khalistan and Tamil Elaam (Bhat and Sahoo 2002; Wayland 2003). Governments, especially "host" and "homeland" ones, attempt to exploit transnational communities in order to both obtain their support and counter such movements and activities.

Global networks complement the networks that exist within the countries of settlement, and the latter can be and usually are just as significant, intense, and strong in the much more individualistic, impersonal societies of the West, especially in the large metropolitan areas (Patel 2000b). Because the strong family and kinship ties among South Asians (discussed below) extend to wherever group members live, there is significant intertwining of the domestic and global networks. Together the two networks reinforce ethnic/kin group identity and consciousness in a hostile/"alien" environment through regular contact, exchange, and support buttressed by the (re)construction of "place," or locality, with its "translocal understandings." Thus these activities cover the range of the six clusters identified by Vertovec.

All of these networks are rooted in South Asian cultures, which place much greater importance than do Western cultures on social relationships governed by specific norms, customs, and rules, especially within one's family, kin group, and community. In South Asian cultures, the individual is usually seen *and* sees him- or herself in this wider social context, which in turn influences his or her behaviour. For those South Asians settled in the West, this transnational socio-cultural context spans not only South Asia, but also other countries where their relatives live; this context is critical to their lives and thus an important factor in understanding them.

Key Role of Families and Communities in Transnational Links
Most South Asian Canadians generally function, especially in their personal lives, within a particular socio-cultural context distinguished by three sets of key features that influence their attitudes and behaviour: a set internal to the group/community, which is the most important set at least initially; a set external to it that originates with the wider society; and a set that results from the interaction between the internal and the external. Given that most South Asian Canadians are recent immigrants, their socio-cultural context is heavily permeated by their transnational links – especially with members of the central institutions of family groups/communities in South Asia and/ or elsewhere – and these links will continue to be important given the continued inflow of new immigrants.

Internal Set

The internal set consists of two parts: (1) transnational social structures and socio-cultural contexts and (2) a view of living, of life, and of the world that differs in significant ways from that of most other groups.[6] At least during the initial period of settlement, South Asian Canadians generally continue for various reasons to be defined by these internal attributes, especially within their own communities, and make considerable effort to socialize their young accordingly. It is therefore important to understand in general these differences between South Asian Canadians and others. Perhaps the most fundamental difference is the pivotal role that the interlocking institutions of extended family and cultural community play among South Asian Canadians, resulting in very divergent sets of obligations, rights, and responsibilities in each case and thus in divergent priorities and actions.

Because of their primacy, these social institutions, whose networks extend across borders, generally play a much larger role in the life of individuals. Indeed, individuals are socialized, as Parekh (1994, 610) notes, "as members of a larger unit to which they are bound by deeper obligations" that they try to meet; these transnational units, which possess what Parekh calls "cultural and moral capital" (603), reciprocate by providing the individual with extensive support of all kinds.[7] Helweg's (1986, 121) point that "most [overseas] Indians want to be recognized for their achievements in their home country" underscores the importance of these units. Add to this desire some of the other Asian values that Parekh (2000, 137) alludes to, such as "social harmony, respect for authority, orderly society, ... and a sense of filial piety," and the differences become even more pronounced. These, combined with related factors such as religion, multiple identities, and the capacity to live with the contradictions and ambivalence that the enormous diversity of South Asia engenders,[8] indicate that Canadians of South Asian origin currently function within a very different set of dynamics than do most other Canadians. Thus transnationalism is important here primarily as a mode of cultural reproduction and as a (re)construction of "place," or locality.

External Set

The external factors consist of two powerful contexts – the historical and the contemporary – that are closely interrelated yet quite distinct because they refer to two very different time periods. The historical context of colonialism, discussed in the next section, was crucial to developing and entrenching both the ideology of European ("white") superiority, which provided the rationale for European domination of non-Europeans, and the Euro-centric perspective.

There have been many changes in the postcolonial era of the last sixty years, the impact of which can be felt today in the form of attitudes and behaviour among both "white" and nonwhite people. However, these contexts are usually ignored or given insufficient attention, the assumption perhaps being that the dawn of the modern postcolonial era of normative equality and universal rights (and its accompanying legislative instruments) has somehow made the historical background irrelevant and the existence of racism a minor leftover aberration that has essentially disappeared or is fast disappearing. The evidence, in the form of contemporary experience of nonwhites generally in Western societies, challenges the validity of this assumption (Ballard 1979; Patel 1980; Radhakrishnan 1996; Handa 1998; Parekh 2000; Frank 1998).

This racism, combined with the related phenomenon of a prevalent Euro/Western-centric perspective in Europe and North America, has an impact on both non-European immigrants and especially their children, who often react by reinforcing or reconnecting to and reclaiming their ethnic identity and heritage, including their families' transnational connections.

Interaction between Internal and External Sets
Although South Asian immigrants to Canada, like all recent migrants, undergo changes as they adapt to their new and different environments, it is still too early to say anything definitive. There appears to be a remarkable degree of stability and continuity despite the changes, tensions and conflict, and even confusion, particularly between generations.

British and other evidence suggests that family/group ties and racism/hostility of the wider society, which drives many South Asian Canadians to retreat into their own groups, are important factors. Weinreich (1979, 88) argues that the special, additional pressures faced by children of ethnic minorities "result from their position in the wider society and not, as it is often assumed, from problems inherent in the minority populations." Ballard (1994, 31) also notes that young South Asian Britons have developed a capacity to "switch codes" – that is, to navigate between two or more languages and cultures in which they have to live, thereby "re-establishing personal dignity in the face of racial and ethnic denigration" (33).

Even young South Asian Canadians who venture out, often distancing themselves (especially in their teen years) from their origins and heritage because they so desperately want to fit in, commonly return to the family and community fold. Some even attempt to learn about their heritage through "Bollywood" movies (Segal 1991). Racism and/or the realization that they are different lead many to begin the often complicated and challenging process of working through the issues around their dual or even multiple cultural identities, including ethnicity.

What this means for them and wider Canadian society remains to be seen. Much will depend on the extent of their integration or even assimilation into this society, particularly through cross-racial/ethnic intermarriage, and on the way that this society and the broader global order evolve in the next few decades (Shankar 1999/2000; Bhat and Sahoo 2002; Patel 2002). One study of Asian youths in Britain concludes that "their continuing allegiance to their ethnic group is in most cases assured – few are likely to reject their ethnic roots" (Weinreich 1979, 101). It remains to be seen whether, given the differences in the immigration situations (e.g., period, type, class, reception, etc.) of South Asians in Britain and North America, South Asian Canadians will follow a similar pattern.

It is noteworthy that in other groups, for example Greek Canadians, even highly educated women born and raised in Canada *choose* to go and live in highly patriarchal Greek society, with its traditional family structure (Panagako 2000). In another case, Vertovec (2000, 85) observes of South Asian Trinidadians of the *fourth generation and later*: "Rather than rejecting their heritage altogether – what some anthropologists predicted young Hindus would do with higher levels of education, greater occupational opportunities, increased exposure to western culture and more wealth ... – Hindu youth plunged further into it."

Similarly, whether second and subsequent generations will maintain transnational connections is difficult to predict. It will depend on how the different variables of transnationalism play out. We cannot assume a repetition of the "assimilative" pattern of other groups, such as the central-, eastern-, and southern-European immigrants whose racial, religious, and cultural backgrounds were closer to those of their host society and who, for various political, technological, and other reasons, were often discouraged and/or not able to maintain significant transnational ties.

For now, early indications are that the struggles with these and other issues faced by young South Asian Canadians involve tensions that are rooted, as Handa (1998, 38) argues, "in a colonial discourse of cultural domination and difference" framed within the Euro-centric perspective of the world in the age of multiculturalism. The increasing ethno-cultural diversity of Canadian society, together with the transnational connections that many Canadians maintain, has potentially significant implications for a redefinition of "Canadian." For Indo/South Asian Canadians it also has consequences for a sense of community identity as well as for the meaning of the terms "Indian" and "South Asian"; much will depend on how the various aspects of transnationalism discussed above unfold for future generations.

Theoretical and Policy Issues

Since the terrorist attacks of 11 September 2001 in New York and Washington, DC, the immigrant context in North America has changed. Increasingly, transnational links and their impacts are capturing the attention of both scholars and policy makers, with certain groups, including South Asians, receiving special attention. This attention, which is likely to continue because of ongoing security concerns, migrations, globalization, and the growth of modern technologies, has significance for a growing number of people across the world.

Thus there is a need to better understand the increasingly important South Asian (and other similar) "diasporas," which are projected to continue to grow (Statistics Canada 2001; Chamie 2000). This understanding can be achieved by recognizing their distinctive transnational situations. The members of these "diasporas," especially the second and subsequent generations, are not just Canadians/"Westerners" or just "South Asians." Rather, they are a part of the growing transnational communities that operate in an era of unprecedented change, generating a unique set of dynamics. Thus going beyond traditional "national" categories in our analysis will greatly enhance our understanding of these groups.

The above discussion provides an indication of why the issue of modern diasporas and transnational "communities" is important to Canada and other Western countries. The case of South Asian Canadians points to some significant features of these "communities," particularly the salience of the "thick," "deep," and close transnational networks that have been developed to maintain social relations with extended family and kinfolk. It is argued that, given the increasingly significant role that members of these "communities" are beginning to play both locally and globally (even though they represent a fraction of the population), those who deal with public policies should examine this particular phenomenon and develop a better understanding of its potential impacts.

There are already signs of these impacts. The pivotal role that transnational high-tech Indo-Americans (as well as Chinese Americans and others) are playing in the rapidly expanding knowledge-based "glocal" economy, noted above, is likely to grow. They are beginning to have an impact on policy. For example, according to one report (Hiebert 2000, 18), "the single most important" factor in changing American policy on India and the warming of relations between the two countries, culminating in an exchange of visits by their leaders, has been the relatively new lobby of Indo-Americans. Of course, such impacts by successful or influential groups are nothing new, but the modern multicultural contexts in which they occur need to be studied systematically.

This gives rise to a number of theoretical and practical issues that need to be addressed. A major critical issue concerns the question of the frameworks or perspectives employed to examine and understand particular phenomena, which in turn will be important to determining the kinds of responses developed (Patel 1980). Thus Levitt and Waters (2002), for example, consider some of the recent efforts to reformulate our approach to migration using a "transnational lens" in the American context.[9]

Another issue is the conceptualization of transnationalism. As this chapter suggests, the several overlapping dimensions of South Asian transnationalism operate simultaneously, rendering it at once a social morphology, type of consciousness, mode of cultural (re)production, avenue of capital, site of political engagement, and (re)construction of "place," or locality.

Much of the data presented here, especially on the Canadian situation, are sketchy, anecdotal, and journalistic. We need to obtain a better picture of this rapidly growing Canadian phenomenon through systematic data collection and analysis.[10] Tambiah's (2000, 172) comment that these activities, which range from the social and cultural to the economic and political, "pose for anthropologists the task of mapping this extended, sprawling, and yet connected social world" can be equally directed to *all* social scientists, not just anthropologists. We need not only to obtain a snapshot of these connections and their impact at one point in time, but also to trace their evolution over time, particularly in relation to later generations. Jones-Correa (2002) identifies a number of issues that need further work, including the activities of the second-generation adults and their marriage choices; the role of religion, power, racial hierarchies, and local contexts and institutions; and changes in receiving contexts.

There are also a number of key policy questions. We can assume that one of the crucial elements for Canada's future well-being will continue to be its ability to attract and retain the best and brightest, especially the highly skilled, who are also in great demand elsewhere. We can also assume that many of these individuals will be of Asian origin, specifically Chinese and South Asian. Not only are many of these people highly mobile, as Parekh (2000, 194) notes, but they also "no longer place much emphasis on their political identity or privilege it over all others," even as they continue to consider Canada home and remain Canadian citizens. Nor are they likely to resist moving their operational base elsewhere to suit their needs. Thus many of them, Portes notes (quoted in Bhat and Sahoo 2002, 3), are at variance with traditional patterns of immigrant adaptation.

A key question is whether policies and programs of the public *and* private sectors, including those related to visitors, immigration, settlement, and longer-term living, meet the needs of transnationals with multiple identities and/or allegiances as well as with strong family and other ties in other countries. One might expect states to accommodate activities of transnational individuals/families across national borders by making the same kinds of adjustments as those made to accommodate transnational corporations and their executives.

Another question relates to the issues around the concept of citizenship in the age of globalization and transnationalism, which, as both de Kerckhove (1995) and Giddens (1999) point out, transfer power or influence from the local or national level to the global while also rekindling local cultural identities (de Kerckhove's "hyperlocalization") or creating new economic or cultural zones *within* and *across* nations. As the existing forms of geopolitics become obsolete, "the nation-state is being reshaped before our eyes" (Giddens 1999, 4), and *nations have to rethink their identities* and approaches. Such rethinking has already begun: the Indian government has completely reversed its historical laissez-faire approach to people of Indian ancestry who are not Indian citizens, referred to as Non-Resident Indians (NRIs); and the Canadian government recently sponsored a discussion in this area (Singhvi 2000; Goldring, Henders, and Vandergeest 2003; Labelle 2002; Patel 2002).

Stephen Castles (2000, 10) contends that "global and regional governance is rapidly gaining in significance, yet transnational democratic institutions hardly exist" and that the growth of transnational communities makes it necessary to adapt institutional frameworks to new forms of social identity. This particularly applies to the model of single and exclusive nation-state citizenship: "Differentiated forms of state membership may be needed to recognize the different types of relationships transmigrants have with different states – such as political rights in one place, economic rights in another and cultural rights in a third" (10). Some of these changes are already happening, albeit in an ad hoc manner (e.g., residency, employment, welfare rights for specific immigrant groups). Indeed, Castles argues that "we need to think about transnational forms of democratic participation – not just for members of transnational communities, but for all citizens affected by the rapid shift in the location of political power" (10).

These are difficult issues, made even more problematic, at least in the short term, by the events of 11 September 2001 and their aftermath. Hopefully, the long-term fallout from these events will not be so damaging as to impede the work that needs to be done to address the issues. For the moment, it looks as though we will be living with the reality described by Meyer and Geschiere (1999, 5): "In a world characterized by flows, a great deal of energy is devoted to controlling and freezing them: grasping the flux often actually entails a politics of 'fixing' – a politics which is, above all, operative in struggles about the construction of identities." One hopes that the "politics of fixing" does not further erode the basic values of democratic citizenship and the evolving global transnational nexus of the twenty-first century.

Notes

1 The opinions and views expressed in this chapter are those of the author and should not be construed as reflecting those of the Department of Canadian Heritage or the Government of Canada.
2 Less than 10% of South Asian Canadians identified themselves by their *regional cultural* identity (Punjabi, Goan, and Gujarati). About 20% identified themselves as Pakistani (8%),

Sri Lankan (7%), Bangladeshi (1.4%), and Nepalese (0.001%). Vertovec (2000) similarly observes an increase in collective self-consciousness in Britain.

3 Sheffer (1986) posits a triadic "home-diaspora-host" relationship and presumably incorrectly includes "Other" in the middle term. For a discussion of the gaps in Sheffer's conceptualization, see Wayland (2003).

4 A. Roy (quoted in Kotkin 1993, 202) estimated in 1990 that at least 300 multimillionaires were based in the United Kingdom; Times News Network (14 May 2003) states that investment firm Merrill Lynch estimated in 2003 that there were 200,000 millionaires of Indian origin in the United States alone. According to P. Shah (cited in Kotkin 1993, 208), the global real estate investment alone of overseas Indians totalled some $100 billion in 1989.

5 Jacob (1993). Walton-Roberts (2000) discusses implications of the transnational socio-economic networks of Indo-Canadian immigration consultants and of the community in Canada.

6 See, for example, Werbner's (1999) comparison of the "English" and "Pakistani" views on "moving places, fixed identity."

7 Although Parekh (1994) is talking here about the Hindu family, these observations would also apply to South Asians in general; see Ballard (1994) and Leonard (1997).

8 For more detailed discussion of these issues, together with their importance to the topic of transnationalism, see Parekh (1994); Saifullah Khan (1979); van der Veer (1995); Bhat and Sahoo (2002); Tambiah (2000); Jacobs (1993); Wolpert (1993); Williams (1992); and Vertovec (2000).

9 Others, like Parekh (2000) and Frank (1998), go much further and argue for new/revised and less Euro-centric approaches to the study of social phenomena in general.

10 The Ethnic Diversity Survey, undertaken by the Department of Canadian Heritage and Statistics Canada, is a good start (Statistics Canada 2003c).

9
The Invisible Transnationals? Americans in Canada
Kim Matthews and Vic Satzewich

> Apparently, you can take an American out of America, but you cannot take America out of an American.
>
> – Dashevsky et al. 1992, v

Scholars based in the United States have been at the forefront of problematizing transnationalism (Portes, Guarnizo, and Landolt 1999; Levitt 2001b; Basch, Glick Schiller, and Szanton Blanc 1994). While scholars in other national contexts are becoming more and more interested in analyzing and theorizing the forms, meanings, and consequences of transnationalism (e.g., Vertovec 1999; Van Hear 1998), America-based scholarship has nevertheless set the tone for much of the original debate around how the concept should be defined, measured, and theorized. There may be good practical reasons why America-based scholars have been at the forefront of carving out this relatively new field of study. Since the United States is one of the world's leading countries of immigration and since transnational practices tend to be seen as something that immigrants "do," it is perhaps natural that this phenomenon first attracted the attention of scholars in America.

If the relatively widespread presence of a phenomenon were scholars' main reason for latching on to an issue, one could reasonably expect that American scholars would also be just as interested in American emigration and the transnational practices of Americans who have moved and settled abroad. Yet this does not appear to be the case. Even though emigration is an important part of American population movements, US-based scholars seem to have been generally disinterested in why Americans might want to leave their country of origin, how they adjust to their lives abroad, and how they maintain transnational ties with their ancestral homeland. Further, for many Americans who believe that there are endless numbers of people clamouring to get into their country, it is truly surprising that native-born

Americans might want to leave the country at all. According to one commentator, "as unbelievable as it may be to late-20th-century citizens of the U.S., emigration may be a more common trend in the next century" (Belsky 1994, 62).

There is, however, a uniquely Canadian twist to the relative silence within US-based literature on Americans as immigrants. In one of the few studies that systematically examines emigration from the United States, American emigration to Canada is portrayed as little more than a form of internal migration to the fifty-first state. According to Dashefsky and colleagues (1992, 29), "the political border [between Canada and the United States] does not generally represent a sociologically significant boundary as far as international migration goes ... The mainstream of this movement [from the United States to Canada] is more akin to internal than international migration."

On one level, this chapter aims to question Dashefsky's assumption that American migration to Canada is, in terms of the lyrics of a popular 1970s song, akin to "taking a trip without leaving the farm." More substantively, this chapter suggests that the concept of transnationalism is in fact relevant for helping us to understand the social realities and life experiences of this large, socially significant, yet relatively invisible component of Canada's immigrant population. Since there are few explicit studies of American immigrants in Canada, the arguments of this chapter are, in many ways, only tentative and suggestive. The chapter begins with a brief examination of the wider context of American emigration to Canada. We then discuss American attitudes toward dual and Canadian citizenship. Finally, we use a case study of the American community of war resisters and a case study of Democrats and Republicans abroad to show how a number of themes within the literature on transnationalism are relevant to understanding the American immigrant experience in Canada.

American Migration and Transnationalism in a Wider Context
Arguably, there are two broad components to emigration from the United States. American citizens and permanent residents either move to places from which they or their families "originally" come or migrate to places where they have no prior family, national, ethnic, or identity connections. The former are part of the traditional transmigrants in the American literature insofar as they are naturalized citizens or permanent or temporary residents who decide to return to their countries of origin after having lived in the United States, but they can also include later generations who "return" to their ancestral homelands. According to one estimate, between 1900 and 1980, approximately 80 percent of emigrants from the United States were former immigrants who were returning to their countries of origin. However, the balance may be shifting. In the 1990s an estimated 50 percent of

those who emigrated were native-born Americans (Belsky 1994). Some may be second- and third-generation individuals who make diasporic returns to their ancestral homelands, but some are simply individuals who leave their ancestral *American homeland* for the same reasons that other people leave their countries of origin: for a new job, to start a new business, to find a place with a different political climate, or because they fall in love and move to a partner's place of origin.

There is a long history of Americans and Canadians choosing to live in greener pastures across the 49th parallel. The world's largest unprotected border is, as it turns out, quite porous, with citizens from each country establishing homes and lives in new frontiers (Hansen 1964). In the 1990s Canada was the fourth-most-important destination for Americans who were leaving, and in 2001 the United States was the sixth-largest country of last permanent residence of immigrants to Canada. The nearly six thousand immigrants from the United States in 2001 made up 2.4 percent of the total flow of immigrants to Canada (Citizenship and Immigration Canada 2002, 8). And there are deep historical roots to American emigration to Canada. Although identifying socially and politically with Britain, the United Empire Loyalists constituted the first major wave of American migration to Canada. The underground railroad is estimated to have brought between thirty and sixty thousand escaped slaves from America to Canada. These waves of migration were followed by subsequent migrations of Americans who came in search of land, business opportunities, and/or employment. Between 1901 and 1907, for example, one-third of the one million immigrants who came to Canada arrived from the United States (Woodsworth 1972, 24-25).

Canada expressed a very strong preference for "white" immigrants from Europe and the United States until the mid-1960s. Between 1954 and 1986, over 468,283 immigrants came to Canada from the United States; they made up 10 percent of the 4.5 million immigrants who arrived at the time (Li 1992a, 154-55). Of this figure, approximately 50,000 American war resisters came to Canada in the late 1960s and early 1970s (Hagan 2001). In the 1970s American academics were actively recruited by universities in order to help cope with the expansion in higher education. Although numerically smaller than other components of American immigration flows to Canada, American-born managers and business owners augmented the postwar corporate elite in this country (Clement 1975, 153-55). By 1996 the Census indicated that with 244,694 individuals, the United States was the third-most-frequent place of birth of Canadian immigrants (Brym 1999, 8).

There are a number of broader aspects of American migration to Canada and of Canada-America relations that make this a rather unique case in the literature on transnationalism. First, many studies of transmigrants have focused on marginalized groups and communities (Appadurai 1990; Basch,

Glick Schiller, and Szanton Blanc 1994; Bhachu 1996; Clifford 1997; Mcmichael 1996; Mittleman 1994; Zolberg 1999). Data suggest that American immigrants in Canada are relatively well off compared to other immigrant groups and to the Canadian population more generally. One study of Toronto shows that American-born immigrants have the highest level of education of all immigrant groups, are significantly overrepresented among the ranks of senior managers and professionals, and are underrepresented among manual and lower nonmanual workers. Furthermore, American-born immigrants are the best paid and have the highest total income and the highest household income of all immigrants in the city (Jansen and Lam 2003, 104-5, 115).

Second, American immigrants have relatively easy access to information about their homeland through the mainstream media. Information about the United States does not have to fight for space on television news or in newspapers. As a result, there is little need to rely on community organizations or on hard-to-access "homeland" news sources to stay in touch with what is happening "back home."

Third, according to Guarnizo and Smith (1998, 19), "transnational flows are not limited to transmigrants' bodily geographic mobility. They also include material and symbolic objects, commodities and cultural values." Culture, Barber (2000, 71) suggests, is more potent than armaments, and the United States is the largest cultural exporter in the world; in Canada, American cultural products are ubiquitous and, more to the point, sought out. American sports and entertainment are well represented on Canadian television screens, and if Americans can be considered an ethnic group, video stores such as Blockbuster and Rogers are the biggest "ethnic" video stores around.

Fourth, even though border controls have become more stringent since the attacks of 11 September 2001 in New York and Washington, DC, the border between Canada and the US is relatively easy and cheap to cross. Flights from Toronto to New York or Los Angeles are often cheaper than flights from one end of Canada to the other, and returning "home" for American transnationals in Canada is oftentimes no more difficult than taking a Sunday drive. And fifth, the United States is Canada's largest trading partner. Orchestrating the movement of goods and services often necessitates both long and short periods of stay in one country or the other.

Citizenship

In some ways, American transnationalism is so ubiquitous that it is often difficult to recognize it as such. As a result, more work needs to be done to tease out how the factors noted above structure American transnational lives in Canada. However, one way to study understandings of place among immigrants is to look at the issue of citizenship and at the extent to which immigrants take up citizenship in their countries of settlement and/or retain dual citizenship.

Americans in Canada are permitted to hold dual citizenship, which provides additional options; an alternative country in which to live, work, and invest; an additional locus and source of rights; and additional obligations and communal ties (Schuck 1998, 163). According to the 1996 Canadian Census, less than 70% of American immigrants to Canada during the 1980s became Canadian citizens. As of 1991 only 55% of all immigrants from the United States who were eligible to apply for Canadian citizenship had become Canadian citizens. For those arriving in Canada in the late 1990s, the rate drops to 16%.

It is ironic that one of the immigrant groups that has historically been preferred within the Canadian immigration system is also among the least likely to take out Canadian citizenship. The ability of American immigrants to "pass" as Canadians may partly explain why this is the case, although the reaffirmation of American culture and values in Canada, through access to American media, is also noteworthy. The identity of Americans is not appreciably threatened in Canada. Conversely, members of more marginalized immigrant groups may find the option of becoming a Canadian citizen quite attractive. Along with the rights that are conferred by citizenship, there is a space to forge a sense of identity and belonging that includes being a Canadian. The reasons for migration also differ. Because conditions in developing countries make gaining a livelihood difficult at best, returning to one's homeland may not be an option. Americans in Canada, and elsewhere, are more like cosmopolitans: they leave the United States for better opportunities with the comfort of knowing that the option of return is open.

In order to investigate the meaning of citizenship for American immigrants in Canada, we conducted a small qualitative pilot study of Americans living in Canada. The American immigrants whom we interviewed indicated that, for the most part, unless they decided to mention that they were Americans, other Canadians did not initially realize that they were from south of the border. When asked, American immigrants had varying responses to the question of citizenship. One American living in Canada explained why she decided to retain her American citizenship rather than have dual citizenship in the following terms: "I believe that you are one citizenship or another. If the United States and Canada were to go to war, I would side with the United States because I am an American. I don't feel like I am a Canadian, so why would I swear allegiance to a country that I do not feel a great national pride in?"

Two other respondents decided to apply for Canadian citizenship after living in Canada for over thirty-five years. Their decision hinged on believing that their votes were needed to help prevent the separation of Quebec from the rest of Canada during the Quebec referendum of 1995. They explained that prior to this, their needs were met in Canada as landed immigrants.

Of the respondents who reported having dual citizenship, all said that they enjoyed the advantage of selectively using their two passports. Specifically, they use their American passport when travelling to the United States and their Canadian passport when travelling overseas. They reported that they feel safer travelling as Canadians, especially since 11 September 2001. This kind of citizenship switching, where dual citizens can selectively use one passport rather than another, is certainly familiar to members of other immigrant and ethnic communities in Canada and to scholars interested in transnationalism. Americans with dual citizenship who circumstantially assert their Canadian identity and underplay their American origins and citizenship do so in situational contexts where they believe that this will be beneficial.

Anti-American attitudes in Canada have arguably intensified with the US-led war in Iraq. A survey conducted in 2002 by the Pew Research Center for the People and the Press (2002), based in Washington, DC, found that 72% of Canadians polled had a "favourable attitude" toward the United States, with 27% holding an unfavourable opinion. When asked about the influence of the United States on the world, 68% reported that American policies are increasing the gap between the rich and the poor, and 54% suggested that the spread of American ideas to Canada is a bad thing. At the same time, 77% indicated a taste for American music, movies, and television.

All of the individuals with whom we spoke affirmed that they felt anti-American sentiment in Canada. Their reactions to incidents of anti-Americanism speak to their understanding of the role that America plays in the global political economy. As one respondent explained, "well most of the time when people have made those [anti-American] comments, people know that I am an American, and they make the comments anyway. It doesn't get a rise out of me, but you have to remember that as Americans we are very secure in ourselves. It is hard for Canadians to understand the deep rooted sense of security."

A thirty-three-year-old respondent who has been living in Canada for the past nine years, has permanent residency status, and is working toward attaining Canadian citizenship described how she felt upon arriving in Canada to study at a major Canadian university: "Well, I took up residence in a graduate student hall, and I was immediately immersed in Canadian graduate students and shocked by the anti-Americanism. And that was the first realization that I wasn't in Kansas any more, so to speak, because there were sort of constant jokes and jibes about Americans and American patriotism or American politics. The American cultural invasion of Canada at the time was a hot topic. I found a lot of it [anti-Americanism] very simplistic and very naive, and it also struck me at the time as simple jealousy."

These examples illustrate the ways that respondents rationalized incidents of anti-Americanism. Although some Canadians express anti-American sentiment, these attitudes do not appear to have a systematic or significant impact on the economic standing of Americans in Canada. The experiences and opinions of some of our respondents support this view. When asked about whether being an American hindered his economic opportunities, one individual noted that the offer of a very attractive position in Canada had encouraged him to leave the United States. Another explained, "you actually get a lot of benefits by being an American. You bring something to the table that other people don't have, both in reality and in perception. I worked on Wall Street before I came here, so I found that my trading-floor experience was really useful when I came to Canada. I had seen a lot of things happen that other Canadians my age, like, sort of my peers that were competing for the same jobs, hadn't experienced."

The economic, political, and military supremacy of the United States also affords American citizens abroad a strong sense of security. As one respondent suggested, "you don't have to justify who you are or what you are doing to the rest of the world because there is so much might." One illustration that the "might" of the United States is on Canadians' radar is that politicians "who wish to be considered important" make their way to New York to "seek out someone – preferably a group of someones – on Wall Street who will talk to them in front of television cameras, so that these images of validation can be transmitted back to Canada" (Cross 1992, 303). Americans in Canada, who enjoy the status gains of being from an economically dominant country, have the added security of knowing that Canadians are generally assimilated into *their* culture and that Canadian political deference to the United States is both common and necessary.

War Resisters as Transnationals
Between 1964 and 1973 an estimated fifty thousand Americans came to Canada as a result of their opposition to the United States' draft and military laws in the context of the Vietnam War. John Hagan's 2001 book, *Northern Passage: American Vietnam War Resisters in Canada,* is one of the only systematic studies of the migration process and settlement experiences of a modern cohort of American immigrants in Canada. Although they are not framed in the context of literature on transnationalism, it is possible to read some of his findings in such a light. Using a combination of secondary sources, interviews, and the results of a survey, Hagan's analysis of American war resisters' migration to Canada and subsequent social incorporation into Canadian society indicates that their experiences bear a strong resemblance to those of the transnational immigrant groups who feature in the

American literature on immigrants to the United States. With respect to two dimensions of transnationalism – namely, (1) multiple identities and attachments and (2) political engagement with one's country of origin – it seems clear that the experiences in Canada of this wave of American immigrants need to be factored into the literature on transnationalism.

First, the American war resisters in Hagan's sample display multiple and overlapping identities and attachments that reflect complicated and ambivalent links to both Canada and the United States. Hagan interviewed 100 men and women for his research. In part, he wanted to know how strongly they had identified with being American or Canadian when they first arrived in Canada and how this compared to their national attachments at the time of the interview (over twenty-five years later). Hagan looked at differences both between men and women and between draft/military resisters and men who had come to Canada for other reasons. He found that, with the exception of one particular arrival cohort, overall identification with Canada increased while national attachment to the United States decreased. The exception to this overall pattern was war resisters who had arrived in Canada in 1970. Hagan (2001, 203-4) argues that they display a markedly stronger attachment to the United States than do individuals who arrived either before or after 1970:

> Those resisters who came in 1970 were most likely to return to the United States; and ... though they displayed the same tendency as other resisters to have changed their national allegiance, increasing their identification with Canada and diminishing their identification with the United States, they also lowered their identification with the United States to the smallest degree ... In short, this group was not as quick to reject the United States as were those respondents coming to Canada in years other than 1970, and they are not as intense in reframing their identities as Canadians.

Hagan attributes the unique attachments of the 1970 cohort to that year's coincidence with the Canadian government's imposition of the War Measures Act in response to the October Crisis, during which the Front de libération du Québec (FLQ) kidnapped the British trade commissioner, James Richard Cross, and Quebec's vice premier and minister of labour, Pierre Laporte. He argues that the wider political circumstances that prevailed in Canada at the time of their arrival left a lasting impression on this particular group and that these circumstances resulted in greater feelings of ambivalence toward Canada than among other arrival cohorts. This suggests that contextual factors play an important role in shaping the transnational practices and identities of immigrants (Levitt and de la Dehesa 2003).

Despite the overall increase in identification with Canada, Hagan (2001) also finds that Americans in Canada maintain close connections to the

United States. Nearly 90% of his sample respondents had travelled to the United States in the previous year, 92% had communication with family members, and 78% had contact with friends. Further, nearly a quarter had lived for a time in the United States since originally coming to Canada (206). Hagan also estimates that 56% of women and 53% of men who came as war resisters between 1967 and 1972 stayed in Canada; the remainder returned to the United States (186). Although their identification with Canada had generally increased, it is clear that respondents in Hagan's sample continued to maintain frequent, socially significant attachments and links to their country of birth.

Second, American war resisters who came to Canada in the 1960s and 1970s did not suddenly lose their interest in American politics when they crossed the border. While not formally considered refugees within the Canadian immigration system, they nevertheless used the relative safety of Canada to continue to involve themselves in American politics, particularly the organization of opposition to the Vietnam War. They also made concerted efforts to shape American policy regarding amnesties for war resisters.

Hagan examines the role that Canada-based resisters played in the amnesty process partly through tracing the dynamics of the struggle over the appropriate orientation and focus of one of the leading periodicals, the newspaper *Amex*, published by American war resisters in Canada. Hagan recounts the struggle within the organization between what were then called the "exiles" and the "expatriates." Expatriates had a "becoming Canadian" orientation and saw little to be gained from continuing to engage in American debates about amnesties for war resisters and deserters from the American armed forces. Those with an "exile" orientation held sway for the first half of the 1970s; the newspaper was seen as a vehicle for the "politics of amnesty in the United States [and] offered an opportunity for exiles to advance American understanding of opposition to the war" (Hagan 2001, 143).

Eventually, individuals involved with the newspaper established links with American war resisters in other parts of the world. Further, they helped to orchestrate the nomination of Fritz Efaw, a war resister resident in England, as a delegate at the Democratic National Convention in Miami in 1976. Through careful planning, Efaw was nominated at the convention as the vice presidential candidate for the Democratic Party. Even though Efaw declined the nomination, the nomination process itself was specifically intended as political theatre designed to put the issue of an amnesty for both "draft dodgers" and "deserters" more squarely on the Democratic Party's national agenda (Hagan 2001, 173).

Although this was only one episode in a complex history of settlement in Canada, it is interesting because of what it says about the transnational connections and attitudes of at least some of the Americans who had moved to Canada. Engagement with the American political process was not an incidental part of their existence; nor was this kind of transnational political activity unimportant to how the American political system eventually dealt with the problem of an amnesty for war resisters. According to Hagan, "American public attention was focused on these issues in ways and to an extent that never would have been possible without the extraordinarily persistent and well-organized efforts of *Amex* in Toronto. These efforts made the concept of resistance through exile a reality, and it helped achieve an unconditional amnesty in the United States for draft resisters" (Hagan 2001, 179).

Democrats and Republicans Abroad

The recognition and cultivation of transnational relationships, identities, and connections have a long pedigree in American politics. Early in their histories, both major American political parties recognized the legitimacy and political importance of the transnational practices and identities of immigrants who moved to the United States. In the early part of the twentieth century, for instance, both the Republican and the Democratic Parties had "nationality divisions" charged with the political incorporation of immigrants, who, while becoming American, also maintained non-American identities and loyalties and remained interested in politics in their countries of origin (Glick Schiller 1999, 106-7). Further, the involvement of ethnic groups with transnational political orientations had significant effects on political outcomes. According to the chairperson of the Democratic Party, after the Second World War, the "nationalities division" within the party was largely responsible for Harry Truman's 1948 presidential victory:

> Although loyal to the United States, many Americans of foreign descent were nevertheless also deeply concerned with the future of the country of their forefathers. Many of them had close relatives still in the old country and they had friends there with whom they corresponded regularly. The welfare of these friends and relatives, still in Europe and Asia, was a matter of great importance ... Before the campaign began, concrete evidence of the President's interest in the problems of the countries menaced and conquered by Communism had been given over and over ... For voters of foreign origin the issues were clearly with the Democratic Party. What remained for us was to carry out an aggressive program of driving the issues home. (Quoted in Glick Schiller 1999, 106-7)

In the 1970s both political parties continued to maintain their ties with American ethnic organizations who were interested in overseas political affairs. The Republicans, for instance, were particularly interested in groups involved in anticommunist transnational political activities and priorities.

For example, in a 1982 speech to the Ukrainian National Association, Republican vice president George Bush told the audience, "Let me assure you that you have not been forgotten. We are a nation of immigrants, descended from those who sought a better world. It was they who helped build this nation; we owe it not only to ourselves and to our children to guard our liberty and our democracy zealously, but to them as well. Their spirit lives on. Their quest for freedom lives on. Meanwhile, as the phrase has it, 'Shche ne vmerla Ukraina' [Ukraine has not died]" (quoted in Kuropas 1996, 562). Clearly, the political engagements that members of "nationality" groups in the United States maintained with their ancestral homelands were regarded not only as legitimate within American political culture, but also as central organizing principles of party politics.

We know less, however, about the other side of American transnational political relationships – that is, about the activities of American transnationals. Although precise statistics are not available, there are probably more than 6 million Americans living outside of the United States. The American presidential campaign of 2000 resulted in a controversial, razor-thin victory for George W. Bush. Representatives of both political parties noted the crucial role that the "expatriate" vote played in the outcome of this election.

Americans living outside of the United States are permitted to vote in federal elections as a result of the Uniformed and Overseas Citizens Absentee Voting Act (UOCAVA) of 1986. Originally designed to facilitate the political participation of American military personnel and their families, it has been extended to Americans living abroad more generally. Citizens use the state where they last resided as their legal voting residence even though they may never intend to return. As a result, both major political parties have organizations that are oriented toward encouraging and facilitating the continued involvement of Americans in the US political system – primarily, although not exclusively, through voting in American presidential elections. Democrats Abroad (DA) and Republicans Abroad (RA) are the two main organizations that provide the medium for American citizens' participation in transnational politics.

Active in over thirty countries with approximately eleven thousand members worldwide, DA is the larger and more established organization. Exact figures for RA are not available, but the number is likely to be in the thousands (RAC 2004). According to a representative of Democrats Abroad Canada (DAC), there are 2,200 members in Canada, its largest branch. This compares to a membership list of 200, with paid members of "less than two dozen" for Republicans Abroad Canada (RAC), according to one of its representatives. DAC and RAC seek to get the vote out for their respective parties partly by distributing voter registration postcards to Americans in Canada. They also seek to cultivate party loyalty, provide a forum for participation in party politics, and bring the concerns of expatriates to candidates.

Unlike other immigrant groups, Americans in Canada tend not to form their own "ethnic" or "homeland-based" associations. Further, compared to other immigrants, Americans in Canada are relatively "invisible." As a result, identifying Americans in Canada is more difficult than in the other regions of the world where DA and RA are active. DAC takes a direct approach, seeking out Americans by attending various events in Toronto, including Word on the Street, the Cabbagetown Festival, the Beaches Jazz Festival, and the Gay Pride Parade. In comparison, an RAC representative noted that "we tend to let them [Americans] find us"; this is done through posters in the consulate, the occasional newspaper article or radio interview, and RA International's website. The RAC representative suggested that connections with the previous Alliance and Progressive Conservative Parties of Canada assist in "ferreting out" Americans. When Jeb Bush spoke in Toronto in July 2003, the Alliance and Progressive Conservatives helped with organization and encouraged people to attend:

> They helped us to do a lot of the legwork to get people out; it is an interesting combination on a number of levels; they really can help us because they have the base, the manpower, the "know how," and the connections that we need help with because we are such a fledgling organization. On the other hand, we are beneficial to them in the sense that we have a very pure reason for existing. We just want to get Americans out to vote, so working through our organization dissuades people from believing that those parties are doing something for political motives.

The political benefit of the association between RA and elements of the former Alliance and Progressive Conservative Parties of Canada may outweigh simple logistics. Whether this association reflects a serious policy level convergence is a question for future investigation.

Regardless of the means employed to recruit Americans in Canada, there are advantages to membership that go beyond having a way to support the Democratic or Republican Parties. Incentives for participation in DA and RA differ. Regular financial support (US$1,000 per year or more) of RA is rewarded with "a personal invitation to attend the Republicans Abroad Annual Meeting in Washington, D.C., where they meet with, and are briefed by prominent Republican leaders" (Dark 2003, 251). Incentives to join DA are rooted in the recognition of DA as a state party that may elect representatives for the Democratic National Committee. "A Democrat living in a foreign country can, through participation in DA, attend stateside Democratic conventions and even serve on the party's National Committee: as a result, the development of a career within American party politics is not foreclosed by residence abroad" (246). Delegates from DA attend the National Nominating Convention and have nine votes shared by twenty-two members who are elected as delegates. Dark notes that the delegation sent to the 2000 convention equalled, or was larger in size than, those sent by the six smallest states and territories (245).

Despite a seemingly broader basis of support, RA appears to be better off financially. A DAC representative noted that the Democratic Party provides a phone and a desk in Washington for the executive director of DA; her salary is paid with the dues from the country committees. These dues are assessed on a per capita basis. As Canada has one of the largest committees, it must pay the maximum, US$1,500 a year, raised through various activities, including plays, concerts, and solicitation letters, which are mailed from Washington. Comparatively, until 2002 RA received generous funding from the Republican National Committee – US$120,000 according to an RA report (RAC 2003). The McCain-Feingold Bill, passed in 2002, makes this type of funding illegal. It also forbids these organizations to solicit non-Americans for funds.

Likewise, DAC and RAC explicitly refrain from interfering in Canadian political matters. An RAC representative was specifically instructed not to speak at any political rallies against the Liberal government's decision not to send troops to Iraq. The organization does not want to be seen as meddling in the affairs of a foreign country, which is ironic given that the American government overtly does this in other contexts. Because Canada has historically been an ally of the United States, there may be a concern with maintaining mutually beneficial relations, a goal that could be compromised by the actions of DAC or RAC members who are linked to the American political framework. In the final analysis, DAC's and RAC's mandate is to encourage Americans in Canada to vote in American elections and, at least officially, not to influence political activities in Canada.

The Americans now living in Canada who were interviewed for this pilot study attached different meanings to voting in American elections. Gladys, a member of DAC who has lived in Canada for the past twenty-five years, votes in US elections because "America is a world power and makes a difference throughout the world with its policies. It also affects Canada. I care what happens to America."

Ingrid, also a member of DAC, has lived in Canada for the past twenty years and has dual citizenship. When asked why she believes that it is important to vote in US elections, she said:

> Because that just affirms my connection to the US. I had an experience that I have kind of shared with many of my compatriots. You get more involved [with the American political process] the longer you stay [in Canada], as you realize that no, I am not Canadian. We care about what happens in the US, and we see the effects first-hand of American foreign policy, and we

want to be able to do more than demonstrate or write letters. We really want to change foreign policy to put it into a direction that is fair, equitable, and beneficial for the United States.

Philip, who has lived in Canada for thirty-five years, suggested that he votes in American elections because "the US economy, and just sheer size, is just so strong in terms of its relationship to Canada, anything Americans can do up here to help shape policy down there will reflect back to Canada." By voting in American elections, these respondents are attempting to influence conditions not only in the United States, but also in Canada and the world more generally. Transnationals are perhaps better suited than most to appreciate the interconnectedness of world activities. The ability to influence political events in the United States provides Americans in Canada with the possibility of maintaining bonds with their home country. American policy, by permitting nonresidents to vote, may foster and maintain their allegiance to the United States. Nonresidents also provide financial contributions to political campaigns in the United States. Transnational social fields are being constructed that acknowledge the value and importance of nonresidents. There is a degree of power associated with this recognition. Governments, through legislative actions that permit voting for nonresidents, are opening the door to organizations such as DA and RA to reframe party politics in a manner that emphasizes both their domestic and their global significance. It remains to be seen whether the needs and wishes of expatriate communities will overshadow those of resident populations, but given American political culture and American emigration patterns, this seems unlikely.

Conclusion

The engagement of Americans who live abroad in political processes in the United States is a salient example of transnational practices that are of considerable importance not only for America, but also for the world more generally. Given the enormous impact of American economic, political, and military power around the globe, it is hard for anyone to not be at least vaguely aware of political developments in the United States. Further, the spread of global media networks such as CNN gives individuals in even the most remote locations outside of the United States an opportunity to see and learn about American society, sport, culture, and politics. In this context, it may be that, of all emigrant groups, American emigrants have the easiest access to information about their homeland and thus the most potential to partake in transnational political activities.

Compared to other immigrant groups in Canada, American immigrants are relatively privileged. Generally, they do not face serious problems with having their American-earned credentials recognized in Canada, and they can parlay these credentials into high-status, well-paid jobs. Notwithstanding the occasional anti-American outburst by Canadian politicians, Americans do not face serious discrimination or prejudice in Canada. If white, they can blend into the so-called Canadian mainstream, and depending on where they are from, with a slight tweak of their accent, it is easy for them to "pass" as Canadians. As a result, American immigrants in Canada are, on the surface, quite different from the racialized and disadvantaged transnational immigrants who have been the object of so many American studies of transnationalism.

However, Vertovec's (1999) review of the various meanings of transnationalism may in fact be just as relevant for individuals who define "America" as their ancestral homeland as it is for individuals and groups who move to the United States. Although we have only scratched the surface of this topic, an argument can be made that Americans are perhaps the most exemplary transnationals of all. Vertovec's cataloguing of the six different "takes" on transnationalism seems relevant here. Americans may not be a "diaspora" in the traditional understanding of the term, but the sense that transnationalism involves social formations that span borders does seem obviously relevant to Americans abroad. They also seem to have either dual or multiple identifications, which are reflected both at the level of dual citizenship and in terms of their identities being linked to more than one nation. Third, the process of cultural blending also seems relevant. Even though they are difficult to measure empirically, there are cultural differences between Canada and the United States; immigrants from the United States experience cultural shock when they move to Canada, and like other immigrants they find that they must go through a period of adjustment. Fourth, flows of capital, in the form of remittances, are often identified as another dimension of transnationalism; it is doubtful whether remittances are a very important part of American immigrants' relationships with their families in the United States. However, the broader dimension to the issue of capital exchanges is of course the flow of goods and capital between the two countries. The United States is Canada's largest trading partner. Capital flows both ways, and there is a transnational capitalist and professional class that moves between the two countries to help manage these investments. Fifth, with respect to transnationalism as a site of political involvement that spans two or more states, it is also clear that Americans, through their participation in organizations such as Democrats Abroad and Republicans Abroad, also qualify as transnationals. And finally, it may also be the case that American immigrants' understanding of locality and their relationship to social space may be changing in the sense that there may be a disjuncture between where people live and where their identities and identifications lie.

Perhaps transnationalism, like the concept of diaspora, is too elastic. If the concept is stretched enough, enterprising researchers can make it fit any group of people who live abroad. Given the paucity of research on Americans as immigrants and on American transnational practices, it is worth investigating the transnational lives of this group in Canada. Further research may in fact demonstrate that the concept of transnationalism does not have to be stretched very far to "fit" American experiences of life abroad.

10
Latin American Transnationalism in Canada: Does It Exist, What Forms Does It Take, and Where Is It Going?
Luin Goldring

This chapter analyzes research on and conceptualizations of Latin American transnational activity in Canada and raises issues for further study.[1] Research on Latin American and Caribbean transnationalism has been central to the development of the literature on migrant transnationalism in the United States. By comparison, there is far less work on Latin Americans in the growing Canadian-based literature on transnational flows, linkages, and practices. Why is this the case? Are Latin Americans in Canada less likely to engage in transnational activities compared to those in the United States? Do they engage in different types of activities compared to their conationals in the United States? Is there something about the Canadian context that makes people from Latin American countries less likely to engage in transnational practices compared to other immigrant groups whose transnational practices have been documented more widely? Is it just a matter of time before Latin Americans in Canada will be engaged in similar kinds of transnational activities as those practised by Latin Americans in the United States? Or have researchers simply not gotten around to documenting the existing or earlier transnational linkages of Latin Americans in Canada, which have somehow gone undetected? A comprehensive response to these questions is beyond the scope of this chapter. However, I hope that beginning to address them will contribute to discussions about transnationalism in Canada.

I begin with a brief introduction to the place of Latin American transnationalism in the American- and Canadian-based literatures on the topic. Next, I review existing survey research on transnational activity in Canada that includes information on Latin Americans. After establishing the narrower range of institutionalized forms of transnational activity that have been documented for Latin Americans in Canada, I review possible explanations for differences between the literatures in these two contexts of reception. These explanations include differences between American and Canadian immigration policy, histories and patterns of migration (including the range of source countries and population concentrations), and settlement policies. A reexamination of the literature on Latin Americans in Canada as well as insights from two case studies that explicitly use a transnational approach in their analyses of Latin American groups in Canada allow me to argue that there is evidence of other configurations of transnational practice. More specifically, solidarity organizations have been a key element of transnational activity in Canada. Although their activities may have been short-lived, their significant role suggests the importance of studying transnational engagements from a combined institutional and social-fields perspective.

The past five to ten years have witnessed dramatic increases in migration from most Latin American countries to Canada. Because of this, I conclude that existing analyses of the experiences of Latin Americans in Canada, whether conducted from a transnational perspective or not, are likely to change. Patterns may move toward convergence with those seen in the United States if chain migration expands beyond the family level in terms of scale and density. However, immigration policies may limit this possibility. Instead, different forms of entrepreneurial, political, religious, and sociocultural transnational practices and capabilities may develop without the village- and place-based collective identities, institutions, and activities that have been prominent in the United States. Further research is needed on Latin Americans in Canada to document their transnational activities more systematically. Such work should contribute to comparative analyses that stress the importance of legal status, migratory history, broader historical context, contexts of departure, and contexts of reception (Al-Ali, Black, and Koser 2001).

Comparing the Literatures on Transnationalism: The Place and Forms of Latin American Transnationalism in American and Canadian Research

The American Context
Research on the transnational practices of Latin American and Caribbean people in the United States helped to establish the field of transnational studies as it emerged there in the mid-1980s (Basch, Glick Schiller, and Szanton Blanc 1994; Rouse 1991). Since then, documentation and analyses of the transnational practices of a number of Latin American and Caribbean groups have grown dramatically (Cordero-Guzmán, Smith, and Grosfoguel 2001; Glick Schiller and Fouron 2001; Goldring 2002; Guarnizo and Diaz 1999; Guarnizo and Smith 1998; Kyle 1999; Landolt, Autler, and Baires 1999; Levitt 2001b; Mahler 1999; Popkin 1999; Portes, Haller, and Guarnizo 2002; Smith 2003).

The transnational engagements of people from other parts of the world living in the United States have also been studied (Espiritu 2003; Ong 1999;

Ong and Nonini 1997b). However, work on the Americas continues to occupy a preeminent position in this literature. This is undoubtedly related to
the geographic proximity of Mexico and other Latin American and Caribbean countries, the comparatively high proportion of immigrants from this
region in the United States, and the long and well-documented history of
economic integration and international migration in the hemisphere.

The study of immigrant transnationalism has become increasingly accepted as a legitimate conceptual and methodological approach (Portes 2003;
Portes, Guarnizo, and Landolt 1999). At the same time, it continues to generate lively discussions in the United States (Levitt, DeWind, and Vertovec
2003). The debates concern a range of issues, including definitions, mea-
surement, prevalence, units of analysis, recency, and causes of transnationalism as well as the role of states and state institutions in shaping migrant
transnationalism (Foner 1997; Itzigsohn and Saucedo 2002; Levitt 2001a;
Levitt and de la Dehesa 2003; Portes 2001; Portes, Guarnizo, and Landolt
1999; Smith 2003; Waldinger and Fitzgerald 2004).

Despite the debates, there is little doubt that several types and forms of
transnational practices have become institutionalized among Latin American and Caribbean immigrants in the United States. Portes and his associates (1999) identified three broad *types* of transnational activity:
socio-cultural, economic, and political. Researchers have also developed
terms to describe variation in the frequency, scale, scope, prevalence, and
institutionalization of various types of transnational activity.[2] These distinctions allow me to identify diverse forms and configurations of
transnational engagement. I use the term "configurations" to draw attention to variation in the combination of specific institutional actors who are
engaged in particular types of transnational practices and identities that
involve one or more counterpart institutional actors. I also use the term to
draw attention to distinctions that specify the scope, frequency, duration,
prevalence, and layering of transnational engagement. My emphasis on the
configuration of transnational engagements allows me to combine attention
to who (institutional actors) is involved in what (types of transnational
engagement) and how (often, institutionalized, widespread, durable).

Portes and his collaborators have found evidence of economic, political,
and socio-cultural transnationalism in research conducted on Dominicans,
Salvadorans, and Colombians, although the degree and patterns of transnational engagement vary across groups (Guarnizo, Portes, and Haller 2003;
Itzigsohn and Saucedo 2002; Portes 2001; Portes, Haller, and Guarnizo 2002).
Using qualitative approaches that do not focus exclusively on individual-
level research, other scholars have analyzed these and other types of
transnational practices and institutions in several United States contexts
relevant to Latin Americans. This body of work includes analyses of political transnationalism (Itzigsohn 2000), religious transnationalism (Levitt

2003), and economic transnationalism in the form of remittances to Mexico and other Latin American countries (Goldring 2004; Orozco 2003; Suro 2003). It also covers various forms of migrant-based transnationalism that connect the United States and countries such as El Salvador (Landolt 2000, 2001; Landolt, Autler, and Baires 1999; Mahler 1999), Guatemala (Popkin 1999), Puerto Rico (Cordero-Guzmán, Smith, and Grosfoguel 2001), the Dominican Republic (Levitt 2001b), Colombia (Guarnizo and Diaz 1999), and Ecuador (Kyle 1999; Miles 2004). The literature on Mexico is particularly rich, with publications on transnational migrant circuits (Rouse 1991), state-migrant relations (Chelius and Saldaña 2002; Goldring 2002; Smith 2003), hometown associations and their activities in the United States and Mexico (Bada 2003; Fitzgerald 2004; Moctezuma 2000; Zabin and Escala 1998), transnational migration and social change (Grimes 1998), and gender relations (Goldring 2001; Hirsch 2003).

The literature on transnational practices that is US-based and oriented toward the Latin American and Caribbean experiences suggests that a relatively modest proportion of people engage intensively in a wide range of types of transnational activity, while others are actively involved in a narrower range, and many more are involved in broad transnationalism – that is, in a few types of activities carried out on an occasional basis. Despite variation in the intensity, frequency, and scope of transnational engagement at the level of individuals, families, and localities of origin, a variety of institutional forms have developed in transnational "social spaces." Many of these are state-mediated, with government programs aimed at courting political and economic support among emigrants and migrant organizations. Although specific government outreach programs and hometown organizations may disappear, to be replaced by others, the institutionalization of such forms seems fairly established. This may be partly due to the growing interest among states and multilateral organizations in remittances (Goldring 2004; Guarnizo 2003; Itzigsohn 2000). To summarize, Latin American transnationalism in the United States is visible, widespread, and institutionalized; there is variation in the distributive scope of different types and levels of activity; and place-based networks are an important element of most configurations of transnational activity.

The Canadian Context

In Canada, the field of transnational studies is somewhat different. Partly because it is more recent, the literature is smaller. It includes valuable conceptual contributions (Hyndman and Walton-Roberts 2000) and covers a wide range of geographic source regions, including East Asia (Wong 1997; Wong and Ng 2002), South Asia (Walton-Roberts 2003), eastern Europe (Winland 1998), the Middle East (Gall 2002), the Caribbean (Duval 2001), and Africa (Wong 2000). With two exceptions (Landolt forthcoming; Nolin

2001, 2004), there are virtually no case studies of Latin Americans in Canada conducted using a transnational framework. There is one survey of immigrant transnationalism that includes information on Latin Americans (Hiebert and Ley 2003). In addition, recent government surveys contain items that cast some light on Latin American transnationalism in Canada.

To situate this in context, it is worth noting that there is relatively little work on Latin Americans in Canada compared to the vast literature on Latin Americans in the United States. The existing Canadian literature can be divided into three broad categories. First, there is earlier work on refugee groups and issues, most of it from the mid-1970s and 1980s. This work documents the needs of and the range of problems faced by refugees in the process of incorporation and the efforts of various groups to assist them (Allodi and Rojas 1983a, 1983b, 1988; Duran 1980; Johnson 1982; Marsden 1977; Neuwirth 1989; Smith and Hess 1985). Second, there are statistical profiles of Latin Americans in Canada or particular cities that rely on Census data. Much of this work focuses on employment, occupational mobility (or lack thereof), and income (Garay 2000; Loaiza Cardenas 1989; Magocsi 1999; Mata 1985, 1988). Third, there is contemporary work on recent Latin American immigrants to Canada, which includes, but is no longer limited to, studies of refugee groups (Kulig 1998; Recalde 2002; Woodill 2000). This work documents the experiences of Latin Americans with particular institutions or sectors, such as education, including training in English as a second language (ESL) (Bernhard and Freire 1999a, 1999b; Rockhill and Tomic 1992), health (Miloslavich 1999), social services (Israelite et al. 1998), and civic engagement (Armony, Barriga, and Shugurensky 2004).[3] It also includes profiles and case studies of particular immigrant groups.[4] This contemporary work concentrates on immigrant incorporation and adaptation, and for the most part, does not use a transnational approach.[5]

Initial Evidence of Latin American Transnationalism in Canada

Quantitative Approaches

Hiebert and Ley (2003) conducted one of the few surveys designed to collect information on immigrant transnationalism in Canada. Adapting a Portes-style approach, they conducted a telephone survey in Vancouver that included 1,479 immigrants from a number of countries and regions. One purpose of the survey was to determine whether transnationalism in Vancouver was associated with successful economic integration, as found by Portes and Guarnizo in the United States, or whether transnational activities were more likely to be practised by people who were less incorporated into Canadian society (Hiebert and Ley 2003). They concluded that in Canada, unlike in the United States, immigrants who are least incorporated are most likely to engage in transnationalism.

Hiebert and Ley (2003) also analyzed the relationship between ethnic origin and transnational activity. The authors broke down their sample into six categories for "ethnic origin," or region of origin: European/Canadian, Arab/West Asian, South Asian, East Asian, Southeast Asian, and Latin American/Caribbean. Unfortunately, the Latin American/Caribbean subsample was the smallest, with only thirty respondents. Respondents in this category were very likely to have family in the home country (90%), as were people in the other categories. Where Latin Americans differed from the other ethnic-origin categories was in their *types* and *forms* of transnational activity. Although 89% kept in touch with family, this was at the lower end of the range for this indicator, which rose to 97% for East Asians. More significantly, Latin Americans were less likely to travel home than were other groups and had low rates of property ownership in the home country. Their transnational business contacts were lowest compared to those of other groups. None had jobs requiring them to travel home, nor did any operate a business in the home country. Nevertheless, their reported visits from the home country were among the highest (63%), and they were among the most likely to send remittances, at 30%, compared to 8% for European/Canadians, 19% for Arab/West Asians, 17% for South Asians, 13% for East Asians, and 36% for Southeast Asians (Hiebert and Ley 2003, 13).

In comparative terms, people in the Latin American/Caribbean category appear to be less transnational than those in other "ethnic" categories in that they engage in fewer types of activities and at lower rates (except for remittances). However, it is difficult to generalize these findings to all Latin Americans in Canada because of the relatively small size of the Latin American/Caribbean subsample and because Hiebert and Ley's (2003) study did not include indicators of other types of transnationalism, such as the political or religious. It is possible that Latin Americans exhibit other types and configurations of transnationalism and that a larger sample and different indicators would reveal different patterns.

Two other government surveys – the Longitudinal Survey of Immigrants to Canada (LSIC)[6] and the Ethnic Diversity Survey (EDS) – also find evidence of socio-cultural transnationalism among Latin Americans in Canada. The indicators show forms of transnationalism associated with the maintenance of family ties over time and space, such as communication with family and friends abroad, the intention to sponsor relatives, migration to Canada based on family and friendship ties, and so forth. These surveys confirm Hiebert and Ley's (2003) finding of transnational activity among Latin Americans in Canada but do not provide firm conclusions about Latin Americans compared to people from other regions.

Special tabulations of the LSIC data show that Latin Americans, at 62%, were more likely than the average of the surveyed population to have relatives at home whom they wanted to sponsor (Statistics Canada 2004).[7] The tabulations also provide information about the respondents' relationship to those they wished to sponsor. Seventy-five percent of the Latin American respondents said that they wanted to sponsor siblings or parents; 37%, in-laws, nephews, or cousins; and 7%, a spouse or children (Statistics Canada 2004).[8] These data are consistent with Hiebert and Ley's (2003) work because they show that Latin Americans have relatives at home with whom they probably maintain contact; in other words, there is a demographic and geographic basis for potential transnational activity.

The LSIC data do not provide much information on specific transnational activities. Respondents were asked whether they sent money to relatives or friends living outside of Canada and whether they sent money abroad as an investment. According to the tabulations, Latin Americans did not report sending money abroad as an investment. However, nearly a quarter of Latin Americans (24.4%) reported sending money to relatives and friends. This is lower than the rate that Hiebert and Ley (2003) reported for Latin Americans and Caribbeans (30%) but higher than the rates that they reported for most other groups, except Southeast Asians (36%). It is also much higher than the 6% of Chinese respondents in the LSIC who reported sending money to relatives and friends outside of Canada.[9] The LSIC data thus confirm that remittances are an important form of economic transnationalism among recent Latin American newcomers, although comparisons across groups are difficult. It is important to remember that these Latin Americans, and many other newcomers, are in the process of adjusting to Canada, finding employment, and so forth and that they may consequently not have much surplus income. The extent to which individuals and immediate family members from various Latin American regions are able to enter Canada also needs to be taken into account. However, such analysis is not possible with the available secondary data.

The Ethnic Diversity Survey (EDS) provides information on ethnic identity, attachment to cultural values, and experiences of racism and discrimination, broken down by visible-minority status. It also includes items on attachment to one's country of origin (birth or ancestry) and on types of contact with relatives in the country of origin (Statistics Canada 2003c). Because the EDS is a post-Censal survey, the weighted responses are generalizable to the population as a whole.[10] The report notes that generation and length of time in Canada made a clear difference in terms of contact with family members abroad, with contact decreasing over time and generation. Seventy-five percent of first-generation immigrants who had arrived since 1990 had contact with relatives in the country of origin at least once a month. The rate declined among those who arrived prior to 1991 to 46%, which is still noteworthy. Among second-generation respondents, the rate of monthly contact with overseas family members declined to 18% (Statistics Canada 2003c).

Using the EDS to examine the relationship between transnational activity and ethnic origin is complicated by the fact that there is no "Latin American" category. However, a tabulation of the EDS data on frequency of contact with family in the country of origin or ancestry does include "Spanish" as a category. Table 10.1 shows that 51% of those who identified as "Spanish" reported contact with family members at least once a month. Among the twenty-one ethnic groups listed, this was the fifth-highest rate of contact.

If we assume that the 148,500 people in the category "Spanish" include respondents from Latin America and/or of Latin American ancestry, then we can infer that the EDS provides corroborating evidence of fairly high levels of contact with family members in the country of origin or ancestry for Latin Americans. This is a safe but imprecise inference. According to the Canadian Census of 2001, only 10,655 immigrants in Canada's immigrant population (0.02%) reported Spain as their country of birth (Migration Policy Institute 2004a).[11] In contrast, 206,955 immigrants (3.7%) were born in South American countries, and 116,500 immigrants (2.1%) were born in Central American countries. Even though these regional groupings include non-Spanish-speaking countries, they still vastly outnumber the population of immigrants born in Spain. If we subtract the Guyanese-born population (67,810), we are still left with 255,645 Latin Americans, not including the Caribbean. Again, because this far exceeds the Spanish-born population, there is a good chance that the Spanish-origin category in the EDS includes a fair share of Latin Americans and people of Latin American ancestry.

These three surveys show that Latin Americans in Canada maintain contact with family members in countries of origin, receive visits from home, and send remittances. The first two are forms of socio-cultural transnationalism, while the last is also a form of economic transnationalism. Hiebert and Ley's (2003) work indicates that Latin Americans and Caribbeans engage in fewer types of transnational activity compared to Asian groups. The government surveys confirm the existence of socio-cultural transnationalism, which might be an indicator of broad transnationalism.

Although they offer a partial picture of Latin American transnationalism, the surveys have limitations.

Case Studies of Transnationalism among Latin Americans in Canada
Catherine Nolin and Patricia Landolt are the only authors that I have been able to identify who explicitly use a transnational framework in their analyses of Latin Americans in Canada. Their analyses help to fill out the picture of transnationalism provided by the quantitative analyses. Nolin (2001, 2004) argues persuasively that Guatemalan transnationalism in Canada may best be characterized as psychological transnationalism because it takes a form different from that seen in the United States. Nolin (2004) finds that Guatemalans in Canada are relatively isolated and not involved in the prevailing

Table 10.1

Frequency of contact with family in the country of origin or ancestry, for the population with such family, Canada, 2002

Ethnic origin	Total	Valid responses	Subtotal: At least once a month	%	At least once a week	At least once a month	At least three times a year	Once or twice a year	Not at all
Punjabi	91,200	91,200	60,400	66	11,500[a]	48,900	9,200[a]	13,100[a]	8,400[a]
Filipino	225,800	225,100	139,800	62	56,300	83,500	31,600	28,900	24,800
East Indian	393,300	390,700	213,400	55	70,800	142,600	65,800	47,900	63,500
African (black, NIE)	97,700	97,400	52,100	54	18,200[a]	33,900	16,700[a]	11,600[a]	16,900[a]
Spanish	148,500	148,500	76,300	51	36,400	39,900	27,900	18,100[a]	26,100
Greek	118,400	117,700	54,700	46	15,100[a]	39,600	20,800	20,200	22,000
Chinese	702,800	697,000	317,900	46	143,900	174,000	113,300	114,700	151,100
Portuguese	255,500	255,400	102,100	40	29,000	73,100	49,000	46,600	57,700
Jamaican	109,600	109,600	41,700	38	11,300[a]	30,400	27,900	21,500[a]	18,500[a]
Russian	146,200	144,800	49,300	34	19,000[a]	30,300	13,300[a]	16,300[a]	65,900
Italian	789,800	787,800	240,400	31	59,300	181,100	142,400	139,700	265,300
Polish	347,800	347,600	97,800	28	36,300	61,500	38,700	48,700	162,400
American (USA)	181,400	181,400	50,100	28	22,100	28,000	23,900	46,700	60,700
French	504,100	500,600	136,300	27	60,600	75,700	47,800	87,800	228,800
British (NIE)	416,200	416,100	104,100	25	35,400	68,700	62,500	100,400	149,200
Dutch	441,800	441,100	107,000	24	35,300	71,700	57,400	92,800	183,900
German	916,400	911,100	185,700	20	62,900	122,800	100,500	162,000	462,900
English	1,532,400	1,528,400	281,300	18	96,900	184,400	155,900	324,500	766,700
Irish	944,600	932,600	161,400	17	57,700	103,700	88,600	184,700	497,900
Scottish	1,184,200	1,178,700	186,700	16	73,800	112,900	132,400	230,500	629,100
Canadian/Canadien	420,700	418,100	50,500	12	11,500[a]	39,000	50,500	94,700	222,300

Notes: Refers to Canada's non-Aboriginal population aged fifteen and over. NIE = not included elsewhere.
a Interpret with caution due to the small sample size.
Source: Ethnic Diversity Survey, 2002 (Statistics Canada 2003c).

forms of associational and organizational life identified in the United States. Immigration policies have admitted refugees, but they have not facilitated the development of village-based or other broader networks and forms of organization. Even networks of extended family seem to be absent, as family reunification is costly and difficult. Thus Guatemalan transnationalism is experienced as a "rupture," rather than a continuation, of social networks and relations, and Nolin argues that people's yearning for connections to home are rarely matched by physical mobility in the form of return visits or permanent return.

Nolin's concept of psychological transnationalism is reminiscent of the distinction made by Al-Ali and colleagues (2001) between transnational practices and transnational capabilities. They argue that in cases of emerging transnationalism, although groups may not display much in the way of measurable transnational activity, they nevertheless construct their identities and orient their lives around attachments to the home country.[12] The Guatemalans with whom Nolin (2001, 2004) worked may be transnational in the sense of disposition and capabilities, even though they do not manifest as much transnational mobility, collective organization, or other more visible activity as do Guatemalans in the United States (Hamilton and Chinchilla 2001; Popkin 1999). Whether they will engage in more visible forms of transnational practice once they become more settled, secure, and less lonely remains to be seen.

Landolt's (forthcoming) comparative analysis of Salvadorans in Los Angeles and Toronto shows that distinct patterns of incorporation and transnationalism developed for immigrants in these two settings.[13] She argues that changes in the contexts of exit and reception in the United States and Canada are fundamental for understanding the emergence of different institutional landscapes that shaped distinct Salvadoran immigrant communities in Los Angeles and Toronto, even though Salvadorans left their country for similar reasons. Differences between the United States and Canada in the process of migration and in state policies meant that there was more undocumented and chain migration to Los Angeles, where Salvadorans established a number of important umbrella organizations as well as many place-based organizations. As a result of context-specific institutional opportunities, Salvadorans in Los Angeles have a strong institutional presence in El Salvador and in Los Angeles. In comparison, Canada's acceptance of Salvadorans as refugees led to different patterns of settlement and organizing. Salvadorans in Toronto have not developed village-level associations or a significant institutional presence in El Salvador or in the "local" Toronto context. In addition to demonstrating the significance of comparative analyses, Landolt's work underscores the importance of using a transnational approach for understanding the constraints and opportunities that shape the trajectory of immigrant institution building and organizing as well as the configuration of transnational engagements.

Rereading the Literature on Latin Americans in Canada: Transnational Solidarity, Political Parties, and Humanitarian Assistance

The insights from Nolin's and Landolt's respective work led me to reread the literature on Latin Americans that was not written from a transnational perspective so that I might uncover practices and institutions that helped to mediate transnational social fields in one way or another, even though they were not labelled as such. Studies of Latin American refugee groups in Canada highlight the importance of homeland-oriented solidarity activity, particularly in cases where a majority of refugees left because of their opposition to a particular regime that remained in power for some time after their arrival in Canada. According to Diaz (1999b), Kowalchuk (1999a, 1999c), and Simalchik (2004), Chileans, Salvadorans, and Guatemalans exemplify this form of transnational engagement. This solidarity work took place in organizations whose members were primarily of the specific national-origin group in question (e.g., political parties) and in groups that included Canadians, other Latin Americans, and others. This last set would include pro-Sandinista solidarity groups (at the time of the Sandinista revolution and immediately afterward), Canadian labour unions, human-rights groups, humanitarian organizations, religious organizations, and ecumenical groups.

Chileans are one of the older Latin American groups in Canada. Nearly half of the current population of Canadian residents born in Chile arrived between 1971 and 1980 (Statistics Canada 2003e). Most of this cohort left for political reasons and arrived as refugees following the 1973 coup against Salvador Allende's government. This is reflected in the community and organizational life that they developed. Chileans worked in "Canadian branches of Chilean left-wing political parties" (Diaz 1999b). They also came together in political organizations until the 1980s to mobilize "Canadian individuals and organizations against the Chilean military regime and [for] solidarity work with the political opposition in Chile" (Diaz 1999b). These organizations disappeared after the process of democratization in Chile, but some Chileans remained active in solidarity work with Central American and other countries (Diaz 1999b). Simalchik (2004) documents the role that Chileans who were in Canada before the coup played in lobbying the Canadian government to bring Chilean refugees to Canada. They worked with faith communities, organized labour, and other groups in civil society and also contributed to the development of refugee-selection policies.[14] These efforts facilitated the admission of subsequent Chilean refugees (during the late 1970s and 1980s) and the admission of refugees from Southeast Asia, Central America, and other regions.

In the late 1990s, Kowalchuk (1999a, 1999c) stated that Guatemalans and Salvadorans also developed a number of organizations and worked with Canadians in labour, human-rights, and other groups. Their indirect transnational activities included lobbying the Canadian government around refugee admissions and foreign policy as well as educating the Canadian public about the situation in their countries. Their more direct transnational activities included raising funds for political groups, humanitarian projects, and women's organizations.

Even though Nicaraguans were a refugee group, Kowalchuk (1999b) contends that they did not engage in pro-Sandinista solidarity activities or participate in related organizations operating during the 1980s. She suggests that this was the case because of the ambivalence that Nicaraguans felt toward the Sandinista regime and its successors and also notes that an important share of Nicaraguans who entered Canada as refugees did so *not* because they were fleeing state violence – as was the case for Chileans, Salvadorans, and Guatemalans – but because of the civil war that began after the Sandinistas lost power. At the time of her writing, there was only one Nicaraguan organization, and it focused on humanitarian aid.

Kowalchuk and Diaz present respective pictures of a fairly dense set of organizations for Chile, Guatemala, and El Salvador, some with direct ties to groups in the home countries and others rooted in Canadian civil-society organizations. Not all of them remained in existence at the time of writing, largely because of political changes in the home countries. The significance of these organizations derives from their being based more on common political values than on identification with a common locality of origin. That is, they were not organizational expressions of transnational village networks but representatives of overlapping yet distinct constituencies: extraterritorial civil-society organizations and actors (e.g., Chilean political parties abroad, Salvadoran opposition groups, and immigrants) and Canadian civil-society groups that were following the well-worn path of international solidarity by acting in an extraterritorial fashion with a membership base that often included immigrants.

Groups without, at least until recently, high proportions of refugees have not had an associational life marked by transnational solidarity activities. Ecuadoreans and Mexicans, for example, have cultural and professional organizations, but at the end of the 1990s comparable solidarity activities had not been reported for them (Goldring 1999; Phillips 1999). However, the expansion of the Caribbean and Mexican Seasonal Agricultural Workers Program, which has increased the number of Mexican workers who spend time in Canada, has raised concerns among Canadians and Mexicans, leading to new solidarity activities.[15] These activities appear to be Canada-based and oriented toward Canadian institutions.

Since the end of the 1990s, these fairly established groups have been joined by increasing numbers of refugees and refugee claimants from a new set of countries. Some of these individuals come from countries that are not generally thought of as refugee-producing (e.g., Mexico and Argentina), while others come from countries that typically are regarded as such (e.g., Colombia). Published research on groups of these individuals is minimal. Although there is no academic documentation of transnational solidarity activity among these groups, there is considerable anecdotal evidence of transnational solidarity activity among Colombian organizations, such as speaking tours to Canada by Colombia-based labour and rights activists sponsored by Canadian activist groups (CERLAC 2004).

Transnational solidarity has thus been an important form of transnational activity, particularly among refugee groups that oppose the regimes in power in their home countries but perhaps also among groups that support a regime. In the past, Canadian foreign policy and immigration policy have been sufficiently autonomous from American policies to allow substantial numbers of migrants from countries such as Chile, El Salvador, and Guatemala to enter Canada with refugee status. However, four points should be noted about these activities. First, many Canadians were involved in these solidarity activities. Second, most of these organizations folded once their immediate purpose was rendered passé due to regime changes. Third, these collective forms of transnationalism were based not on village- or locality-specific identities but on political projects and shared values. Fourth, migrants' legal status as refugees or exiles, with its associated emotional state, had a profound influence on these organizational forms.

The differences between the American and Canadian contexts are fairly clear. In the United States the literature on Latin American transnationalism focuses on migrant-only transnationalism while paying relatively little attention to solidarity activities and the participation of nonimmigrants (and non–Latin Americans) in these activities.[16] Undocumented status is the main category of legal status addressed in the US-based literature, with comparatively less attention being paid to refugees.[17] Place-based identities, such as those facilitated by village-based networks, dominate the literature. It may be that Canada-based Latin American forms of transnational practices are less durable, but one can imagine conditions under which the organizations might take on new objectives and/or conditions under which members might move on to other organizations with transnational components. Further research can address this question as well as others that emerge from an analysis of different forms of transnational activity. Clearly, solidarity and related forms of transnational activity deserve serious consideration if analyses are to be grounded in historical context.

Latin Americans and Transnationalism in the United States versus Canada

There are various explanations for the differences between the patterns of Latin American transnational engagement identified in the literatures on Canada and on the United States. This section compares histories and patterns of migration, settlement and immigration policy, and geographic location.

The Numbers: Share of Population and Timing of Migration

Canada and the United States are both known as countries of immigration. Both have large foreign-born populations. In the United States the numbers of both the total population and the foreign-born population are considerably higher. However, the proportion of foreign-born is higher in Canada. In 2001 there were 5.1 million foreign-born in Canada, representing 19% of the population. In the same year, the United States had 31.1 million foreign-born, but this accounted for only 11% of the population (Migration Policy Institute 2004b). In addition to the difference in magnitude, there have been important historical and contemporary differences in nation building, geopolitics, immigration patterns, and immigrant and refugee policy, leading to differences in the history and position of Latin American immigrants and refugees in the two countries.

Latin American migration has been far more integral to economic and historical development in the United States than in Canada, where the presence of Latin Americans is much smaller and more recent. The Americas have been, and continue to be, an important source region for the immigrant population of the United States. In 2001, 54% of all immigrants in the United States were from the Americas (including Canada). Mexico, El Salvador, and Cuba were important source countries. In declining order in terms of size, Asia and Europe followed as source regions, accounting for 26% and 16% of immigrants respectively. Relatively small shares of immigrants came from other regions such as Africa, at 3%, and Oceania, at 1% (Migration Policy Institute 2004b).

In contrast, Europe remains the main source region for the immigrant population of Canada, accounting for 41% of immigrants in 2001. Asia, with 32% of immigrants, was in second place, while the Americas accounted for only 15.6% of immigrants. Africa and Oceania were the source regions for 5% and 1% of immigrants respectively. Compared to the United States, Canada has a much lower proportion of immigrants from the Americas and a higher proportion of immigrants from Africa (Migration Policy Institute 2004b).

The Importance of Mexico

Another way to illustrate the difference in immigration patterns between the two countries is to compare the largest foreign-born groups in 2001. In the United States, Mexico alone accounted for 29.5% of the foreign-born population. In Canada, the United Kingdom tops the list with 10.9% of the foreign-born population (Migration Policy Institute 2004c). No single group dominates the list in the way that Mexicans do for the United States. Mexico's geographic proximity to the United States and the historic process of migration have contributed to Mexico's unique migratory relationship with the United States.

The Mexican presence in the United States predates the contemporary national boundaries, since much of the contemporary southwest of the country belonged to Mexico until the 1848 Treaty of Guadalupe Hidalgo. Mexicans' migration to the United States continued, then declined during the Mexican Revolution, and then rose again with the Bracero Program (1942-64), a bilateral contract-worker program designed to import workers for American agriculture during the Second World War. The migrants who went north through this program established the social networks that would lay the bases for a post-1960s boom in Mexican migration and settlement, both documented and undocumented. The cumulative nature of this migration system led analysts to coin the phrase "cumulative causation" to describe the exponential growth of chain migration from multiple localities (Massey et al. 1987). Despite periodic efforts to reduce Mexican migration by various means, including border enforcement and employer sanctions, migration continued. The 1990s were a time of anti-immigrant sentiment and stepped-up border control, but Mexican migration continued, despite the rising cost and risk of crossing the border. Recent data indicate no end to Mexican migration. Instead, there has been a diversification of sending regions within Mexico, a rise in permanent US settlement (Canales 2003), and an increase in the volume of remittances.

In 2002 Mexico continued to overshadow the proportion of foreign-born, with 29.8% of the total. Other groups with national origins that were Latin American or Spanish-speaking Caribbean each accounted for between 2% and 3% of the foreign-born population in the United States (Migration Policy Institute 2004c). Despite this element of continuity, there have been changes. Traditional areas of immigrant concentration are shifting as new immigrants settle in new "gateways" in the Midwestern and Southeastern United States and increasingly in suburbs throughout the country (Singer 2004).

Timing and Diversity

In contrast, migration from Latin America to Canada is relatively recent and more diverse. The large number of different Latin American groups represented in Canada is an indicator of this diversity, particularly since there is no single group that dominates as Mexicans do in the United States. According to the 2001 Census, El Salvador, Mexico, and Chile were the top three countries represented in the immigrant population. The Census also tracks nonpermanent residents, who include refugee claimants and temporary workers. In this category, Mexico, Colombia, and Argentina were the top three source countries. Although Mexicans do not represent as large a share of the Latin American population in Canada as in the United States, the Mexican population ranks first in size when permanent and nonpermanent residents are combined (Statistics Canada 2003e).

Table 10.2 presents 2001 Census data on Latin American immigrants by period of entry to Canada (not including nonpermanent residents). Key differences exist among countries in terms of when migration began and peak periods of immigration to Canada. Different contexts of departure are also reflected. Mata (1985) characterized Latin American migration to Canada as occurring in four waves, each related to changes in Canadian immigration policy and events taking place in the countries of origin. First was the "lead wave" of European-origin migrants, who arrived through the early 1960s; second was the Andean wave of Ecuadorean, Colombian, and Peruvian economic migrants during the late 1960s and early '70s; third was the coup wave of political refugees from Chile, Argentina, and Uruguay, which started in 1973 and continued through the 1970s; and fourth was the Central American wave comprising individuals who left civil wars during the 1980s.

Table 10.2 confirms that the largest share of Chileans arrived between 1971 and 1980, the period following the 1973 coup and military intervention (Diaz 1999a). Similarly, it indicates the movement of Central Americans who left countries marked by violence and civil war during the 1980s (Kowalchuk 1999a, 1999c). This is also the period during which large proportions of Dominicans, Bolivians, and Ecuadoreans arrived, leaving countries affected by early neoliberal restructuring (Phillips 1999). The so-called Andean wave appears to peak somewhat later in time than in Mata's scheme and includes non-Andean source countries.

The 1990s brought about important changes in Latin American migration patterns to Canada. Migration from El Salvador and Guatemala declined compared to the previous decade. Most significantly, substantial proportions of Latin Americans who now live in Canada entered the country between 1991 and 2001. For example, 54% of Costa Ricans, 63% of Hondurans, 71% of Cubans, 50% of Mexicans, 49% of Peruvians, 43% of Bolivians, 54% of Colombians, and 56% of Venezuelans entered Canada during this time.

The last column in Table 10.2 presents the proportional change between the periods 1981-90 and 1991-2001. The majority of groups experienced substantial increases in immigration. Cuba, Colombia, Venezuela, Panama, and Honduras stand out, with increases ranging from 130 to 388 percent. In some of these cases, there was relatively little migration prior to 1991 (e.g., Honduras); in others, such as Colombia, the recent surge is actually a

Table 10.2

Period of entry to Canada by country of birth for Latin American immigrants (pre-1961 to 2001) and rate of change between 1981-90 and 1991-2001

Country of birth of Latin American immigrants	Total Latin American immigrants	Before 1961	%	1961 -70	%	1971 -80	%	1981 -90	%	1991 -95	%	1996 -2001	%	Total (%)	Change 1981-90 to 1991-2001 (%)
Costa Rica	2,230	30	1.3	60	2.7	75	3.4	850	38.1	610	27.4	605	27.1	100	+42.94
El Salvador	38,460	15	0.0	60	0.2	1,145	3.0	23,780	61.8	10,690	27.8	2,770	7.2	100	-43.40
Guatemala	13,670	40	0.3	125	0.9	930	6.8	6,215	45.5	4,360	31.9	2,000	14.6	100	+2.33
Honduras	4,335	0	0.0	50	1.2	355	8.2	1,190	27.5	1,690	39.0	1,050	24.2	100	+130.25
Mexico	36,225	1,445	4.0	2,140	5.9	4,865	13.4	9,660	26.7	6,650	18.4	11,465	31.6	100	+87.53
Nicaragua	9,375	0	0.0	45	0.5	125	1.3	4,695	50.1	3,560	38.0	950	10.1	100	-3.94
Panama	2,405	30	1.2	60	2.5	220	9.1	640	26.6	1,130	47.0	325	13.5	100	+127.34
Cuba	4,930	150	3.0	275	5.6	295	6.0	715	14.5	960	19.5	2,535	51.4	100	+388.81
Dominican Republic	4,970	65	1.3	80	1.6	310	6.2	1,670	33.6	1,695	34.1	1,150	23.1	100	+70.36
Puerto Rico	240	20	8.3	30	12.5	65	27.1	50	20.8	45	18.8	30	12.5	100	+50.00
Argentina	12,015	645	5.4	1,200	10.0	3,180	26.5	2,790	23.2	2,140	17.8	2,060	17.1	100	+50.54
Bolivia	2,275	50	2.2	160	7.0	320	14.1	775	34.1	475	20.9	495	21.8	100	+25.16
Brazil	11,700	500	4.3	1,090	9.3	1,765	15.1	2,345	20.0	2,630	22.5	3,370	28.8	100	+155.86
Chile	24,500	155	0.6	515	2.1	10,995	44.9	7,190	29.3	3,550	14.5	2,095	8.6	100	-21.49
Colombia	15,510	175	1.1	520	3.4	3,520	22.7	2,935	18.9	1,880	12.1	6,480	41.8	100	+184.84
Ecuador	10,900	65	0.6	385	3.5	4,285	39.3	2,165	19.9	2,195	20.1	1,805	16.6	100	+84.76
Paraguay	4,955	785	15.8	1,210	24.4	1,115	22.5	1,075	21.7	280	5.7	490	9.9	100	-28.37
Peru	17,110	180	1.1	585	3.4	2,330	13.6	5,660	33.1	5,275	30.8	3,080	18.0	100	+47.61
Uruguay	6,095	55	0.9	790	13.0	2,285	37.5	1,385	22.7	1,015	16.7	565	9.3	100	+14.08
Venezuela	7,055	270	3.8	525	7.4	805	11.4	1,490	21.1	1,660	23.5	2,305	32.7	100	+166.11
Total	228,955	4,675	2.0	9,905	4.3	38,985	17.0	77,275	33.8	52,490	22.9	45,625	19.9	100	+26.97
Total immigrants entering Canada	5,448,480	894,465		745,565		936,275		1,041,495		867,355		963,325			

Note: Does not include temporary residents.
Source: Elaborated from the 2001 Census of Canada, Table 9 (Statistics Canada 2003i).

renewed increase, spurred by ongoing violence and insecurity in the country. Even without these more extreme cases, it is clear that migration from Latin America took off dramatically in the period between the last two Censuses. Seven countries exhibited increases ranging from 40 to 100 percent during this time period. In only two cases was there relative continuity: Guatemalans show a slight increase, while Salvadorans show a slight decline. Salvadorans, Nicaraguans, Chileans, and Paraguayans are the only groups whose rates of immigration declined between 1981-91 and 1991-2001.

Although the presence of some groups of Latin American national origin dates to the 1960s, the majority of Latin Americans currently in Canada arrived in the past twenty years. More specifically, the past five to ten years have been a time of dramatically higher entry for most groups. The economic situation in a number of countries helps to explain much of this increase, but Canadian immigration policies also contributed in several ways. The numbers of nonpermanent residents, temporary workers, refugees, and refugee claimants from Mexico, Argentina, and Colombia have increased considerably. The Mexican figures reflect Canada's growing use of temporary workers, a well-documented trend (Basok 2002; Preibisch 2004; Sharma 2001). Latin Americans are well represented among refugee claimants in Canada. In 2002, 32,466 refugee claims were finalized. Of these, 1,407 claims were from Colombians, 1,207 from Mexicans, and 1,011 from Argentines (Canadian Council for Refugees 2003).

Immigration Policy, Refugees, and Networks
Starting in the 1960s, Canadian immigration policy, like that of the United States and other northern countries, began to accept authorized immigrants from a wider range of source countries. This represented a shift from more-or-less explicitly racist policies that excluded non-European immigrants (Simmons 1998). Since that period, Canadian immigration has undergone several changes. However, two trends have been evident in the country's immigration policies since the late 1970s: relatively generous targets for refugee admission (once the category was created in 1976) and an emphasis on the economic contribution and employability of prospective immigrants. Family reunification has been accommodated in immigration policy, but the definition of the family has become more restrictive. The Canadian "point system" gives preference to people with specific skills, occupations, and education, while the investor and business programs admit immigrants who can contribute to the Canadian economy. In the past, significant numbers of Chileans, Salvadorans, Guatemalans, and to some extent, Nicaraguans entered Canada as refugees. They arrived as individuals or with relatives but not through a process based on or leading to chain migration.

For Latin Americans, and perhaps other groups with disproportionately high shares of recent immigrants, this has generated a context of reception that differs from that of the United States. Rather than having large, established, residentially concentrated conational and coethnic communities created in large part through chain migration and consisting of dense locality- or region-based networks, Latin Americans in Canada are more likely to be embedded in different configurations of social networks. They may be relatively isolated, as Nolin (2004) argues, part of smaller (non-extended) family units, and embedded not in place-of-origin networks but in social networks based on shared religious commitment, membership in political parties, union membership, sports, country of origin, or language (i.e., Spanish). That is, transnational village networks appear to be rare. Therefore, forms of Latin American immigrant organization that predominate in the US-based literature, such as hometown associations and their umbrella organizations, are less evident in Canada.

However, as indicated, other forms of community organization and associational life have developed, and some have been documented. Latin Americans in Canada have been and/or are involved in national-origin or pan–Latin American organizations, such as housing cooperatives (Allodi and Rojas 1988), sports clubs (Romero 1985), political parties, and cultural groups, including music and dance troupes. They have also been involved in various non-ethno-specific institutions such as solidarity, humanitarian, and religious organizations (Diaz 1999b; Kowalchuk 1999a, 1999b, 1999c).

Conclusion and Directions for Research
The dearth of research on the topic makes it difficult to provide a more extensive description or analysis of Latin American transnationalism in Canada since it is not possible to determine systematically whether certain forms of transnationalism do not exist in this country, exist on a small scale, or simply have not been analyzed. However, a comparison of Latin American migration patterns to Canada and the United States, together with a brief analysis of Canadian immigration policy, allowed me to suggest that one of the key differences between the two contexts of reception rests upon differences in the migration process and the kinds of social networks in which Latin Americans have been embedded upon arrival in Canada. These may have led to a narrower range of types of transnational engagements in the past, but this may change.

The extremely rapid increase in Latin American migration to Canada in the past ten years, the continued national-origin diversity of these movements, and the growing importance of Mexico as a source country have significant but unpredictable and perhaps geographically uneven implications for Latin American incorporation and transnationalism in Canada. The most obvious implication is that current practices, in whatever form, are very likely to change because growing concentrations of Latin Americans will transform the context of reception. Major urban areas, which are key settlement destinations for Latin Americans, may become more residentially concentrated. Even if this process does not take place rapidly, ethnic enterprises, whether transnational or not, are likely to continue to develop. There are already areas of Toronto with high concentrations of Latin Americans, which also have a number of businesses that offer Latin American products and services aimed at this population. Neighbourhoods in Toronto and other cities are becoming increasingly "Latinized." The market for home-country products will grow, as will the demand for other services consumed by migrants who maintain homeland identities and/or contact with their homelands. As a result, current types and forms of transnational involvement are likely to become more institutionalized and diverse.

Latin American transnationalism in Canada may be best characterized by Al-Ali and colleagues' (2001) phrase "emergent transnationalism," which they use in reference to situations where full-blown "transnational communities" appear to be in the process of developing but have not yet done so, such as among Eritreans and Bosnians in Europe. Whereas Chileans, Salvadorans, and Guatemalans were clearly engaged in transnational activities following the arrival of early refugee cohorts, this no longer appears to be the case with respect to these groups' political transnationalism. Still, further research is needed to assess the extent of various configurations of transnational engagement among these and other groups, particularly those with large shares of recent arrivals. In addition, it is possible that the consulates of some Latin American countries will make more of an effort to reach out to their diasporas in Canada, seeing them as relevant constituencies and sources of remittances, not simply as small populations whose political, economic, and numerical significance is dwarfed by that of their co-nationals in the United States. This may also shape the future course of Latin American transnationalism in Canada.

Future research on Latin Americans in Canada will clarify the relationship between incorporation and transnationalism in a context marked by selective immigration policies, changing refugee policies, and multiculturalism. To achieve this outcome, such research can pursue various objectives. First, it can clarify the demographic bases for transnationalism by gathering data on the geographic dispersal of families. Unfortunately, existing secondary data do not permit this (Bernhard, Goldring, and Landolt 2004). Second, it can examine the kinds of networks in which newcomers and more established Latin Americans are embedded, with particular attention to whether chain migration has developed and whether there is evidence of networks based on place of origin that go beyond the immediate family. This may allow researchers to investigate the relationship between village-based, political, or other networks and those without a homeland orientation. Third, the specificity of the Canadian context offers an opportunity to investigate more systematically the effects of government support for multiculturalism, the presence of refugee and refugee-like concentrations, and the work of active solidarity coalitions. Any of this research will have to deal with the challenge of working with an extremely diverse and sometimes divided population to whom the term "community" does not always apply (Recalde 2002).

Acknowledgments
I am grateful to Lloyd Wong and two anonymous readers for comments on earlier drafts of this chapter, which is informed by research taking place as part of a project funded by the Social Sciences and Humanities Research Council of Canada (SSHRC) on "International Migration in a Globalizing Era" (directed by Michael Lanphier). Three coinvestigators on this project (Patricia Landolt, Judith Bernhard, and Catharine Nolin) and I have formed the Latin American Research Group (LARG) as a subgroup. I am grateful for their comments and intellectual community. However, I am responsible for the chapter's contents.

Notes
1 In this chapter, I use the term "Latin American" in reference to people from Spanish-speaking Latin American and Caribbean countries as well as from Brazil.
2 Guarnizo, quoted in Levitt (2001a), uses the term "core transnationalism" to describe activities that are undertaken on a regular basis and that are an integral part of people's habitual life, and he uses the term "expanded transnationalism" to describe behaviour that migrants engage in only occasionally.
3 This pioneering study of political participation among Latin Americans in Toronto and Montreal (Armony, Barriga, and Shugurensky 2004) examines the relationship between pre- and postmigration political participation and civic engagement. The research focuses on the political integration of immigrants in Canada and thus pays more attention to activities oriented toward the host country and does not employ a transnational conceptual framework.
4 *The Encyclopedia of Canada's Peoples* (Magocsi 1999) contains entries on Chileans (Diaz 1999a), Salvadorans (Kowalchuk 1999c), Guatemalans (Kowalchuk 1999a), Ecuadoreans (Phillips 1999), Nicaraguans (Kowalchuk 1999b), and Mexicans (Goldring 1999).
5 Veronis (2002) argues against using a transnational approach to analyze Latin Americans in Canada because she found little evidence of contemporary transnational activity.
6 The Longitudinal Survey of Immigrants to Canada (LSIC) is being conducted jointly by Statistics Canada and Citizenship and Immigration Canada. It is a "comprehensive survey designed to study the process by which new immigrants adapt to Canadian society."
7 I am grateful to Lloyd Wong for facilitating access to the special tabulations and to Mary Decuypere of Statistics Canada for producing them. The special tabulations were produced for Latin Americans, not for a comprehensive set of source regions. Therefore, I cannot compare the responses of Latin Americans to those of other regional groups.
8 These percentages do not add up to 100 because respondents could check more than one category of people whom they wanted to sponsor.
9 See special tabulations of the LSIC data developed for Chapter 13 of this volume. Given Hiebert and Ley's (2003, 13) finding that 12.7 percent of East Asians reported sending remittances, the LSIC data appear to confirm these authors' finding that in Canada Latin Americans are more likely to send money than are East Asians.
10 The sampling frame was constructed using the 2001 Census's long-form responses (Statistics Canada 2003f).
11 The Canadian Census data reported here are from the Migration Policy Institute (2004a). They are also available from Statistics Canada.
12 This is also similar to Levitt and Glick Schiller's (2004) distinction between ways of *being* and ways of *belonging* in transnational social fields.

13 This excellent analysis, which became available after I completed the first version of this chapter, reinforces my arguments.

14 In the late 1970s a distinct admission class was implemented for refugees, separate from immigrant admissions (Simalchik 2004).

15 These include ENLACE, a group founded by Mexican women in Toronto to assist Mexican farmworkers, and Justicia for Migrant Workers (2005), a social-justice collective that advocates on behalf of migrant workers.

16 Research on Salvadorans is an exception to this statement (Coutin 1998; Hamilton and Chinchilla 2001).

17 Al-Ali and colleagues (2001) argue that relatively secure legal status among Eritreans in Europe facilitated their transnational activities, whereas the more ambiguous and insecure legal status of Bosnians made such engagements more difficult. However, in Canada, the cases of Nicaraguans (earlier refugees with limited transnational organizations) and contemporary Mexicans and Argentines (current refugee claimants with little evidence of transnational organization beyond the family level) suggest that the relationship between secure legal status for refugees and engagement in transnational solidarity is less than uniform.

11
The New "In-Between" Peoples: Southern-European Transnationalism
Luis L.M. Aguiar

In this chapter, I discuss how a transnational framework coheres with the contemporary experiences of Italians, Greeks, and Portuguese who immigrated to Canada largely between the end of the Second World War and the mid-1970s. Although the general focus is southern-European immigrants, I discuss in more detail the case of the Portuguese and transnationalism. My focus on this regional emigrant group is important since it is entering the second and third generation of immigrants in Canada. Ancestral amnesia has arguably come to characterize the consciousness of the children of immigrants, who now possess only a nostalgic curiosity about their parents' and grandparents' immigrant roots. In other words, transnationalism is sometimes understood as mainly a first-generation phenomenon that quickly fades once the first generation dies and subsequent generations are assimilated. This makes sense only if we see ethnic minorities in Canada as internally homogeneous. In this chapter, I argue that with respect to southern-European immigrants, transnationalism is regional, is often orchestrated from above, and extends beyond the first generation. At the same time, this chapter also notes that there are factors militating against the emergence of transnational identities and practices and that participation of southern-European immigrants in the political affairs of their respective homelands is far from an uncontested process.

Transnationalism
Capitalist globalization compresses space and time (Harvey 1989) through new technological innovations and techniques. These shorten the "turnover time between investment and the taking of profit" (Kearney 1995, 551). Thus barriers to the flow of both investment and ideology as well as to the accumulation of capital are shrunk. Furthermore, some places are "revalorized" while others are "devalorized" in an intense, competitive, global market pitting one place against another for the attention of capital invest-

ment. In the global economy, working classes are increasingly mobile and need to be "flexible" in order to meet capital demands, both on and off production sites. Workers are part of a global migration system that shifts people from place to place so that they can produce, service, serve, and consume in an increasingly interdependent global labour market (Moody 1997). Further, immigrants are no longer predominantly unskilled or semi-skilled white labourers for manufacturing industries but increasingly "racially" diverse men and women employed in the global North's high-tech industrial parks and in its engineering and telecommunications industries (Florida 2002; Hardt and Negri 2000; Iredale 2001; White and Hurdley 2003). Many suffer racism and downward mobility (Aguiar 2001) and thus end up performing tasks in care work, in paid domestic and janitorial work, and in the service sector more generally (Aguiar 2000; Bakan and Stasiulis 1997; Hondagneu-Sotelo 2001; Macdonald and Sirianni 1996).

But whereas capital has a footloose status due to malleable international borders and technological developments in communications and transportation, the mobility of the working classes across borders is still policed and controlled by new and ever-more-invasive technologies and corporeal state agencies and policies (Satzewich and Wong 2003; Wong 2002b).

Economic globalization is complemented by a hegemonic neoliberalism favouring free trade and social reengineering that imperils many populations across the globe (Bright 2003), forcing them to migrate in search of economic and social alternatives (Castles 2002). The shrinking of space through rapidly improving communications technologies has given rise to easier and more intimate relations between some immigrants and their countries of origin. It has facilitated immigrants' dual existence across nation-states. In some cases, these improved relationships are used to negotiate better working and living conditions in the society of immigration (Levitt 2001b; Wong 2000). But if labour-market vulnerability has been globalized to the extent that unprecedented numbers of people face an uncertain future (Bright 2003), so, too, has the understanding of "home" become precarious due to capital's shifting interests in the production of place (Harvey 1989). In this context of double uncertainty, some immigrants keep their options open by "continuously translat[ing] the economic and social position gained in one political setting into political social and economic capital in another" (Glick Schiller, Basch, and Szanton Blanc 1992, 12). Transnationalism, in this view, is a reflection of the conscious and unconscious strategies that migrants develop in order to place themselves in less insecure and disadvantageous positions regardless of where they may "settle." They achieve this not by severing links between places but by grounding these links in economic, cultural, and familial relations in an attempt to carve out their lives in dual contexts.

Scholars have "increasingly recognized that immigrants do not simply settle, [but] maintain important linkages with their places of origin" (Kelly 2003, 209). However, Madeleine Wong (2000) points out that because some of the research on transnationalism is gender-blind, it gives the impression that only men practise transnationalism. Some researchers have overlooked the translocal networks of immigrant women and have thus failed to recognize the critical role that these networks play in the lives of immigrant women who are socially and spacially marginalized in the country of settlement (Wong 2000). In her research on Ghanaian immigrant women in Toronto, Wong found that they maintained ties with Ghana *regardless* of when they emigrated. These ties are secured via telephone, remittances, presents, letters, and pictures. However, she points out that the maintenance of ties across borders has contradictory consequences: "on the one hand, the network represents one way for the women to resist the barriers they encounter in Canada. On the other hand, they are responsible for sustaining home and family across national boundaries, as they are expected to care for dependents and immediate and extended family members" (64). For women who are frequently the only members of their families to emigrate, the social, economic, and psychological burdens can be overwhelming. The geographic separation caused by competitive spatial expectations regarding women's responsibilities and obligations means that "the women are expected to meet the needs of those who live in Ghana and those who live in Canada" (64-65). As others have also described, this double burden can be exhausting. Hondagneu-Sotelo (2001, 25) shows how immigrant women from Central America enact "transnational motherhood" functions by raising the children of professional couples in Los Angeles while struggling to care for their own "back home." In this transnational role, Central American women "cope with stigma, guilt, and others' criticism." Wong's (2000) article is an important corrective to the literature on transnationalism not only because of the gendered critique she offers, but also, and as importantly, because of her suspicion that many writers glorify and romanticize experiences with transnationalism. Transnationalism, in the form of the *va-et-vient* (Campani 1992) of immigrants, can be exhausting for the mind and body. The romanticization of transgressing borders (Ilcan and Phillips 1998) becomes apparent as participants grow fatigued by its repetition and "schizophrenic disjunction" (Jameson 1992, 29).[1]

Southern-European Immigration to Canada
Many Italians (Iacovetta 1992; Painchaud and Poulin 1988; Wood 2002) and to a lesser extent Greeks (Chimbos 1999) and Portuguese (Anderson and Higgs 1976; Teixeira and Pereira da Rosa 2000b) had a presence in Canada prior to the Second World War. Italians migrated to Canada in large numbers in the early twentieth century "as seasonal workers in railways, mines

and construction, [and] after accumulating some cash, returned to Italy" (Iacovetta 1992, xix). Sojourning did not threaten Canadian "white" nation building, nor did it make demands on the state for citizenship rights already enjoyed by other immigrants. Later in the twentieth century this intermittent migration turned into a movement for permanent settlement, and migrants' desire to remain in Canada was aided by capital's need for labour to operate the expanding production system in an emerging post–Second World War regime of accumulation (Lipietz 1987). But this presence, even in the midst of the postwar social contract, was contested by the "biological eugenics" of Anglo-Saxon Canadian culture, which sought to restrict entry to Canada to those emigrants who originated from designated preferred "white" countries and who could "nation build" (Abu-Laban 2002, 271).

As a result, southern-European immigrants were discouraged from entering during the interwar period on the basis of their "unassimilability" to Canadian culture and society. Not only was their "backward" culture suspect in a modernizing Canadian economy and society, but their not-quite-white skins were also a source for discrimination (Frye 1998; Troper 2003, 24). In the 1940s and 1950s capital regularly relied on the help of the state to import immigrant labour, warning that failure to do so threatened the developing postwar economic boom. Capital's attitude, however, was economically selfish rather than "racially enlightened," as was evident in its preference for assigning immigrants to the least desirable and most dangerous jobs in the Canadian economy. In doing so, capital legitimized the discourses of ethnics' "natural" abilities for specific jobs and relegated them to the labour market. Waldinger and Lichter (2003, 8) tell us, "In a racialized society like the United States, entire ethnic groups are ranked according to sets of socially meaningful but arbitrary traits; these rankings determine fitness for broad categories of jobs." In Canada, Ottawa pursued its racialized practices by seeking to attract immigrants from the North of Italy because they were "Germanic-like" and thus fit the preferred model for Canada (Iacovetta 1992; Troper 2003, 32). Italians from elsewhere were said to be "swarthy," unclean, and thus undesirable (Iacovetta 1992). Despite concerns about whether they would be suitable raw material for Canadian citizenship, today "nearly 60% of all Italian immigrants [in] Canada" are from southern farming regions of Abruzzi, Molise, Basilicata, Campagnia, Puglia, Calabria, and Sicily (xxii). Similarly, the Portuguese were racialized and called "greasers" and "pork-chops" with all that these epithets imply "racially" and hygienically (Aguiar 2001; Alves 1997).

This hegemonic biological eugenics lasted into the 1960s. Between 1954 and 1967 only 5 percent of immigrants to Canada were from Asia and Africa (Li 1996, 103). White British women were welcomed as the "future mothers of the nation," but the temporary work status of women of colour was the government's way of imposing severe restrictions on their abilities to stay and reproduce biologically (Abu-Laban and Gabriel 2003; Calliste and Dei 2000). Troper (2003, 31) writes that a "racial leavening" and a "whitening" of Euro-ethnics took form in the early postwar years "spurred on by a repudiation of eugenically based notions of racial boundaries and by public revulsion at the excesses of Nazi racism."[2] Since 1967 "Canada's immigration policy has become officially nondiscriminatory *in terms of* race and ethnicity, as potential immigrants are mainly assessed on how their educational and professional skills may contribute to Canada's labour market" (Abu-Laban 2002, 271, emphasis added). Consequently, southern Europeans find themselves "in between" the biological eugenics of earlier immigration policy and the "social eugenics" of the point-system regime of immigrant-selection criteria. The latter encourages, promotes, and selects middle- and upper-class immigrants with capital (and, to a lesser extent, language skills) that they can invest in Canada as well as such immigrants who possess entrepreneurial experience that they can draw on in mentoring Canada-based businesses.

The government's practice of social eugenics is evident in its tightened policy regarding access to the country via sponsorship and family-reunification routes. Concerned about ensuring the "quality" of the immigrants who enter the country by means of this "self-selecting" immigrant option, the government has over the years put in place measures to restrict the use of sponsorship and family-reunification programs. During the early postwar years, these were the two ways that most southern-European immigrants arrived in Canada (Chimbos 1999, 617; Teixeira 1999). Murdie and Teixeira (2003, 147) note Iacovetta's estimate that family members sponsored "more than 90 per cent of post-war Italian immigrants in Toronto." Thus, by tightening "back-door" entry to Canada, the federal policy sought to curtail the entry of less skilled southern-European immigrants while at the same time developing an "entrepreneurial frame" that sought "designer immigrants" (Simmons 1999, 53). Simmons writes that the reduction in the number of family-reunification and sponsorship numbers is evidence of the government's elimination of "certain categories of automatic admission," including family members over twenty-one years of age, "even if they have never been married." In addition, there has been a reduction in the "number of points an applicant can accumulate through sponsorship from relatives in Canada" (61). Where family sponsorship is possible, the government requires affidavits indicating one's ability to take care of sponsored immigrants, a feature introduced only recently with the ascendance of neoliberalism in the Canadian state.

During the 1960s and 1970s, southern-European immigrants adopted the now-familiar strategy of chain migration. Because network chains functioned not only among family members and acquaintances, but also among townsfolk more generally, in some cases entire communities were brought out of stark poverty to "the land of milk and honey." Consider Franca Iacovetta's (1992) description of the Izzos and their immigration to Canada. In 1950 Giuseppe received a contract with a Quebec farmer and emigrated thanks to an uncle who was already in Canada. In 1952 he sent for his wife and two sons under the Canadian sponsorship program. By 1953 the family had been reunited. What happened next is instructive of the pattern and practice of many southern-European immigrants. As Iacovetta describes it, "over the next few years, the couple [Giuseppe and Angela] sponsored twenty relatives. As each of the families, in turn, sponsored more kin, the Izzos were ultimately responsible for the arrival of more than forty Italians, all of whom hailed from the same cluster of towns in the southern Molisan province of Campobasso" (20). As this case suggests, immigration may result in the complete displacement of entire communities and family members to another place. It also implies that once communities settled in Canada, few individuals were left behind with whom to maintain contact. In this context, one must raise the question of whether transnational connections are mediated, in this first instance, by family connections.

Campani (1992) points out that communities retain contacts with their place of origin, but this is contingent on spatial differences between communities of settlement. She compares Italian immigrants to France and Quebec and, like Iacovetta, points out that "entire villages left and settled down in another country" (188) via networks of chain migration between the sending and the receiving countries. But how are these networks maintained across generations once chain migration has ceased (190)? In the case of migration to France, Italians maintained and nurtured associations with their villages of origin by embedding kinship in the local society's system of relations and by forming alliances within local communities via relationships such as godparentage. Moreover, holidaying and regular visits to the place of origin nurtured the networks, as did the expressed desire of some "to be buried there" (191). The Italian experience in Quebec is quite different. "Even if the distances have been 'shortened' thanks to air transportation and to the lower fares, trips both ways are not as frequent [as those of Italians in France], properties have often been sold, and holidays are usually spent in Canada" (191). Campani does not attribute this difference to spatial (France and Italy) or cultural (Latin and Catholic) proximity between the two countries. She argues that to emphasize "distance" would mean overlooking "distances" within the Mediterranean region and inside each country – for example, between the North and the South of Italy (194-95). Furthermore, arguments about cultural similarities between the two groups can have racial overtones that posit some people as culturally similar and others (e.g., Muslims) always as outsiders and "unassimilable" (194-95). Instead, Campani explains the difference between the two groups of

Italians in terms of the longevity and strength as well as the maintenance and reproduction of social networks.

By comparison, Harney (1998) argues that Italian identity in Toronto is constantly "remade and reproduced" and that transnationalism and the globalization of culture, including Italian culture, is an important feature of this process. For him, "air travel, electronic media, telephones, video and audio cassettes, multiple citizenships, and a mobile employment market serve to enhance connections and diminish distances between people in the same Diaspora" (6). In addition, Italian television stations, satellite trans-missions, football clubs, and cultural icons link Italians in Canada with events, people, and processes in Italy. Nonetheless, Harney points out that there is "an ambiguity" in the Italian Canadian identity insofar as the "emer-gence of subethnicities" leads many to identify first with their region of origin (e.g., Calabreze, Abruzze, or Veneti) and only second with the Italian nation (50).

New immigration from Portugal to Canada has virtually ceased. Between 1996 and 2001 just 2,875 Portuguese arrived in Canada. The numbers are just as low for Italians (2,595) and Greeks (1,085) for the same period (Gov-ernment of Canada 2001b).

In addition, the Portuguese find themselves in an increasingly difficult economic position as a result of economic restructuring and deindustrial-ization (Giles and Preston 1996; Preston and Giles 1997). Those with jobs are enmeshed in a climate of eroding industrial citizenship because the re-structuring of labour relations by the provincial and federal states denies unionization opportunities for many and encourages decertification for others. This precariousness has the ideological intent of disciplining work-ers – Portuguese included – to accept poor working conditions, poor wages, and reliance on employers' paternalism in the new "peer pressure" labour-relations system being proposed by, for example, the minister of labour in British Columbia (Aguiar 2004). It is not surprising that the Portuguese in Canadian society are overrepresented in some class categories (e.g., by 18.4 percent in the proletarian category), but underrepresented in all others: semi-autonomous workers, managers and supervisors, petty bourgeoisie, and employers (Liodakis 2002, 93). In his investigation of the "vertical mosaic" within ethnic groups in Canada, Liodakis shows that the Portuguese "ex-hibit the most proletarianized class structure among the Southern Euro-pean groups" (93). He concludes that the respondents of Portuguese origin are overrepresented in the proletariat category and underrepresented in every other class *irrespective* of gender and/or nativity dimensions. Portuguese Canadians are distinctive when compared to other southern-European groups (Greeks and Italians), even though they share the same general dates of arrival in Canada and have about the same percentage of native-born (112). According to Liodakis, Portuguese Canadian class disadvantage is more in line with that of "visible" minority groups in Canada. Thus Filipinos are the most proletarianized group in Canada, at 74.9%, with the Portuguese a close second, at 74.7%. By comparison, 69.9% of Caribbean Canadians, 63.8% of South Asians, 58.4% of Italians, and 56.1% of Greeks are proletarianized (112, Table 3.36). In another survey, Mata (2002) reports that the Portuguese are among the groups least satisfied with life in Canada. Given their position in the Canadian class structure, one must ask how transnationalism can contribute to ameliorating the lives of Portuguese right here in Canada. This question has become increasingly relevant in light of research showing that the middle classes engage in transnational practices (Guarnizo, Portes, and Haller 2003) rather than the socially marginalized and those who face discrimination (Foner 2001c).

Transnationalism and Southern-European Immigrants
The above discussion points to some key themes that need to be recognized in relation to transnationalism's applicability to southern-European immigrants. First, there is no longer a significant wave of southern-European immigrants coming to Canada. Immigration has dwindled to the point that replenishing communities and strengthening their links to countries of origin cannot happen through the arrival of new members (Kelly 2003). Second, whole communities and towns left countries of origin during the chain migration of the postwar period, mostly through family reunification and sponsorship. Thus, even if southern-European immigrants wanted to establish links, no one remains in their home countries with whom they could correspond. Third, given changes in Canadian immigration policy that tightened the family-reunification route and prevented further southern-European immigration, southern Europeans are slowly being distanced even further from their countries of origin. Finally, the poor socio-economic location of this group and the effects of capitalist restructuring on its communities, particularly the Portuguese, raise questions about what transnationalism means, if anything, in this context. What does transnationalism mean to southern Europeans in light of rapid transformations in Canadian society and the Canadian economy, and what does it mean given that the bulk of new immigrants now come from Asia, the Caribbean, and Latin America? How should we interpret the "in-betweeness" of southern-European immigrants? In the limited literature on southern-European immigrants in Canada, some of these questions are addressed. However, some require more research and will hopefully set the agenda for future work.

Thus far, distinctions have been made between Portuguese, Greek (discussed less), and Italian experiences of migration. It is important to understand that there are also many distinctions within these broad groups (Campani 1992; Cole 1998; Harney 1998; Labelle et al. 1987). These distinctions must be recognized since they highlight the different collectivities within groups and allow us to better investigate who, within a particular immigrant group, exhibits transnational practices.

For example, Sally Cole (1998) identifies three groups of Portuguese constituting different communities in southwestern Ontario. Her investigation of the Portuguese in Wheatly, Leamington, and Kingsville reveals three regional groups with different relations both to each other and to their country of origin. The groups are Nazarenos, from the region of Nazare in central Portugal; Trasmontanos, from the northern part of the country; and Acorianos, from the islands of the Azores. She describes tensions between the groups and quotes an Acoriano's comments about Nazarenos: "'The women are domineering. The men are drunkards. We Azoreans would rather have nothing to do with the nazarenes'" (86). Her description of a union drive exposes the class composition of the Nazarenos and the conflict between members of the bourgeoisie who own fishing boats and their fishers from the same Nazare community. The relevance of Cole's work lies in what she says about how each of the groups has positioned itself vis-à-vis transnational links with Portugal. Cole writes, "Acorianos return rarely, if at all, to Portugal. They are committed to building their futures in Canada, serve on the local town council, and intermarry with members of other ethnic groups in the area including Italians and Anglo-Canadians" (82). They are, therefore, culturally assimilated. But "unlike acorianos, who are firmly committed to a future in Canada, and nazarenos, who plan to return permanently to Portugal, trasmontanos build retirement homes in Portugal with the intent of living part of the year there and part of the year in Canada" (83). Part of the explanation lies in the fact that, historically, Azoreans have characterized their homeland as a source of poverty, neglect, and restrictive social roles for women. Her assessment of the Azoreans as indifferent to the "old" country is applicable to most Azoreans in Canada (Teixeira 1999). This is significant since the large majority of Portuguese in Canada either come from the Azores or are descendants of Azoreans. In Toronto – where the largest community of Portuguese can be found – 70 percent of immigrants come from the Azores (Carey 1999).

Cole (1998, 83-84) also argues that the overwhelming majority of those who return to Portugal are from the mainland. In the case of returnees, Klimt's (1989, 49) argument about the Portuguese in Germany (who are rarely Acorianos) applies. She writes that the Portuguese immigrant in Germany tries to balance "temporariness" in the land of residence with a discourse of "permanence" in a future return to Portugal. But among those who return, reintegration into the community in the country of origin is often not easy and not welcomed (Brettell 1982). Therefore, different groups of Portuguese articulate different discourses about their "grounding" in the society of residence as well as about their transnational links with the country of origin. At best, one can say that a transnational regionalism has some validity in the case of the Portuguese (and Italians) in Canada.

Of course, this does not mean that no transnational links have emerged as a result of the history of these three southern-European groups of migrants to Canada. Even when entire families and towns have moved to Canada, it is not clear that connections have been irreparably severed (Harney 1998). In the case of the Portuguese, particularly among those of Azorean origin, transnationalism does exist, although it appears to be increasingly orchestrated from above. Giles (2002, 113) explains why the Portuguese federal state is so interested in developing and maintaining these links. The state's emigration frameworks seek to encourage "emigrants to remain elsewhere, in order to remit needed infusions of foreign capital [and to] ensur[e] émigrés continued allegiance and ties to Portugal in order to secure the endurance of these remittances." With migrants' annual transfers of remittances to their countries of origin now approaching $75 billion worldwide (Vertovec 1999, 452), it is easy to see why immigrants' "national" governments are eager to solidify links across diasporas. The regional autonomous government of the Azores has created a number of cross-border activities, from summer courses for students in the islands to conferences and workshops with business personalities and academics in order to build bridges with Azorean communities in Canada, the United States, and Brazil. Several years ago the regional autonomous government created a program called A Descoberta de Raizes (In Search of Roots). This program seeks to bring educators and community leaders to the Azores from abroad so that they can learn about the history, culture, and recent developments in the political economy of the archipelago. Although the number of participants varies from year to year, on average thirty to forty people are flown to the Azores each year at the government's expense (100,000 euros in the summer of 2002) to partake in this transnationalism from above (Mahler 1998). Implicitly, the program assumes that "roots" have been lost since people are selected to come to the islands so that they can rediscover themselves and their backgrounds.

This is a laudable initiative. However, its reach into the Azorean diaspora is limited. For example, all participants must speak Portuguese. This excludes many from the second and third generations in Canada and the United States who have no Portuguese language skills or who speak too poorly to communicate comfortably and effectively. Therefore, most participants are middle-class, middle-aged, first-generation immigrants with long ties to the homeland. Moreover, many Azoreans are not aware that such a program exists. This is not because information is lacking but because there has been little effort to make the project's availability widely known. As a result, the information circulates among a select group of community leaders who often are the same people who enrol in the program. During my participation in this program in 2002, the majority of community personnel were teachers, many of whom were making their second or and even third trip under the program! This program has tremendous potential to teach cultural history as well as to establish links between widely dispersed Azorean diasporic communities. However, initiatives need to be undertaken in order to avoid making this program overly teacher-dependent and so restrictive that "sao sempre os mesmos, os elites da comunidade" (it's always the same people, the elites of the community) who take advantage (Carlos Teixeira, personal communication).

In reviewing the various approaches to transnationalism, Vertovec (1999, 454) writes that transnationalism is often discussed as a "site of political engagement." By this, he means that migrant communities have presented new political issues that must be addressed in terms of transnationalism because they are beyond the "national frames" of conventional politics (454). It is not always clear, however, what sort of issues these might be, although Vertovec points out the examples of political parties establishing offices abroad to be closer to immigrants as well as of immigrants lobbying home governments for support of their causes.

The explicit nature of this lobby has not yet surfaced with respect to Azoreans in Canada. For example, in 2001 the president of the Azores, Carlos Cesar, visited several Azorean communities across Canada for the first time, celebrating and dining with their members while assuring them that they were integral to the the Azorean "identity," the so-called Acorianidade. In addition, the president met with Prime Minister Jean Chrétien as well as with provincial government leaders or their representatives. The goal of these meetings was to make the Azorean communities visible within a Canadian political culture absent of Portuguese politicians (Black and Lakhani 1997). In this regard, a sense *of* the community was presented to members of the Canadian political system, and some of the community's grievances were presumably highlighted. Missing, however, was a political agenda anchored in a sense *for* the community. Such an agenda would outline the poor economic location of the community and articulate the political steps necessary to begin to address the most appropriate and efficient ways of dealing with the challenges and barriers that Azoreans endure in Canadian society. If the Azorean government does in fact have a dynamic agenda for the Portuguese in the Canadian political scene, it is difficult to recognize (Aguiar 2002). Finally, one cannot disregard that much of this campaigning is a display, or a politics of image, for the voters back home (Fitzgerald 2004).

Levitt and de la Dehesa (2003, 588) use the case of Ireland as an example of a state that maintains contact and links with immigrants in order to "encourage emigrants' continued sense of membership in and loyalty to the sending state." They write that Ireland is "decoupling residence and membership and extending [its] boundaries to those living outside [its] borders" (588). Through the creation of economic, political, and social opportunities for the Irish diaspora, distance to the "homeland" has been rendered a nonissue. Portugal, Greece (Chimbos 1999), and Italy (Allemang 2003) have also extended electoral participation to their members abroad, although in the case of Portugal, only since 2001 have such members been granted the right to vote for the president of the country. It is estimated that approximately 4 million Portuguese reside outside Portugal (Medeiros 2004). In terms of national elections to the General Assembly, Portuguese immigrants in Europe are allowed three representatives, while those in the rest of the world (except for South Africa) have two. However, this modest representation may be inadequate because political parties in Portugal often appoint who will run and potentially represent immigrants, meaning that politicians elected for this purpose are often not immigrants themselves and not residents of the diaspora but residents of Portugal. More important is the lack of participation in the general and presidential elections of Portugal by Portuguese transnationals. According to the Government of Portugal (31 December 2003), participation in general elections has been granted to Portuguese living outside the country since 1975, although with some limitations. To participate, Portuguese must first get on the voting list, which can be done through the Portuguese consulate. In the general election of 1999, 9,648 registered but only 2,361 (24.6%) voted. This is seemingly quite low for a community of 350,000 to 375,000 in Canada (Teixeira and Pereira da Rosa 2000a, 7). Only in 2001 were Portuguese abroad allowed to vote for the election of the president of the country. Here again the participation rate was quite low: across Canada 8,754 registered but only 957 actually voted (10.9%), and in Montreal 721 registered but only 80 (11.1%) cast ballots. Significant here is the identification of reasons for the lack of interest in participating in elections "back home." In a telephone interview, the editor of the Portuguese community newspaper in Montreal, *Lusopresse*, indicated that discussions are under way in the Azorean Legislature regarding granting the right to vote in regional elections to those Azoreans living outside the islands. One stumbling block is that the Left parties are reluctant to support such a move, as they claim that the immigrant vote is a conservative one. But as noted above, the participation rate is so low that it is difficult to believe that the Azorean vote from abroad would have an impact on the political landscape of the islands.[3]

This participation in the elections of the country of origin is not unique to the Portuguese. Last year the Italian Parliament decided to award three seats to Italians living in Canada.[4] This was part of an overhaul that created eighteen seats for Italians living outside the country. And though candidates are working hard for an election that at the time of writing is still years away, representatives of the Italian community in Toronto question its usefulness. Toronto Liberal member of Parliament Joe Volpe says that someone campaigning in Canada for a seat in the Italian Parliament could create problems (Allemang 2003, M5). Tony Carella from the National Congress of Italian Canadians is even more categorical: "'We don't believe any of these people [candidates] have a right to say that they represent the community. For the first generation who came here for a better life, one of the things they miss least is Italian politics. And as for the second and the third generation, no one cares'" (M5). While this may be the dominant position within the Italian community, some argue that participation in the election will mean ridding themselves of the "paternalistic approach" that Italy has consistently displayed in its relations with compatriots abroad (M5). It is clear that while there is intent to link across borders, not everyone who moves and settles abroad buys into such efforts.

Conclusion
One of the challenges in writing about transnationalism among southern Europeans in Canada is that there is so little literature to examine. This is particularly the case with the Portuguese in Canada, given the paucity of research regarding either their Canadian experiences or their connections across the Atlantic (Noivo 1997, 4-5). There is, then, a need for research that examines the transnational links, opportunities, and challenges within and between southern-European immigrant groups. However, as the discussion in this chapter shows, links are particular, rather than general, within each of the groups. That is, transnationalism is practised within limited segments of these communities. In addition, states are playing an increasingly prominent role in establishing and maintaining transnational ties (Giles 2002), especially in the case of the Portuguese from the Azores, although Acorianos participation remains limited. This is not to say that further development is not taking place. Rather, the transnational practices of southern-European Canadians may increase as the forces of globalization, geographical effacements, and extended identities circulate within Canada. It is also the case that some within these communities have always been transnational, such as some businesspeople, community liaisons, cultural workers, and community journalists. But in general transnational practices are not common among the large majority of Italians, Greeks, and Portuguese. At the same time, however, links with the country of origin have remained, and attempts are being made to establish new ones.

Several aspects of transnationalism and southern-European immigration that are not discussed in this chapter need to be the subject of more research. First, we need to know about the functioning (or not) of grass-roots transnational links. Who is participating in such links in and across groups, and what forms are these links taking? Second, there is a need to investigate the transnational activities of the second, third, and fourth generations of southern-European immigrants. The same questions apply here as those regarding grass-roots links but without ignoring gender in the process of investigation. Third, what is the purpose of transnationalism, particularly cross-border politics, and what opportunities does it offer communities in the countries of settlement? In the case of the Portuguese, their socio-economic position remains among the lowest in the class structure of Canada. What has transnationalism done to remedy this depressing state? Can transnationalism be a vehicle by which the Portuguese improve their opportunities within the Canadian class structure? Arguably, transnationalism should provide another vehicle for Portuguese Canadian economic militancy. Engagement in Canadian politics should be coordinated with other ethnic-minority communities in order to define issues broadly and inclusively rather than narrowly and in divisive ways. To this end, we must ask what role might be played by a transnational approach linking countries of origin and communities in the country of settlement. Focusing on these areas of concern will go a long way toward strengthening the validity and credibility of transnationalism as a framework for our times as well as toward ensuring a relevant role for communities in the political scene.

Notes

1 Thanks to Paty Tomic and Ricardo Trumper, who are examples of transmigrants, for this point.
2 Elsewhere, I have argued that the Portuguese remain nonwhite in contemporary Canada (Aguiar 2001; see also Noivo 1997, 59).
3 Telephone conversation with Norberto Aguiar, editor of the Portuguese newspaper *Lusopresse* in Montreal, 1 January 2004.
4 However, according to Professor Nick Liodakis (e-mail, 16 November 2004), Greeks outside of Greece cannot vote in national elections; nor does the National Assembly reserve seats for the representation of Greeks abroad. This contradicts information contained in Chimbos (1999). Unfortunately, a lack of time has prevented me from pursuing this issue further.

12
Whose Transnationalism? Canada, "Clash of Civilizations" Discourse, and Arab and Muslim Canadians
Sedef Arat-Koc

In this chapter, I look at Arab and Muslim communities in Canada as communities under siege. The reality of siege has implications for the ability of individuals and groups not only to safely *cross* borders, but also to live in safety and as equal citizens *within* borders. The specific context in which the chapter is being written necessitates that we pose a set of critical questions about *what* gets to be studied as transnationalism and *how*, as well as about what does and *does not* get to be asked and about *whom*. In the environments of racism, anti-immigration, and anti-multiculturalism that prevail in many Western states today, the transnational identities of many ethnic minorities get discussed as a way to interrogate and question their "loyalties" to the nation-state in which they are living. In the political environment that has prevailed since the terrorist attacks of 11 September 2001 in New York and Washington, DC, identities and loyalties of Arabs and Muslims are especially suspect. What are rarely, if ever, interrogated in this context are the "loyalties" as well as the various material transnational connections – economic, cultural, political, and even military – of dominant groups and of the state.

Since the 1990s in Canada, but more specifically since 11 September 2001, we have been in a period of retreat from multiculturalism and a politics of inclusion. During this period racism has not only intensified, but also, and more important, been legitimated through public discourse and mainstream institutions. Precisely at this historical moment, it may be useful, as Enakshi Dua has suggested, to ask "what it means to recodify immigrants and some ethnic and racialized groups as 'transnationals'" as well as to question "whether the concept itself does not contribute to the *dis*location of immigrants from the nation in new ways."[1] There is a danger that the commonly used term "transnational" will be applied almost exclusively to racialized groups in order once again to question their belonging and even their loyalty. Only since the 1960s in Canada, after long struggles by people of colour, has the concept of "Canadian nation" started to include the histories and present experiences of the many peoples that make up this nation. Only recently have "immigrants" – a term used almost exclusively to refer to racialized minorities – become part of the concept of the nation. However, this inclusion has been of a very fragile and tentative nature. The conceptualization – and isolation – of immigrants and most racialized groups as transnational subjects makes their inclusion even more fragile. Their membership in the nation can be more readily questioned and even their deportation more easily legitimated because it may appear to be ethically unproblematic.[2]

Since 11 September 2001 we have witnessed a renewal of nationalism in Canada. This nationalism is of a transnational kind, a white nationalism confirming *some* Canadians' place in "Western civilization." In Canada, Europe, and the United States this reconfigured notion of the nation, based on a "clash of civilizations" perspective (Huntington 1996), effectively serves to exlude those of Arab and Muslim background from Western nations and Western civilization altogether.

As we contemplate the nature and significance of transnationalism, we must not naively approach or celebrate it as a free movement of people around the world. As Ong (1999, 15) has pointed out, it is essential to remember that the state's continuing role is "to define, discipline, control, and regulate all kinds of populations, whether in movement or in residence." Since 11 September 2001 states obsessed with national security have increased and intensified such disciplinary and regulatory roles. In addition, there has also been a reconfiguration of regulatory regimes at the transnational level through cooperation on "antiterror" legislation, intelligence, and border control.

In Sassen's (1996) frequently cited words, economic globalization is "*denationaliz(ing)* national economies," whereas immigration is "*renationalizing* politics" (59, emphasis added). If borders were already important as conceived by "Fortress Europe" and "Fortress North America" when Sassen wrote these words, they have gained more significance since 11 September 2001 in an increasingly securitized world.

For the vast majority of people, borders were already far less permeable than optimistic theoreticians of transnationalism might have assumed. They are even less permeable today. We are living at a time when the transnational ties of Arabs and Muslims – whether social, familial, financial, political, or involved in shaping a general sense of identity – are perceived as suspect, if not directly criminalized. While the transnational ties of some groups may be increasing, those of Arabs and Muslims are subject to intense forms of surveillance.

There are empirical as well as ethical difficulties inherent in doing research in communities under siege. Rather than keeping "the gaze" on the diasporic Arab and Muslim "community" in the period since 11 September

2001, this chapter returns "the gaze" and raises questions about the often unscrutinized and unnamed dominant transnationalisms in Canada, transnationalisms that are not just reconfiguring Canadian national identity and its boundaries, but also changing "national" institutions, such as borders, immigration, justice, and the military. I start the chapter with a description of the siege that has gripped Arabs and Muslim Canadians since the attacks on New York and Washington, DC, and the effects of this siege on their identities and transnational connections. I then focus on the nature of the dominant transnationalisms that create and reproduce the siege. I end with a discussion of "alternative transnationalisms" – that is, trans-ethnic and non-ethnic solidarities that are developing to challenge the current national and transnational order.

The category "Arab and Muslim" is problematic because it often does not recognize the complexity and the heterogeneity of the categories "Arab" and "Muslim" but conflates the two. As Suad Joseph (1999) argues, representations of Arabs, Muslims, and Middle Easterners are underpinned by multiple conflations. Even though the categories sometimes overlap, the conflated category makes the diversity of Arabs invisible. Arabs are not just Muslims, but also Christians and Jews. In popular representations in Western countries, "Arab" may be used to include other ethnic groups, such as Turks, Armenians, Persians, or Roma – groups with different languages and ethnic or national backgrounds who do not identify as Arab. Conflations overlook that the category "Muslim" encompasses many ethno-cultural and linguistic groups, the majority of whom are neither Arab nor Middle Easterner but Indonesian, Malaysian, Filipino, Sudanese, Indian, or Chinese. Joseph argues that in the American context, the inaccurate conflations *erase* difference in order to "serve the *creation* of another difference: the difference between the free, white, male American citizen and this constructed Arab" (260, emphasis in the original).

However, despite the inaccuracy of the conflations and their racist connotations, I make references to the category "Arabs and Muslims." As the category has become "real" socially and politically, I do so in making references to specific racialization. Discourses on "Arabs and Muslims" have become "real" in the subjection of a category of people to specific forms of racialization and *political* designation in North America. The category, which has been politicized by Palestinian resistance to Israeli occupation since 1967, gained special significance in the 1990s during and after the Gulf War and in the post–Cold War political discourses in search of a new enemy of "the West" or globalizing capitalism. Since 11 September 2001 the category, as a concept of racialization, has been raised to the status of "common sense" in depictions of "the enemy," resulting in attacks on many non-Arab and non-Muslim people, often of South Asian background, who are thought to "look like Muslims."

Transnationalism and Identity for Arab and Muslim Canadians

The heterogeneity and complexity of the categories "Arab" and "Muslim" – separately and conflated – suggest that it is impossible to form a simple set of assumptions about a type of identity among Arabs and Muslims. There are further complications in conceptualizing the identity of Arabs and Muslims in Canada because the already existing diversity in people's backgrounds is multiplied by different experiences and adaptations to living in the diaspora. The current climate of intensified racialization and vilification also yields different types of responses from people and different ways of *being* Arab and Muslim in Canada.

Different authors have articulated why it is analytically essential to use a transnational perspective in studying immigrants. Spivak (2000, 354) points out the shortcomings of "focusing on the migrant as an effectively historyless object of intellectual and political activism." She argues that one cannot simply treat the postcolonial migrant as a "blank slate," pretending that he or she can be analyzed simply using a class-gender-race calculus that begins and ends in the First World metropolis. While I agree with Spivak that the migrant is not a blank slate, I also think that it is important to conceptualize the history and connectedness of the migrant in non-essentialist ways. When Ong and Nonini (1997a, 327) argue that identities are "constituted through transnational systems," they also offer an approach to identity "as a politics rather than as an inheritance ... as fluidity rather than fixity, as based in mobility rather than locality, and as the playing out of these oppositions across the world."

For the majority of people, racialization, rather than a common national or religious identity, provides the basis for identification and organizing. As one Muslim has stated: "For me, my whole life is now demarcated by 9/11. It is now pre-9/11 and post-9/11 ... The attacks were a break with our past as Muslims. Sept. 11, 2001 is not a defining moment in the history of North American Muslims but *the* defining moment" (quoted in Safieddin 2003, B2, emphasis in the original).

As W.E.B. Du Bois (cited in Winant 1997) brilliantly argues, race operates both to assign and to deny people their identities. Hours after the horrific events of 11 September 2001, Arab and Muslim Canadians found themselves racialized in new ways. No longer considered just "exotic" subjects or bearers of irrational traditional cultures, they were now "the enemy." The words of a New York lawyer summarize how many Arab and Muslim Canadians felt: "Before last week, I had thought of myself as a lawyer, a feminist, a wife, a sister, a friend, a woman on the street. Now I begin to see myself as a brown woman who bears a vague resemblance to the images of terrorists we see on television ... As I become identified as someone outside the New York community, I feel myself losing the power to define myself" (quoted in Deaux 2001).

In an environment where Islam became loaded with political connotations, people of a Muslim background who had never seen religion as a central part of their identity suddenly found others imposing this identity on them:

> For me, Islam was not a factor in structuring my identity at an early age. My parents were both secularists. I wasn't brought up according to Islamic tradition ...
>
> Sept. 11, 2001 all of a sudden changed that. People started to identify me as a Muslim. They would ask: You are from the Middle East, are you Muslim?
>
> For a while, it was incredibly confusing. It was not a question that I could answer simply. It needed a lot of qualification that people did not have the patience for ...
>
> It was as if I woke up one day to find that a special type of a Muslim identity was imposed on me. (Quoted in Safieddin 2003, B3)

Racialization is not a recent phenomenon for Arab and Muslim Canadians. In certain periods, such as during the Gulf War, they experienced an intensification of the white gaze and criminalization of their communities as the "enemy within." There were several prevailing racist discourses in Canada prior to 11 September 2001 – some used for Arabs and Muslims and some not. These discourses frame immigrants or people of colour as "taking advantage of Canada," as "bogus refugees," and as "welfare cheats." According to Thobani (2004b), after 11 September 2001 discourse on security became *the* racist discourse. Since security is an issue that concerns everyone, it makes the new racist discourse an especially powerful one.

What has been new for Arab and Muslim Canadians since 11 September 2001 is not the experience of racism but its growing public legitimacy, spread, and mainstreaming in all major institutions, from the media to law and policy. Overt acts of violence and expressions of hatred in civil society in the aftermath of 11 September 2001 were soon followed by government "security" measures that not only justify, but also further fuel, racialization and a suspicion of most Arab and Muslim Canadians. Once considered an illegitimate practice, racial profiling has not only become de facto policy, but also gained significant popular legitimacy. A recent survey by Ekos Research Associates revealed that, at 48 percent, close to half of Canadians find it acceptable that "security officials give special attention to individuals of Arabic origin" (Alghabra 2003, A24).

Although negative and politically loaded portrayals of Arabs and Muslims in the media are by no means new or rare, this racialized group has been defined as the "enemy within" since 11 September 2001. George Jonas of the *National Post,* for example, fanned the flames of hatred that were rapidly spreading when he argued that "not all the terrorist caves are in

Afghanistan ... some are in Quebec and Ontario" (quoted in Kutty and Yousuf 2002, A13). The view that Arabs and Muslims belong to a radically different civilization – or perhaps even to a different species! – with a very different set of values than those of "Canadians" has become the basis for news stories and commentaries. In the media – in contrast to white Canadians' portrayal of themselves as rational, civilized, liberal, democratic, and peaceful – depictions of Muslims and Arabs as "extreme, vengeful, irrational, suicidal and fanatical people pathologically predisposed to violence with an incorrigible mindset" (Alghabra 2003, A24) have become regular fare.

Immediately following 11 September 2001 there were countless cases of harassment, intimidation, and violence directed at Arabs, Muslims, and those who were thought to "look like Muslims." Arson at mosques and Sikh temples was accompanied by physical and verbal attacks or by dirty looks directed at Muslims, Arabs, Sikhs, and Hindus. Darker people and those with visible signs of religion or ethnicity – such as women wearing the hijab – bore the brunt of attacks. The Canadian Islamic Congress advised Muslims to stay home from school and to take measures to avoid harassment. It also urged Muslims to avoid crowded areas "where a mob mentality may develop" (Small and DeMara 2001, A2). Perhaps even more disturbing than the actual harassment, intimidation, and violence that took place was that many people who experienced these assaults were so distressed and so insecure about their place in Canada that they did not report them to the police (Raja Khouri, national president of Canadian Arab Federation, personal interview).

Also, Muslim and Arab Canadians faced a number of pressures that differed from blatant attacks on their physical safety. Some business owners and corporate employees were pressured to change their Arab names to more non-Arab or "Anglo-sounding" names (Jamal 2002, 46; Khouri, personal interview). In one case, a business owner decided not to personally conduct the more public aspects of his business and instead sent a "white Canadian" to meet with his clients (Jamal 2002, 46).

Although some political leaders made political statements appealing to "Canadians" – a category that did not seem to include "Arab and Muslim Canadians" – to stop the violence and harassment, they seemed to give double and conflicting messages, as they themselves were participating in a discourse of clashing civilizations and moving rapidly toward legitimization of racism through institutionalization of racial profiling and new anti-terrorism, immigration, and border policies.

A recent survey conducted by the Canadian Arab Federation (2002) in the Arab Canadian community paints an unsettling picture of where Arabs see themselves in the larger Canadian society. According to the survey, 41.3% of the respondents believe that Canadians "don't like Muslims," and 84% believe that Canadians think Muslims and Arabs are violent (17). Although these responses are subjective, they clearly raise questions about Arabs' and

Muslims' sense of reception and belonging in Canada. The respondents to the survey almost unanimously agreed that "in general Canadians know very little about Arab culture" and that "what Canadians know about Arab culture stems from negative stereotypes and myths" (17). Thirty-eight percent of the respondents said that they are made uncomfortable by the way that white Canadians look at them, and almost half said that they encounter racism in daily interactions (18).

For 28.1% of respondents, perceptions of racism in the media and experiences of racism in schools and workplaces were accompanied by identification of institutional racism as a problem.[3] The examples that they gave included detentions following 11 September 2001 and interrogations by the Canadian Security and Intelligence Service (CSIS), the introduction of Bill C-36 (the antiterrorism bill), the Immigration Department, and employment in the public sector (Canadian Arab Federation 2002, 18). Nearly three-quarters of the respondents, at 73.9%, strongly or somewhat disagreed with the statement that "the Canadian government is concerned with what Canadian Arabs want from it." The level of dissatisfaction both with the federal government and with foreign policy was particularly high (21).

These responses are especially ironic when juxtaposed with the responses that Arab immigrants gave about why they chose Canada as their immigration destination: 71.9% of the respondents said that it was for Canada's human rights and freedoms, and 51.5% said that it was for its multiculturalism (Canadian Arab Federation 2002, 13). Given the expectations of Arab and Muslim immigrants in Canada, it is not surprising that the intensification of racialization and demonization following 11 September 2001 was a shock to them: "Anxiety, fear, alienation, marginalization, betrayal and disillusionment: This is how Sept. 11, 2001 and its aftermath have left Arab and Muslim Canadians feeling – indeed reeling" (Khouri 2003).

The implications of the racialization and victimization of Arabs and Muslims are very serious not just for members of the communities, but also for the larger society. Reflecting on these implications for Canadian multiculturalism, the current national president of the Canadian Arab Federation, Raja Khouri, is grim:

> Our country has effectively engaged in an exercise of self-mutilation: stripping away civil liberties it holds dear, trampling on citizens' rights it had foresworn to protect, and tearing away at its multicultural fabric with recklessness.
>
> Arab Canadians are today convinced that there is a bigger threat to our way of life from the security agenda than there is from terrorism itself.
>
> The question that remains is: Given that multiculturalism is premised on the equal treatment and respect of all citizens, will multiculturalism survive the security agenda? (Khouri 2003)

Recent research shows that even though children of Arab Canadians born in Canada were "Americanized ... their Arab identity has been raised as a result of [the] events" of 11 September 2001 (Jamal 2002, 47). I suggest that for Arabs and Muslims in the diaspora, the environment during this period has created a specific *positionality* but not necessarily an *identity* with specific outcomes. This positionality is created in an environment of intensified racism that, partly due to the commonly used "clash of civilizations" discourse, posits every Arab and Muslim as guilty by association, thereby increasing Arabs' and Muslims' sense of exclusion from mainstream notions of what/who constitutes "Canada." The "clash of civilizations" discourse and logic constructs a monolithic conception of both "the West" and some of the communities that live within it. The implications of such monolithic conceptions and of the notion of a naturalized, inevitable "clash" are catastrophic for some diasporic communities who suddenly find themselves outside the borders of what is conceived of as "the West."

Despite the potent role that intensified racialization and exclusion have played in the development of a sense of "we" – forcefully and/or voluntarily – among Arab and Muslim Canadians, this community's racialized positionality has not automatically translated into an identity. Rather, this positionality has given rise to the formation of different identities.

For some, a process of intense racialization has led to identification with others of the same ethnic or religious background with whom one might not have had much in common before: "Prior to 9/11, I never identified with women who wear the veil ... But all of a sudden, I take the public transportation in the week following the attacks, and the driver allows me in but closes the door in the face of a veiled woman waiting at the bus stop. This happened a number of times. At a certain point I started thinking it could have been my cousin or a member of my family, some of whom cover their hair with a scarf" (quoted in Safieddin 2003, B3).

For others, the connotations of the category "Arab and Muslim" were too painful to lead to identification with their racialized coethnics. Some Arabs interviewed by Jamal (2002, 49) regrettably observed that "misunderstanding of [their] culture and prevalent stereotypes have led to a confused Arab identity. Fear has led to people suppressing their Arab identity." Instead of self-identifying as Arab or Muslim, some – especially those whose social class, appearance, accent, or level of assimilation enables them to "pass" as non-Arabs/non-Muslims – have attempted to distance themselves from ethnic identity and community. Some Christian Arabs have tried to distance themselves from their vilified Muslim coethnics – for example, by wearing large, visible crosses to emphasize non-Muslim identity (Khouri, personal interview). As one of Jamal's (2002, 49) interviewees notes, "some ... retract and retrench from society while others throw away their Arab culture and become fully 'Canadian' by changing their names, habits, and values to the extreme – and neither is happy."

Although some Arabs and Muslims have continued to nurture multiple identities and multiple connections to different communities, for others intensified racialization and othering has led to a rigidness and defensiveness regarding essential identities. Those who are religious Muslims have found themselves especially isolated. Demonization of their religion has been particularly painful, as religion has long been a central part of their identities.

Many Muslims in the diaspora, especially refugee survivors of fundamentalist regimes, find themselves in a bind. Although they are inclined to continue to articulate a critique of fundamentalism, they also find themselves under a new type of attack based on racism and Islamophobia in Canadian society (Tahmasebi 2004). One response to this dilemma has been to emphasize the universal in condemning all forms of hatred and violence. As one Muslim has explained, "what became clearer to me post-Sept. 11 is that everyone should be against hatred, whatever it is, if it is happening from the pulpit or from the government or from ordinary people on the street" (quoted in Safieddin 2003, B2).

The environment of suspicion in which Arab and Muslim Canadians have found themselves since 11 September 2001 has served to create a climate of intimidation and fear. Several members of Arab and Muslim communities have made references to internment in describing what this environment has felt like: "Ghettoization since 9/11 became clear. In reality we could have been physically interned. Instead we have been interned by fear – psychological internment" (quoted in Jamal 2002, 48).

Intimidation has led to different responses by individuals in Arab and Muslim Canadian communities. For some, intimidation has resulted in depoliticization. They have found security in the image of the "good Muslim" and "good immigrant," which has come to be defined in this context as someone who makes generalized negative statements – approaching racism – about Islam and Arabs, gives unconditional support to everything the Canadian government does, and is forever grateful to Canada.

Despite the environment of vilification and intimidation, many Canadian Muslims and Arabs have felt compelled to express their disagreement with the war in Afghanistan, in which Canada continues to participate. Jehad Aliweiwi, the executive director of the Canadian Arab Federation, has observed an intense scrutiny of the loyalties, actions, and beliefs of Arab and Muslim Canadians since 11 September 2001, which he regards as amounting to "a new form of internment." He describes the costs of dissent for people from communities already suspected of disloyalty: "We're perceived as the enemy and as responsible collectively ... And now, we're seen as guilty because we don't support the bombings. It's a frightening position to be in" (quoted in Mitchell 2001).

Despite the intimidation, some people consider it their duty as Canadian citizens to express what they see as the truth, even if doing so is risky. As Mohamed Elmasry, the president of the Canadian Islamic Congress, states: "Some people feel it may be time to have a low profile and just support the government, no matter what ... Others feel it is their duty to be a good citizen and voice their opinion" (quoted in Mitchell 2001).

Transnationalism of Communities under Siege

Discussing the translocal or transnational character of Islam, we come across wide discrepancies between representation and reality. On the one hand, both the media and much of the academic literature are saturated with claims about the cultural uniqueness of Islam as a relatively static, reactionary, and violent religion. On the other hand, there is the reality of a very complex and diverse "Muslim world" that occasions a multiplicity of interpretations and expressions of what it means to be Muslim. Heterogeneous in its local forms, Islam becomes even more diverse as it "travels." As Mandaville (2001) argues in his research on transnational Muslim politics, Islam is no more or less fixed, monolithic, or fluid in its transnational forms than are its religious or cultural counterparts. Even though Mandaville limits his analysis to "individuals whose self-descriptions and identities ... involve ... Islam as a key ... component," thus excluding those of a "Muslim background" who do not share this component (111), he still finds Islam to be widely plural in its historical and spatial practices as well as variable and changing as it moves into new locations in the diaspora.

In discussing the transnationalism of diasporic subjects, we must recognize class differences in the amount of freedom and mobility that distinct transnational subjects enjoy (Ong 1999). It is also important not to exaggerate the deterritorialization of the state and to recognize the monopoly that states enjoy over the exercise of legitimate force within their borders. Depending on their class, race, and political status, binational subjects "may be doubly empowered or doubly subordinated, depending on historically-specific local circumstances" (Guarnizo and Smith 1998, 9).

For many ethnic groups, transnational affiliations cannot be interpreted as voluntary and politically neutral results of globalization and travel. They need to be seen in their political contexts, which are sometimes hostile owing to racism, exclusion, discrimination, and even criminalization. In an environment of racism, isolation, and exclusion supported by hostile, or at least insensitive, foreign policy toward the peoples in the lands of origin, transnational identifications with the "homeland," or with people of shared ethnic or religious background, seem to be of significance for Arabs and Muslims. Writing about the British context, Kabbani (2002) states: "We still read our old countries' papers. We were ravaged by news from Bosnia, Iraq, Kashmir or Palestine and increasingly infuriated by Britain's hostile policies on these matters of grave import to 2 million of its citizens. The umbilical cord with home had not been cut and there was no soothing local midwife to help."

In the American context, Cainkar (2002, 26) mentions that since the Gulf War in 1991, exclusion of Arabs from American civil society and government has led Arabs toward "transnational affiliations, rather than the affiliations sought by minorities able to participate in democracy." As a result, there has been "a major shift in identification, affiliation and behaviour ... among a significant proportion of Arab Muslims ... Their primary affiliation changed from secular to religious."

When we talk about transnationalism, it is useful to distinguish between transnational identification and practical transnational ties. Although the "civic exclusion, political voicelessness and popular denigration" of Arabs in the United States have pushed them toward transnational affiliations, Cainkar (2002, 26) predicts that "these homeland ties – return travel, family visits, foreign students, family reunification, remittances and charitable donations – are likely to drop significantly due to changes in policies, the social climate and Arab-American fears after September 11." Even though we have no corroborating or quantifiable data, spokespersons for Canadian Arabs and Muslims observe a decline in practical transnationalism in their communities due to the intimidation that intense surveillance creates over return travel, charitable donations, and even remittances (Khouri, personal interview).

Limitations to travel occur not just at the individual level, but sometimes on a larger scale. Just before Air Canada was about to launch direct flights between Montreal and Beirut in the summer of 2003 – a route that the airline had thought would be popular and profitable – it learned that the Canadian Transportation Agency had cancelled the flights. Arab Canadians interpreted the decision as one imposed by the United States. They also saw it as sending yet another message about Arabs as dangerous and violent (Jamal 2003).

Transnationalism is not just restricted to connections between the home country and the new home. Since 11 September 2001 many Arab and Muslim Canadians have also found that their travels to the United States include intense questioning and harassment at the border. This is something that affects not only people's ties with family and relatives in the United States, but potentially also their employment security. As one Arab Canadian notes, "I am worried that these new measures adopted by the American authorities are going to create a new culture in corporate Canada. A lot of Arab-Canadians cross the border frequently ... Once corporate Canada begins to realize that Arab-Canadians create a hassle for them when they cross the border, next time they hire somebody who needs to be traveling to the U.S., inadvertently or not, they may prefer to hire a non-Arab" (quoted in Safieddin 2003, B1).

Dominant Transnationalisms: Transnational Identity of the Canadian State and "Ordinary Canadians"

> It is a banal fact of contemporary existence that economic forces, communication systems, military interventions, and ecological disasters continually transcend nation-state boundaries, yet state authorities remain deeply suspicious of all international movements, loyalties, and relationships they cannot regulate.
>
> – Asad 1993, 266

There is an irony in the political discourses that have dominated the mainstream since 11 September 2001. Although there has been an inflation in nationalist discourses that interrogate the belonging and loyalties of suspect "ethnics," mainstream "Canadian identity" is more than ever defined in transnational terms and specifically in relation to the United States. The disproportionate focus in the literature on the transnationalism of – often racialized – minorities is misguided. This focus tends to ignore or make invisible the transnationalism of the dominant racial/ethnic groups as well as the transnationalism of the state. The latter has become particularly important in Canada since 11 September 2001, as Canada's already close ties with the United States – in terms of investment, trade, culture, tourism, and so on – have not only solidified, but also reconfigured and redefined, a number of other areas, such as national identity and the harmonization and integration of military policy, security legislation, and immigration and border controls. In the next section, I start by focusing on the redefinition and reconfiguration of Canadian identity as denoting one's belonging in "the West." These changes in Canadian identity, which are constantly fed and refuelled by mainstream media, play a significant role in making possible the racialization and othering of Arab and Muslim Canadians. More important, they continue to legitimize institutional racism.

"Canadian Identity" as "Western" Identity

Even though both President George W. Bush in the United States and former prime minister Jean Chrétien in Canada declared that Islam was not the enemy, the mainstream media in both countries continued to write as though it were. In specifically targeting Arabs and Muslims not just externally, but also in the diaspora, security policies in both countries also strengthened the idea that this image corresponded to reality. The entire discursive framing of the attacks of 11 September 2001 was based on the notion of a "clash of civilizations." After the attacks on New York and Washington, DC, Samuel Huntington's book with this phrase in its title was praised as visionary, ingenious, and brilliant. Five years after its publication in 1996, it rose to the bestseller list. Its thesis was taken up wholeheartedly by the media and came to be used as the common-sense explanation for what had happened.

With the conclusion of the Cold War at the end of the 1980s, some American intellectuals deeply embedded with the state started actively redrawing maps of international conflict and identifying who the new enemy would be in the new world order being created. The concept of a "clash of civilizations" was first introduced by Bernard Lewis to explain what he saw as the conflict between political Islam and "the West" (Lewis 1990). It was then taken up by Samuel Huntington – a long-time Cold War warrior – who initially used the term with a question mark in the title of a 1993 article. Huntington expanded the concept into a universal thesis on the state of the world after the end of the Cold War. In the title of his 1996 book, Huntington got rid of the question mark and suggested that the world was now divided along *civilizational* lines – as opposed to the ideological ones of the Cold War – based on ethnic, cultural, and religious differences. Defining eight major civilizations in the world today – "Western, Confucian, Japanese, Islamic, Hindu, Slavic-Orthodox, Latin American, and 'possibly African'" – Huntington (1996, 128) highlighted the increased significance of ethnic identifications in the post–Cold War world and expressed his expectation that the most serious threats to "the West" would come from the "Islamic" and Chinese civilizations. Huntington articulated the nature of civilizational conflict in this new era in military and potentially catastrophic terms: "In a world where culture counts, the platoons are tribes and ethnic groups, the regiments are nations, and the armies are civilizations."

Huntington's book has been criticized from a number of angles. He uses a very monolithic conception of culture and "civilization identity" that ignores their diversity, internal contradictions, and historical variability. He conceptualizes cultures and civilizations as sealed-off, isolated entities whose historical relationship to each other consists of wars and conflict rather than exchange, interaction, and cross-fertilization. This perspective on cultures denies the significance of a shared history between cultures, even ignoring the recent interconnections through colonization, imperialism, and globalization. Huntington's simplified and monolithic perspective on cultures leads to an exaggeration, absolutization, and mystification of cultural differences. Exaggeration of cultural differences implies that – at least some – cultural differences are irreconcilable, leading Huntington to naturalize conflict (Arat-Koc 2002b).

It is interesting to observe how rapidly the notion of civilizational clash became the dominant framework in which political leaders and the media interpreted developments leading up to and following 11 September 2001.

Columnists in mainstream media made constant references to how "they" – used in a very slippery way to refer sometimes to the terrorists and sometimes to the culture to which they belonged – hated "our" freedoms, democracy, human rights, and women's rights. The article "Why Do They Hate Us So Much?" by *Globe and Mail* columnist Margaret Wente (2001, A13) represents a discourse that was – and continues to be – very common in the media. Wente rejects any reflection on "root causes" stemming from a history of the relations between countries. Opting instead for the essentialism of the cultural-clash perspective, she writes – with the confidence of those who think they speak common sense – that "we" in "the West" have "a culture of peace," while "theirs" is "a culture of violence." Referring to suicide bombers, she declares: "The poison that runs through the veins of the suicide bombers does not come from America. It comes from their culture, not ours. The root causes are in their history, not ours." By the end of October 2001, some columnists were predicting that the war in Afghanistan would only be an "opening battle" in a long war that would "spread and engulf a number of countries in conflicts of varying intensity." They declared that this war would "resemble the clash of civilizations everyone had hoped to avoid" (Kristol and Kagan, quoted in Alam 2003).

The Canadian media played a very significant role in creating an imaginary conception not just of the nation, but also of transnational alliances (Thobani 2002). As the "clash of civilizations" thesis began to be employed daily to define "us" and "them," the definition of "Canada" and Canadian identity rapidly evolved into a transnational one emphasizing Canada's and its citizens' place in "the Western civilization" (Arat-Koc 2002a, 2003; Thobani 2002, 2004a). Of importance here is that this notion of "the West" excluded not only other civilizations, but also the histories and cultures of "non-Western" diasporas living in "the West." Thus the redefinition of Canadian identity as part of "the West" implied a rewhitening of Canadian identity after decades of multiculturalism. In Canada, given its geography and its history, belonging to "the West" also came to mean strongly identifying with the United States in particular. The repeated statement "we are all Americans now" represented not just an expression of temporary solidarity with an apparently victimized, terrorized neighbour, but also an identification with a white, imperial power.

The new borders of Canadian identity were so rigidly drawn that in the immediate aftermath of 11 September 2001, there was no tolerance among the new "ordinary Canadians" for dissent against strong identification and unquestioning cooperation with the United States. In this environment, Sunera Thobani, the former president of the National Action Committee on the Status of Women, was demonized for remarking that the United States, through its foreign policy, has blood on its hands and that we need to be able to extend the same sympathy shown for the victims of the terrorist attacks of 11 September 2001 to victims of American aggression in many different parts of the world. Not even some "mainstream Canadians" were spared questions about their degree of belonging given this newly defined national identity. A letter to the editor, for example, called Alexa McDonough, then the leader of the New Democratic Party, "un-Canadian" for her opposition to Canada's participation in the war in Afghanistan (Lafond 2001, A25).

Institutionalization of "Western" Identity

> If some "ethnics" were showing the sort of loyalty to another
> country as Canadian right-wingers are to the United States, they
> would have been branded traitors to Canada.
>
> – Siddiqui 2003, F1

A significant number of Canada's business, political, and media elites have been pushing hard since 11 September 2001 for an integration of Canada's military, borders, and policies with those of the United States. These elites, who have played an active role in redefining Canadian identity in transnational terms, are also actively pursuing a materialization of this new identity in the form of concrete institutions.[4] Even though I refer to the constitution and institutionalization of this identity as "transnational," it is important to recognize that this is not a transnationalism of equal partners but one based on an agenda defined specifically by the United States and on a union in which Canada is erased. This is a reality that even the proponents of this integration recognize: "Our condition of virtual sovereignty is like that of all the member states of the European Union. With one difference. The political construct that is developing here isn't a comparable North American union. It's just an American union" (Gwyn 2001b, A13).

The discourses used to justify the desire for integration with the United States often conflate business interests and concerns about "security" (Canadian Council of Chief Executives 2004). State discourses explaining new forms of integration with the United States also accept and naturalize this conflation by speaking about trade and security in one breath. For example, the Smart Border Declaration, signed by Canada and the United States on 12 December 2001, states:

> The terrorist actions of September 11 were an attack on our common commitment to democracy, rule of law and a free and open economy. They highlighted a threat to our public and economic security ...
>   Public security and economic security are mutually reinforcing. By working together to develop a zone of confidence against terrorist activity, we

create a unique opportunity to build a smart border for the 21st century; a border that securely facilitates the free flow of people and commerce; a border that reflects the largest trading relationship in the world. (Government of Canada 2002)

Military Alliance or Integration?
Just a few days after 11 September 2001, columnists in the mainstream Canadian media started presenting – or rather advocating – a fatalistic picture of Canada's "inevitable" integration with the United States:

On the anti-terrorist war ... it goes without saying that the U.S. will take for granted our full political and diplomatic support, as well as, of course, military and intelligence. We will have to operate on the assumption that the U.S. will simply not accept, and at best angrily reject, any criticisms we might make about its excessive use of force or about actions it engages in that cause "collateral damage" to innocent bystanders.

At least for the time being, and probably for some time to come, those terrorists have fused the U.S. and Canada together. (Gwyn 2001a, A1, A10)

When Canada first committed its troops to the war in Afghanistan, they went under the operational control of the United States Army. Even though Canada did not directly participate in the subsequent invasion of Iraq, the Canadian Navy went to the Gulf early in the Iraq War to provide "protection" for the United States Army.

The nature of Canada's transnational military cooperation has serious implications for the citizenship and belonging of Arab and Muslim Canadians. In his discussion of Australia's participation in the Gulf War and the implications of this for Arab Australians, Hage (2002a, 2) elaborates on the meaning of *belonging*. In emphasizing the need to go beyond a rights-based conception of citizenship, he introduces the concept of *honourability*: "belonging is not about citizenship as rights but about citizenship as 'holding your head high.'" Reflecting on the rapidity of the decision of the Australian government to participate in the Gulf War, Hage suggests that in today's world, where most nations are multicultural in their composition, making war does not fit the model of distinct ethno-national states, as "it is very hard to have an enemy that is totally 'not us.'" As he notes, "because there will always be cultural groups of citizens who will be personally in a state of trauma as a result of a decision to go to war, the government of a multicultural country ought to always 'pause' and 'reflect' a bit more than others before going to war" (10). Hage argues that the heritage of a multicultural nation extends beyond the national territory and therefore involves recognizing the worthiness of a migrant culture beyond the borders of the nation-state (11-12).

Antiterrorism Legislation

In the days and weeks following 11 September 2001, Canada was under immense pressure from the United States to develop tough new legislation and policies demonstrating that it was doing all it could in the "war against terrorism." One of the significant developments came in the form of Bill C-36, the antiterrorism bill, which was hastily passed even though it posed major challenges to basic civil liberties.

Although the proponents of the bill argued that it was "necessary" in this time of crisis, the bill was not a response to a national crisis or tragedy. In fact, as Audrey Macklin (2001, 399) ironically recalls, Canada had experienced the deadliest terrorist attack in aviation history prior to 11 September 2001: the Air India tragedy of 1985, in which a bomb placed on board flight 182 departing Toronto en route to London, England, exploded off the coast of Ireland, killing all those onboard, almost all of whom were Canadian citizens and permanent residents. Yet Canada never treated this attack as "a fundamental assault on our nation, our values, our people." Proponents of Bill C-36 did not demonstrate that Canada in particular was under an imminent terrorist threat. Rather, complete identification with the United States and with the logic of "civilizational clash," which had become germane to the newly articulated Canadian identity, made people accept as "common sense" that Canada, as part of "the West," was a potential target. Even the fact sheet that the Department of Justice produced on the proposed bill failed to make nationally specific arguments about the necessity or the constitutionality of the bill. The fact sheet was titled "Canada's Proposed Anti-Terrorism Act: *Working with Our International Partners*" (Government of Canada 2001a, emphasis added).

During the very short time in which the bill was proposed and passed, critics insisted – unsuccessfully – that "Canada must reflect on its specific needs and legal structure" and that it should move with "caution and calm deliberation" (Canadian Arab Federation 2001). According to Amina Sherazee (2004), Bill C-36 was the most controversial legislation in the history of Canada, yet it passed in less than a month. Even legislators who voted for the bill were surprised to learn of its implications from the newspapers after the bill had passed.

Bill C-36 uses a very broad definition of "terrorism," endangering a number of basic rights and liberties guaranteed by the Canadian Charter of Rights and Freedoms, such as freedom of expression, freedom of association, the right to be secure against unreasonable search and seizure, the right not to be arbitrarily detained or imprisoned, and the right to a fair trial. At the same time, however, it uses a very selective definition of "terrorism." Antiterrorism legislations are framed in civilizational and racialized terms. Although the definition can be interpreted to include civil disobedience or even boycotting products, it explicitly excludes state terrorism (Sherazee 2004). The simultaneous broadness of the definition, on the one hand, and its selectiveness, on the other, have led many people to question exactly *what* and *who* the legislation targets.

Although the effectiveness of the legislation is questionable, one of its unquestionable consequences has been the intimidation and silencing of critical and oppositional voices. Bill C-36 gives local police forces, the Royal Canadian Mounted Police (RCMP), and CSIS new powers to increase surveillance of persons, suppression of protests, monitoring of e-mail and listservs, and spying on protestors and political activists during rallies, meetings, and conferences (Sherazee 2002). One of the most significant implications of this legislation has been "criminalization of dissent," "the creation of a climate in which even those who are not specifically targeted are still affected and are either silenced or silence themselves" (20).

Another aspect of the legislation is that it criminalizes transnational fundraising or humanitarian aid for organizations or groups that are or may be included on a list of designated terrorists. Some groups have argued that creating such a list is inherently discriminatory, as such "blacklisting" is always open to the government's "discretion to determine, depending on its own changing foreign policy needs, which groups are legitimate and which are not" (Canadian Arab Federation 2001).

There is widespread belief among Arab and Muslim Canadians that Bill C-36, despite its universal language, specifically targets their communities. In particular, Bill C-36 gives extraordinary discretion to police and to immigration officers. In a period of intensified racialization and demonization of Arab, Muslim, and South Asian Canadians, it is not surprising that they are the people being targeted for "random checks" or treated as suspect by law enforcement and intelligence agencies (Canadian Race Relations Foundation n.d.; Macklin 2001, 395).

Even though Bill C-36 and similar measures are generally defended as "a small inconvenience" or "a small price to pay in exchange for security," people in targeted communities are questioning who is inconvenienced and who is paying the price for "security." Many Arab and Muslim Canadians believe that there would have been widespread opposition to the bill and that it would not have passed if it did not target specific communities (Jamal 2002, 48). Given the history in Canada of targeting specific communities in the interest of ensuring an abstract "security" of "Canadians" in general (see, for example, Chapter 3 in this volume on Japanese Canadian transnationals), Audrey Macklin (2001) cautions about the implications of this bill: "while many look to the criminal law to protect us from the enemy within, I urge us to attend to the law's role in *producing* the alien within" (398, emphasis added).

Transnationalization of Justice or Transnationalization of Torture?
As demonstrated by the well-publicized case of Maher Arar, a Canadian citizen of Syrian origin, it appears that in situations when the Canadian intelligence agencies find the task of preparing a case against suspected terrorists under the antiterrorism legislation cumbersome, they may be downloading the work of detention and questioning to foreign governments. In what some are calling "torture by proxy" (Kutty 2004), Canadian intelligence agencies are accused of passing erroneous information about Arar to American authorities, who in turn are accused of Arar's removal to Syria, where he was tortured. In a more recent case, another Canadian citizen, Dr. Khawaja, has argued that he was detained – but not tortured – by Saudi authorities at the request of Canadians. Dr. Khawaja also asserts that the Canadian authorities asked his interrogators to ensure that he would not be able to contact the Canadian consulate in Riyadh (Kutty 2004).

The Arar and Khawaja cases have received some attention in the media, as both men are Canadian citizens. As Wright argues (2003, 2004), much less known and less controversial are the cases of noncitizens, including those with no legal status in Canada. So far, there are at least five known cases of noncitizens detained indefinitely without charge on security certificates. As they are held on the grounds of secret evidence, their lawyers have no access to the evidence against them and therefore no effective way to prepare a defence. There is also the case of more than twenty young Pakistani and Indian nationals arrested in August 2003 under Project Thread. Even though there has been no case for charges, they were detained until most were deported.[5] The question some ask in these cases is, "If there is evidence then why not charge, arrest and prosecute them in Canada to the full extent of the law?" (Kutty 2004). Macklin (2001, 397) may have the answer: when Bill C-36 was introduced, she predicted that criminal prosecution under the antiterrorism law would be difficult, leading her to conclude that in those cases involving noncitizens, the state would use its powers under Bill C-36 to investigate individuals but then issue security certificates under the Immigration and Refugee Protection Act, as it would be "easier to deport than to imprison" suspects.

These and other similar cases reveal a disturbing new form of transnationalization in the treatment of suspected terrorists by Canada. This may be part of a new global pattern of human-rights violations led by the United States. It includes offshore prisons, cross-border arrests that verge on kidnappings, and the rendition of terror suspects to countries where they face torture.

Transnationalization of Immigration and Border Issues
Within just weeks of 11 September 2001, the Canadian government moved toward harmonizing immigration and border issues with the United States

and toward creating a "security parameter" that would encompass both countries when, on 12 December 2001, the Canadian foreign minister and the American director of Homeland Security signed the Smart Border Declaration.

The security perimeter was clearly dictated and defined by the United States, and its proponents were aware of its implications for Canadian sovereignty. However, this did not prevent "a coterie of Canadian media commentators and right-wing politicians [from] tripp[ing] over each other in the rush to blame Canada's allegedly lax refugee policies for September 11 in particular and global terrorism in general" (Macklin 2001, 388). Some openly acknowledged the sovereignty issue yet defended the security perimeter as "inevitable" and as the only significant contribution that Canada – given its perceived weak military capacity – could make to the "war on terrorism": "The Chretien government's decision this week to adopt a common North American perimeter – U.S. standards applying everywhere, that's to say – for security and intelligence, for immigration and for our refugee systems represents one of the most significant abandonments of our sovereignty in our history. Abandonment is the wrong term. Accepting the inevitable would be the right way to put it ... A common North American security perimeter is the single substantial contribution we can make to the war against terrorism" (Gwyn 2001b, A13).

As mentioned, the notion of a "smart border" is based on a conflation of "security" and business concerns. The declaration outlines a thirty-point action plan to "secure" flows of people and goods. It establishes "border cooperation" in a number of areas, including immigration, crime and security, and transportation and customs. The plans involve reviewing and working toward harmonizing several policies and procedures, such as refugee/asylum processing, visa policy, the issuing of identity cards for permanent residents, the development of joint immigration databases, border policing, and the standards for biometrics to be used on identity cards.[6]

Sharryn Aiken (2001b, A17) argues that a "security perimeter" would "give primacy to the unfettered movement of goods and investment capital" but lead to a situation where "the border intrudes into everyday life of all non-citizens and the periphery is mapped by high fences in the name of safeguarding those on the inside from dangerous foreigners." Aiken draws analogies between policies today and harmonization of policies with the United States regarding treatment of Japanese Canadians after the attacks on Pearl Harbor: "An inclination to get closer to America in this time of crisis merely exposes Canadians to greater risk. We will come to regret reflexive policy responses, just as we did, eventually, our wartime policies in the wake of Pearl Harbor."

The move toward creating a North American perimeter is based on the notion that immigrants and refugees are the problem. It is not an accident that the introduction of a discourse of a "common security parameter" coincided with the hasty passage of the Immigration and Refugee Protection Act, which is likewise based on the assumption that immigrants and refugees are security threats.

Alternative Transnationalisms? Transethnic and Non-Ethnic Identifications and Solidarity

> We are not lumps of clay, and what is important is not what people make of us but what we ourselves make of what they have made of us.
>
> – Jean-Paul Sartre, *Saint Genêt*

In a world that is increasingly multicultural and transnational, for the state and dominant ethno-cultural groups to approach diversity in terms of a "clash of civilizations" – à la Huntington (1996) – would have catastrophic consequences. Such an approach could, in the least, be used to justify deportations, exclusion, and criminalization and could potentially lead all the way to an all-out holocaust to exterminate those identified as the civilizational "others." In this section, I argue that though such apocalyptic possibilities are not inconceivable, there have been significant developments in Canada and abroad of a positive kind that constitute a resistance and challenge to the dominant transnationalisms mentioned in the previous section. I suggest that the kind of transnational, transethnic, and non-ethnic bonds of solidarity established in response to a climate of war, hatred, and racism promise to subvert the logic of a "clash of civilizations" discourse.

In the past decade, several important concepts have been developed to deal with the complexity of identities produced in the context of transnationality. Two of these concepts are hybridity and diaspora. However, even though these concepts represent important attempts to complicate and de-essentialize identity, they do not go far enough, as they continue to privilege "culture" as the central element of identity and community (Anthias 2001, 2002). Specifically, the concept of diaspora privileges a notion of "origin" and thus "fails to pay adequate attention to *transethnic, rather than transnational, processes*" (Anthias 2002, 37, emphasis added). Moreover, I would add, it fails to account for *non-ethnic* processes in making sense of the new identities that emerge.

While an atmosphere of racism, and specifically a discourse of "clash of civilizations," attempts to fix racial, religious, national, and civilizational identities, a politics of solidarity – organized around principles of antiracism, anticolonialism, anti-imperialism, peace, or civil rights – has the potential to counter this fixing of identities, leading to the emergence of new democratic subjects.

In a world that has been shaped by "clash of civilizations" discourse since 11 September 2001, there are enormous pressures not just on minorities, but also on the dominant ethnic group, to adopt a fundamentalism of identities. As Ella Shohat (2002, 469) succinctly puts it, "war is the friend of binarisms, leaving little place for complex identities." Thus there is a danger that the widespread acceptance of "clash of civilizations" discourse by "ordinary Canadians" and its internalization by isolated and alienated Arab and Muslim Canadians can turn the discourse into a self-fulfilling prophecy by creating mutual distrust and mutual isolation. The tendency now of some "ordinary Canadians" to see their neighbours with suspicion and fear has been accompanied by a great sense of disappointment and betrayal among Arab and Muslim Canadians who previously enjoyed a sense of belonging based on the professed Canadian ideals of multiculturalism and democracy:

> Our failure as a society in this regard was in not sending a clear signal to the contrary – society did not come to the aid of this maligned minority ... by and large, Arab and Muslim Canadians were left on their own, having to explain themselves and prove their loyalty; defend their religion and demonstrate its goodness; and at times hide their ethnicity and deny their heritage in a bid to escape scrutiny.
>
> The effect on our communities is that, like our Japanese-Canadian counterparts during World War II, we, too, have become victims of psychological internment. In the meantime, our mainstream institutions, including governments, simply looked the other way. (Khouri 2003)

However, despite the sense of disappointment and betrayal in the community, there have been unprecedented levels of mobilization among Arab and Muslim Canadians. According to Raja Khouri (personal interview) of the Canadian Arab Federation, marginalization has forced some people in the community to become more politicized and, ironically, has led them to be more integrated politically. Activism among Arab Canadians has increased substantially. Participating in interfaith activities and working in civil-rights, antiwar, and antiracist coalitions with other groups, some Arab Canadians have also started to work toward developing a voice in some of Canada's political parties.

There is an indeterminacy about the transational politics of ethnic groups and their implications for the larger society. Analyzing conflicts in Britain surrounding both the first Gulf War and the Rushdie affair – that is, the controversy and death threats to Salman Rushdie following the publication of his book *The Satanic Verses* – Pnina Werbner (2000, 309) observes that "far from revealing ambiguous loyalties or unbridgeable cultural chasms, British Muslim transnational loyalties have challenged the national polity ... to explore new forms of multiculturalism and to work for new global human rights causes."

Already reeling from the demonization and attacks that came in the aftermath of 11 September 2001 and during the bombing of Afghanistan, Arab and Muslim Canadians again braced themselves for hostilities in the period preceding the Iraq War. Some Iraqi Canadians even feared internment if Canada participated in the war. There was great relief in the community when the Canadian government decided against participation. Just as important as the decision of the government was the sense of solidarity that developed as a result of the antiwar demonstrations in Canada and worldwide. During the heavily attended antiwar demonstrations in Canada, Arab and Muslim Canadians felt a sense of belonging for the first time since 11 September 2001 (Khouri, personal interview). Because of enormous diversity among the organizations that took part in demonstrations, teach-ins, and various kinds of meetings – including ethnic as well as church, labour, antipoverty, and women's groups – rather than clashing as essentialized civilizational subjects, as had been expected, participants learned from each other, made connections between the various issues that were concerns to different groups, and developed new political subjectivities. In a sense, the emerging picture looked like a multiculturalism based more on intercommunal coalitions than on monoculturalist identities, a configuration proposed by Ella Shohat (1995, 177): "Rather than ask who can speak ... we should ask how we can speak together ... How can diverse communities speak in concert? ... In this sense, it might be worthwhile to focus less on identity as something one 'has,' than an identification one 'does.'"

The worldwide demonstrations against the Iraq War on 15 February 2003, which involved a total of 12 million people, represented a historic moment of transnational solidarity. Subverting the very logic of the discourse of civilizational conflict, these demonstrations were a show of solidarity against imperial power gone out of control and beyond accountability.[7]

Accompanying the widespread violence and harassment of Muslims and Arabs that followed 11 September 2001 were many expressions of support and solidarity from interfaith groups. Some church groups even offered to protect mosques. Although organizations such as the Canadian Muslim Civil Liberties association received many hate e-mail messages, they received five to six times as many messages of support (Kutty and Yousuf 2002, A13).

Several groups expressed support for notions of a Canadian nation that are different from those based on a supposed "clash of civilizations." As early as October 2001, having observed that Arab and Muslim Canadians were being blamed for terrorism and increasingly victimized, the Canadian

Federation of Nurses Unions expressed its solidarity by declaring "we are all Muslim Canadians until this crisis is over" (Connors 2001). Shared experiences of racial profiling have sometimes brought different ethnic and racialized communities together. In the United States, soon after 11 September 2001, there were solidarity demonstrations against the racial profiling that they predicted would follow. The National Asian Pacific American Legal Consortium invited Arab Americans to join it at the National Japanese American Memorial (Stein 2003). In Canada, on the issue of racial profiling, there have been some attempts to express mutual solidarity and to establish transethnic ties between black communities and Arab and Muslim groups.

Writing a few weeks after 11 September 2001, Brah (2002, 41-42) made some observations about what she sees as the emergence of a novel transnational political subject. Listing a diverse range of organizations that participated in rallies for the International Day Against War and Racism in San Francisco and Washington, DC, on 29 September – including Women for Afghan Women; Mexican Support Network; Collective for Lesbian, Gay, Bisexual and Trans-Gender Rights; Pastors for Peace; Action for Community and Ecology; Black Voices for Peace; Healthcare Now Coalition; and AFSCME, of the labour movement – Brah sees "a new collective subject being constituted, as speaker after speaker made connections across many different experiences, forms of differentiation and social divisions." Finding this political subject "simultaneously diasporized and localized," Brah suggests that the current conjuncture creates a space for "imagining and negotiating alternative transnational conceptions of the person as 'holder of rights' that are distinct from the current notions of citizenship."

Conclusion

Edward Said (1998) argued that what we usually have instead of a "clash of civilizations" is a "clash of definitions" over the nature of a civilization, culture, and identity. Even though wars, as Shohat (2002, 469) suggests, do tend to be "the friend of binarisms, leaving little place for complex identities," the present reality reveals a state of indeterminacy. On the one hand, we have seen a diverse range of responses from Arab and Muslim Canadians: some have defensively embraced more narrowly defined ethnic and religious identities, while others have perhaps become more politically active than ever, working with myriad other Canadian groups toward antiracist, anti-imperialist, and antiwar coalitions. On the other hand, if we look at the institutionalization of this identity, we can say that the attempt by Canadian elites to define Canadian identity along transnational civilizational lines has been a hegemonic *attempt,* no doubt largely successful, but not necessarily a hegemonic *success story* altogether. The significant resistance in Canada to the Iraq War and the growing cynicism since then about American foreign policy suggest that a new hegemony has not necessarily been established – at least not in terms of the consensus dimension of hegemonies. Even though, thus far, many acts of resistance and demonstrations of solidarity have not necessarily been long-lasting, what might be emerging out of the worst aspects of the fear, suspicion, and hatred unleashed in the aftermath of 11 September 2001 is a loose but strong antiracist, anti-imperialist, antiwar, pro-democracy movement and a new alternative transnational political subject in the making.

Acknowledgments

I would like to thank Enakshi Dua, Mustafa Koc, Mary-Jo Nadeau, and Cynthia Wright for discussing aspects of this chapter with me. I am grateful to Raja Khouri, the national president of the Canadian Arab Federation, for an interview and to Audrey Jamal, the executive director of the Canadian Arab Federation, for sharing some of the federation's documents as well as her MA thesis with me.

Notes

1 Dr. Enakshi Dua, York University, in personal conversation, April 2004.
2 As demonstrated by calls in April 2004 for the deportation of members of the Khadr family – accused of links to al-Qaeda – and for denial of their citizenship rights. Despite the existing legal status of citizenship in Canada, even the membership of some citizens can be open to questioning.
3 Among parents, 11.8% mentioned that their children were teased and called names by fellow students, and 13.2% indicated differential treatment by teachers or school administrators. Examples given from the survey included one case where a teacher called a child "a little terrorist" (Canadian Arab Federation 2002, 18).
4 At the time of writing, Canadian prime minister Paul Martin was planning a trip to the United States. A few weeks before his visit, the Canadian Council of Chief Executives, a group made up of the leaders of Canada's biggest corporations, released a "discussion paper" and headed to Washington for a discussion of their vision of the "Canada-United States Partnership" with some high-level American politicians and bureaucrats. The council proposes a "partnership" with the United States that includes "a common security agenda, joint military institutions, an integrated energy market and harmonized tariffs and regulations" (Goar 2004, A18; Canadian Council of Chief Executives 2004).
5 See the website of Project Threadbare, a group formed in response to the arrest and detention of the South Asian men: http://threadbare.tyo.ca.
6 See http://www.canadianembassy.org/border/declaration-en.asp and http://www.canadianembassy.org/border/index-en.asp.
7 There are numerous examples of diverse groups being brought together by this kind of organizing. For instance, the groups that were starting to organize a protest against a planned visit by George W. Bush to Ottawa in May 2003 – a visit that was subsequently cancelled – were the Anti-Capitalist Community Action and the Committee for Peace in Iraq, groups that were themselves very diverse internally.

13
Chinese Transnationalism: Class and Capital Flows
Lloyd Wong and Connie Ho

The transnationalism of the Chinese in Canada is usually characterized in terms of their ethnic social formations and their modes of cultural adaptation and reproduction. These include the formation of Chinatowns, voluntary associations, and ethnic businesses. However, it is the flow of financial capital that facilitates their social formations, adaptation, and reproduction. This chapter documents transnational capital flows associated with the Chinese in Canada and the relationship of these flows to social class. The chapter also attempts to show that public discourse and policy have utilized these flows to structure discussions of Chinese Canadians' citizenship and sense of belonging. Transnationalism here is conceived of as an avenue of capital (Vertovec 1999, 452-53).[1] Capital moves across borders via social networks created by Chinese migrants. These migrants are mostly from the working and middle classes, and a few are part of an elite segment of a transnational capitalist class. The terms "migrant" and "immigrant" are used interchangeably, and the assumption here is that many Chinese Canadians are engaged in transnational practices.[2] Recent research has concentrated on flows of human capital associated with transnationalism (Saxenian 2002; Devoretz and Ma 2002), while there has been little exploration of flows of financial capital. Typically, the transnational flows of financial capital provide for migrant adaptation and/or for economic maintenance or development in countries of origin. This international flow of capital also has transformative potential for migrants in that it facilitates a transnationalism "from below" or "from above" depending upon their class position.

This chapter begins with a historical analysis of Chinese transnationalism in terms of social class and capital flows. Then the chapter moves to a contemporary analysis by examining the Chinese as part of a transnational capitalist class. This class includes small-, medium-, and large-scale entrepreneurs; business tycoon Victor Li is described as an example of a transnational Chinese capitalist. The chapter ends with an analysis of recent data on the flow of capital associated with contemporary Chinese immigration to Canada.

History of Chinese Migration and Transnationalism in Canada

The history of Chinese migration to Canada can be divided into three different periods, although in the latter two periods there is considerable overlap. The first period was one of labour migration that began in the late 1800s and lasted until 1923, when the Chinese Immigration Act (commonly known as the Exclusion Act) effectively halted Chinese migration to Canada. Thus, between the first and second periods, there was a time of relative immobility that lasted from 1923 until 1947, when the Exclusion Act was rescinded. The second period occurred during the postwar decades from the late 1960s to the 1980s, when significant numbers of middle-class Chinese entered Canada, particularly after the liberalization of Canadian immigration policy in 1967. They did so as members of the independent class of migrants and complemented the continuing labour migration of working-class Chinese who were entering under the family class. Although Chinese working- and middle-class immigration has continued during the past two decades, the third, and current, period is marked by significant numbers of Chinese entrepreneurs and capitalists who began arriving in Canada in the early 1980s as part of the Canadian Business Immigration Program.

In all three periods the original class positions of the Chinese were approximately replicated in Canada. In the case of labour migration in the 1800s, it was Chinese from the peasant class who became working-class "coolies," agricultural workers, and servants in Canada. The contemporary Chinese migration, which began in the late 1960s, has been primarily one of middle-class skilled workers and professionals initially from Hong Kong and now from the People's Republic of China, who also occupy the middle class in Canada. Similarly, the class positions of wealthy entrepreneurs and investors have been replicated in Canada. This situation is one of transnationalized class, whereby class has been transferred from one place to another. In some cases, where transnational practices are particularly prevalent, there are manifestations of transnationalism "from below" and "from above."

Chinese Transnational Labour History

Aside from the few thousand Chinese who came to Canada in the mid-1800s during the Gold Rush, the first significant cohort came as low-wage contract labourers for the Canadian Pacific Railway in Canada's nation-building construction project. Approximately twenty thousand Chinese males came to Canada during the 1880s for the construction of the western sections of the railway. After it was completed, the Canadian state imposed a head tax to reduce and further control Chinese migration. While some workers returned to China during this period, many others remained in Canada, providing labour in agricultural and manual-service sectors of the labour market. At the same time, growing racist public opinion and working-class racism led to overt forms of state-sanctioned institutional racism that barred Chinese from many jobs and occupations. This systemic racism forced some Chinese out of the wage-labour sector and into a noncompetitive ethnic service sector, in which, as ethnic entrepreneurs, they operated small laundries, vegetable gardens, and Chinese restaurants. These business establishments, in turn, employed Chinese wage labourers.

During this first period of Chinese labour history, it was the flow of human labour into Canada and the flow of capital out of Canada, in the form of remittances to China, that characterized their transnationalism and transnational practices. Because transmigration among these Chinese males was infrequent due to the high cost of transportation, they lived a "bachelor" life, enduring separation from their spouses and families for decades (Li 1998, 66-70). The flow of capital in the form of remittances is impossible to calculate precisely, as is the case in the United States, because the money was in private hands and official statistical information was limited (Hsu 2000, 40, 42). A Canadian journalistic account in 1875 cited a figure of approximately Cdn$800,000 a year in remittances to China (Morton 1974, 51). As the number of Chinese in Canada grew, so did the flow of capital in the form of remittances. Based on the estimates from the American literature circa 1900, an approximate total annual remittance for the Chinese in Canada at the time would be Cdn$10.6 million.[3] This figure is very significant given the size of the Chinese Canadian population and the purchasing power of the dollar at the turn of the century. When considered in the context of today's dollar, this amount would well exceed Cdn$177 million in 2004 dollars.[4] Because the number of Chinese in Canada was only about seventeen thousand, this would equal approximately Cdn$10,400 per person in 2004 dollars. Since this was an annual figure and since remittances continued to be sent for many decades by these Chinese workers, the total sum over this period was substantial, if not astounding. Since remittances were an example of capital leaving Canada, they were used in public discourse as evidence of a lack of commitment and allegiance to Canada among the Chinese population. This provided a rationale for their designation as noncitizens and aliens as well as for discriminatory legislation, such as the head tax and other measures that attempted to ensure that their money was spent in Canada (Con et al. 1982, 81).

Seldom mentioned was that Chinese transnationalism was also an avenue of capital *into* Canada. Chinese labourers and merchants directly paid monies to the Canadian state treasuries through import duties, head taxes, and other iniquitous taxes, municipal fees, land taxes, and the like. Although these amounts were not as high as the remittances leaving Canada, they were significant. For example, in the City of Victoria, Chinese businesses paid over Cdn$148,000 in customs duties in 1901 (Chan 1983, 97). In the period between 1890 and 1898, a member of the provincial government in British Columbia stated that the Chinese head tax comprised 2.07 percent of the country's total revenue (Morton 1974, 182). Through the Chinese head tax, the total amount of money collected by the Canadian government between 1886 and 1923 was Cdn$23 million,[5] which is approximately equivalent to Cdn$1.2 billion in 2004 dollars.[6]

At the end of this first period of migration, the Chinese in Canada were mostly denizens of the working class, although a few were self-employed. Due to the Exclusion Act, this first period was followed by a time of relative immobility among Chinese who may have otherwise come to Canada, leaving the relatives of Chinese Canadians and other potential migrants *in situ* in China. Shortly after the Second World War, the Exclusion Act was rescinded, which, aided by legislative changes in immigration policy in the 1960s, led to a more diverse class composition in Canada.

Contemporary Chinese Transnational Middle-Class Workers, Entrepreneurs, and Capitalists

The second period is one of middle-class Chinese migration that began in the late 1960s and continues today. In the two decades after the Second World War, Chinese migration to Canada was again flowing but consisted of relatively small numbers of previously excluded family members of Chinese men in Canada. However, after the liberalization of Canadian immigration policy in 1967, which introduced the point system for the independent class of migrants, the number of Chinese coming to Canada started to increase substantially. Many were highly skilled and highly educated workers from Hong Kong destined for professional or semiprofessional occupations, while others continued to enter Canada under the family class of migrants and were destined for working-class occupations in clerical, sales, construction, and service work. What is most notable about this period of Chinese migration is the large numbers of those who were from the middle class. This migration led to the emergence of a new and upwardly mobile Chinese middle class in Canada (Li 1990) as well as in other parts of the world where many Chinese emphasized business and education (Wang 2000, 98-103). Their numbers grew significantly in the 1980s, both in absolute terms and as a proportion of all Chinese Canadians in the labour force, as a direct result of Canada's "designer" immigration policy, which emphasizes human capital in the form of skills and credentials (Li 1998, 129, 131). A large proportion of them were in managerial, administrative, science, and health occupations. Some of them would eventually become self-employed independent entrepreneurs, as immigrants to Canada with higher amounts of human capital are more likely to be engaged in self-employment (Li 2001b). The Chinese have a higher propensity for self-employment than most other ethnic groups and the native-born due not only to blocked mobility, but also to their tendency to regard self-employment as an option of first choice (Li 2001a). In addition to the second period of recent and ongoing Chinese middle-class migration, which in recent years has been from the People's Republic of China, a third period of migration can be identified as that comprising Chinese businesspeople under the Canadian Business Immigration Program. In contrast to the working-class and middle-class migrations of previous periods, this type of migration was particularly prominent in the 1980s and 1990s and has only recently declined in popularity. Of the business immigrants who came to Canada during these two decades, the majority was from Hong Kong and Taiwan, engaging in business enterprises in Canada as self-employers, as entrepreneurs (employing others), or as investors (with commitments of specified amounts of capital). The transnational practices among many of these Chinese, particularly those with small- and medium-sized enterprises, have been substantially documented (Wong and Ng 1998, 2002). In some cases their transnationalism has emerged after the fact as an ethnic business strategy, while in other cases it was predetermined as part of increasing transnational flows related to globalization. Chinese transnational businesses are not new in Canada. In the late 1800s and early 1900s, for example, a few wealthy Chinese merchants were engaged in transnational businesses that imported Chinese goods such as rice, sugar, and tea. In the contemporary period, it is not just a few wealthy merchants who are engaged in transnational business practices but a sizable proportion. A recent survey of Chinese businesses in Vancouver and Calgary estimates that approximately 19%, or one in five, are transnational (Wong 2003). Although this figure is lower than the figure of 58% for Latin American entrepreneurs in the United States (Portes, Haller, and Guarnizo 2002, 285), it is still significant. Thus, in contrast to earlier times when transnational business practices were a privilege for a wealthy few, currently they have become much more pervasive and now involve many small- and medium-sized Chinese businesses.

This diversification of Chinese businesses has shifted the explanation for Chinese business in Canada from a debate premised on "structural" versus "cultural" determinants to a consideration of new contextual factors (Li 1993). The net effect of this overall growth in Chinese immigration to Canada has been the transformation and reproduction of Chinese culture in many of Canada's larger cities, such as Toronto, Vancouver, and Calgary. Li's (1992b) study of Richmond, British Columbia, a city within the Greater Vancouver area, documents the rapid growth both of the Chinese population and of Chinese business in the 1980s, a transformation that continued into the 1990s. During this period substantial amounts of Chinese financial capital from Hong Kong and Taiwan fuelled a Chinese ethnic economy in Canada's

246 Lloyd Wong and Connie Ho·

larger cities and also allowed many Chinese to participate in the mainstream economy.

The Chinese Transnational Capitalist Class

The conceptualization of transnationalism as an avenue of capital has largely focused on multinational corporations. As a result, a few wealthy Chinese tycoons and their multinational enterprises have been clearly identified with global capital. However, as Vertovec (1999, 452) points out, in addition to the "Big Players" in the global economy, the "little players," in a cumulative fashion, have an even greater impact in terms of transnational capital flows. Thus many Chinese who are engaged in small- and medium-sized cross-border business circuits contribute to this form of transnationalism. Transnational practices among the Chinese in terms of diasporas, cultural politics, deterritorialized relations, the disembedding of gender and family structures, racialized discourse, and flexible citizenship have received scholarly attention in recent years.

Nonini and Ong's (1997) framework of "alternative modernity," which defines Chinese transnationalism as different from the transnational experiences of other ethnicities, is a useful one on a general conceptual level. On another level, however, such as among those who are extremely wealthy and part of an elite global capitalist class, transnational practices are not unique and are purely class-based.

Chinese transnationalism is facilitated by "flexible citizenship," which Ong (1999, 6) defines as the "cultural logics of capitalist accumulation, travel, and displacement that induce subjects to respond fluidly and opportunistically." Although flexible citizenship is not uniquely a Chinese practice, it certainly is highly associated with Chinese transnationality. As a result, Chinese transnational capitalists manage both to circumvent and to benefit from different nation-states' regimes by selecting different sites for investment, work, and family relocation. This fluid form of citizenship enables them to navigate their business lives in innumerable ways conducive to the smooth flow of financial capital.

Chinese transnationalism is also facilitated through the geographical dispersal and extension of family and *guanxi* (special personal relationships of long-term mutual benefit) (Wu 2000, 38). Chan (1997) points out that the dispersal of the Chinese family, while seemingly paradoxical, is a rational decision that contributes to the strengthening of the family. In this sense, family dispersal can be conceptualized as a spatial resource (Ma Mung 1999). The practice of dispersal is also not uniquely Chinese, but among the Chinese it is a fairly widespread practice. Thus family and guanxi represent a long-standing tradition of reciprocity (Ong 1999) whose very flexibility has enabled Chinese entrepreneurs to achieve their capitalist pursuits and also, in many cases, their transnationalism. For instance, Wong (1998) describes how in California many Chinese professionals capitalize on the family to deploy their global strategies. By engaging in extensive transmigration, or "astronauting," in different parts of the world, these migrants exploit opportunities in the global village, while the family remains stationed in the receiving country. Likewise, Chinese transnationals also exploit guanxi. However, it must be recognized that firms do not necessarily operate smoothly just because they are family-run and that guanxi also carries with it very high levels of risk (Smart and Smart 2000). Further, although the practice of guanxi is not a uniquely Chinese form of interpersonal relationship, it does serve as the foundation for cooperative relationships in Chinese business networks (Yeung and Olds 2000, 15). Thus family and guanxi are indispensable mechanisms that facilitate Chinese transnationalism.

Contemporary Chinese transnationalism involves the United States and Canada and relies on a Pacific shuttle (Ong 1999, 110-36) that utilizes transnational capital circuits, family networks, guanxi, and the logics of flexibility. These transnational practices and processes are comparable among powerful elites in the capitalist class, medium- and small-sized entrepreneurs, and professionals.

Small- and Medium-Sized Transnational Entrepreneurs
With the media's popularization of public discourse centred on Chinese tycoons who are multimillionaires and billionaires, what tends to be overlooked are the flows of capital generated by small- and medium-sized entrepreneurs. The number of extremely wealthy elite Chinese who have significant influence in the global economy is small,[7] but the cumulative impact of all the non-elite small- and medium-sized entrepreneurs is very significant, as their capital moves back and forth along transnational circuits and transnational family networks. In many cases, these are ethnic-embedded businesses based on strong and intense family and/or social networks for whom ethnicity is a resource for capital and labour.

Any attempt to understand contemporary Chinese transnationalism must take into account both elite and non-elite strategies of accumulation under capitalism while at the same time grounding transnational activities in specific times and spaces (Nonini and Ong 1997, 4-5).

Research conducted in the mid-1990s on non-elite small- and medium-sized Chinese entrepreneurs found that they had significant transmigration between Asian Pacific countries and Canada, as they spent a significant proportion of their time outside Canada and circulated among transnational social fields (Wong 1997, 346). In many cases, their transnationalism was an adaptive business strategy necessitated by barriers and obstacles faced in Canada (Wong and Ng 1998). More recent research has verified the emergence of small-sized transnational Chinese enterprises in Vancouver, described their different transnational forms, and demonstrated that they represent a new phenomenon in contrast to the transnational practices of Chinese merchants in the period of migration to Canada during the late 1800s and early 1900s (Wong and Ng 2002). This research also showed the importance of transnational family and kinship networks as forms of social capital and how they were interwoven into these entrepreneurs' business operations. Overall, these transnational networks and the flows of capital along their avenues can be thought of as transnational social spaces. Faist (2000a, 2) defines transnational social spaces as the "ties and the unfolding strong and dense circular flows of persons, goods, ideas, and symbols within a migration system." He further delineates three basic forms of transnational spaces: kinship groups, circuits, and communities, the typical cohesive resources of which are "reciprocity," "exchange," and "solidarity" respectively (203). For the Chinese in Canada, all three forms are prevalent, and Chinese immigrant entrepreneurs in particular include transnational kinship groups and transnational circuits in their trading networks. In the case of the former, the family is the manifestation of transnational ties, and family members' demographic characteristics and their human and economic capital facilitate their mobility. However, in the initial instance, the immigration policies of nation-states facilitate this mobility. The Canadian Business Immigration Program has the objective of attracting both human capital and financial investments, and Chinese immigrants have participated considerably in this form of immigration over the past two decades. The last section of this chapter provides documentation of capital flows associated with immigration, including business immigration. Since 1986, with the introduction of the investor category of business immigration, the cumulative sum of capital brought into Canada by migrants has increased substantially.

Large-Scale Transnational Capitalists
Chinese immigration in the late 1980s and early 1990s brought with it a substantial flow of capital into Canada to the extent that popular journalists began writing about Chinese Canadians' participation in a "hidden establishment" in Canada (Milner 1992) and their participation in a more general global economy along with other ethnicities (Kotkin 1993) via ethnic business networks. For example, by the mid-1990s James Ting, the founder of a small Canadian electronics-manufacturing company called Semi-Tech in the 1980s, was hailed as a transnational entrepreneur with global operations in places such as Tokyo, New York, and Toronto after taking over well-known companies such as Singer Sewing Machines and Sansui Electric. Although James Ting's fortunes have fallen dramatically since the late 1990s, at the time he was portrayed as exemplary of an ambitious immigrant who had established himself in Canada with connections to foreign financial capital from Hong Kong and other places.

Recent theorizing by Robinson (2004, 37) suggests that under global capitalism a distinction has emerged between transnational and national classes. Moreover, working from a broadened definition of the traditional Marxist notion of a capitalist class, Sklair (1991, 1998) conceptualizes a new transnational capitalist class (TCC) comprising "people who see their own interests and/or the interests of their nation, as best served by an identification with the interests of the capitalist global system, in particular the interests of the countries of the capitalist core and the transnational corporations domiciled in them. The TCC holds certain transnational practices to be more valuable than domestic practices" (1991, 8). This broadly defined and abstract class includes four factions: (1) the corporate faction of TCC executives and their local affiliates, (2) the state faction of globalizing bureaucrats and politicians, (3) the technical faction of globalizing professionals, and (4) the consumerist faction of merchants and media players (Sklair 2001, 17; 2002, 99). According to this conceptualization, many corporate executives, highly skilled professionals, and merchants are part of a transnational capitalist class. For instance, Mr. John Lau, the chief executive officer of Husky Energy of Canada – which is controlled and mostly owned by Li Ka-Shing's Cheung Kong (Holdings) Ltd. via Hutchison Whampoa Ltd. – would be an example of a very influential TCC executive and member of the corporate faction. In 2004 Mr. Lau earned a salary of Cdn$895,000 and a bonus of Cdn$875,000 (Haggett 2004, E2). In a different vein, many of the Chinese who have come as investors and entrepreneurs under the Canadian Business Immigration Program are examples of the merchant faction. Employing this broad definition of a transnational capitalist class, we can argue that some Chinese in Canada have been part of this class's formation over the past two decades.

Recently, other scholars who use a narrow definition of a transnational capitalist class and who examine interlocking directorships among those in the world's largest corporations, such as Carroll and Carson (2003), have also concluded that there is some evidence of a transnational capitalist class. Regardless of which definition is used, Victor Li is a powerful global capitalist and a member of the transnational capitalist class. He is the eldest son of Li Ka-Shing, who was ranked by *Forbes* (2004) as the nineteenth richest person in the world in 2004 with an estimated new worth of US$12.4 billion.

The Case of Victor Li: Transnational Hegemony of Class and Capital
Victor Li is a Canadian citizen, and his involvement in his family's businesses includes being the deputy chairperson of Cheung Kong (Holdings) Ltd. His family holds the controlling interests in Cheung Kong (Holdings) Ltd. and many other transnational corporations. These include Hutchison Whampoa Ltd., TOM Group Ltd., Hong Kong Electric Holdings Ltd., and

CK Life Sciences Int'l (Holdings) Inc., to name a few. As noted earlier Husky Energy Inc. of Calgary is held by Cheung Kong. This business conglomerate has a market capitalization of almost HK$600 billion and includes property development, property investment, a real estate agency, estate management, hotels, telecommunications, e-commerce, finance and investment, retail and manufacturing, ports and related services, energy, infrastructure projects and materials, media, and biotechnology. Cheung Kong's website states that it has operations in forty countries throughout the world and employs over 175,000 staff. It ranks among the top 100 corporations in the world.

Victor Li is no stranger to the Canadian scene. His high-profile moves include the Vancouver condominium projects on Expo '86 land, control of Calgary-based Husky Energy, and a recently proposed injection of Cdn$650 million into Canada's cash-strapped national carrier, Air Canada (Chipello 2003), although this bid was ultimately withdrawn. This investment would have been funded via a company called Trinity Time Investments Ltd., which he controls. Victor Li is a graduate of Stanford University and became a Canadian citizen in the 1980s. His arrival in Canada was based on a family decision to pursue dispersal as a means of finding a country where their investments would be safe and their property ownership protected under British law (Milner 1992, 244). As a consequence, for more than a decade, Victor Li had a residence in Vancouver, where he supervised businesses with holdings in the Canadian Imperial Bank of Commerce (CIBC) and Concord Pacific Developments. Moreover, Li holds top posts in the family conglomerate in Asia and around the globe and has controlling interests in diverse sectors such as real estate, finance, manufacturing, infrastructure, and telecommunications. The success of transnational capitalists often depends on the prudent observation of geopolitics. Li is keenly aware of this and has opportunistically and flexibly utilized his Canadian citizenship. Since becoming a Canadian citizen in the 1980s, Li has managed to jump-start a run of business ventures, thus enabling him to ensure the smooth flow of capital and expertise across national borders. These transnational practices are crucial for exploiting the vicissitudes of the global economy and the diversification of capital. His status as a Canadian citizen became the grist for the mill in the bid for control of Husky Oil in 1987 (which became Husky Energy in 2000). His father, Li Ka-Shing, bought a 43% interest in the firm, and Victor acquired 9%. This gave the family a majority stake. Since Victor Li is a Canadian citizen, the Government of Canada ruled that the combined purchase did not amount to a foreign takeover. Likewise, his Canadian citizenship helped him to win out as a prospective buyer of Air Canada, something that would have otherwise been impossible due to the law that caps foreign ownership at 25%. Through Trinity Time Investments, he had proposed investing Cdn$650 million in Air Canada, which would have given him a 31% stake in the airline as it attempted to restructure itself under bankruptcy protection (Westhead 2003). At the time, Li's offer was selected by Air Canada's board over the offer of a rival bidder, a New York firm called Cerberus Capital Management.

Victor Li is described as a very private and demure person who shuns publicity (Stainsby 1989). He is a loyal disciple of his father, and his personal life is kept secret. For example, he has not confirmed or denied whether his wife is from Vancouver. All that is publicly known is that she and their children are Canadians. Despite the secrecy of his personal life, Li's public business moves demonstrate how guanxi has facilitated his transnationalism. His transnational forays and takeovers of key Canadian businesses relied on an intricate network of social and interpersonal ties. For instance, Fraser Elliot, the founder of the well-known law firm Stikeman Elliot, helped Li to secure the Expo land deal. In addition, his firm represented Li in the acquisition of Husky Oil. So powerful were these business and friendship ties that Stikeman Elliot itself eventually opened an office in Hong Kong on the eighteenth floor of the China Building, two floors above Li Ka-Shing's headquarters (Chan 1996). As a master of long-term relationships, Li has also been intimate with the CIBC, of which his father is reported to be the largest individual shareholder. The partnerships with the CIBC gave Li instant credibility in Canadian banks and the Canadian business community. Another nexus for Li's relationships in Canada is Robert Fung, a successful Toronto financier. Fung's wide corporate ties have connected Victor Li to some of the most powerful people in the nation, such as Jean Chrétien and Paul Martin (Lee-Young 2004). These connections have paved the way for Li's continued presence in and control of many enterprises in Canada. Thus it is apparent that Victor Li's success in Canada is intricately tied to his shrewd reliance on transnational social networks facilitated by guanxi.

Victor Li's corporate transnationalism is clearly illustrative of transnationalism "from above," whereby, as a powerful transnational capitalist who owns and controls major transnational corporations, he is engaged in hegemonic capitalist practices aimed at ensuring economic dominance in many parts of the world. An example of such practices is the recent attempt by Victor Li's Trinity Time Investments company to alter the pension plans of many of Air Canada's employees as part of its efforts to take over the airline. The type of pension plan that Victor Li proposed to the unionized Air Canada workers is called a defined-contribution plan, which provides no guaranteed or specific amount of pension payout, in contrast to one that does (called a defined-benefit plan). Li's proposal would have transferred the investment risk to the workers while lessening his company's investment risk in purchasing Air Canada. Li made acceptance of this proposed pension plan a condition of his investment in Air Canada (CBC News 2004) and ultimately withdrew his offer to purchase the airline based on lack of support of his position by Air Canada workers. He had also proposed that Air Canada employees pay 30 percent of their health-care costs. These initiatives, which would have made Air Canada more profitable for Victor Li, are illustrative of transnational capitalist hegemony and capitalist financial logic.

Victor Li's business dealings are exemplary of Chinese transnationalism "from above." Few transnational Chinese are engaged in this form of trans-nationalism, and it remains unclear whether they are part of a national elite or increasingly part of a transnational capitalist class of hybrid cosmopoli-tans. Growing evidence from cases such as that of Victor Li suggests the latter. Although these Chinese transnational capitalist tycoons provide for the flow of many billions of dollars to and from Canada, the case of Victor Li also demonstrates that their reliance on family networks, guanxi, and the logics of flexibility is akin to the transnational practices of other non-elite entrepreneurs and capitalists. The cumulative capital flows generated by the non-elites and the "little players," which are examined in the next section, also involve very substantial sums.

Chinese Transnational Capital Flows and Circuits

Chinese Immigration and Flows of Capital into Canada

The data for this section come from two sources. One source is landing data from Citizenship and Immigration Canada (CIC), to whom immigrants pro-vide information upon entering Canada. With respect to the "money in possession" of immigrants from selected countries of origin, CIC produced special tabulations of the landing data specifically for this chapter. Another source of data is "wave one" of the Longitudinal Survey of Immigrants to Canada (LSIC), which focused on immigrants six months after their arrival and was conducted by Statistics Canada from October 2000 to September 2001. The target population for "wave one" was approximately 165,000, and the sample size was approximately 20,000 where the method of data collection was personal interviews (Statistics Canada 2003g).

Capital in Possession upon Arrival in Canada

Over the past decade and a half, from 1986 to 2002, Chinese immigrants have brought into Canada at the time of their immigration a total of Cdn$14.9 billion. This amount is approximately 1.6 times the Cdn$8.9 bil-lion brought into Canada by non-Chinese immigrants during the same pe-riod (see Table 13.1). More specifically, from 1988 to 1994 the annual amounts of capital in Chinese possession upon arrival were either double or triple the non-Chinese amounts. This was due to the large and significant number of immigrants from Hong Kong (compared to the number from the People's Republic of China, Taiwan, and other countries) who relocated capi-tal to Canada in anticipation of the 1997 British handover of Hong Kong to China. For example, in 1994 Hong Kong immigrants constituted 67% of all

Table 13.1

Chinese immigrants to Canada: Sum and mean money in possession, 1986-2002

Year	Chinese immigrants[a]			Non-Chinese immigrants		
	Count (#)	Sum (Cdn$)	Mean (Cdn$)	Count (#)	Sum (Cdn$)	Mean (Cdn$)
1986	9,076	220,124,599	24,253	90,913	229,575,133	2,525
1987	21,674	589,361,939	27,192	131,690	372,075,449	2,825
1988	31,248	867,369,488	27,757	131,529	395,730,411	3,009
1989	31,466	1,187,995,433	37,755	161,507	522,660,431	3,236
1990	44,895	1,150,444,723	25,625	172,924	351,091,500	2,030
1991	43,349	914,654,315	21,100	190,054	372,818,244	1,962
1992	58,847	1,159,804,529	19,709	195,385	362,185,351	1,854
1993	57,742	1,290,602,112	22,351	199,053	339,764,325	1,707
1994	65,393	1,271,483,117	19,444	159,028	441,494,557	2,776
1995	53,630	844,140,815	15,740	282,575	900,992,346	3,189
1996	61,154	968,106,575	15,831	164,923	666,451,245	4,041
1997	54,957	911,920,381	16,593	161,091	716,477,382	4,448
1998	35,409	592,709,734	16,739	138,804	857,584,527	6,178
1999	39,002	879,434,647	22,548	150,986	1,010,318,309	6,691
2000	43,941	761,772,716	17,336	183,529	1,365,910,436	7,442
2001	46,510	712,803,348	15,326	204,287	1,391,467,009	6,811
2002	39,058	575,671,014	14,739	190,142	1,178,047,031	6,196
Total	737,351	14,898,399,485	20,205	2,908,420	11,474,643,686	3,945

a Includes immigrants from the People's Republic of China, Hong Kong, Taiwan, Singapore, Malaysia, and Macao.
Source: Compiled from special tabulations of landing data provided by CIC (2004).

Chinese immigrants from Hong Kong, the People's Republic of China, Taiwan, Singapore, Malaysia, and Macao. By 1998 Hong Kong immigrants constituted only 23%, and by 2002 a mere 4%. Thus the post-1997 amounts indicate that Chinese immigrants had lower annual sums of capital in their possession upon arrival than did non-Chinese immigrants. Overall, even though the number of new Chinese immigrants each year was significantly lower than the number of new non-Chinese immigrants, the mean amounts of capital in the possession of Chinese migrants upon arrival per year and for the whole period are considerably higher. Although the Chinese mean is consistently higher than the non-Chinese mean, the discrepancy has dwindled over time. From 1986 to 1993 the mean amount of money in the possession of arriving Chinese immigrants was approximately ten times more than that in the possession of new non-Chinese immigrants. However, the Chinese mean has dropped since then, particularly during the post-1997 era, to approximately double the non-Chinese mean. Nevertheless, there was still a significant difference in the mean amounts in recent years, indicating that capital flows associated with Chinese immigration are much higher than those associated with non-Chinese immigration at a ratio of slightly over 2:1 for the years 2000, 2001, and 2002.

Further analyses of CIC landing data show that for the period from 1986 to 2002, immigrants from Hong Kong made up the largest proportion (approximately 45%) of all immigrants, but in the post-1997 era their numbers and their proportion have dropped dramatically. Although their mean worth in the post-1997 era increased a bit, to Cdn$33,864 in 1999, it now ranges from Cdn$22,000 to $25,000. This is based on only a few thousand immigrants, compared to the tens of thousands in the pre-1997 era. As well, in the immediate post-1997 years, the total sum of money in their possession upon arrival dropped to less than Cdn$200 million from pre-1997 levels that ranged from Cdn$600 million to $1 billion; in recent years this total has dropped further, to just tens of millions of dollars. In contrast, the number of immigrants from the People's Republic of China has been increasing, and in recent years they have comprised over 90% of all Chinese immigrants to Canada.

In terms of a breakdown of the amount of capital in Chinese immigrants' possession based on their "class" of immigration (not including the "other" category), it is not surprising to find that immigrants in the business/independent class had the highest total sum (Cdn$5.35 billion) and highest mean (Cdn$33,046), followed by those in the skilled-worker/independent class, family class, and refugee class. While both the family class and the refugee class are considered humanitarian forms of immigration, a closer analysis of the family class reveals that substantial amounts of capital are brought into Canada via this form of immigration and that this capital has an economic impact. As Table 13.2 shows, the total sum for the family class

Table 13.2

Chinese immigrants to Canada: Sum and mean money (Cdn$) in possession by class, 1986-2002

Year	Family class			Skilled-worker/ independent class			Business/ independent class			Refugee class			Other classes[a]		
	Count (#)	Sum ($)[b]	Mean ($)	Count (#)	Sum ($)[b]	Mean ($)	Count (#)	Sum ($)[b]	Mean ($)	Count (#)	Sum ($)[b]	Mean ($)	Count (#)	Sum ($)[b]	Mean ($)
1986	4,464	35,797	8,019	1,236	39,119	31,650	2,850	113,694	39,893	13	0	0	501	31,514	62,902
1987	6,885	65,718	9,545	9,496	241,026	25,382	4,182	204,418	48,880	16	2	125	1,074	282,606	263,134
1988	7,130	119,453	16,754	16,054	327,684	20,411	6,278	314,965	50,170	7	0	0	1,601	105,267	65,751
1989	8,506	199,241	23,424	12,466	227,635	18,260	8,352	527,424	63,149	31	35	1,129	2,111	233,661	110,687
1990	14,535	259,468	17,851	18,430	398,545	21,625	10,170	379,883	37,353	93	86	925	2,240	112,463	50,207
1991	17,043	275,744	16,179	12,348	105,975	8,582	10,048	271,149	26,985	524	90	172	3,386	149,697	44,210
1992	27,517	415,197	15,089	6,655	67,221	10,101	19,513	501,599	25,706	649	37	57	5,208	198,559	38,126
1993	22,296	219,021	9,823	6,000	67,631	11,272	21,765	597,947	27,473	264	38	144	7,417	404,945	54,597
1994	29,592	436,323	14,745	35,716	132,958	3,723	17,342	357,901	20,638	200	14	70	7,400	344,287	46,525
1995	29,917	441,072	14,743	11,983	134,207	11,200	10,444	255,729	24,486	506	127	251	780	13,005	16,673
1996	24,145	423,057	17,522	20,408	212,709	10,423	13,353	327,410	24,520	527	279	529	2,721	4,652	1,710
1997	20,339	298,968	14,699	21,512	237,268	11,030	11,240	373,782	33,255	328	192	585	1,538	1,710	1,112
1998	12,010	138,322	11,517	15,364	280,741	18,273	6,517	172,079	26,405	453	164	362	1,046	1,404	1,342
1999	10,874	103,855	9,551	22,502	480,808	21,367	4,812	293,911	61,079	488	137	281	326	724	2,221
2000	10,612	92,332	8,701	27,667	412,404	14,906	4,938	256,831	52,011	647	173	267	77	34	442
2001	11,192	96,254	8,600	28,599	369,482	12,919	5,928	246,666	41,610	760	398	524	31	3	97
2002	12,729	115,082	9,041	20,978	308,026	14,683	4,059	151,198	37,250	1,227	1,178	960	60	23	383
Total	269,786	3,734,904	13,844	287,414	4,043,439	14,068	161,791	5,346,586	33,046	6,733	2,950	438	37,517	1,884,554	50,232

a Includes the classes designated live-in caregiver, retired, deferred removal orders, in-Canada, and designated.
b In thousands and rounded to the nearest thousand.
Source: Compiled from special tabulations of landing data provided by CIC (2004).

was Cdn$3.73 billion, and the mean was Cdn$13,844, which is comparable to the figures of Cdn$4.0 billion and Cdn$14,068 for the skilled-worker/independent class.

Capital Flow after Arrival in Canada

Data from the LSIC reveal that approximately 10% of all Chinese immigrants and 25% of Chinese business immigrants received income from sources outside of Canada within the six-month period after their arrival (Statistics Canada 2003h). More detailed analysis of the sources and sums of the capital flowing into Canada (see Table 13.3) for all Chinese immigrants indicates that the main sources reported were (1) a job, (2) self-employment, (3) a foreign government, and (4) investments. The total sum of capital that flowed into Canada was Cdn$38.5 million for the six-month period after their arrival, most of which was generated by their transnational jobs and self-employment. Other data from the LSIC reveal that these self-employment figures represent a large proportion of Chinese business immigrants, as 71% of them reported receiving income from this source outside of Canada, at a total of Cdn$12.9 million (Statistics Canada 2003h). This figure constitutes approximately 90% of the Cdn$14.3 million generated by this source, as indicated in Table 13.3, and reflects the geographical diversity of these immigrants' labour and entrepreneurship.

The LSIC also has data on Chinese immigrants' reported capital in possession at the time of their arrival in Canada, and these data are presented here to supplement the landing data collected by CIC. At the time of their immigration, most Chinese immigrants (91%), including those who are business immigrants (94%), brought money, such as savings, into Canada. Chinese immigrants brought in a total of Cdn$1.4 billion, of which approximately one-third, or Cdn$0.5 billion, belonged to business immigrants.[8]

Table 13.3

Chinese immigrants: Source and sums of the flow of capital into Canada after arrival[a] (N = 36,200)

Source outside of Canada	Reporting (%)	Sum (Cdn$)
Job	33	20,419,400
Self-employment	23	14,307,300
Foreign government	13	849,500
Investments	13	2,325,200
Other sources[b]	6	569,900
Total		38,471,300

a   These figures are for the six-month period after their arrival in Canada.
b   Thes include child support, alimony, rental income, and scholarships.
Source: Compiled from special tabulations of LSIC data provided by Statistics Canada (2003h).

The other side of the flow of capital into Canada is the capital *in situ* in these immigrants' countries of origin and elsewhere in other countries. Chinese immigrants maintained approximately Cdn$760 million in their countries of origin when they immigrated, of which one-third, or Cdn$235 million, belonged to business immigrants. Further, 23% of all Chinese immigrants reported having capital in a third country (i.e., a country other than their country of origin or Canada) at the time of their arrival. In the case of business immigrants, 44% had capital in a third country. The total amount in a third country was Cdn$395 million, of which Cdn$167 million belonged to business immigrants. In total, approximately Cdn$1.2 billion was *not* brought into Canada by Chinese immigrants at the time of their immigration, an amount just slightly below the Cdn$1.4 million that they did bring in. In the early 1990s the Canadian government assumed that the considerable amounts of capital and assets held abroad by immigrants would be patriated within ten years (Statistics Canada 1991, 17); however, given the rise of transnationalism and transnational practices among many immigrants, this assumption is likely to be a false one. A possible indication of this is the figures in Table 13.4 for the amount of capital still left in third countries after six months, which indicate very little movement. Overall, the figures on the capital *in situ* and elsewhere indicate that Chinese immigrants were not prepared to risk bringing all of their capital to Canada, thus demonstrating, on one level, their commitment to transnationalism. On another level, this trend implies a geographical diversification of financial investment. Thus the Chinese proverb that "the clever

Table 13.4

Chinese immigrants and business immigrants: Capital in flow, *in situ*, and elsewhere at time of arrival in Canada

Activity of capital	All immigrants[a] %	All immigrants[a] Sum (Cdn$)	Business immigrants[b] %	Business immigrants[b] Sum (Cdn$)
Brought capital into Canada	91	1,379,563,000	94	495,608,157
Capital remaining in country of origin	–	760,467,600	–	235,377,609
Had capital in a country different from country of origin at time of arrival	23	395,333,300	44	166,904,347
Total capital remaining in country different from country of origin six months after arrival	–	372,491,600	–	158,453,313

a N = 36,200
b N = 3,600
Source: Compiled from special tabulations of LSIC data provided by Statistics Canada (2003h).

rabbit has three burrows" may be reflected here in the multiple sites of capital for Chinese immigrants in Canada.

It should be recognized that it is not only immigrants who provide a venue for the flow of Chinese capital into Canada. Those who come into Canada temporarily on a more short-term basis, such as temporary workers, students, and tourists, are also important. In the case of international students, there were 10,247 from China, Taiwan, and Hong Kong in 2000, 14,563 in 2001, and 14,901 in 2002 (CIC 2003b, 17). Many international students establish social networks during their stay in Canada and a sense of connectedness that often contributes to transnationalism after their graduation.

The Flow of Chinese Capital from Canada

Determining the flow of Chinese capital from Canada to other countries is much more difficult, and data are not readily available. For example, remittances sent by Canadian immigrants to their home countries are not calculated by the International Monetary Fund (IMF), whereas they are for many other countries, such as the United States. In 2001, US$28.4 billion flowed out of the United States to other countries in the form of remittances (IMF 2002). Given Canada's relatively large proportion of foreign-born, remittances from Canada are also likely to be fairly significant. Between 2000 and 2002 China, India, Pakistan, and the Philippines were consistently ranked the top four source countries of immigrants to Canada, comprising approximately 35% of all new immigrants (CIC 2003b, 8). These same countries are among the top twenty countries cited by the IMF in 2001 as recipients of remittances, with India receiving US$10.0 billion, the Philippines US$6.4 billion, Pakistan US$1.5 billion, and China US$1.2 billion (IMF 2002). Thus, though figures are not readily available on remittances sent from Canada, the amounts are probably substantial, with a good proportion coming from the Chinese in Canada. One estimate for Western Union, one of the larger money-transfer companies, is that in 2001, approximately 10% of the estimated US$5.2 billion in total money transfers originated in Canada (Monzón and Tudakovic 2004, 6). Western Union has 2,800 outlets across Canada and considers the Chinese one of its strongest customer communities (Thomas 2004). Since the late 1980s, the vast majority of Chinese immigrants have come to Canada for economic reasons, making the likelihood of their sending remittances high.

Although the LSIC data indicate that 14% of all recent immigrants sent remittances to family and friends in their countries of origin, only 6% of the Chinese immigrants reported doing so, and only 1% reported sending money outside of Canada as an investment. However, as mentioned earlier, this survey took place only six months after their arrival in Canada. It may well be that this initial period is one of immigrant settlement and adaptation and that the proportion of those who send remittances increases over time after they gain greater economic security.

Conclusion

The flow of capital associated with Chinese transnationalism in Canada has been, and continues to be, substantial. In the earlier period of Chinese labour migration in the late 1800s and early 1900s, the flow of capital out of Canada via workers' remittances was extensive. This fact became, in part, the rationale for racism and social exclusion, as it was viewed as demonstrating a lack of commitment to Canada among the Chinese. Seldom mentioned, however, is that the Chinese also brought substantial amounts of capital into Canada in the form of migration costs, the head tax, import duties, and other taxes. The newer transnationalism of contemporary Chinese migrants, from the late 1960s to the present, also consists of substantial flows of capital. While aspects of contemporary Chinese transnationalism, particularly that of Chinese professionals and entrepreneurs, are depicted as constituting an alternative modernity characterized by capital accumulation, instrumentality, and flexible citizenship, a fundamental aspect is the flow of capital in a transnational social space. This space includes kinship networks, business circuits, and social organizations among transnational communities. The flow of capital associated with the hegemony of the powerful elites of a global capitalist class, such as Victor Li, is without question a form of transnationalism "from above." However, the cumulative flow of capital associated with non-elites is often overlooked. The magnitude of capital flow is much greater among ordinary Chinese immigrants than among non-Chinese immigrants. Paradoxically, and in contrast to earlier times and remittances, these cumulative and large flows of capital into Canada have not enjoyed a public discourse that touts Chinese immigrants' allegiance and loyalty to Canada. This chapter has demonstrated that contemporary capital flows are related to immigration class, country of origin, and the sources of capital. That *more* capital is brought into Canada by Chinese immigrants than is left behind in other countries confirms their commitment to Canada. However, the other side of the coin is that the sizable capital left behind by Chinese immigrants in their countries of origin, as well as in third countries, confirms their commitment to transnationalism.

Notes

1 While the term "capital" has many definitions, it is used in this chapter to more narrowly mean "financial" capital, a medium that is liquid and that represents a form of wealth. The term here is used primarily to mean "money," as the chapter's many examples of capital flows indicate.
2 In this sense, transnational migrants or immigrants are those who maintain multiple contacts with other countries, their countries of origin, and/or perhaps their countries of last departure.

3   This figure is calculated using sources cited in Hsu (2000, 41) and in Li (1998, 67) as well as population figures from the Chinese American Data Center. Estimates based on the sources in Hsu indicate that total remittances to China from the United States in 1903 were approximately Ch$110 million, which, given the exchange rate at that time, was equal to approximately US$55 million. With a Chinese population of 89,863, this equals a per capita remittance of US$612. If we assume a similar remittance rate for the Chinese in Canada, who, according to Li's figures, totalled 17,312 in 1901, and given that there was a very narrow exchange rate between the American and Canadian dollars at the time, annual remittances from the Chinese in Canada totalled approximately Cdn$10.6 million.

4   The amount was calculated using the Bank of Canada's Inflation Calculator. Due to limitations of the program, the estimate of Cdn$10.6 million was actually based on a 1914 dollar, not on a 1900 dollar; see http://bankofcanada.ca/en/inflation_calc.htm.

5   This figure is cited in a news release dated 12 March 2004 by the Chinese Canadian National Council (CCNC) entitled "UN Report Calls on the Canadian Government to Redress Chinese Head Tax and Exclusion Act" and is excerpted from a report by the Special Rapporteur for the United Nations. The figure is also mentioned on the CCNC website: http://www.ccnc.ca/redress.

6   This figure of Cdn$1.2 billion is a very conservative estimate based on the total head taxes collected from 1885 to 1923 (Cdn$23 million) and on a calculation of this total's "investment value." If the Cdn$23 million had been invested in 1923 in long-term Canadian government bonds, with the investment cashed out and reinvested once per year, it would be worth approximately Cdn$1.2 billion today. This is a conservative estimate because (1) while the head tax was collected over a period of thirty-eight years, only the final year, 1923, was used as the starting point for calculating "investment value" and (2) since government bonds are very low risk, they have lower returns compared to other investment vehicles. Government long-term bonds were used because data are readily available on their yields dating back to 1923. Professor Jeremy Rudin did the original calculation for the Chinese Canadian National Council back in 1988, producing a figure of Cdn$896 million (Victor Wong and Avvy Go, Chinese Canadian National Council, personal communication, 23 June 2004).

7   Only twenty-one Chinese are included in *Forbes* magazine's listing of the world's richest five hundred people; see http://www.chron.com/cs/CDA/printstory.mpl/side2/2422081.

8   These figures are higher than the ones in Table 13.1 for Chinese immigrants for the years 2001 and 2002. This is because Chinese immigrants were determined by their countries of origin for Table 13.1, whereas for the LSIC data in Tables 13.3 and 13.4, Chinese immigrants were selected out as a subsample by the question on visible-minority status. Given that this criterion allows for a much broader definition of "Chinese" than does country of origin, it is not surprising that the figures from the LSIC data are higher.

14
Raising the Iron Curtain: Transnationalism and the Croatian Diaspora since the Collapse of 1989

Daphne Winland

The collapse of state socialism throughout central and eastern Europe and the dissolution of the Soviet Union, events that ended the Cold War division of the world and changed the political map of the globe, are among the most significant historical transformations of the twentieth century. The "transition," as this period is most commonly (albeit problematically) called, has been examined from a multitude of analytical perspectives across disciplines. But though the contributions of academics in the region since 1990 have, in many cases, been challenging and innovative, most of this research focuses on the macropolitical and economic impacts of transition – for example, global capital and labour flows as well as civil and political turmoil. These interests extend into analyses of transnationalism and its effects on the new postsocialist nation-states. Key transnational actors identified include major political, financial, and humanitarian institutions as well as diaspora/exile populations. Thus, to date, studies of transnationalism and diaspora in the region have been limited to examinations of, for example, diaspora efforts to influence foreign policy (Shain 2000), the creation of "near-abroad" diasporas in post-Soviet successor states (Motyl et al. 1998), or external national homelands in borderland states (e.g., Latvia and Lithuania) (Brubaker 1996). Less attention has been devoted to the impact of the developments of the past decade on the reconfiguration of transnational affiliations, ties, and loyalties.

In this chapter, I focus on the everyday effects of transnationality for diasporic Croats in Toronto in the context of their experiences related to the "transition" in 1990 of the Croatian homeland from a republic in the Yugoslav socialist federation to an independent nation. The chapter relies on research conducted with Toronto Croats since 1992, the year that Croatia was officially recognized by the European Union. Compared to other diasporic groups in Canada, Croatians are, as Wong and Satzewich state in the Introduction to this volume, "comparatively privileged" and are not a subaltern group "subject to racial or other forms of exclusion," or at least they have not been so in recent years. Nonetheless, diasporic Croats in Canada share some attributes with those groups that have experienced the upheaval of war and dislocation in their homelands, such as Tamils, Sikhs, and Ethiopians. For example, they are generally highly committed and connected to the homeland socially, economically, and often politically. It is this latter political dimension that I engage here.

The involvement of diasporas in political activity geared toward homelands has long been recognized as a central factor in diasporic life, although it hasn't generated theoretical enthusiasm until recently. For example, Tölölyan (2000) makes the argument that, among other things, political issues of internal power are often absent from the analysis of diasporic politics. In a similar vein, Jusdanis (2001, 205-8) states that the shortcoming of studies that celebrate multiculturalism, globalization, and the post-communist moment is the lack of work on politics. I argue, following Ong (1999, 23), that "the pressures to cope with the social and political contradictions between cultural homeland and host country ... the politics of imposed identity and of ... self-positioning reflect the logics and ambivalence" that shape Croatian identifications in Canada.

While it has become axiomatic in ethnic studies that attention must be given to the often changing ethnic projects of the host nations within which groups are identified, it is also clear that, in the case of diasporas, attention must likewise be paid to projects of the homeland. Similarly, ties to the homeland play a crucial, ongoing, and often central role in shaping the relationships of diasporic groups to the host country and vice versa. The impact of homeland independence on Croatian identities in the diaspora is thus best understood in the context of current theoretical debates both on transnationalism and diaspora and on the politics of location and representation.

Although, as stated above, there is little research on the effects that recent changes in the former Eastern Bloc have had on eastern-European immigrants to Canada, the research that does exist provides a glimpse into the key dynamics of immigrant identity during precommunist and communist eras. For example, the rich history of immigration of eastern-European groups to Canada over the past 150 years provides invaluable testimony to the centrality of transnational linkages. The contexts within which transnationalism was a factor for eastern-European immigrants were mitigated by particular Cold War circumstances that, for most, prevented open and frequent contact with family in communist states and made it difficult or impossible to visit the home country.

For example, Isajiw (1991, 1992), Subtelny (1991), and Hryniuk and Luciuk (1993) all provide essential insights into the impact of the socialist period on Ukrainians in Canada. As Subtelny has argued, Ukrainians are more politicized than other ethnic groups in Canada. Ukrainians share a sense of "historical mission," as they have, for generations, been the self-appointed "guardians of ancestral cultural heritage" (Subtelny 1991, 259). Other Ukrainian Canadian writers have discussed the "burden of loyalty" for those Ukrainians who have historically felt it their responsibility to preserve their cultural traditions until such time as Ukraine would be free. The politics of eastern-European immigrant groups spanned the ideological spectrum from radical left-wing to radical right-wing political philosophies. These philosophies were revealed, for example, in support campaigns for Russian dissidents such as Alexander Solzhenitsyn; in Ukrainian campaigns to exonerate John Demjanjuk, accused of being Ivan the Terrible, the notorious gas-chamber operator at the Treblinka concentration camp in Poland during the Second World War; and more recently in the Croatian diaspora's efforts to do the same for General Ante Gotovina, indicted by the International Criminals Tribunal of the Former Yugoslavia in the Hague.

During the Cold War, immigrant groups originating from the Union of Soviet Socialist Republics (USSR), including Estonians, Lithuanians, and Armenians, experienced tremendous anxiety over the fate of family and nation. Representatives of these communities regularly organized pickets at Russian consulates across Canada and organized or participated in counter-demonstrations at antinuclear rallies. Hungarians, particularly those who arrived in Canada as refugees from communism in 1956 (known as the "56ers"), have also been closely connected to developments in the communist homeland (Patrias 1994; Dreisziger 1982; Keyserlingk 1993), as were Czechs, Poles, Russians, and other immigrants of eastern-European descent (Gellner and Smerek 1968). Hungarians in Canada were also deeply affected by the execution on 16 June 1958 of Imre Nagy, former prime minister of Hungary. Here was one case where the politics of contested memory promoted social cohesion. The Hungarian émigré population in Canada, some of whom have ties to the large number of Hungarians in Transylvania, was also key to the dissolution of Ceauçescu's regime.

The case of Yugoslavia differs from other eastern-European contexts in several important respects. First, Yugoslavia was a multinational, multi-cultural, and multiconfessional state (similar in selected respects to the USSR but vastly different in others) where multiple national groups coexisted under a policy of pan-Slavic or South Slavic unity. While most European communist states achieved independence with a minimum of bloodshed (e.g., the Czech Republic's Velvet Revolution), the breakup of Yugoslavia resulted in war after independence was proclaimed by republics such as Slovenia and Croatia. Although certain republics such as Macedonia, Montenegro, and Slovenia did not go through the trials of war, the rest of the country was involved in the bloody wars of secession. Most Bosnians, many of whom self-identified as Yugoslav to Canadian immigration authorities prior to the war, came to Canada after 1992, many as refugees. Canadian Serbs, many of whom have resided in Canada for at least several generations, have been heavily involved in lobbying the Canadian government and in maintaining communication with the homeland during and after the war. In 1999, for example, during the NATO bombing campaign in the former Yugoslavia, Canadian Serbs expressed their anger with Canadian government involvement in the North Atlantic Treaty Organization through large demonstrations and rallies in major Canadian cities. According to Danforth (1995, 85), "Greeks and Macedonians of the diaspora, often living side by side in suburbs of Toronto and Melbourne, just as they once did in villages in northern Greece, participate actively in the conflict over Macedonian identity that dominates the politics of their homelands."

In this chapter, I focus on the case of Croatians from the former Yugoslavia, as transnational political linkages have consistently played a decisive role in the progress of war and of nation building in Croatia. I begin with an analysis of the Toronto Croatian diaspora's response to homeland war and independence before considering how this response coheres with the politics of identity in Canada.

The Yugoslav Context: The Case of Croatia

Few international political events captured the world's attention during the 1990s as did the war in the former Yugoslavia. By the late 1980s and especially following the rise to power of Slobodan Milošević in 1987, signs of the tragedy that was to unfold became apparent. Apart from the looming political and economic crises facing Yugoslavia, the fragility of the state was evidenced in faltering support for the preservation of Yugoslav unity (Woodward 1995; Ramet 1996). With the erosion of Yugoslav institutions and the lack of independent ones to take their place, steps were taken in Croatia to found independent political parties, all of which sought, in different ways, to deal with the Croatian national question. The threat of a Croatian multiparty democratic system to Slobodan Milošević's hold on the federal Yugoslav state led to the rapid deterioration of relations between the two. Milošević's truculence proved decisive in Croatia's decision to pursue the path of independence rather than opt for the earlier Croatian offer of a compromise giving Croatia more autonomy under Yugoslav rule. The war that erupted shortly after caused untold damage, the human costs of which are inestimable.

While several scholars have mentioned the role that transnational processes played in the diaspora's involvement in the ascent to power in 1990 of the first Croatian president, Franjo Tudjman (Pusić 1997; Tanner 1996; Goldstein 1999), few have gone beyond brief descriptions of the political and financial influence of the diaspora during and immediately following war and independence (Skrbiš 1995, 1999; Kolar-Panov 1997). The events of the past dozen years have had an enormous impact on the symbolic, social, and in some cases, material worlds of diasporic Croats. I begin with an analysis of the Croatian diaspora's involvement in homeland affairs in order to ascertain the nature and degree of transnational connections and affiliations.

Toronto Croats

Since the outbreak of war in the former Yugoslavia, Croatians, who have historically maintained a low (ethnic) profile in Canada, have begun to assert their ethno-national pride primarily by identifying with the political cause of their compatriots in the former Yugoslavia. For Croatians in the diaspora, the combination of images of war, their fears and anxieties over the fate of family and friends in Croatia, and the urgency with which they have become interested and/or involved in homeland affairs has had a significant impact not only on the configuration of social relationships in the Croatian community, but also on the ways that Croatians "remember, reconstruct, and lay claim" to their homeland (Hannerz 1992).

Regardless of their specific relationship to the mother country, Croatians now speak of their collective transformation from a historically repressed minority group in the former Yugoslavia to a proud new nation that successfully shrugged off the yoke of communist rule and asserted a new sense of purpose and pride. As expected, then, the impact of national independence in the homeland on the diaspora introduced new elements into the analysis of the politics of Croatian diasporic identity. Croatian independence provided the opportunity to publicly celebrate Croatian identity in Canada, thanks in part to the (initially favourable) media attention generated by the war. It gave the community a legitimacy and visibility that it had never known before. Although the initial effects of this increased profile were positive – as Croatians were largely portrayed as the victims of the war, notably during the Serb assault on Croatia during the war's early stages (1991-92) – they later came under criticism particularly because of the interventionist and aggressive military policies of the new Croatian state in Krajina and (pre–Dayton Accords) Bosnia and Hercegovina.

Independence and the war resulted in a flood of information and new avenues for transnational communication between homeland and diasporic Croats, including the establishment of news services and newspapers, the proliferation of amateur videos (see Kolar-Panov 1997), the emergence of numerous publications on the war (among them nationalist treatises and medical journals chronicling the human toll of war), and the creation of websites, many of which have come and gone.

Although their diasporic history is marked in part by fragmentation and discord, stemming from differences in political viewpoint, economic status, region of origin, and time of arrival in Canada, Croatians have been galvanized by the issue of independence in an unprecedented fashion. For example, Croatians tirelessly mobilized support for Croatian relief by fundraising and by volunteering their services. In particular, student brigades were sent to rebuild war-torn areas and to serve in the Croatian military. Narratives of renewal replaced those of displacement and oppression. Such revitalization and reinvention of Croatian diasporic discourses and the intensification of transnational links as a consequence of Croatian independence resulted in a movement to reclaim and redefine Croatian origins and affiliations.

The "people production" (Balibar 1991, 86) needs and efforts of the new state have also meant that, to a certain degree, the Croatian diaspora has been implicated in the new Croatian state-building *(državotvorna)* program (Winland 2002). For example, the diaspora has been referred to as the "third pillar of the Croatian national budget" (Sopta 2001, 8-9). In their quest to reshape the contours of Croatianness, national elites have reached beyond their borders to the diaspora. For example, an integral component of the Croatian state-building program and one that draws further attention to the ethno-nationalist emphasis of Franjo Tudjman's regime was an active campaign to attract diasporic Croats to the homeland. Although Croatia has always been a nation of emigration, soon after independence it strove to become a nation of immigration by implementing policies aimed primarily at diasporic Croats living abroad.

Although the series of changes that propelled Croatia toward its independence in 1991 are to be found in the long and turbulent history of the region, there is no doubt that one of the most important forces fuelling the momentum of these changes is to be found in the diaspora. Central to Tudjman's success in 1990 was his ability to drum up considerable financial and political support in the diaspora, representatives of whom he recruited for his new national Cabinet. Most diasporic Croats enthusiastically embraced homeland efforts to involve them in Croatian national affairs. It soon became clear, then, that for those who had the resources, diaspora-homeland relations were shifting from largely personal family- and region-based ties to more public economics- and politics-based involvements in Croatia.

Internationally, diasporic Croats played a central role in the success of the Hrvatska Democratska Zajednica (HDZ). According to Misha Glenny (1992, 63), US$4 million was raised by emigrant Croats (primarily in Canada, the United States, Germany, and Australia) in support of the HDZ's political campaign in 1990. By 1992 Croats in Canada were the first diasporic group to have raised over US$1 million for Tudjman's electoral campaign. According to one of my Croatian Canadian contacts, who moved to Zagreb in 1996, "we bankrolled the revolution" (interview, 12 December 1998). It is common knowledge among Toronto Croats that the money raised in Toronto was instrumental in putting the HDZ leadership in power in Croatia (Sopta

1994, 78). However, some went further in suggesting that the involvement of Toronto Croats was decisive for Croatian independence. For example, a prominent Toronto Croat stated that "if it was not for the diaspora, Croatia would not be independent today" (interview, 10 September 1999). Another proclaimed that "we expatriates helped to save Croatia" (interview, 15 May 1998). The HDZ enjoyed a broad base of diasporic support in Croatia primarily because it was seen as largely responsible for shepherding Croatia toward long-sought independence. The continued importance of diasporic support was evidenced in the steady stream of Croatian government officials featured as keynote speakers at Croatian fundraisers in Toronto. This strategy has been widely used by leaders of nations with large expatriate communities, who often "actively [engage] in nation-building projects that [bind] transmigrants into the body politic of their states of origin" (Basch, Glick Schiller, and Szanton Blanc 1994, 267).

For close to ten years, diasporic Croats were courted by the HDZ regime; some were given choice political appointments, and others were extended investment opportunities. However, as a result of the January 2000 elections, when a left-of-centre coalition replaced the HDZ, the influence of the Croatian diaspora on homeland political and economic affairs diminished considerably, particularly given the resounding defeat of the HDZ, which received over 60 percent of the diaspora's vote. The perceived need of the new coalition to distance itself from the legacy of the HDZ was expedited in part through the marginalization of diasporic Croats, many of whom directly or indirectly supported the HDZ. Coalition members were concerned about the right-wing, nationalist influence of the diaspora on Croatian politics and the corruption that seemed to taint diasporic Croats alongside HDZ political leaders. They soon began to institute the changes necessary to limit diasporic involvement. Measures included closing the Ministry of Return and Immigration; delays in tabling a Bill of Returnees, modelled on the Israeli Law of Return; closing some consulate offices in the United States and Australia, which have the largest diasporic Croat populations; and a parliamentary review of the "special diaspora ticket," a provision added to the Croatian Constitution in 1995 by the HDZ that reserved twelve seats in the Croatian Parliament for diasporic representatives. Almost immediately after Tudjman's death in December 1999 and the subsequent replacement of the ruling HDZ with the left-of-centre coalition in January 2000, efforts were under way to make a definitive move away from an ethno-nationally based vision. However, this period (between 2000 and 2003) was short-lived, as the HDZ regained its majority status in the 23 November 2003 federal elections and has since continued as the ruling party.

The key question, however, is how diasporic Croats have negotiated these changes in light of Canadian political culture and as Canadian citizens. Although the postindependence politics of identity among diasporic

Croatians have been expressed largely in the language of culture and citizenship, they are also articulated from a position of indeterminacy and via an array of positionalities in Canada that, at times, conflict and challenge each other. I therefore provide a brief overview of Croatian immigrant experience in Canada before considering the central role that politics, both in Canada and Croatia, have played in determining the particularities of Croatian identity in Canada.

"Multikulturu Zivota"† and the Politics of Representation in Canada

As Croatians in Canada diversified along economic, generational, and even cultural lines, they began to negotiate their way into the socio-political and economic fabric of Canadian society. Early on in their settlement history, diasporic Croats were inward-looking, largely due to mainstream attitudes and treatment of Croatian immigrants, but they didn't remain so for long. In the early years of settlement, Croatians actively took part in politics not only in the Croatian community, but also in mainstream Canadian politics. Croatians at the time were linked to the trade-union movement, the Communist Party, and the left-leaning New Democratic Party of Canada (Bubrin 1994; Rasporich 1982).

By the end of the Second World War, they were no longer (publicly or politically) vilified as members of "inferior eastern-European stock" and began to define themselves as Europeans. Many began to see themselves as equal to, although distinct from, mainstream Canadians. This process was greatly facilitated by postwar immigration and changing attitudes in Canada on issues of diversity and cultural pluralism.

The Politics of Visibility

A key mitigating factor in self-identification as Croats in Canada has been the issue of visibility (see Dyer 1997; Mackey 1999). Thus, for older generations, obstacles and/or struggles encountered upon emigrating to and settling in Canada defined their experiences, as did their positioning in relation to other minority and/or immigrant groups. For most early immigrants, conditions of recognition in Canada have been negotiated largely *not* on their own terms. Further, during their struggles over the years to establish a presence in Canada, Croats have been at the margins of wider debates on the Canadian nation-building project due in large part to their equivocal relationship to the former Yugoslav state.

Over time, Croatians have responded in ways that reflect their acceptance of, ambivalence toward, or rejection of the terms (ethnic, national, etc.) under which recognition has been extended. However, the Canadian demographic landscape has shifted dramatically since the liberalization of

---

† "Multicultural life"

immigration rules in the late 1960s began to allow entry to immigrants from predominantly nontraditional (i.e., non-European) source countries. Whereas during the early decades of the twentieth century, Croatian immigrants were distinguished from the "we" (i.e., Anglo and northern Europeans) of the Canadian nation-state, they have since become subject to a "politics of recognition" (Taylor 1994) that has enabled them, as Europeans rather than the previously vilified *eastern* Europeans, to begin negotiating the terms of English/white equivalence privileged by the Canadian nation-state. Croats have thus seen their ethnic status improve relative to more "visible" newcomers; they have become part of the white invisibility of the social mainstream of Canada. The degree to which Croatians have embraced the opportunities afforded by these changes has been influenced by the complex history of Croatian settlement in Canada and by the vagaries of class, status, region, and other particularities of being Croatian in Canada. Despite changes in Canada that were generally favourable to ethnic groups like Croats, the Croation community has not tried to assert a highly visible public profile, even during the past thirty years of government-sanctioned multiculturalism.

Even though Croatians, by and large, have always placed importance on Croatian cultural heritage through Croatian religion, language and heritage classes, folklore ensembles (called *tambourica*), and recreational facilities (most of which were established by earlier immigrants) and even though Croats have maintained some degree of involvement in politics, the community in general has been characterized by a vague sense of ethnic pride and insularity (Rasporich 1982). Many Croatians interviewed and surveyed for this project concur with the assessment that Croats seem to have suffered for years from what some referred to as an "inferiority complex." When asked why this was the case, particularly first-generation Croatian informants argued that this was the result of negative stereotypes and fear generated by the Yugoslav government's years of monitoring Croatian expatriates as well as by negative portrayals of Croatians as fascists and extremists in the Canadian media and on the part of some Canadian politicians.

With the introduction of federal multicultural policies and initiatives in 1971, Croatian language and heritage programs as well as music and folklore groups flourished. Examples include the Croatian folklore ensemble Zrinski Francopan and the Croatian Canadian Artists Society (established in 1984), which sponsors the annual Croatian music festival in Canada. Among the services available to Croats are the Croatian Credit Union and Croatian language schools that have been in operation since the mid-1960s. Croatians were extremely proud when, in 1981, Awde Street in downtown Toronto was renamed Croatia Street. Sports, particularly soccer, are a major source of community identity and involvement. The Croatian national sports club, named Croatia, was established in Toronto in 1956. The centrality of

Croatian accomplishments and contributions to Croatian community life is epitomized in Croats' pride over the Metros-Croatia soccer team's win in the 1976 North American soccer championships. But, as is common in many ethnic-based social organizations, the potential for rifts and dissension is ever present. For example, the founding mandate of the Croatian Soccer League (established in 1955) was to promote the Croatian name and to remain politically neutral on the fate of Croatia as part of the Yugoslav federation. The commitment to political neutrality was, however, overshadowed by a history of acrimony and division regarding political issues. Over the years, political differences have thus pitted some Croatians against others and led to abiding feelings of mistrust. These internal political differences seemed to dissolve with the creation of the new Croatian state.

Although, like other ethnic immigrant groups, Croatians have developed a variety of different organizations over the years to meet religious, social, and cultural needs, intragroup relations have never been characteristically harmonious. Although many Croatian social clubs were gradually depoliticized in the 1970s and 1980s as a means of detaching themselves from negative political factionalism and achieving cultural objectives in line with those of Canadian multiculturalism (Rasporich 1982), disagreements over political views were common. Members who had political affiliations with, for example, the Croatian Peasant Party (CPP) did not agree with the political views of other more radical Croatian organizations (Sopta 1994, 136). "Any individual or group that dealt with Yugoslavia in any way were labeled as 'traitors' or 'Yugoslavs' by many mainstream Croats" (138).

An examination of commemorative activities among Toronto Croatians over the years also reveals their intrinsically political significance. Croatians in Toronto have a long history of celebrations and festivities of deep religious, historical, and community significance. But though a full calendar of anniversaries, testimonials, and religious and cultural festivals suggests the presence of a vibrant, proud, and united community, the reality is often more complex. Gillis (1994, 5) states that "commemorative activity is by definition social and political ... whose results may appear consensual when they are in fact the product of processes of intense contest, struggle, and, in some instances, annihilation." In many cases, the political significance of Croatian cultural/social events was explicit. For example, throughout the years, Toronto Croatians have gathered to commemorate the anniversary (8 August) of the 1928 assassination of Stjepan Radić, leader of the Croatian Peasant Party; the Day of All Souls (2 November) at a Croatian cemetery in northwest Toronto to honour friends and family killed in Croatia; the Annual Memorial Day in May marking the Bleiburg massacre of Croatian soldiers and civilians by Serbs in 1945; and finally, the anniversary of the Ustaše's seizure of power in Croatia on 10 April 1941, an event traditionally celebrated with religious masses and banquets. Thus, given that ethno-cultural festivals produce an abiding sense of identity through the concretization and essentialization of culture (Shukla 1997), a large percentage of Croatian commemorative occasions has had a deeply nationalist significance.

Postcommunist Change and the New Visibility

The images that dominated media accounts of atrocities and extensive destruction in the former Yugoslavia, particularly in places such as Croatia and Bosnia and Hercegovina, misleadingly depicted the region as condemned to endless cycles of violence due to age-old ethnic hatreds (Kaplan 1994; Ignatieff 1998; Kimball 1991). In the early stages of the war, Croatians emerged as victims of "Serb aggression" (i.e., the high-profile destruction of Vukovar and the occupation of one-third of Croatian soil), but they soon became the object of international condemnation for their role in the conflict, particularly for their alleged complicity in ethnic cleansing in parts of Croatia (e.g., Krajina) and parts of Bosnia and Herzegovina. The homeland war and Croatian independence fundamentally transformed the lives of many Croatians both in the diaspora and in the homeland while generating or reviving forms of association and identification for Croatians locally and globally – such as tortured and torturers, oppressed and oppressors, war victims and warmongers. In addition, the appellation "Balkan," historically associated with stereotypical and Orientalist assumptions of ancient ethnic hatreds and tribal animosities (for critiques of this view, see Todorova 1997; Halpern and Kideckel 2000; Lampe 2000), which gained currency in the early 1990s, resurrected unwanted associations for Croatians that were common in the early years of Croatian settlement in Canada. Memories of earlier condemnation and stereotyping by mainstream Canadians resurfaced with the onset of war in Croatia in 1990. This also had the effect of complicating efforts to publicly promote their vision of Croatians as central and western Europeans. Thus Croatians were once again made visible *not* on their own terms.

Consequently, though independence and the promise of a future free of communism have given Croatians an outlet for articulating positive nationalistic sentiments and ethnic pride, they have also become a means of renegotiating the terms on which their sense of belonging in Canada is based. For example, by promoting the Croatian state's efforts to establish a pluralist society modelled on Western liberal-democratic traditions, Croatians not only affirm their loyalty to the new Croatian state, but also demonstrate their commitment to and stake in the traditions and values of Canadian political culture. International recognition of Croatia as a sovereign and democratic state also provides Croatians with a new sense of pride and pedigree: as members of the new Croatian nation-state, they are no longer officially lumped together with all other nationalities from the former Yugoslavia. Croatians, therefore, continue to negotiate their identities as Canadians and/or Croatians on terms dictated by a Canadian state that discourages explicitly nationalist affiliations with homelands.

For example, the transnational interplay of political values is evidenced in the attitudes of many diasporic Croats toward the political future of the new Croatian homeland. Although diasporic Croats generally argue that Croatians in the new state should be left to chart their own national course, many interviewed felt that homeland Croatians should look to *them* for inspiration and guidance in their "transition to democracy." This attitude asserts not only their commitment, as Croatians, to the future of Croatia (as they imagine it), but also their view of themselves as the exemplars of a democratic (in this case, Canadian) political culture. As one Toronto Croat observed, "Croatians at home don't know the meaning of democracy. They have been under the communists for so long. They have a lot to learn" (interview, 21 October 2003). This view may also reflect a long-held insecurity concerning the perceived Canadian view of Croatians as Balkan peoples – a view reinforced during the war by Canadian and international media reports of "Balkan tribal hatreds" and the like – as well as Croatians' desire to free themselves from association with communist eastern Europe and Yugoslavia.

The composition and direction of diasporic organizations have changed somewhat since 1990 to reflect the shifting configurations and conditions of diasporic Croat life and meaning as well as the making and unmaking of diasporic forms of identity and affiliation. For example, the socio-demographic profile of Croatians in Canada, including data on self-identification, has shifted since Croatian independence, as indicated in the 1996 and 2001 Censuses, to reflect a marked decrease in identification as Yugoslav in favour of Croatian.

Not surprisingly, the past decade has also seen a significant gearing down of initiatives aimed at the Croatian homeland, such as wartime relief and fundraising. The Croatian Canadian Congress has incorporated many smaller Croatian organizations, and its mandate has changed since its inception. It was established to work for Croatian independence through relief efforts and to aid displaced peoples, but it has now affirmed its commitment to helping displaced Croats to get back to their homes. Although some organizations have been disbanded, many still exist and, in some cases, thrive.

Although less numerous than before independence, there are presently branches and/or representatives in Canada of four Croatian (homeland) political parties, the majority of which have maintained a presence in the three Croatian government regimes since independence (elected in 1990, 2000, and 2003). The existence and/or vitality of these organizations can be attributed to a variety of factors reflecting not only changes in homeland circumstances, but also changes in Toronto Croats' relations with one another as members of a postindependence community and changes in diaspora-homeland relations.

The language of citizenship also provides a new vocabulary for emigrant leaders, as it constitutes the ground for the formation of diasporic identity in Canada. In his analysis of Croatian involvement in Canadian politics, Bubrin (1994, 73) states that, "in most cases, a candidate's Croatian ethnicity was an incidental biographical detail that did not play a role in his or her candidacy." The two exceptions that he cites are John Šola and Mary Sopta (the wife of Marin Sopta, a diaspora returnee from Toronto who was instrumental in the election of Franjo Tudjman as the first president of Croatia). The case of Šola, a provincial politician of Croat descent in Ontario, provides an interesting example of how homeland events had an impact both on local Croatian politics and on the management of Croatian public image in Toronto. In 1987 John Šola was elected as a Liberal member of the provincial Parliament in Ontario. He was so well known for his vocal support of a free and independent Croatia that a reporter for a local Mississauga weekly newspaper commenting on the election results stated that "voters in Mississauga East have elected a man who seems to think he's gone to Queen's Park to free his Croatian homeland" (quoted in Bubrin 1994, 71). He enjoyed the financial and political support both of Croats in his Mississauga East constituency, which has a large Croatian population, and of Toronto Croats in general.

During the war, Šola became more involved and hence visible in Croat efforts for the homeland. He was present at many Croat functions and fundraisers in his capacity not only as the legislative representative for his constituency, but also as a Croatian nationalist. He first ran into trouble in 1991 for his comments about the war in Croatia when he stated in an interview aired on the current-affairs program *The Fifth Estate*, "I don't think I'd be able to live next door to a Serb" (CBC, 14 December 1991). Such comments provoked outrage from the Serb community in Toronto, some of whom lived in his riding. He was subsequently ousted from the Ontario Liberal caucus by the then Liberal Party leader, Lyn McLeod, due to what were seen as inappropriate remarks and, in the view of some critics, as crude nationalist invective. Šola continued to make controversial remarks, including those videotaped during his speech to Croatian students at York University in 1993, in which he stated that Serbian Canadians had shown that "they support ethnic cleansing, that they support mass rape, that they support mass murder." He sat as an independent until 1995. What this case makes clear is that the tolerance of the Canadian public for sentiments and practices that betray strong transnational interests and involvements on the part of diasporas in Canada is increasingly limited. Since the terrorist attacks of 11 September 2001 in New York and Washington, DC, the message of loyalty (to Canada) and belonging has been reinforced in a political climate of heightened suspicion where values of social cohesion are enunciated alongside those that champion the rights of ethnic, racial, and other minorities.

Although remittances and travel to the home country have been the traditional focus of scholars assessing transnational linkages, the introduction of computer-mediated communication into the lives of diasporic Croats has intensified the nature and quality of linkages between Croats worldwide. The recent development of far-reaching forms of information dissemination and communication linking Croatians internationally includes (1) a digital communication system that allows worldwide reception of Croatian television and radio programs that are particularly attractive to older, often first-generation Croatians, and (2) the proliferation of Internet sites ranging from electronic billboards and chat rooms/groups to online Croatian media, used extensively by the younger generation and/or by those who have the economic means to afford Internet technology. That these developments have coincided with major changes in the political fortunes of the homeland is significant. The prevalence and accessibility of electronic technologies has permitted many diasporic Croats to foster and maintain relatively easy and continuous contact. The significance of computer-mediated diasporic public spaces in particular (Castells 1996; Mitra 1997; Poster 1998; Rai 1995) is revealed in the politicized interpolation of "homeland" across geographical boundaries. The numerous and diverse interactive and noninteractive Croatian-themed websites have been aimed at or generated mainly by diasporic Croats.

One particularly important dimension of enhanced communication has been the use of the Internet as a conduit through which to disseminate the conservative politics of the homeland (see Rai 1995). This complex discursive field reveals positions ranging from those that reproduce rhetorical right-wing, ethno-nationalist discourses to those that link Croatians working for peace and human rights in postcommunist Croatia (Stubbs 1998). These include issue-oriented temporary sites, such as that generated in Australia in response to President Tudjman's efforts in 1996 to shut down Radio 101, an independent station in Zagreb, because of its critical stance on the HDZ; cultural and historical sites; and numerous others that contain lists of personal homepages of Croatians internationally.

One of the most significant effects – other than those that have necessarily followed from the establishment of an independent Croatian state (i.e., the dissolution of fundraising, political lobbying, and some relief efforts) – has been the persistence and, in some cases, reinvigoration of ties based on historical links to the homeland, such as region. For example, some organizations are still named after regions in Croatia: Klub Bosiljevo (a town in the county of Karlovac), Grupa Livno, Klub Karlovac, Klub Medjimurje, and

Klub Zagorje. Although their mandates are focused primarily on charity work, the names of these clubs underscore the continued relevance of ties of locality and region. Of interest is how the diasporic Croats interviewed reacted to the prevalence of regional affiliations as defining features of Croat organizations compared to the perceived state of affairs before 1990. The regionalism evidenced in clubs and other recreational associations identified by Toronto Croats is not looked upon favourably by many diasporic Croats. Some point out the irony inherent in perpetuating intragroup ties that often separate Croats, even after Croatian independence. Some lament the temporariness of the unifying effect that the war and independence had on Toronto Croats: "There is also a difference in defining Croatians. During and after the war we were all the same – people from Croatia – but now we differentiate between regions ... I mean people from Istra see ourselves as separate from the rest of Croatians; we don't really belong to Croatia, and we also don't belong to Italy" (interview, 14 May 2000).

Another important dimension of diasporic life that inevitably arises is the impact of the war in the former Yugoslavia on Croat-Serb relations in Toronto. Although clearly the war had a strong impact on people's sense of loyalty and allegiance, the effect on Croat-Serb diasporic relations on a more personal level often escapes critical attention. Over the course of this research, I found several cases of family discord resulting from, for example, Croat-Serb (and sometimes Croatian–Bosnian Muslim) marriages. The sensitivity of these situations made it extremely difficult to contact and/or interview Croats who had personally gone through this experience. Further, although I was not able to acquire any information that would lead to verification of some kind of pattern, Croats with whom I spoke both during and after the war all mentioned how family or social circles involving Serbs had changed significantly. The extent of acrimony over homeland politics between Croats and Serbs ranged from ambivalent to intense. One Croatian woman said: "My husband doesn't trust them [Serbs]. We don't want them to come to our house any more" (interview, 9 November 1999). Another commented: "After independence Croatians and Serbs have broken up: my father used to meet a Serbian family, but now they just say 'hi'" (interview, 12 May 2000).

One difficulty often framed as highly problematic when it arose in interviews was the pressure for mixed Croat-Serb families to take sides in the conflict. Neutrality was often considered a liability and, in some cases, was not tolerated. Relationships at times became so strained that a husband or wife left for Croatia, Serbia, or Bosnia to join family back home. Although tensions have decreased significantly since the war ended in 1995, *rapprochement* between the two communities has not gained significant momentum. However, the relatively neutral social and political space available to both Croats and Serbs of all generations in Canada provides both groups opportunities to work through their political views and to reflect on their social relationships. Thus some, particularly younger second- and third-generation Croats, have established close friendships with Serbs and Bosnians.

In some cases, the domestic politics of Croatian families have also been significantly affected by independence. For example, whereas the basis for loyalty, affiliation, and identity as Croatians among first-generation Croatians is often the localized space of shared villages or regions of origin, among those Croats who have grown up in Canada, the ways of being Croatian have been disciplined by the accessible and familiar language of ethnicity and by identity production consistent with the cultural logics of citizenship and belonging in Canada. Thus contemporary expressions of Croatian identity among many young Croatian Canadians are often entrenched in the concretization and essentializing of a distinctively Croatian culture. Even so, many second- and third-generation diasporic Croats are often ambivalent and/or conflicted over the issue of identities and allegiances.

Perhaps the most interesting insights into transnationalism and its relationship to the politics of diasporic identity can be seen in the attitudes and experiences of Croatian diasporic youth. For them, their primary socialization has taken place in the cross-currents of social fields that differ from those of their parents. For example, when asked to reflect on how they identified themselves as Canadians, over half of the fifty-seven university students whom I surveyed in 1996 mentioned multiculturalism as a key reference point. Intergenerational differences on the issue of multiculturalism, and the impact of these differences on perceptions of multiculturalism's role in identity claims, are evident. For example, multiculturalism does not factor heavily into personal identifications for older first-generation Croats, as evidenced in the following remarks: "Multiculturalism has not affected our Croatian identity – we have survived through our own choice to uphold our heritage with our own sweat and expense" (interview, 7 June 1993). By comparison, second- and third-generation Croat youth have grown up with the apotheosis of multiculturalism in the form of multicultural instruction (e.g., public-education programs) and the ubiquitous efforts of all levels of government to disseminate the multicultural message of mutual tolerance and respect for interethnic, racial, and cultural differences. Nevertheless, although second- and third-generation Croat youth are cognizant of the centrality of multiculturalism in discussions of Canadian identity, not all of their responses reflected an unqualified embrace of multicultural ideals.

Conclusion

Despite the heterogeneity that defines the Croatian diaspora in Toronto, all Croats have had to play the "politics of recognition" (Taylor 1994) in Canada according to terms set by the Canadian state, which foreground ethno-cultural traditions as part of the Croatian contribution to the (cultural) fabric of Canadian society, conceived of ideologically as a multicultural "mosaic" (Fleras and Elliott 1992). Croatians have had a range of strategies of identity formation from which to choose. Many chose the terminology and historical precedents of ethnicity (either as Yugoslavs or as Croatians, *culturally* defined) to construct themselves as an ethno-cultural group within the Canadian political and cultural landscape. However, since independence in 1990, diasporic Croats have had to negotiate a new reality marked by independence and its impact, either positive or negative, on their relationships with one another and on their sensibilities about who they are in relation to the host country and homeland. The context of Croatian homeland independence has provided diasporic Croats with an opportunity not only to express their newfound pride, but also to test the limits of tolerance for the expression of homeland loyalties in Canada.

Croatian Canadian responses to homeland independence thus provide the context for reexamining the premises upon which notions of identity are based, premises that assume permanent rupture between immigrants and their countries of origin and that hinge on the apparent fixity of these identifications, political and otherwise. The Croatian case demonstrates a highly complex relationship between different perceptions of and links to the homeland, the historical and contemporary dynamics of the diasporic community's structure and processes, and diasporic involvements in Croatian affairs. Although it is difficult to speculate on the degree to which social and political changes in Canada and in Croatia have contributed specifically to changes in Croatian self-perceptions, most Croats use terms of reference that reflect key conceptual categories of Canadian and Croatian identification. Therefore, it is important to investigate the degree to which identifications with the homeland are reflective and/or reactive and how they cohere with the politics of representation in Canada.

15
Canadian Jewry and Transnationalism: Israel, Anti-Semitism, and the Jewish Diaspora
Stuart Schoenfeld, William Shaffir, and Morton Weinfeld

The *Canadian Jewish News (CJN)*, one of Canada's weekly Jewish newspapers, regularly features a number of articles, notices, and advertisements linking Canadian Jewry to Israel and informing the readership, in considerable detail, of unfolding political, cultural, and economic events in the Jewish state. (Not coincidentally, the same can be said of the *Jewish Tribune*, another Canadian Jewish weekly newspaper.) For example, a headline in the 7 August 2003 edition of the *CJN* reads, "Thornhill couple adapts to a new home in Israel." The article tells of a couple who left "a comfortable life ... to realize their dream of making *aliya* [literally, 'ascending' via migration to Israel] with their five children" (6). According to the article, nearly a thousand North Americans had decided to immigrate to Israel the previous summer and, where necessary, had received financial assistance for the move. Another headline in this same edition announces, "*Aliya* program offers free schooling in Israel." The readers learn of a program that provides airfare, tuition, and free room and board for North American teens so that they can attend religious or secular schools while also matching students with a foster family for weekends and holidays.

Virtually each front page of these weekly papers either highlights or includes stories connected to Israel. Page after page details aspects of life in Israel, offers announcements of prominent Israelis who will be visiting and speaking in Toronto, Montreal, or elsewhere in the country, or includes advertisements seeking to connect Canadian Jews to Israel.

Indeed, throughout the past millennia, Jews remained intimately connected to their biblical homeland – Palestine and then Israel – and countless generations of diasporic Jews have traditionally prayed for a return to the Holy Land, recited "Next Year in Jerusalem" at the end of the Passover Seder, and prayed daily for a return to the Holy Land. Waller's (1981, 353)

This chapter is dedicated to the memory of Daniel J. Elazar, the foremost scholar of the Jewish diaspora.

observations about Zionism in Canada still ring true: "There can be no doubt that Canadian Jewry is very interested in Israel; in fact, identification with it is probably the strongest bond uniting Jews from sea to sea. It brings together individuals of all religious and political persuasions in such a general commitment that a kind of civic religion of orientation to Israel seems to have supplanted both the religious and the Zionist affirmation of earlier generations."

Attending to the links and commitments between Canadian Jewry, Canada, and Israel, this chapter looks at three case studies: Levitt and Shaffir on Canadian Jews making aliya but eventually returning to Canada; Cohen and Gold on Israelis in Toronto; and Schoenfeld, Schoenfeld, and McCabe on South African Jews in Toronto. Each illustrates how such connections unfold in everyday life and in the movements of persons from one society to another. However, we first set the stage with an account of Canadian Jewry as a diasporic community and, following the presentation of the studies, focus on how this community has been transformed by the establishment of the State of Israel and by new forms of anti-Semitic activity that manifest themselves through opposition to Israel, Israeli policies, and the basic idea of an independent Jewish state.

Canadian Jewry as a Modern Diaspora

Many Jews to Canada came with the wave of immigrants at the turn of the twentieth century. From about 4,000 Canadian Jews counted by the Census of 1881, the number grew to over 125,000 in 1921. At the turn of the century, Jewish migrants came almost entirely from central and eastern Europe. Millions of Jews were in flight after the outbreak in 1881 of widespread mob violence directed at Jews, which continued intermittently for forty years. Jews settled across Canada – in small towns and even in a few farming colonies but mostly in the largest cities. Together Montreal and Toronto have long accounted for over 70 percent of the Canadian Jewish population, and Vancouver has overtaken Winnipeg to become the Canadian city with the third-largest Jewish population.

In these settings, Canadian Jews followed the modernist strategy of compartmentalizing private and public life while combining this with selective cultural synthesis. They pursued integration into Canadian society through entrepreneurial capitalism, education, and advocacy of nondiscriminatory government policies.

In addition to pursuing integration, Canadian Jews established continuing connections to the transnational Jewish diaspora. Immigrant Canadian Jews established *landsmannschaften* (associations of Jews from the same place), which functioned as self-help organizations assisting in the adjustment of immigrants to Canada and also maintained ties with the European places of origin. Landsmannschaften often established Orthodox synagogues, linking themselves through ritual and study to the diaspora's history and religious practices. Canadian Jews took it for granted that their religion was transnational and would have considered any proposal for a locally produced "Canadian Judaism" to be peculiar and heretical.

Espousing sentiments paralleling those of other diasporas, Canadian Zionists did not consider their movement to be in conflict with their Canadian loyalty. The high drama of the first World Zionist Congress in Basel in 1897 was followed in 1899 by the coalescence of Canadian supporters into the Zionist Organization of Canada. The Canadian Zionist movement included individuals who personally dreamed of participating in the return to Zion. Mostly, however, it was composed of those who supported a Jewish homeland as a legitimate movement of self-determination and as a place of refuge for eastern-European Jewish masses experiencing severe intensifications of poverty, discrimination, and violent attack.

The Yiddish-speaking unions of early-twentieth-century Montreal and Toronto also played some role in maintaining a diasporic orientation. Members and leaders had personal connections with the Yiddish workers' movements in Europe. The formal ideology of Yiddish socialism was cosmopolitan, but there were strong emotional ties to the Jewish workers of eastern Europe. The Zionists among the workers had ideological, organizational, and emotional ties to the Zionist socialists who were doing the practical work of settling in the ancient Jewish homeland. Jews were among the leaders of the communist and social democratic movements in Canada and were conscious of themselves as a faction ("progressive Jews") within Canada, the Canadian Jewish community, and the world Jewish community.

The consciousness of being a diasporic people in Canada was further fostered by Jewish patterns of residential concentration, intragroup marriage, and community organization. These social patterns maintained a distinctive identity in private life as a counterpoint to integration as citizens with equal rights in public life. Jews remain one of the most residentially concentrated of Canadian ethnic groups (Balakrishnan and Hou 1999). Residential concentration has been paralleled by very high rates of intragroup marriage. Jews are still much more likely to marry among themselves than are Protestants and Catholics as well as members of most other ethnic groups whose presence in Canada goes back three generations (Weinfeld 2001, 372-75).

Residential concentration and kin ties have also formed a basis for communal organization. The network of charitable and social-service organizations found in other modern diasporas also developed in Canada. Jewish federations were created not only in the places with the largest Jewish populations (Montreal, Toronto, Winnipeg, and Vancouver), but also in cities with much smaller Jewish concentrations (Ottawa, Hamilton, London, Windsor, St. Catharines, Calgary, and Edmonton) (Elazar and Waller 1990).

Probably 95 percent of Canadian Jews live in a "federated" community. The federations are affiliated with the continent-wide United Jewish Communities. Canadian federations plan and support local activities, with social-welfare services and Jewish education as the common priorities. They support national institutions such as the Canadian Jewish Congress and the Jewish Immigration Aid Society and allocate funds to the needs of Israel and world Jewry.

Another example of the congruence of the national and the diasporic is the Canadian Jewish Congress, founded in 1919. On one hand, this organization advances the integration of Jews into Canadian society by representing the views of its Jewish citizens to Canadian governments. On the other hand, the Canadian Jewish Congress was founded in the context of a non-Canadian event: the post–First World War debates over minority national rights in Europe. In the 1930s and 1940s, the Canadian Jewish Congress vigorously but unsuccessfully tried to persuade Canada to alter its policy of refusing refuge to those fleeing Nazi genocide (Abella and Troper 1983). The congress agenda has always mixed an interest in Canadian issues with an interest in the Canadian role on the international scene. In particular, with the creation of Israel, the congress shifted its agenda away from national integration and toward stronger transnational ties (Elazar 1989). Indeed, in Jewish communities around the world, Israel-diaspora relations are constantly at the centre of attention and action in Jewish organizational life.

The connection to Israel is not just an expression of identification and shared fate. Israel is joined to Jews elsewhere through social and communications networks. The older social networks facilitated by membership in Zionist organizations still exist but are overshadowed by a broad range of relationships: familial, economic, professional, cultural, and philanthropic.

A few examples indicate the extent of the connections. Transnational family networks have been established by migration patterns. Hundreds of thousands of Holocaust survivors were resettled in the 1940s and 1950s. Hundreds of thousands of Jews fled Arab countries and other parts of the Islamic world. Larger numbers have left the former Soviet Union. Emigration has also been significant in many smaller Jewish communities, such as those in Ethiopia, South Africa, and South America. Israel, as a developing society and place of refuge since 1948, has admitted the majority of these migrants. However, many have gone to Europe and North America, and hundreds of thousands of Israelis now live overseas. North America and Europe have become both receivers and senders of Jewish migrants. Both Israel and the diaspora have become Jewish multicultural societies, with many members with family in other countries.

Economic ties sometimes take the form of direct investment. The Canada-Israel Chamber of Commerce and Industry stimulates bilateral trade and investment. The Canada-Israel Industrial Research and Development Foundation, established in 1993 and funded by the Canadian and Israeli governments, promotes joint research and development projects. A free-trade agreement between Canada and Israel – the first such agreement between Canada and a trading partner outside of the North American continent – came into effect in 1997. Business relationships are not limited to Canadian Jews, of course, but Jews are more likely than other Canadians to be involved. For example, a member of the Koffler family, which built the Shoppers Drug Mart chain in Canada, moved to Israel and built up Super-Pharm, Israel's major chain of drugstores (Arnold 1999).

Philanthropic ties link Canadian Jews and Israel. The United Jewish Appeal in Canada raises many millions of dollars each year, with about half going to local Jewish needs and about half going to social welfare overseas, mostly in Israel. In Canada, Israeli universities, hospitals, social services, and religious institutions of all sorts have established "Canadian Friends of ..." to raise funds directly and to cultivate ties with specific sectors of the Canadian Jewish population.

Religious groups have parallel, cooperating organizations in both Israel and Canada. Many of the teachers and some of the administrators in Canadian Jewish schools are Israeli. The Hebrew language and identification with Israel are part of the formal and informal curricula of Canadian Jewish schools. Missions to Israel, which combine touring and fundraising, involve thousands of Canadian Jews each year, and programs of touring and study offer young Canadian Jews their personal experience of Israel.

These varied relationships are maintained by travel, telephone, and the Internet. Families visit relatives, sometimes celebrating bar/bat mitzvahs or weddings. Canadians who have retired to Israel travel back and forth, as do Canadians who have bought homes in both countries. Students spend a year at an Israeli university or other educational institutions. Youth and other groups tour. Israeli tourists visit Canada; businessmen, rabbis, and professionals travel in both directions. In the 2000 Israeli election, political parties subsidized charter flights of Israelis returning to vote. Not to be outdone by these charters, El Al offered a special fare to overseas Israelis who flew in for the election and stayed no more than a week.

Telephone rates to Israel are competitive. Just as the travel agents and airlines advertise in the *Canadian Jewish News,* so, too, do phone companies. The Internet is rich with English-language sites that connect Israelis and the diaspora. Canadian Jews have easy access to Israeli organizations through websites – including two Israeli daily papers in English – and to individuals through e-mail.

This brief sketch of transnational ties between Israel and the diaspora illuminates an apparent paradox. Although a focus on the importance of the nation-state is a preoccupation of modern politics, the reality of the

State of Israel has been that of a small state in which transnational networks are of fundamental importance. Life in Israel can be understood only by reference to what is happening outside its borders in the Jewish world and even more so in the world at large. The State of Israel has drawn Jews in the other parts of the world away from a consciousness of themselves as identifying only with their countries of citizenship and toward an identity that continues to link them to a global social network and a self-conscious globalized identity. The establishment of a Jewish state has been associated with the promotion of a transnational perspective rather than a national one (Schoenfeld 1999).

Three Case Studies

Aliya and Return

In research on aliya, usually focusing on standard push-and-pull models (Goldberg 1985; Tabory and Lazerwitz 1977), Jewish commitments are the primary pull factors, representing a basically ideological attraction to Israel, while the push derives from some form of dissatisfaction with one's community or lifestyle in North America (Antonovsky and Katz 1979; Berman 1979). This claim is borne out in research conducted by Cyril Levitt and William Shaffir (1990) that examined Canadian Jews' decisions to make aliya and the circumstances prompting their return migration to Canada following a series of unsuccessful aliya experiences.

Although offering various reasons for the decision to embark on aliya, all respondents mentioned a desire to live in the Jewish state and to realize the long-standing dream of leading a Jewish life in a Jewish homeland. However, they did not claim that they felt driven out of Canada because of rising levels of anti-Semitism or feelings of second-class citizenship. On the contrary, they spoke appreciatively about the range of freedoms and opportunities available in Canada while nevertheless expressing a sense of unease about the Christian character of the country, especially the public celebration of Christian holidays. By contrast, Israel was expected to offer a milieu where the celebration of Jewish festivals, even if undertaken in a secular mode, would no longer situate them in a minority position.

Apart from one person in the sample, all those who had emigrated to Israel had lived in comfortable circumstances in Canada. They had visited Israel, had consulted not only with friends or relatives living in Israel, but also with Israeli government officials, and were generally aware of the range of difficulties that they were likely to encounter.

A common denominator for all respondents preparing for aliya was their perception of approaching, or having already reached, a turning point in their lives (Strauss 1969). All stated that a break in their pattern of living was imminent or was advisable. One such case was a Toronto businessman who said: "I just seemed to be getting more and more bogged down in my work. I was in a real rut. When we decided to go for a brief vacation to Israel, I began to see a way out. It could be my place of renewal. The country was alive, and I was dead. Here I could make a fresh start."

Some respondents pointed out that when they took stock of their particular circumstances, including the long-term future of their children, they were confident that they would be able to settle without great difficulties in Israel. A mother of three young children recalled, "We moved in 1983. Our kids were at an age that unless we did it at that point, we would have to do it when we retired." In another case, the impetus was provided by the changes that were reshaping the political landscape of Quebec: "We always had considered aliya, but we never had either the push or the pull. [René] Lévesque [then premier of Quebec] gave us the push. We were getting the hell out of Montreal, not because we had to. There was nothing wrong with my practice, and my French was fluent, too. So we said, 'We're leaving' ... Then we said, 'Since we talked about aliya potentially, for many years already, so now that we're leaving, there's only one place we can go. And that's Israel.'"

Levitt and Shaffir's respondents were aware that the announcement of their plans to settle in Israel would cause some surprise, and they were particularly concerned about the effect that their decision might have on their close relatives, friends, and business associates. Toward this end, they learned to craft a set of convincing arguments that the decision to make aliya had not been arrived at impulsively, as both the advantages and disadvantages had been carefully weighed. As one person observed, "The truth is that you have to come up with a story, but in a way, the story is as important for yourself as for others." People developed a script with a storyline, which was carefully and continually rehearsed, modified, and refined as the aliya plans crystallized.

In an unpublished paper that focuses on several of the challenges faced by Canadian *olim* (immigrants) when integrating into Israeli society, Shaffir (2001) emphasizes the positive features of the experience identified by the respondents. Immersed in the process of acclimatizing to a different style of life, olim took stock of how the experience impacted favourably on their self-image and on the new directions that they were pursuing in their lives. Although focusing most immediately on friendships and interpersonal relationships, they were also philosophical about matters of Jewish identity. Said one: "This isn't an easy country, but it's our country, it's the homeland of the Jewish people. My kids feel very Jewish here, and our family is far more Jewish here than we were in Montreal. You feel Jewish by everything around you ... I live my life as a Jew, and you just can't do it in the same way anywhere but in Israel."

Although not pushed out by anti-Semitism and while appreciative of the opportunities available in Canada, the vast majority of respondents claimed to miss little about Canada, save for some people left behind. "Maybe the odd good lobster," says Gerry, "but I really have no yearnings, or losses, or desires. I don't miss the weather. Israel has everything."

Although respondents not infrequently emphasized the years of planning required to finally realize their dream to live in Israel, unexpected circumstances in Israel compelled numbers of them to reevaluate the decision and to reluctantly return to Canada. For those, the conditions experienced living in Israel progressively deteriorated over time to such an extent that, in the end, they found life there almost intolerable. This was revealed by the phrase "dropping the bottom line," which virtually every respondent either used or implied. For example, "The ground rules, or the bottom line, kept changing. You put your bottom line here [outlining the process with table cutlery], and then here, but then we kept dropping the bottom line ... And you can only drop the bottom line so far until things fall apart."

The final firm decision to return was apparently not precipitated by any one dramatic event but was the result of a series of setbacks over a period of time. In one case, the decision to return to Canada after two and a half years in Israel "was the culmination of seven or eight months of thinking and seeing what the alternatives might be to stay. Because there's no discussion that we would have preferred to stay ... One day we made the decision; we had already explored all the other possibilities." Following meetings with government officials and discussions with relatives and friends, this couple was forced to admit that financial constraints had become severe, adversely affecting their marital relationship.

In most cases, economic considerations led olim to reassess their position and prospects. As one respondent explained: "I was involved in work for which I was getting more than the national average but which was considerably below our lifestyle. We adjusted it considerably in Israel, but we had not adjusted enough to compensate. And basically, any kinds of savings we had, we went through it completely ... And the only asset that we had when we came back to Toronto was through the sale of our apartment in Israel."

Another respondent, who had been a successful real estate agent in Toronto and had gone to settle in Israel in 1982, commented that he and his wife had been prepared to reduce their standard of living but had not expected the drastic reduction that became necessary: "My wife saw the writing on the wall long before I did. And she's saying, 'This isn't going to work; we're losing money every month' ... We figured out what it costs to live there, and it came out [to] ... about $2,500 a month, Canadian. Who makes $2,500 a month in Israel? So if you make $2,200 Canadian a month, you're losing $300 a month. So we see it's not working."

None of the respondents stated that the decision to return to Canada had been chiefly motivated by the unstable political situation or by the fear of physical danger. Although some referred in passing to the violence occasioned by the ongoing conflict with the Palestinians or to aging family members left behind who needed their support, all spoke about failed dreams. "I had a dream," laments one individual about the return to Montreal. "The dream was that I would come to Israel, find some place in the business community, and I would be able to send tickets to my children in Montreal to visit once a year, and Janice [his wife] and I would visit them once a year. The dream is shattered." And another: "I always believed that I was returning to my real home, and that is why we came on aliya ... I'm among Jews, the bond is tangible ... you feel it all the time. [But] we have to return ... My heart is broken."

To a person, though critical of some of their experiences during the course of their aliya – be these in the realms of politics, encounters with the bureaucracy, or daily interactions with Israelis – all continued to identify strongly with Israel. And for all, Israel would remain at the core of their Jewish identity; they would feel connected to it in a manner that Canada, despite its material advantages, could not duplicate.

Israelis in Toronto

In a series of insightful articles, Rina Cohen and Gerald Gold have explored the origins, structure, and dynamics of the Israeli immigrant community in Toronto, which has remained distinct from the Jewish Canadian diasporic community. They gathered their data primarily through informal interviews and participant observation and divided their research into three phases between 1991 and 1997. Although precise figures for the number of Israelis are unavailable, the authors estimate the number at between 25,000 and 35,000. Observing that immigrants can maintain multiple linkages, including emotional ties to their homelands (Goldring 1996; Al-Rasheed 1994), they focus on the mechanisms employed by the Israeli diaspora in Toronto to remain connected with their Israeli homeland.

The Israelis, we are informed, stress that they remain loyal Israeli citizens who have every intention of returning to Israel. Their task is far from simple. The conceptualization of the Israeli diaspora as *yordim* (literally, those who have gone down) reflects a Zionist ideology that derogatorily describes those who have "descended" from a higher place, the land of Israel, to a lower one, the diaspora. In this respect, Israeli emigrants have been stigmatized. Having internalized the Zionist ideology, they must rationalize their decision to leave, realizing, as they do, the vulnerability of Israel, whose existence remains threatened. As Cohen and Gold (1996, 17) observe, "The *yordim* cope with their sense of guilt about deserting Israel by asserting that they have firm plans to return, and that since their absence is purely temporary, they do not need to take any steps to become integrated into the life-style of the new country." And, indeed, they do not. Although Israelis in Toronto send their children to Jewish schools, live in Jewish neighbourhoods, and participate in locally organized Jewish communal activities, they remain marginal in the community and "have developed distinctive Israeli communal activities involving politics, recreation, culture, and entrepreneurship" (Cohen 1999, 121).

Jointly and separately, Cohen's and Gold's work (Cohen 1999; Cohen and Gold 1996, 1997; Gold 1992; Gold and Cohen 1996) examines how the Israeli community in Toronto has failed to integrate more fully into the larger Jewish community. In their 1996 publications, they identify features that distance Israelis from this larger community, including language, their life experiences growing up in Israel, and stereotypes held by each group about the other that provide boundary markers reinforcing the Israelis' distinct identity. They note that their respondents stressed their intention to return to Israel and that, unlike diasporic Jews, they did not intend to remain permanently in their non-Jewish native land. Impressively, only three of the sixty-two first-phase respondents identified themselves as yordim. However, they observe that while attempting to coordinate the requisite logistics, they continuously postpone their return to Israel. The development of a plan to return, a return that is mythical in nature and, therefore, never materializes, paradoxically enhances the social construction of an Israeli ethnicity and contributes to the formation of this ethnic community. Gold (1992, 235) contends that a mutual rejection among North American Jews and Israeli immigrants both shapes and reinforces "an emergent ethnic boundary ... and nurtures the formation of a distinctive and situational Israeli ethnicity which coalesces around ties which link Israelis into network-based communities that circuitously avoid the labyrinth of the highly-organized Jewish communities." In a later article, Cohen (1999) addresses the two major components that are responsible for the emergence of this distinctive community. First, whereas the ethnic identity of the "host" Jewish community is essentially shaped by matters of religious affiliation, support of Israel, and involvement in Jewish institutions, the bases of Canadian Israelis' identity are national affiliation and fluency in the Hebrew language and culture; the second concerns the extant tension between the organized Jewish community, largely committed to Israel and to Zionism, and the expatriate Israelis who have left the ancestral homeland to pursue their careers on Canadian soil. Although Israelis in Toronto share certain characteristics with the host community – for instance, certain cultural and religious practices and identification with Israel – there remains a fundamental distinction between these communities. Cohen (1999, 127) observes, "When Israelis migrate to Canada, they carry with them the national-cultural ethnic identity. Consequently, an incongruity develops between their ethnic identity and the religious-based (Orthodox, Conservative, or Reform) identity of Canadian Jews; this incongruity is the basis for some tension between the two groups."

These differences have led Israelis to coordinate their own activities and institutions, "including synagogues, seniors' organizations, a school, day-care centres, Israeli chapters of philanthropic associations, specialty stores, travel agencies, restaurants, night clubs, health clubs, book clubs, folk-dancing clubs, and other activities, effectively creating an Israeli *shikun* [denoting a crowded Israeli area] at the corner of Bathurst Street and Steeles Avenue" (Cohen 1999, 123). As well, roughly half of Israelis in Toronto read an Israeli newspaper or weekly magazine that can be purchased in Jewish areas of the city. Additionally, numbers of them access Hebrew newspapers and Israeli radio through the Internet.

Thus it is not entirely surprising that most Israelis in the study (78 percent) socialized exclusively with other Israelis, that this socialization pattern extended to those who had lived in Toronto for more than twenty years, and that the resulting networks were instrumental in helping Israelis to find both new friends and employment.

Interestingly, Cohen and Gold detect an important change among second-generation Israelis. Cohen (1999, 131) writes: "While adult immigrants ... describe themselves as unhyphenated Canadians, the younger generation feel that they are Canadian, part of the larger Jewish community in Canada." Raised in Canada, they connect to Judaism differently from their parents; their ethnic identity is centred more around Judaism than around Israeli nationalism. "The parents of these children, immigrants from Israel to Canada, define themselves ethnically as Israelis ... Their children, however, are engaged in gradually developing a Diasporic Jewish identity" (132). Practically speaking, they are more comfortable expressing themselves in English than in Hebrew, and the majority attend public schools and, much like the children of other Jews in Toronto, attend the same summer camps and participate in Jewish organizations. In the process, "they have gradually detached themselves from the Israeli community of immigrants and immersed themselves in the general Jewish population" (133).

Nevertheless, despite this apparent shift leading toward integration into the mainstream Jewish community, the presence of a sizable Israeli population in Toronto has changed the cultural politics of the diaspora.

South African Jews in Toronto

Interviews with over two hundred Jews who moved from South Africa to Canada between 1971 and 1990 (Schoenfeld, Schoenfeld, and McCabe 1999) show the significance of transnational ties and the ambivalence of diasporic identities. During these years almost 40,000 Jews left South Africa, a significant out-migration from a community that totalled not quite 120,000 persons in 1970. Of that number, almost 4,000 settled in Canada. The migrants left a small, closely knit community, which had grown slowly after the mass Jewish emigration out of Europe at the turn of the twentieth century.

As in Canada, many organizations founded by Jews in South Africa were both local and transnational. The substantial majority of Jewish congregations were founded as Orthodox. Although some provision was made for local training of religious functionaries, Orthodox Judaism in South Africa established ties to Orthodox Judaism elsewhere. Similarly, those who established the small number of Reform congregations joined this broader network. B'nai B'rith lodges linked their members to a worldwide Jewish service organization.

Zionism was the basis of much organizational activity in South Africa. Zionist groups formed the South African Zionist Federation in 1905, which was the first all-national Jewish group. Membership in Zionist youth movements, which functioned as social clubs, became a common part of growing up Jewish in South Africa. The Women's Zionist Organization of South Africa, like Hadassah in the United States, became a mass-membership organization active in fundraising for services directed at women and children. The United Israel Appeal was founded to raise funds in support of Zionist work. After Israel attained independence, other organizations were established to support specific institutions, to promote tourism, and to encourage aliya.

The election of the National Party in 1948 put South Africa on a course of intensified segregation and apartheid. Jews began leaving. Following the antiapartheid riots that began in 1976, Jewish emigration increased. Many went to Israel, which is not surprising given the strength of the Zionist movement among South African Jews. However, over two-thirds chose to migrate elsewhere, primarily to the United States, Australia, the United Kingdom, and Canada.

Migrants to Canada spoke about the combination of English-language economic opportunity and a strong Jewish community. Family ties were important in the choice of Canada, mentioned more than any other factor. Many had close relatives who had already immigrated to Canada. Some had moved elsewhere first, including Israel. More than half of the South African immigrants to Toronto considered themselves Zionists. Those who had previously lived in Israel almost always explained their aliya in Zionist terms. Even though they spoke of the difficulty of living in Hebrew, of the lower standard of living, of the divisiveness of Israeli politics, and of the tension occasioned by the ongoing conflicts in the Middle East, they continued to consider themselves Zionists. Respondents spoke of friends and relatives in Israel and some looked forward to retiring there.

Some reported being even stronger Zionists in Canada. One commented: "Since meeting Holocaust survivors in Canada, I've become even more for the existence of Israel." Compare the answers to a question on the Holocaust. Asked whether "all Jews everywhere should see themselves as if they had survived the Holocaust," over half strongly agreed (55 percent of the respondents rated their agreement at 8 or over on a 10-point scale). Others became more critical. One respondent expressed it this way: "In South Africa there was total devotion [to Israel] in any circumstances. In Canada, one examines more the approach to Israel. In terms of support and love, there is no change."

Those who did not consider themselves to be Zionists in South Africa mostly kept the same self-identification in Toronto. They distinguished being Zionist and being pro-Israel. As one said, "I still support them in spite of everything. We have to have a homeland, but I couldn't live there." Among many, the identification as "Zionist" seems restricted to a clear commitment either to making a new life in Israel or to formal membership in a Zionist organization. "Pro-Israel" has a different meaning. No one interviewed questioned the legitimacy of the State of Israel, its importance to the Jewish people, or the importance of the relationship between Jews living in the diaspora and Jews living in Israel. Among the respondents, Zionist or not, there was very strong agreement with the statement that "Jews, regardless of where they live, have a special obligation for the welfare of the State of Israel" (almost 70 percent gave responses of 8 and over on a 10-point scale).

The decision to migrate to Canada while maintaining emotional and practical ties to Israel may be seen in the context of what it means to be Jewish in the diaspora, to be a Zionist, and to be an Israeli. Diasporic Jewish migration choices are pragmatic, being guided only partly by ideology. The South African Jewish immigrants to Canada, like other diasporic Jews, negotiate the Zionist dream and the Israeli reality. Most attend synagogues, where they join the congregation in reciting the ancient prayers for the return to Zion and the contemporary prayer for the welfare of Israel. They make financial contributions to support Israel. Many are members of Zionist organizations, just as they were in South Africa. They visit Israel, read about Israel, and send their children to schools in which they are taught to identify with Israel. Many consider aliya, if not for themselves, then for their children. The choice to live in Canada is not a choice to cut ties with Israel but to express them through means other than residence.

Israel, Anti-Semitism, and Canadian Jews

Support for Israel has emerged as a focal point of the contemporary Jewish diaspora and as a central feature of Canadian Jewish political activity (Taras and Weinfeld 1993; Taras and Goldberg 1989). But many observers, and certainly most Jews in Canada and elsewhere in the diaspora, now feel that as traditional measures of anti-Semitism decline, a new form of anti-Jewishness tied to hostile attitudes about Israel and Zionism has emerged. Websites of the Canadian Jewish Congress, B'nai B'rith Canada, and international Jewish organizations such as the World Jewish Congress document this concern (for the British case, see Kosmin and Iganski 2003 and Penslar, Marrus, and Stein 2005; for the Canadian case, see Weinfeld 2001).

The impact of homeland conflicts on Canadian diasporic communities is not new. Japanese, Italian, and German Canadians suffered during the Second World War to varying degrees. Since the terrorist attacks of 11 September 2001 in New York and Washington, DC, Canadians of Islamic and/or Arabic background have experienced new expressions of hostility or government scrutiny rooted in potential terrorist acts and threats emanating from the Middle East. Jews have wrestled with allegations of dual loyalty for some time. Pro-Israel advocacy is an important element in the activities of many of the major national Jewish organizations in Canada. For Canadian Jews today, anti-Semitism is increasingly rooted to the Jewish tie with Israel.

B'nai B'rith provides annual counts of acts of anti-Semitism, and in recent years the numbers have risen, although not in a linear fashion. For the year 2002, the number reached 459, which included a troubling 60 percent jump over the figures for 2001. The long-term rise has reflected better reporting; the dramatic recent one-year gain was probably caused, in the view of B'nai B'rith officials, by tensions in the Middle East related to the second Palestinian-declared *intifadah* (literally, uprising) against the State of Israel (Canadian Press 2003).

Events such as the Concordia University riot in September of 2002, which led to the cancellation of a speech by former Israeli prime minister Binyamin Netanyahu, and the 2004 Concordia decision preventing former premier Ehud Barak from speaking on campus are seen by many Canadian Jews as expressions of or linked to anti-Semitism. Some Canadian Jews see anti-Israel bias on the part of some Canadian media. Norman Spector, former Canadian ambassador to Israel, took the unprecedented step of publicly accusing the Canadian Broadcasting Corporation (CBC) of a systematic anti-Israel bias in its Middle East coverage, which had helped to spread currents of anti-Semitism. Indeed, *Globe and Mail* columnist Jeffrey Simpson glibly refers to "Likudniks" in the Bush administration, Likud being current Israeli prime minister Ariel Sharon's right-of-centre governing party (Simpson 2003, A15; Eden 2003).

Most of the traditional indicators, with the exception of reported incidents, suggest that Canadian anti-Semitism has been declining since the 1950s and is relatively low by comparative standards. Nevertheless, there is a palpable concern among some in the Canadian Jewish community that despite their economic success in the diaspora, anti-Semitism is a real and growing danger (see Penslar, Marrus, and Stein 2005). Many Canadian Jews fear that a "chilly climate" is spreading regarding the defence of Jewish or Israeli interests. *Globe and Mail* science columnist Stephen Strauss (2002) wrote an anguished column on the spectre of anti-Semitism in Canada. Minister of Justice Irwin Cotler (2002, 1) described a "new, virulent, globalizing, and even lethal anti-Jewishness reminiscent of the atmospherics of the 1930s."

It is important to distinguish between "Canadian anti-Semitism" and "anti-Semitism in Canada." The former refers to the traditional motifs of Canadian anti-Semitism: the social, cultural, and economic exclusions that are part of the historical record in all parts of Canada. The latter refers to worldwide trends in anti-Semitism that impact the entire Jewish diaspora, including Canada, in similar ways. Multiple phenomena converge in the globalization of anti-Semitism: the movement of peoples, as migrants, refugees, and visitors, both around the world and into Canada; the increased salience of the Middle East conflict in Canada as articulated by diasporic Jewish/Israeli and Arab/Muslim communities, which are increasingly mobilized on foreign policy matters; and the role of the Internet and communications generally in spreading anti-Semitism and in multiplying the impact of anti-Semitic acts (e.g., the beheading of American Jewish journalist Daniel Pearl in Pakistan by Islamic terrorist groups), in linking anti-Jewish and anti-Israeli forces, and in providing competing sources of information and worldviews. Both Jews and their enemies are now virtual communities.

The central aspect of this new globalized anti-Semitism is the linkage between anti-Semitism, anti-Zionism, and opposition to Israeli policies. It is often hard to tell when "protests" against Israel are criticism of policy, part of a campaign of delegitimation, or part of a war against "the Jews."

Anti-Zionism in current discourse can be defined as opposition to the legitimate existence of the Jewish State of Israel and support for efforts to dismantle the state or undermine its existence. In fact, such intellectual anti-Zionism can provide cover and respectability to terrorist groups and states that seek actively to attack and eventually destroy Israel. Anti-Zionism does not exist in a real-world vacuum. The anti-Zionist position is perceived by diasporic Jews as anti-Semitic because it denies the Jewish people the right to national liberation and self-determination, rights accorded to most other peoples (King 1967, 76).

In earlier decades opponents of Israel were very careful to couch their discourse as anti-Zionist or anti-Israel. Militant Islamist websites, which tend to support terrorist attacks by militant Islamic groups, do not make this distinction but often condemn Jews and their supporters. The firebombing of a Jewish school library in Montreal, reports of blatantly anti-Semitic sermons in a British Columbia mosque, and comments by the head of the Canadian Islamic Congress that any Israeli adult, male or female, is a legitimate target for terrorist attacks are Canadian manifestations (CBC 2005; Wikipedia 2005; Jiminez 2004). These kinds of events are linked by Jews to increasing Muslim/Arab migration to Canada. Today, the anti-Zionist idea sustains a campaign to delegitimate Israel in the world community and, by extension, all the diasporic Jewish communities that support Israel. It offers a rationale for unacceptable levels of violence, whether in terror attacks, in suicide bombings, or in other forms.

There is no clear link between anti-Semitism and criticism of Israeli policy. Canadian Jews who see themselves as Zionists are themselves sharply divided, from left to right. The charge of anti-Semitism should never be used as a knee-jerk response to stifle vigorous criticism and debate about Israeli policies in Canada. Canadian Jews and non-Jews alike have the right to criticize Israeli policy, without fear of moral censorship. But equally, others have the right to object when critics of Israeli policies ally themselves with, support, and promote those who condemn Israel as always guilty and make war against the Jews. There are occasions when harsh, one-sided criticism of Israeli policies is indeed anti-Semitic in its consequences and possibly in its motive. Many criticisms of Israeli policies are made not for any constructive purpose but to delegitimate Israel itself. These criticisms often have a fervour bordering on Judeophobia (see Kosmin and Iganski 2003). As criticism of Israel grows louder and as Israel is made a pariah among nations, Canadian Jews are attacked for being supporters of Israel.

Demographic changes also matter. The Canadian Jewish population is growing slowly, while Arab and Muslim communities are growing rapidly, mainly through recent immigration. These changes are noticeable on Canadian campuses and in major cities, especially Montreal and Toronto. They have consequences for the atmosphere on campuses (e.g., Concordia University in Montreal) and for political life in terms of mobilizing a Canadian "Muslim" vote (Elmasry 2004; Ouellette 2004).

Changes in the global political environment worry Canadian Jews. Attacks on Israeli policies have led to greater isolation for the Jewish community. Liberal Jews in particular feel not only discomfort with the aggressive policies of the Israeli government, but also abandonment by former allies on the left. This trend has intensified since 1967. In the prevailing "progressive" discourse on geopolitics, Israel is seen as Western/colonial, white, and tied to the United States – three serious strikes.

The diasporic tie to Israel may be more problematic for Canadian Jews than for their American counterparts. The United States has for years been recognized as Israel's staunchest ally and supporter. The United States is more likely to vote with Israel – often alone – on contentious United Nations resolutions than is Canada, for which abstentions have been the more "even-handed" response. Despite the magnitude of Canadian trade with the United States, there remains a reflexive anti-Americanism among many in Canada's political and cultural elite, who would seek to distance Canadian from American foreign policy on matters such as the conflict with Iraq and the Israeli-Palestinian dispute. Anti-Americanism in Canada works to the detriment of Canadian Jews who support Israel and, by apparent extension, the United States. Israel is at the core of the Jewish diaspora, and Canadian anti-Semitism today is intertwined with attacks on Zionism and Israel, reflecting global forces and ideologies.

Conclusion

Place of residence looms large in consciousness. However, as these studies show, the lives of Jews in Canada are deeply affected by transnational networks and identities. Jews have long thought of themselves, and been thought of by others, as a people with a transnational identity and social networks. The oldest use of the word "diaspora" is usually traced to the Septuagint, the Greek translation of the Torah (the five books of Moses) made over two thousand years ago. Although the word is now used more widely in academic circles, the most common dictionary definitions of "diaspora" continue to refer to the dispersal of the Jews from the time of the Babylonian exile to the present.

As periods of toleration turned to periods of persecution, centres of Jewish population and cultural creativity moved from place to place: from Babylonia to Spain, to Germany, and in the early modern period, to eastern Europe. The cultural centrality of the eastern-European diaspora ended with mass murder in the 1940s. From the 1950s onward, the centres of Jewish life have been the communities in the United States and in the newly re-created Jewish state. The Canadian diaspora, now one of the larger communities outside of the two centres, represents about 3 percent of world Jewry.

Our review of transnational ties among Canadian Jews has implications for contemporary understandings of transnationalism in general. Analytical accounts of the meaning of diaspora have usually presented the Jews as a "classical" case, contrasted with more recent emergent forms. The Jewish diaspora, however, has not been an invariant structural type.

On the one hand, it is possible to see a continuing theme in the Jewish diaspora: a cultural emphasis on the transcendent importance of Jewish belief and way of life that has justified the refusal to assimilate into the surrounding societies. On the other hand, in many visible features of daily life – food, clothing, language – Jews have adopted the practices of their host societies. Jewish ideas have been reshaped in deep dialogues with the ideas of host cultures.

As Jews moved to different cultural milieus, they engaged in intricate debates about the meaning of their dispersion. Rather than perpetuating an identity fixed at the time of their departure from their homeland, Jews were like the shape-shifter of folklore, whose different forms are adaptations to different circumstances. The ancient dispersion before the destruction of the Second Temple was unlike the exile after the loss of Jewish sovereignty. Jewish culture changed in Christendom and in somewhat different ways in the Muslim world. The politics of modern nationalism in turn changed the social structure and culture of the Jewish diaspora. Historical events in the mid-twentieth century and contemporary social trends again transformed the diaspora. The variations in contemporary Jewish diasporas, as the three case studies examined in this chapter indicate, reflect contingent, emergent forms rather than stages in a standardized model of the evolution of diasporic communities.

The variable, reflexive reinvention of the Jewish diaspora has implications for how diasporas in general are approached analytically. It may be useful to think of diaspora as a metaphor or as a sensitizing concept. Even if there is an explicit recognition that real diasporas combine the characteristics of more than one type, there are limitations to sketching out the characteristics of various types, as Robin Cohen (1997) has proposed. Typologies inevitably give the impression of fixed characteristics, drawing attention away from continuing change. An analytical perspective more attentive to change could come from a focus on various kinds of transnational relationships – familial, political, economic, religious, and so forth – and on the processes that originate, sustain, and change them. The Jewish case suggests the importance of attending to transformations in diasporas and to how historical events change patterns of transnational networks. In shifting the analytical gaze to the transnational, the concept of diaspora is powerful simply for directing our attention to those processes through which local structures and meaning systems are embedded in the global.

Acknowledgments
A section of this chapter originally appeared in Morton Weinfeld, "The Changing Dimensions of Contemporary Canadian Antisemitism," in Penslar, Marrus, and Stein (2005). We wish to thank the University of Toronto Press for authorizing reproduction of this material.

Conclusion:
Directions for Future Research
Vic Satzewich and Lloyd Wong

The approaches to transnationalism presented in this book help to focus attention on an important and arguably growing dimension of Canadian social life. At the same time, we hope that the material presented here will help to generate further multifaceted research on transnationalism. In our very brief closing comments, we want to outline at least a few of the possible directions for further research.

First, we hope that this collection will help to set the stage for more comparative analysis and a better understanding of the social forces driving transnationalism. One kind of comparison is historical. Although contemporary transnational practices *may* be different from the transnational practices and identities that immigrants engaged in between the late nineteenth and mid-twentieth centuries, these differences have tended to be asserted rather than demonstrated. As a result, more focused comparisons dealing with the similarities and differences in transnational practices between "then" and "now" could help to establish whether contemporary transnational practices are in fact qualitatively different from those engaged in by groups in the past and what factors in contemporary society drive these new forms of transnationalism.

Another kind of comparison would involve groups who have broadly similar patterns of migration to, and settlement in, Canada. Some of this comparative work is already reported in this volume. However, the collection of more medium- and large-scale survey data, along with qualitative data, will help researchers to answer questions about how involvement in transnational practices varies by gender, age, generation, class, region, and the conditions that have led to emigration.

Yet another, and perhaps more ambitious, comparison would be international in scope and examine groups from the same ancestral homeland who have settled in different countries. In this context, we think that comparisons of Canada and the United States could be fruitful. The two countries share the world's longest undefended border, and despite some similarities in their immigration flows and policies, relatively little comparative research has been conducted on topics related to immigration and settlement. In their book *Illusion of Difference* (1994), Jeffrey Reitz and Raymond Breton compare the nature and extent of racism and ethnic and racial inequality in the two countries. Further, in relation to issues of immigrant incorporation, they argue that the stereotypical differences between "multicultural" Canada and the American "melting pot" are dramatically overstated. Further comparative work on the transnational practices and identities of immigrants in the two countries who are from the same places may help to determine the extent to which different ideologies of immigrant incorporation and different structural contexts shape the nature, intensity, and meaning of transnational practices and identities.

A second useful line of inquiry could focus on the transnational practices and identities of relatively privileged groups. Although the vertical mosaic, as described by John Porter (1965) in the mid-1960s, no longer appears to be a completely accurate description of contemporary Canada, individuals of British and French origins still arguably occupy relatively privileged positions in Canada. Further, Canada continues to bear a strong imprint of these immigrants' historical colonial mother countries. Despite considerable historical research on Canada's charter groups and Canadians' historical ties to the once great colonial powers of Britain and France, little research has examined the contemporary meanings of these respective "homelands" for individuals of British and French descent. Among other things, this kind of work can tell us whether transnational practices and identities are necessarily fostered by social exclusion in the country of settlement and whether the transnationalism of privileged groups is qualitatively different from that of the less privileged.

A third focus for research could examine families and the children of immigrants. Most of the examples and cases in this collection focus on the immigrant generation. But as some of the chapters have shown, transnational practices and identities are not the exclusive domain of first-generation immigrants. A focus on generations and families would also help to advance the understanding of transnationalism as a socially negotiated process. Analyzing transnationalism through the lens of family dynamics is a fruitful way to unpack the dilemmas, contradictions, and conflicts that surround both real and imagined transnational connections to an ancestral homeland. Hoerder, Hébert, and Schmitt (2004) have, in their recently edited book, just begun to explore the transcultural lives and multiple belongings of youth in Canada and in Europe.

The question of the extent to which generations beyond the immigrant generation either embrace or resist engaging in certain forms of transnational ties, and with what consequences, has started to be posed in the United States. Alejandro Portes (1999) outlines some of the possible consequences, in terms of patterns of assimilation, of transnational ties for second-generation im-migrants in the United States. For example, in some formulations "trans-nationalism" and "assimilation" are understood as opposite points on a continuum. As some of the chapters in this volume point out, it is possible that the two dynamics are complementary rather than mutually exclusive. As a result, more research is needed on how participation in transnational networks and transnational social fields may facilitate the process of immi-grant and ethnic-group incorporation.

This question is part of the wider problem of how to understand the rela-tionship between transnational and local social fields. Certainly, some as-pects of social reproduction undertaken by immigrants and ethnic groups may occur outside of Canada in the context of transnational ties and connec-tions. However, immigrants and others who are participants in transnational social fields are also simultaneously embedded in more locally based net-works, situations, and relationships.

Finally, as we note in the Introduction, the tone of some of the literature on transnationalism tends to be implicitly or explicitly celebratory. As Vertovec (1999) points out, there is a potentially darker side to transnation-alism that should not be overlooked. Some writers celebrate the deterri-torialization of nation-states and the concomitant rise of transnational identities, relationships, and linkages. Some sending and receiving coun-tries, for different reasons, look very favourably on and encourage certain kinds of transnational links and identities. However, what are the limits to some states' tolerance and encouragement of transnational activities and practices? Further, in an era of shifting global alliances when yesterday's international ally can quickly turn into today's "rogue state" (and vice versa), there may be good reasons for individuals and organizations to be cautious about the kinds of transnational relationships, connections, and identities that they cultivate or are perceived to cultivate. In a world shaped by the terrorist attacks in the United States on 11 September 2001, individuals can be seen as disloyal or subversive because of their past citizenship, who they have coffee with, or the kinds of overseas causes that they support or for which they have sympathy.

By no means are these the only questions about transnationalism requir-ing further research. This collection is part of the opening salvo of much more good work to come.

References

Abella, I., and H. Troper. 2000. *None is too many: Canada and the Jews of Europe, 1933-1948.* 3rd ed. Toronto: Key Porter.

Abu-Laban, Y. 2002. Challenging the gendered vertical mosaic: Immigrants, ethnic minorities, gender, and political participation. In J. Everitt and B. O'Neill, eds., *Citizen politics: Research and theory in Canadian political behaviour,* 268-82. Toronto: Oxford University Press.

–, and C. Gabriel. 2003. Security, immigration and post-September 11 Canada. In Janine Brodie and Linda Trimble, eds., *Reinventing Canada,* 290-306. Toronto: Pearson Education Canada.

Abu-Lughod, J.L. 1989. *Before European hegemony: The world system A.D. 1250-1350.* New York: Oxford.

Adachi, K. 1991. *The enemy that never was.* Toronto: McClelland and Stewart.

Aguiar, L.L.M. 2000. Restructuring and employment insecurities: The case of building cleaners in Toronto. *Canadian Journal of Urban Research* 9 (1): 64-93.

–. 2001. Discarding credentials, expertise and talent: The marginalization of foreign-trained immigrants in Canadian society. Prepared for the Okanagan Social and Community Research Centre, Okanagan University College.

–. 2004. Resisting neoliberalism in Vancouver: An uphill struggle for cleaners. *Social Justice* 31 (2): 105-29.

Aguiar, N. 2002. Carlos Cesar deixa *mensagem* as varias Comunidades Portugueses do Canada. *Lusopresse,* 1 August, 20-21.

Aiken, S. 2001a. *Comments on Bill C-11 related to national security and terrorism.* Centre for Refugee Studies, York University. Submission to the House of Commons Standing Committee on Citizenship and Immigration. http://www.web.net/~ccr/crsbrief.htm.

–. 2001b. The enemy within. *Globe and Mail,* 24 October, A17. http://www.globeandmail.com/servlet/ArticleNews/prinarticle/gam/20011024/COAIKEN.

Akenson, D. 1995. The historiography of English-speaking Canada and the concept of diaspora: A sceptical appreciation. *Canadian Historical Review* 76 (3): 377-410.

Al-Ali, N., R. Black, and K. Koser. 2001. The limits to transnationalism: Bosnian and Eritrean refugees in Europe as emerging transnational communities. *Ethnic and Racial Studies* 24 (4): 578-600.

Alam, M.S. 2003. Is this a clash of civilizations? *Counterpunch.* http://www.counterpunch.or/alam02282003.html.

Aleinikoff, T.A. and D.B. Klusmeyer, eds. 2001. *Citizenship today: Global perspectives and practices.* Washington, DC: Carnegie Endowment for International Peace.

Alghabra, O. 2003. A chance to lift the veil of ignorance about Arabs. *Toronto Star,* 17 October, A24.

Allemang, J. 2003. Meet the candidates for 2006. *Globe and Mail,* 8 November, M5.

Allodi, F., and A. Rojas. 1983a. *The health and adaptation of victims of torture from Latin America and their children in Toronto.* Toronto: Ministry of Multiculturalism with the support of the Department of Psychiatry, University of Toronto, and Toronto Western Hospital.

–, and A. Rojas. 1983b. *A study of mental health and social adaptation of Hispanic American refugees in Toronto.* Toronto: Ministry of Multiculturalism, with the support of the Department of Psychiatry, University of Toronto, and Toronto Western Hospital.

–, and A. Rojas. 1988. Arauco: The role of a housing cooperative community in the mental health and social adaptation of Latin American refugees in Toronto. *Migration World* 16 (3): 17-21.

Al-Rasheed, M. 1994. The myth of return: Iraqi Arab and Assyrian refugees in London. *Journal of Refugee Studies* 7 (2-3): 199-219.

Alves, C.M. 1997. Between a pork and a mungy cake. *Silva Magazine* 1 (2): 21-23.

Anderson, A. 2001. The complexity of ethnic identities: A postmodern re-evaluation. *Identity: An International Journal of Theory and Research* 1 (3): 209-23.

Anderson, G., and D. Higgs. 1976. *A future to inherit.* Toronto: McClelland and Stewart.

Anthias, F. 1998. Evaluating diaspora: Beyond ethnicity. *Sociology* 32 (3): 557-80.

–. 2001. New hybridities, old concepts: The limits of culture. *Ethnic and Racial Studies* 24 (4 July): 619-41.

–. 2002. Diasporic hybridity and transcending racisms. In F. Anthias and C. Lloyd, eds., *Rethinking anti-racisms: From theory to practice,* 22-43. London: Routledge.

Antonius, R. 2002. Un racisme respectable. In J. Renaud, L. Piandrantonio, and G. Bourgeault, eds., *Les relations ethniques en question: Ce qui a changé depuis le 11 septembre 2001,* 253-71. Montreal: Les Presses de l'Université de Montréal.

Antonovsky, A., and D. Katz. 1979. *From the golden to the promised land.* Darby, PA: Jerusalem Academic Press.

Appadurai, A. 1990. Disjuncture and difference in the global cultural economy. *Public Culture* 2 (2): 1-24.

–. 1996. *Modernity at large: Cultural dimensions of globalization.* Minneapolis: University of Minnesota Press.

–. 2003. Grassroots globalization and the research imagination. In A. Appadurai, ed., *Globalization,* 1-21. Durham: Duke University Press.

Arat-Koc, S. 2002a. Clash of civilizations? Anti-racist, multicultural feminism and diasporic Middle Eastern identities post September 11th. Paper presented at the conference "Unsettling Imaginations: Towards Re-configuring Borders," Vancouver, 22-24 March.

–. 2002b. Orientalism and the cages of civilizations: Re-articulations of nation, race and culture in Canada, post September 11th. Paper presented at the conference "Critical Race Scholarship and the University," Toronto, 25-27 April.

–. 2003. Tolerated citizens or imperial subjects? Muslim Canadians and multicultural citizenship in Canada after September 11th. Paper presented at the annual meeting of the Canadian Sociology and Anthropology Association, Halifax, 1-4 June.

Armony, V., M. Barriga, and D. Shugurensky. 2004. Citizenship learning and political participation: The experience of Latin American immigrants in Canada. *Canadian Journal of Latin American and Caribbean Studies* 29 (57-58): 17-38.

Arnold, M.S. 1999. Freedom in chains. *Jerusalem Post,* 12 August. http://static.highbeam.com/ j/jerusalempost/august061999/freedominchains/index.html.

Asad, T. 1993. *Genealogies of religion.* Baltimore: Johns Hopkins University Press.

Avery, D.H. 1983. *Dangerous foreigners: European immigrant workers and labour radicalism in Canada, 1896-1932.* Toronto: McClelland and Stewart. Revised as *Reluctant host: Canada's response to immigrant workers, 1896-1994.* Toronto: McClelland and Stewart, 1995.

Bada, X. 2003. Mexican hometown associations. *Citizen Action in the Americas,* No. 5. http:// www.americaspolicy.org/citizen-action/series/05-hta.html.

Baily, S.L. 1992. The village-outward approach to the study of social networks: A case study of the Agnonesi diaspora abroad, 1885-1989. *Studi Emigrazione (Rome)* 19 (105): 43-67.

–, and F. Ramella, eds. 1988. *One family, two worlds: An Italian family's correspondence across the Atlantic, 1901-1922.* New Brunswick: Rutgers.

Bakan, A., and D. Stasiulis. 1997. *Not one of the family: Foreign domestic workers in Canada.* Toronto: University of Toronto Press.

Balakrishnan, T.R., and Feng Hou. 1999. Residential patterns in cities. In Shiva Halli and Leo Dreidger, eds., *Immigrant Canada: Demographic, economic and social challenges*, 116-47. Toronto: University of Toronto Press.

Balibar, E. 1991. The nation form: History and ideology. In E. Balibar and I. Wallerstein, eds., *Race, nation, class: Ambiguous identities*, 86-106. London: Verso.

Ballard, C. 1979. Conflict, continuity and change. In V.S. Khan, ed., *Minority families in Britain: Support and stress*, 109-29. London and Basingstoke: Macmillan.

Ballard, R., ed. 1994. *Desh Pardesh: The South Asian presence in Britain.* London: Hurst and Company.

Barber, B. 2000. Jihad vs. McWorld. In F.V. Moulder, ed., *Social problems of the modern world: A reader*, 69-76. Toronto: Wadsworth Thompson Learning.

Basch, L., N. Glick Schiller, and C. Szanton Blanc. 1994. *Nations unbound: Transnational projects, postcolonial predicaments and deterritorialized nation-states.* Langhorne: Gordon and Breach.

Basok, T. 2002. *Tortillas and tomatoes: Transmigrant Mexican harvesters in Canada.* Montreal and Kingston: McGill-Queen's University Press.

Belsky, G. 1994. Escape from America: Citizens who leave the country. *Money Magazine* 23 (7): 60-66.

Berman, G. 1979. Why North Americans migrate to Israel. *Jewish Journal of Sociology* 21 (2): 135-44.

Bernhard, J.K., and M. Freire. 1999a. Supporting parental involvement in schools: An ethnographic study of the Toronto Latin American parent support group. Centre of Excellence for Research on Immigration and Settlement (CERIS), Toronto.

–, and M. Freire. 1999b. What is my child learning at school? Culturally contested issues of Latin American children and families. *Canadian Ethnic Studies Journal* 31 (3): 72-94.

–, L. Goldring, and P. Landolt. 2004. Latin American families and transnational practices. Paper presented at the 7th National Metropolis Conference, Montreal, 25-28 March.

Bezza, B., ed. 1983. *Gli Italiani fuori d'Italia: Gli emigrati italiani nei movimenti operai dei paesi d'adozione, 1880-1940.* Milan: Angeli.

Bhabha, H. 1994. *The location of culture.* New York: Routledge.

Bhachu, P. 1996. The multiple landscapes of transnational Asian women in the diaspora. In C. Knowles and V.A. Talai, eds., *Resituating identities: The politics of race and culture*, 283-303. Peterborough, ON: Broadview.

Bhat, C.S., and A.K. Sahoo. 2002. Diaspora to transnational networks: The case of Indians in Canada. Occasional Paper. University of Hyderabad, Centre for Study of Indian Diasporas. http://www.uohyd.ernet.in/sss/cinddiaspora/centre1.html.

Bigo, D. 1998. Sécurité et immigration. *Cultures et conflits* (31-32): 1-13. http://conflits.revues.org/article.php3?id_article=32b.

–. 2002. Éditorial: La voie militaire de la guerre au terrorisme et ses enjeux. *Cultures et conflits* (44). http://conflits.revues.org.

Black, J., and A.S. Lakhani. 1997. Ethnoracial diversity in the House of Commons: An analysis of numerical representation in the 35th Parliament. *Canadian Ethnic Studies* 29 (1): 1-21.

Bloemraad, I. 2000. Citizenship and immigration: A current review. *Journal of International Migration and Integration* 1 (1): 9-37.

–. 2004. Who claims dual citizenship? The limits of postnationalism, the possibilities of transnationalism, and the persistence of traditional citizenship. *International Migration Review* 38 (2): 389-426.

Brah, A. 2002. Global mobilities, local predicaments: Globalization and the critical imagination. *Feminist Review* 70 (1): 30-45.

Braziel, J., and A. Mannur. 2003. Nation, migration, globalization: Points of contention in diaspora studies. In J. Braziel and A. Mannur, eds., *Theorizing diaspora*, 1-22. Malden: Blackwell.

Breton, R. 1997. Social participation and social capital: Introductory lecture. *Immigration and civic participation: Contemporary policy and research issues*. Ottawa: Multiculturalism Program, Department of Canadian Heritage.

Brettell, C. 1982. *We have already cried many tears*. Cambridge, MA: Schenkman.

Bright, C. 2003. A history of our future. In L. Starke, ed., *State of the world*, 3-15. New York: Norton.

Brubaker, R. 1992. *Citizenship and nationhood in France and Germany*. Cambridge: Harvard University Press.

–. 1996. *Nationalism reframed: Nationhood and the national question in the new Europe*. Cambridge: Cambridge University Press.

Brym, R. 1999. *Canadian society and the 1996 Census*. Toronto: Harcourt Brace.

Bubrin, V. 1994. The involvement of Croatians in the political life of Canada. In M. Sopta and G. Scardellato, eds., *Unknown journey: A history of Croatians in Canada*, 65-76. Toronto: Multicultural History Society of Ontario.

Buchignani, N., D.M. Indra, and R. Srivastava. 1985. *Continuous journey: A social history of South Asians in Canada*. Toronto: McClelland and Stewart.

Burnet, J., et al., eds. 1992. *Migration and the transformation of cultures*. A Project of the Unesco World Decade for Cultural Development. Toronto: Multicultural History Society of Ontario (MHSO).

Cainkar, L. 2002. No longer invisible: Arab and Muslim exclusion after September 11. *Middle East Review* (Fall): 22-29.

Calliste, A., and G. Dei, eds. 2000. *Anti-racism feminism*. Halifax: Fernwood.

Campani, G. 1992. Family, village, and regional networks and Italian immigration in France and Montreal. In V. Satzewich, ed., *Deconstructing a nation: Immigration, multiculturalism and racism in '90s Canada*, 183-207. Halifax: Fernwood.

Canadian Arab Federation. 2001. Submission to the Standing Committee on Justice and Human rights on the proposed Bill C-36: Anti-Terrorism Act.

–. 2002. *Arabs in Canada: Proudly Canadian and marginalized*. Report. Toronto: Canadian Arab Federation.

Canadian Council for Refugees. 2003. *Immigration and Refugee Board, convention and refugee determination, calendar year 2002*. http://www.web.net/~ccr/crdd02.html.

Canadian Council of Chief Executives. 2004. New frontiers: Building a 21st century Canada-United States partnership in North America. Discussion Paper. http://www.ceocouncil.ca.

Canadian Press. 2003. Anti-Semitic incidents up 60%: B'nai B'rith. Montreal *Gazette*, 7 March, A10.

Canadian Race Relations Foundation. N.d. *Racial profiling: Information sheet*. Toronto: Canadian Race Relations Foundation.

Canales, A.I. 2003. Mexican labour migration to the United States in the age of globalisation. *Journal of Ethnic and Migration Studies* 29 (4): 741-61.

Carey, E. 1999. The city that works could be even better. *Toronto Star*, 1 May, A1.

Carroll, W. and C. Carson. 2003. The network of global corporations and elite policy groups: A structure for transnational capitalist class formation? *Global Networks* 3 (1): 29-57.

Castells, M. 1996. *The rise of network society*. Cambridge: Blackwell.

–. 1999. *Le pouvoir de l'identité*. Paris: Fayard.

Castles, S. 2000. Transnational communities: A new form of social relations under conditions of globalization. Paper presented at the 5th International Metropolis Conference, Vancouver, 13-17 November.

–. 2002. The international politics of forced migration. In L. Panitch and C. Leys, eds., *Socialist register 2003, fighting identities: Race, religion and ethno-nationalism*, 172-92. London: Merlin Press.

–, and Mark J. Miller. 1998. *The age of migration: International population movements in the modern world*. 2nd ed. New York: Guilford.

CBC/Canadian Broadcasting Corporation. 2005. BC Muslim leader faces security probe. http://www.cbc.ca/story/canada/national/2005/07/21/cleric-rcmp050721.html.

CBC/Canadian Broadcasting Corporation News. 2004. Trinity Time threatens to bail out of Air Canada investment. http://www.cbc.ca/news.

CERLAC/Centre for Research on Latin America and the Caribbean. York University. 2004. Upcoming CERLAC events. http://www.yorku.ca/cerlac/EVENTS.html.

Chamie, J. 2000. Demographic change and the coming global competition for immigrants. Paper presented at the 5th International Metropolis Conference, Vancouver, 13-17 November.

Chan, A. 1983. *Gold mountain*. Vancouver: New Star Books.

–. 1996. *Li Ka-Shing, Hong Kong's elusive billionaire*. Toronto: Macmillan.

Chan, K.B. 1997. A family affair: Migration, dispersal, and the emergent identity of the Chinese cosmopolitan. *Diaspora* 6 (2): 195-213.

Chelius, L.C., and J.M. Saldaña. 2002. *La dimensión política de la migración Mexicana*. Mexico City: Instituto Mora.

Cheran, R. Forthcoming. Transnationalism, development and social capital: Tamil community networks in Canada. In Luin Goldring and Sailaja V. Krishnamurti, eds., *Organizing the transnational: The experience of Asian and Latin American migrants in Canada*.

Chimbos, P. 1999. Greeks. In P.R. Magocsi, ed., *Encyclopedia of Canada's peoples*, 615-26. Toronto: University of Toronto Press.

Chipello, Christopher. 2003. Air Canada gets lift from Li family. *Wall Street Journal*, 10 November, A12.

Chiu, Y.N.G. 1998. Birds of a feather flock together. Major research paper, Department of Geography, York University, Toronto.

Chui, T., J. Curtis, and R. Lambert. 1991. Immigrant background and political participation. *Canadian Journal of Sociology* 16 (4): 375-96.

CIC/Citizenship and Immigration Canada. 2002. *Immigration overview: Facts and figures 2001*. Ottawa: Minister of Public Works and Government Services.

–. 2003a. *Landed Immigrant Database System (LIDS)*. Ottawa: Minister of Public Works and Government Services.

–. 2003b. *Statistical overview of the temporary resident and refugee claimant population: Facts and figures 2002*. Ottawa: Minister of Public Works and Government Services.

–. 2004. *Special tabulations on landing data*. Ottawa: Minister of Public Works and Government Services.

Clement, W. 1975. *The Canadian corporate elite*. Toronto: McClelland and Stewart.

Cleveland Project. 1986-91. Conflict and cooperation among East European immigrants in Cleveland, Ohio, 1880s-1930s. Unpublished research. University of Bremen, Germany.

Clifford, J. 1994. Diasporas. *Cultural Anthropology* 9 (3): 302-38.

–. 1997. *Routes: Travel and translation in the late twentieth century*. Cambridge: Harvard University Press.

Cohen, Rina. 1999. From ethnocultural enclave to diasporic community: The mainstreaming of Israeli Jewish migrants in Toronto. *Diaspora: A Journal of Transnational Studies* 8 (2): 121-37.

–, and G. Gold. 1996. Israelis in Toronto: The myth of return and the development of a distinct ethnic community. *Jewish Journal of Sociology* 38 (1): 17-27.

–, and G. Gold. 1997. Constructing ethnicity: Myth of return and modes of exclusion among Israeli families in Toronto. *International Migration* 3 (1): 373-93.

Cohen, Robin. 1995. Fuzzy frontiers of identity: The British case. *Social Identities* 1 (1): 35-62.

–. 1996. Diaspora and the nation-state. *International Affairs* 72 (3): 507-20.

–. 1997. *Global diasporas: An introduction*. Seattle: University of Washington Press.

Cole, S. 1998. Reconstituting households, retelling culture: Emigration and Portuguese fisheries workers. In S. Ilcan and L. Phillips, eds., *Transgressing borders*, 75-92. Westport: Bergin and Garvey.

Comité permanent de la Citoyenneté et de l'Immigration. 1994. *La citoyenneté canadienne: Un sentiment d'appartenance*. Ottawa: Chambre des Communes.

Con, H., et al. 1982. *From China to Canada*. Toronto: McClelland and Stewart.

Connor, W. 1986. The impact of homelands upon diasporas. In G. Sheffer, ed., *Modern diasporas in international politics*, 16-45. New York: St. Martin's.

Connors, K. 2001. Canadian nurses: Until this crisis is over, we are all Muslims. http://www.labornotes.org/archives/2001/1001/1001f.html.

Conseil des relations interculturelles. 1999. *L'équité en emploi: De l'égalité de droit à l'égalité de fait*. Montreal: Conseil des relations interculturelles.

Conzen, K.N., et al. 1992. The invention of ethnicity: A perspective from the U.S.A. *Journal of American Ethnic History* 12 (1): 3-41.

Cordero-Guzmán, H.R., R.C. Smith, and R. Grosfoguel. 2001. *Migration, transnationalization, and race in a changing New York*. Philadelphia: Temple University Press.

Correspondence. 1945. National Archives of Canada, Record Group 27, Department of Labour, Japanese Division, vol. 1529, file 23-2-17-6.

Cotler, I. 2002. New anti-Jewishness. Alert paper. *Jewish People Policy Planning Institute*, No. 1. Jerusalem.

Coutin, S.B. 1998. From refugees to immigrants: The legalization strategies of Salvadoran immigrants and activists. *International Migration Review* 32 (4): 901-25.

Cross, M.S. 1992. Towards a definition of North-American culture. In S.J. Randall, H. Konrad, and S. Silverman, eds., *North America without borders*, 303-6. Calgary: University of Calgary Press.

Dafoe, J.W. 1931. *Clifford Sifton in relation to his times*. Toronto: Macmillan.

Danforth, L. 1995. *The Macedonian conflict: Ethnonationalism in a transnational world*. Princeton: Princeton University Press.

Dark, T., III. 2003. The rise of a global party? American party organization abroad. *Party Politics* 9 (2): 241-55.

Dashevsky, A., et al. 1992. *Americans abroad: A comparative study of emigrants from the United States*. New York: Plenum.

de Kerckhove, D. 1995. *The skin of culture: Investigating the new electronic reality*. Toronto: Somerville House.

De Séve, M., and C. Maillé. 2004. Un mouvement des femmes en voie de mondialisation? In M. Labelle and F. Rocher (with the collaboration of A.M. Field), eds., *Contestation transnationale, diversité et citoyenneté dans l'espace québécois*, 107-53. Sainte-Foy: Presses de l'Université du Québec.

Deaux, K. 2001. Negotiating identity and community after September 11. http://www.ssrc.org/sept11/essays/deaux.htm.

Devoretz, D., and J. Ma. 2002. Triangular human capital flows between sending, entrepot and the rest of the world regions. *Canadian Studies in Population* 29 (1): 53-69.

Dewitte, P. 2002. Homo cybernatus. *Hommes et migrations* (1240): 1-6.

Dexter, B. 1995. Chinese demand apology for Bell's "racist" remarks: Political veteran says the majority support her view. *Toronto Star*, 11 August, NY1.

Diaz, H. 1999a. Chileans. In P.R. Magocsi, ed., *Encyclopedia of Canada's peoples*, 347-55. Toronto: University of Toronto Press.

–. 1999b. *Chileans*. Toronto: University of Toronto Press.

Drache, D. 2004. *Borders matter. Homeland security and the search of North America*. Halifax: Fernwood.

Dreisziger, N.F. 1982. *Struggle and hope: The Hungarian-Canadian experience*. Toronto: McClelland and Stewart.

Dugger, C. 2000. Web mogul's return passage to India. *New York Times*, 29 February, A1.

Duncan, C. 2003. Spiritual Baptists in multicultural Canada. In Barbara A.C. Saunders and David Haljan, eds., *Whither multiculturalism? A politics of dissensus*, 205-24. Leuven: Leuven University Press.

Duran, M. 1980. Life in exile: Chileans in Canada. *Multiculturalism* 3 (4): 13-16.

Duval, D.T. 2001. When hosts become guests: Return visits and transnational identities among members of the Commonwealth eastern Caribbean community in Toronto, Canada. PhD dissertation, York University, Toronto.

Dyer, R. 1997. *White*. London: Routledge.

Eden, A. 2003. Israel's role: The elephant they're talking about. *Forward* 1 (17). http://www.forward.com/issues/2003/03.02.28/news4.html.

Editorial. 1995. Intolerance in Markham. *Toronto Star*, 19 September, A20.

Elazar, D.J. 1989. *People and polity: The organization and dynamics of world Jewry*. Detroit: Wayne State University Press.

Elazar, D.J., and H. Waller. 1990. *Maintaining consensus: The Canadian Jewish polity in the postwar world.* Lanham: University Press of America.

Ellis, P., and Z. Khan. 1998. Diasporic mobilization and the Kashmir issue in British politics. *Journal of Ethnic and Migration Studies* 24 (3): 471-88.

Elmasry, M. 2004. Why Muslims should vote. *Globe and Mail,* 7 June, A19.

Espiritu, Y.L. 2003. *Home bound: Filipino American lives across cultures, communities, and countries.* Berkeley: University of California Press.

Fagan, D. 2003. Government unveils public-safety department. *Globe and Mail,* 12 December, A13.

Faist, T. 1999. Developing transnational social spaces: The Turkish-German example. In L. Pries, ed., *Migration and transnational social spaces,* 36-72. Aldershot: Ashgate.

–. 2000a. *The volume and dynamics of international migration and transnational social spaces.* Oxford: Oxford University Press.

–. 2000b. Transnationalization in international migration: Implications for the study of citizenship and culture. *Ethnic and Racial Studies* 23 (2): 189-222.

Fitzgerald, D. 2004. Beyond transnationalism: Mexican hometown politics at an American labour union. *Ethnic and Racial Studies* 27 (2): 228-47.

Fleras, A., and J. Elliott. 1992. *Multiculturalism in Canada: The challenge of diversity.* Scarborough: Nelson Canada.

-, and J. Elliott. 2002. *Engaging diversity: Multiculturalism in Canada.* Toronto: Nelson.

Florida, R. 2002. *The rise of the creative class.* New York: Basic Books.

Foerster, R.F. 1919. *The Italian emigration of our times.* Cambridge: Harvard University Press; reprint, New York: Arno, 1969.

Foner, N. 1997. What's new about transnationalism? New York immigrants today and at the turn of the century. *Diaspora* 6 (3): 355-75.

–. 2001a. Immigrant commitment to America, then and now: Myths and realities. *Citizenship Studies* 5 (1): 27-40.

–. 2001b. New immigrants in a new New York. In N. Foner, ed., *New immigrants in New York,* 1-32. New York: Columbia University Press.

–. 2001c. Transnationalism then and now: New York immigrants today and at the turn of the twentieth century. In H.R. Cordera-Guzman, R.C. Smith, and R. Grosfoguel, eds., *Migration, transnationalization, and race in a changing New York,* 35-57. Philadelphia: Temple University Press.

Forbes. 2004. The world's richest people, 2004. http://www.forbes.com/maserati/billionaires2004/bill04land.html.

Foster, C. 1995. *Caribbana: The greatest celebration.* Toronto: Ballantine.

Fouron, G., and N. Glick Schiller. 2001. All in the family: Gender, transnational migration, and the nation-state. *Identities: Global Studies in Culture and Power* 7 (4): 539-82.

-, and N. Glick Schiller. 2002. The generation of identity: Redefining the second generation within a transnational social field. In P. Levitt and M.C. Waters, eds., *The changing face of home: The transnational lives of the second generation,* 168-208. New York: Russell Sage Foundation.

Frank, A.G. 1998. *ReOrient: Global economy in the Asian age.* Berkeley: University of California Press.

Frauenheim, E. 1999. India Inc. *TechWeek.* http://www.tie.org. 20 September.

Frideres, J.S. 1997. Civic participation, awareness, knowledge and skills. In *Immigrants and Civic Participation: Contemporary Policy and Research Issues.* Ottawa: Multiculturalism Program, Department of Canadian Heritage.

Friedmann, J. 1986. The world city hypothesis. *Development and Change* 17 (1): 69-83.

Frye, M.J. 1998. *Whiteness of a different colour.* Cambridge: Harvard University Press.

Gabaccia, D. 1994. *From the other side: Women, gender and immigrant life in the U.S., 1820-1990.* Bloomington: Indiana University Press.

Gabaccia, D.R., and F. Ottanelli, eds. 2001. *Italian workers of the world: Labor, migration and the making of multi-ethnic states.* Urbana: University of Illinois Press.

Gall, J.L. 2002. Le lien familial au coeur du quotidien transnational: Les femmes shi'ites libanaises à Montréal. *Anthropologica* 44 (1): 69-81.

Garay, E. 2000. *Integrated settlement planning project: Social, economic and demographic profile of the Hispanic community*. Toronto: Hispanic Development Council.

Gellner, E. 1983. *Nations and nationalism*. Oxford: Oxford University Press.

Gellner, J., and J. Smerek. 1968. *The Czechs and Slovaks in Canada*. Toronto: University of Toronto Press.

Giddens, A. 1999. *Runaway world: Lecture 1: Globalization*. British Broadcasting Corporation (BBC) Reith Lectures. http://news.bbc.co.uk/hi/english/static/events/reith_99/.

Giles, W. 2002. *Portuguese women in Toronto*. Toronto: University of Toronto Press.

–, and V. Preston. 1996. The domestication of women's work: A comparison of Chinese and Portuguese women homeworkers. *Studies in Political Economy* 51 (Fall): 147-81.

Gillis, J., ed. 1994. *Commemorations: The politics of national identity*. Princeton: Princeton University Press.

Gilroy, P. 1991. *There ain't no black in the Union Jack: The cultural politics of race and nation*. Chicago: University of Chicago Press.

–. 1993. *The black Atlantic: Modernity and double consciousness*. Cambridge: Harvard University Press.

–. 2000. *Against race: Imagining political culture beyond the colour line*. Cambridge: Belknap Press of Harvard University Press.

Gionas, S. 1995. Bell's remarks still prompt debate within community. *Toronto Star*, 5 October, NY1.

Glenny, M. 1992. *The fall of Yugoslavia: The third Balkan war*. London: Penguin.

Glick Schiller, N. 1999. Transmigrants and nation-states: Something old and something new in the U.S. immigrant experience. In C. Hirschman, P. Kasinitz, and J. DeWind, eds., *The handbook of international migration*, 94-119. New York: Russell Sage Foundation.

–, L. Basch, and C. Szanton Blanc. 1992. Transnationalism: A new analytic framework for understanding migration. *Annals of the New York Academy of Sciences* 645 (July): 1-24.

–, L. Basch, and C. Szanton Blanc. 1995. From immigrant to transmigrant: Theorizing transnational migration. *Anthropological Quarterly* 68 (1): 48-63.

–, and G. Fouron. 1999. Terrains of blood and nation: Haitian transnational social fields. *Ethnic and Racial Studies* 22 (2): 340-61.

–, and G. Fouron. 2001. *Georges woke up laughing: Long-distance nationalism and the search for home*. Durham: Duke University Press.

Goar, C. 2004. Odd way to build a consensus. *Toronto Star*, 12 April, A18.

Gold, G. 1992. Israeli immigrants and Canadian Jews in Toronto. In S. Fishbane, S. Schoenfeld, and A. Goldschlager, eds., *Essays in the social scientific study of Judaism and Jewish society*, vol. 2, 214-51. Hoboken: Ktav.

–, and R. Cohen. 1996. The myth of return and the emergence of Israeli ethnicity in Toronto. In J. Simpson and H. Adelman, eds., *Multiculturalism, Jews, and the Canadian identity*, 166-91. Jerusalem: Magnes.

Goldberg, A.I. 1985. A new look at *aliya* influences among North American Jews. *The Jewish Journal of Sociology* 27 (2): 81-102.

Goldring, L. 1996. Blurring the borders: Constructing transnational community in the process of Mexico-U.S. migration. *Research in Community Sociology* 6: 69-104.

–. 1998. The power of status in transnational social fields. In M.P. Smith, and L.E. Guarnizo, eds., *Transnationalism from below*, 165-95. New Brunswick: Transaction.

–. 1999. Mexicans. In P.R. Magocsi, ed., *Encyclopedia of Canada's peoples*, 975-79. Toronto: University of Toronto Press.

–. 2001. The gender and geography of citizenship in Mexico-U.S. transnational spaces. *Identities: Global Studies in Culture and Power* 7 (4): 501-37.

–. 2002. The Mexican state and transmigrant organizations: Negotiating the boundaries of membership and participation in the Mexican nation. *Latin American Research Review* 37 (3): 55-99.

–. 2004. Individual and collective remittances to Mexico: A multi-dimensional typology of remittances. *Development and Change* 35 (4): 799-840.

–, S. Henders, and P. Vandergeest. 2003. *The politics of transnational ties: Implications for policy, research, and communities*. YCAR-CERLAC Workshop Report. York University, Toronto.

Goldstein, I. 1999. *Croatia: A history.* Montreal and Kingston: McGill-Queen's University Press.

Gordon, M. 1981. Models of pluralism: The new American dilemma. *Annals of the American Academy of Political and Social Science* 454 (1): 178-88.

Gordon, M.M. 1964. *Assimilation in American life: The role of race, religion, and national origins.* New York: Oxford University Press.

Government of Canada. 2001a. *Canada's proposed anti-terrorism act: Working with our international partners.* Fact sheet. Ottawa: Department of Justice.

–. 2001b. *Immigrant status and period of immigration and place of birth of respondents for immigrants and non-permanent residents, for Canada, provinces, territories, Census metropolitan areas and Census agglomerations, 2001 Census.* 20% sample data. Catalogue No. 97F0009X CB01002.

–. 2001c. *Landed immigrant data set, 1980 to 2001.* Ottawa: Citizenship and Immigration Canada.

–. 2002. *The Smart Border Declaration.* http://www.canadianembassy.org/border/index-en.asp.

Government of Portugal. 2003. Portuguese no Canada e eleicoes em Portugal. Fax communiqué. Ministerio dos Negocios Estrangeiros. 31 December.

Green, N.L. 1997. The comparative method and poststructural structuralism: New perspectives for migration studies. In J. Lucassen and L. Lucassen, eds., *Migrations, migration history, history: Old paradigms and new perspectives,* 57-72. Bern: Lang.

Grimes, K.M. 1998. *Crossing borders: Changing social identities in southern Mexico.* Tucson: University of Arizona.

Guarnizo, L.E. 1998. The rise of transnational social formations: Mexican and Dominican state responses to transnational migration. *Political Power and Social Theory* 12: 45-94.

–. 2003. The economics of transnational living. *International Migration Review* 37 (3): 666-99.

–, and L.M. Diaz. 1999. Transnational migration: A view from Colombia. *Ethnic and Racial Studies* 22 (2): 397-421.

–, A. Portes, and W. Haller. 2003. Assimilation and transnationalism: Determinants of transnational political action among contemporary migrants. *American Journal of Sociology* 108 (6): 1211-48.

–, and M.P. Smith. 1998. The locations of transnationalism. In M.P. Smith and L.E. Guarnizo, eds., *Transnationalism from below,* 3-34. New Brunswick: Transaction.

Gwyn, R. 2001a. Canada will have to go ahead with whatever US does next. *Toronto Star,* 14 September, A1, A10.

–. 2001b. We must accept the inevitable. *Toronto Star,* 30 September, A13.

Hagan, J. 2001. *Northern passage: American Vietnam War resisters in Canada.* Cambridge: Harvard University Press.

Hage, G. 2002a. Citizenship and honourability: Belonging to Australia today. In G. Hage, ed., *Arab-Australians today: Citizenship and belonging,* 1-15. Melbourne: Melbourne University Press.

–. 2002b. Postscript: Arab-Australian belonging after September 11. In G. Hage, ed., *Arab-Australians today: Citizenship and belonging,* 241-48. Melbourne: Melbourne University Press.

Haggett, S. 2004. CEOs at Imperial, Husky pulling in bigger bucks. *Calgary Herald,* 20 March, E2.

Halpern, J., and D. Kideckel, eds. 2000. *Neighbors at war: Anthropological perspectives on Yugoslav ethnicity, culture and history.* University Park, PA: Pennsylvania University Press.

Hamilton, N., and N.S. Chinchilla. 2001. *Seeking community in a global city: Guatemalans and Salvadorans in Los Angeles.* Philadelphia: Temple University Press.

Handa, A. 1998. Caught between omissions: Exploring culture conflict among second generation South Asian women in Canada. PhD dissertation, University of Toronto.

Handlin, O. 1951. *The uprooted: The epic story of the great migrations that made the American people.* Rev. ed., Boston: Little, Brown, 1973.

Hannerz, U. 1992. *Cultural complexity: Studies in the social organization of meaning.* New York: Columbia University Press.

Hansen, M.L. 1964. *The immigrant in American history*. New York: Harper Torchbooks.

Hardt, M., and A. Negri. 2000. *Empire*. Cambridge: Harvard University Press.

Harney, N. 1998. *Eh, Paesan! Being Italian in Toronto*. Toronto: University of Toronto Press.

Harney, R.F., ed. 1985. *Gathering place, peoples and neighborhoods of Toronto, 1834-1945*. Toronto: Multicultural History Society of Ontario (MHSO).

Harvey, D. 1989. *The condition of postmodernity*. Cambridge: Blackwell.

Harzig, C., ed. 1997. *Peasant maids, city women: From the European countryside to urban America*. Ithaca: Cornell.

–, D. Hoerder, and A. Shubert, eds. 2000. Negotiating nations: Exclusions, networks, inclusions. *Histoire sociale/Social History* 33 (66): 361-89.

Helweg, A.W. 1986. The Indian diaspora: Influence on international relations. In G. Sheffer, ed., *Modern diasporas in international politics*, 103-29. New York: St. Martin's.

Henry, F. 1994. *The Caribbean diaspora in Toronto: Learning to live with racism*. Toronto: University of Toronto Press.

–. 1999. *The racialization of crime in Toronto's print media: A research project*. Toronto: Ryerson Polytechnic University, School of Journalism.

Hiebert, D. 1999. Immigration and the changing social geography of Greater Vancouver. *BC Studies* (121): 35-82.

–. 2003. Are immigrants welcome? Introducing the Vancouver Community Studies Survey. Working paper 03-06. Centre for Research on Immigration and Integration in the Metropolis, University of British Columbia, Vancouver.

–, et al. 1998. Immigrant experiences in Greater Vancouver: Focus groups narratives. Working paper 98-15. Centre for Research on Immigration and Integration in the Metropolis, University of British Columbia, Vancouver.

–, and D. Ley. 2003. Characteristics of immigrant transnationalism in Vancouver. Working paper 03-15. Vancouver Centre of Excellence, Research on Immigration and Integration in the Metropolis, Vancouver.

Hiebert, M. 2000. Patriot games. *Far Eastern Economic Review,* 23 March, 17-18.

Hirsch, J.S. 2003. *A courtship after marriage: Sexuality and love in Mexican transnational families*. Berkeley: University of California Press.

Hoerder, D. 1992. Labour migrants' views of America. *Renaissance and Modern Studies* 35 (1): 1-17.

–. 1996. From migrants to ethnics: Acculturation in a societal framework. In D. Hoerder and L.P. Moch, eds., *European migrants: Global and local perspectives*, 211-62. Boston: Northeastern University Press.

–. 1997. Segmented macrosystems, networking individuals, cultural change: Balancing processes and interactive change in migration. In J. Lucassen and L. Lucassen, eds., *Migrations, migration history, history: Old paradigms and new perspectives*, 73-84. Bern: Lang.

–. 1999. *Creating societies: Immigrant lives in Canada*. Montreal and Kingston: McGill-Queen's University Press.

–. 2002. *Cultures in contact: World migrations in the second millennium*. Durham: Duke University Press.

–, C. Harzig, and A. Shubert, eds. 2003. *The historical practice of diversity: Transcultural interactions from the early modern Mediterranean to the postcolonial world*. New York: Berghahn.

–, Y. Hébert, and I. Schmitt. 2004. *Negotiating transcultural lives: Belongings and social capital among youth in comparative perspective*. Gottingen: V and R Unipress.

Hondagneu-Sotelo, P. 2001. *Domestica*. Berkeley: University of California Press.

Hryniuk, S., and L. Luciuk, eds. 1991. *Canada's Ukrainians: Negotiating an identity*. Toronto: University of Toronto Press.

–, and L. Luciuk, eds. 1993. *Multiculturalism and Ukrainian Canadians: Identity, homeland ties, and the community's future*. Polyphony, No. 13. Toronto: Multicultural History Society of Ontario.

Hsu, M.Y. 2000. *Dreaming of gold, dreaming of home*. Stanford: Stanford University Press.

Hughes, E.C., and H. MacGill Hughes. 1952. *Where peoples meet: Racial and ethnic frontiers*. Glencoe: Free Press.

Hull House Residents. 1895. *Hull House maps and papers.* New York: Thomas Y. Crowell.

Huntington, S. 1993. The clash of civilizations? *Foreign Affairs* 72 (Summer): 22-49.

–. 1996. *The clash of civilizations and the remaking of world order.* New York: Simon and Schuster.

–. 1997. American identity: The erosion of American national interests. *Current History* 397: 8-9.

Hutchinson, E.P. 1950. *Immigrants and their children, 1850-1950.* 1st ed. Reprint, New York: Russell and Russell, 1976.

Hyndman, J. 1997. Border crossings. *Antipode* 29 (2): 149-76.

–, and M. Walton-Roberts. 2000. Interrogating borders: A transnational approach to refugee research in Vancouver. *Canadian Geographer* 44 (3): 244-58.

Iacovetta, F. 1992. *Such hardworking people.* Montreal and Kingston: McGill-Queen's University Press.

–, R. Perin, and A. Principe, eds. 2000. *Enemies within: Italian and other internees in Canada and abroad.* Toronto: University of Toronto Press.

Icart, J.C. 2001. *Perspectives historiques sur le racisme au Québec.* Montreal: Conseil des relations interculturelles.

Ignatieff, M. 1998. *The warrior's honor: Ethnic war and the modern conscience.* Toronto: Penguin.

Ilcan, S., and L. Phillips, eds. 1998. *Transgressing borders.* Westport: Bergin and Garvey.

IMF/International Monetary Fund. 2002. *Balance of payments statistics yearbook 2002.* Washington, DC: International Monetary Fund Publication Services.

Intercepted Letters. 1943-45. National Archives of Canada, Record Group 27, Department of Labour, Japanese Division, vols. 528, 655, 661, 662, 1527.

Iredale, I. 2001. The migration of professionals: Theories and typologies. *International Migration* 39 (5): 7-26.

Isajiw, W. 1991. The changing community. In L. Luciuk and S. Hryniuk, eds., *Canada's Ukrainians: Negotiating an identity,* 254-70. Toronto: University of Toronto Press.

–. 1992. *The refugee experience: Ukrainian displaced persons after World War II.* Ed. W. Isajiw, Y. Boshyk, and R. Senkus. Edmonton: Canadian Institute of Ukrainian Studies, University of Alberta.

–. 1999. *Understanding diversity, ethnicity and race in the Canadian context.* Toronto: Thompson.

Isin, E., and M. Siemiatycki. 2002. Making space for mosques: Struggles for urban citizenship in diasporic Toronto. In S.H. Razack, ed., *Race, space, and the law, unmapping a white settler society,* 185-210. Toronto: Between the Lines.

Israelite, N.K., et al. 1998. *Voices of recent Latina immigrants and refugees: Effects of budget cuts on their settlement experiences.* http://ceris.metropolis.net/Virtual%20Library/community/israekute1/israelite1.html.

Itzigsohn, J. 2000. Immigration and the boundaries of citizenship: The institutions of immigrants' political transnationalism. *International Migration Review* 34 (4): 1126-54.

–. 2001. Living transnational lives. Review of the book *Transnational villagers. Diaspora* 10 (2): 281-96.

–, et al. 1999. Mapping Dominican transnationalism: Narrow and broad transnational practices. *Ethnic and Racial Studies* 22 (2): 316-39.

–, and S.G. Saucedo. 2002. Immigrant incorporation and sociocultural transnationalism. *International Migration Review* 36 (3): 766-98.

Jackson, J.H., Jr., and L.P. Moch. 1989. Migration and the social history of modern Europe. *Historical Methods* 22: 27-36. Reprint in D. Hoerder and L.P. Moch, eds., *European migrants: Global and local perspectives,* 52-69. Boston: Northeastern University Press, 1996.

Jacob, R. 1993. Overseas Indians make it big. *Fortune,* 15 November, 68 and 174.

Jacobson, M.F. 1998. *Whiteness of a different color: European immigrants and the alchemy of race.* Cambridge: Harvard University Press.

Jamal, Audrey. 2002. Arab-Canadians: The other within. MA thesis, Royal Roads University, Victoria, British Columbia.

–. 2003. Anti-Arab prejudice flies again. *Globe and Mail,* 4 June, A15.

Jameson, F. 1992. *Postmodernism or the cultural logic of late capitalism.* Durham: Duke University Press.

Jansen, C., and L. Lam. 2003. Immigrants in the Greater Toronto area: A sociodemographic overview. In P. Anisef and M. Lanphier, eds., *The world in a city*, 63-131. Toronto: University of Toronto Press.

Jedwab, J. 2001. Leadership, governance, and the politics of identity in Canada. *Canadian Ethnic Studies* 33 (3): 4-38.

–. 2004. Intersecting identities and dissecting social capital in Canada. *Canadian Diversity* 3 (1): 17-19.

Jiminez, M. 2004. Israelis legitimate target. *Globe and Mail*, 23 October, A22.

Johnson, S. 1982. Institutional origins in the Chilean refugee community in Winnipeg. *Prairie Forum* 7 (2): 17-31.

Jones-Correa, M. 2002. The study of transnationalism among children of immigrants: Where we are and where we should be heading. In P. Levitt and M.C. Waters, eds., *The changing face of home: The transnational lives of the second generation*, 221-41. New York: Russell Sage Foundation.

Joseph, S. 1999. Against the grain of the nation: The Arab. In Michael W. Suleiman, ed., *Arabs in America*, 257-71. Philadelphia: Temple University Press.

Jusdanis, G. 2001. *The necessary nation*. Princeton: Princeton University Press.

Justicia For Migrant Workers. 2005. http://www.justicia4migrantworkers.org/index.htm.

Juteau-Lee, D., ed. 1983. Enjeux ethniques: Production de nouveaux rapports sociaux. *Sociologie et sociétés* 15 (2): 1-174.

Kabbani, R. 2002. Dislocation and neglect in Muslim Britain's ghettos. *Guardian (London)*, 17 June. http://www.guardian.co.uk/comment/story/0,,738807,00.html.

Kamphoefner, W.D., W. Helbich, and U. Sommer, eds. 1991. *News from the land of freedom: German immigrants write home*. Trans. Susan Carter Vogel. Ithaca: Cornell University Press.

Kaplan, R. 1994. *Balkan ghosts: A journey through history*. New York: Vintage Books.

Karim, K.H. 2003. *Diasporas and their communication networks: Exploring the broader context of transnational narrowcasting*. http://www.nautilus.org/virtual-diasporas.

Karpathakis, A. 1999. Home society politics and immigrant political incorporation: The case of Greek immigrants in New York City. *International Migration Review* 33 (1): 55-78.

Kasinitz, P., et al. 2002. Transnationalism and the children of immigrants in contemporary New York. In P. Levitt and M.C. Waters, eds., *The changing face of home: The transnational lives of the second generation*, 96-122. New York: Russell Sage Foundation.

Kazal, R.A. 1995. Revisiting assimilation: The rise, fall, and reappraisal of a concept in American ethnic history. *American History Review* 100: 437-71.

Kearney, M. 1995. The local and the global: The anthropology of globalization and transnationalism. *Annual Review of Anthropology* 24: 547-65.

Keck, M., and K. Sikkink. 1998. *Activists beyond borders: Advocacy networks in international politics*. Ithaca: Cornell University Press.

Kelly, P.F. 2003. Canadian-Asian transnationalism. *Canadian Geographer* 47 (3): 209-18.

–. Forthcoming. Pathways to politics: Integration and activism among Filipinos in Canada. In Luin Goldring and Sailaja V. Krishnamurti, eds., *Organizing the transnational: The experience of Asian and Latin American migrants in Canada*.

Keohane, R.O., and J.S. Nye, eds. 1971. *Transnational relations and world politics*. Cambridge: Harvard University Press.

Keyserlingk, R.H., ed. 1993. *Breaking ground: The 1956 Hungarian refugee movement to Canada*. Toronto: York Lanes Press.

Khouri, R. 2003. Can multiculturalism survive security agenda? *Toronto Star*, 9 March, A9.

Kimball, J.C. 1991. *The USSR and eastern Europe: The shattered heartland*. New York: Foreign Policy Association.

King, Martin Luther, Jr. 1967. Letter to an anti-Zionist friend. *Saturday Review* 47 (August): 76.

Kitagawa, M. 1985. *This is my own: Letters to Wes and other writings on Japanese Canadians, 1941-1948*. Vancouver: Talonbooks.

Kivisto, P. 2001. Theorizing transnational immigration: A critical review of current efforts. *Ethnic and Racial Studies* 24 (4): 549-77.

Kleßmann, C. 1985. Polish miners in the Ruhr district: Their social situation and trade union activity. In D. Hoerder, ed., *Labor migration in the Atlantic economies: The European and North American working classes during the period of industrialization,* 253-76. Westport: Greenwood.

Klekowski, A., and R. Ohliger. 1997. Membership reconsidered: (Ethnic) migration as a challenge to German citizenship. Paper prepared for GAAC Summer Institute on Immigration, Integration and Incorporation into Advanced Democracies.

Klimt, A. 1989. Returning home: Portuguese migrant notions of temporariness, permanence, and commitment. *New German Critique* 46 (Winter): 47-70.

Knight, A. 2002. Conceptualizing transnational community formation: Migrants, sojourners and diasporas in a globalized world. *Canadian Studies in Population* 29 (1): 1-30.

Kolar-Panov, D. 1997. *Video, war and the diasporic imagination.* London: Routledge.

Koopmans, R., and P. Statham. 2003. How national citizenship shapes transnationalism: Migrant and minority claims-making in Germany, Great Britain and the Netherlands. In C. Joppke and E. Morawska, eds., *Toward assimilation and citizenship: Immigrants in liberal nation-states,* 195-238. London: Palgrave.

–, and P. Statham, eds. 2000. *Challenging immigration and ethnic relations politics: Comparative European perspectives.* Oxford: Oxford University Press.

Koslowski, R. 2005. International migration and the globalization of domestic politics: A conceptual framework. In R. Koslowski, ed., *International migration and the globalization of domestic politics,* 5-32. London: Routledge.

Kosmin, B., and P. Iganski, eds. 2003. *A new anti-Semitism? Debating Judeophobia in 21st century Britain.* London: Institute for Jewish Policy Research.

Kotkin, J. 1993. *Tribes: How race, religion, and identity determine success· in the new global economy.* New York: Random House.

Kowalchuk, L. 1999a. Guatemalans. In P.R. Magocsi, ed., *Encyclopedia of Canada's peoples,* 626-30. Toronto: University of Toronto Press.

–. 1999b. Nicaraguans. In P.R. Magocsi, ed., *Encyclopedia of Canada's peoples,* 1008-12. Toronto: University of Toronto Press.

–. 1999c. Salvadorans. In P.R. Magocsi, ed., *Encyclopedia of Canada's peoples,* 1109-15. Toronto: University of Toronto Press.

Krivel, P. 1995a. Bell stands her ground. *Toronto Star,* 22 August, A6.

–. 1995b. Councillor sparks racism protest. *Toronto Star,* 21 August, NY1.

–. 1996. Racism report released, Markham residents urged to be more sensitive. *Toronto Star,* 4 July, NY1.

Kulig, J.C. 1998. Family life among Salvadorans, Guatemalans, and Nicaraguans: A comparative study. *Journal of Comparative Family Studies* 29 (3): 451-67.

Kuropas, M. 1991. *The Ukrainian Americans: Roots and aspirations, 1884-1959.* Toronto: University of Toronto Press.

–. 1996. *Ukrainian-American citadel: The first one hundred years of the Ukrainian National Association.* Boulder: East European Monographs.

Kutty, F. 2004. Globalizing the harassment of Muslims: The dirty work of Canadian intelligence. http://www.counterpunch.org/kutty04282004.html.

–, and B. Yousuf. 2002. Climate of distrust threatens our basic values. *Hamilton Spectator,* 11 September, A13.

Kwak, M.J. 2002. Work in family businesses and gender relations: A case study of recent Korean immigrant women. MA thesis, York University, Toronto.

Kyle, D. 1999. The Otavalo trade diaspora: Social capital and transnational entrepreneurship. *Ethnic and Racial Studies* 22 (2): 422-46.

Labelle, M. 2002. Re-reading citizenship and the transnational practises of immigrants. http://www.ceri-sciencespo.com/archive/mai02/artml.pdf.

–. 2005. À propos de la reconnaissance de la diversité dans l'espace national québécois: Exclusion ou incorporation segmentée? In J.Y. Thériault, ed., *Petites sociétés et minorités nationales: Enjeux politiques et perspectives comparées,* 27-47. Ottawa: Centre de recherche sur la citoyenneté et les minorités et Presses de l'Université du Québec.

–, et al. 1987. *Histoires d'immigrées*. Montreal: Boréal.

–, and J.J. Lévy. 1995. *Ethnicité et enjeux sociaux: Le Québec vu par les leaders de groupes ethnoculturels*. Montreal: Liber.

–, and F. Midy. 1999. Re-reading citizenship and the transnational practices. *Journal of Ethnic and Migration Studies* 25 (2): 213-32.

–, and F. Rocher, eds. 2004. *Contestation transnationale, diversité et citoyenneté dans l'espace québécois*. Sainte-Foy: Presses de l'Université du Québec.

–, and D. Salée. 1999. La citoyenneté en question: L'état canadien face à l'immigration et à la diversité. *Sociologie et sociétés* 31 (2): 125-44.

Lafond, R. 2001. Alexa's view un-Canadian. *Toronto Star*, 16 October, A25.

Laguerre, M. 1999. *Minoritized space: An inquiry into the spatial order of things*. Berkeley: University of California Institute of Governmental Studies Press.

Lakshmi, R. 2003. India reaches out to emigrants. *Washington Post*, 12 January, A21.

Lal, V. N.d. Reflections on the Indian diaspora in the Caribbean and elsewhere. http://www.sscnet.ucla.edu/southasia/Diaspora/reflect.html.

Lam, L. 1994. Searching for a safe haven: The migration and settlement of Hong Kong Chinese immigrants in Toronto. In R. Skeldon, ed., *Reluctant exiles? Migration from Hong Kong and the new overseas Chinese*, 163-79. Armonk: M.E. Sharpe.

Lampe, J.R. 2000. *Yugoslavia as history: Twice there was a country*. Cambridge: Cambridge University Press.

Landolt, P. 2000. *Exploring the spaces of political transnationalism: Insights from Salvadoran transnational migration*. Miami: Latin American Studies Association.

–. 2001. Salvadoran economic transnationalism: Embedded strategies for household maintenance, immigrant incorporation and entrepreneurial expansion. *Global Networks* 1 (3): 217-42.

–. Forthcoming. The institutional landscapes of Salvadoran transnational migration: Translocal views from Los Angeles and Toronto. In L. Goldring and S.V. Krishnamurti, eds., *Organizing the transnational: The experience of Asian and Latin American migrants in Canada*.

–, L. Autler, and S. Baires. 1999. From Hermano Lejano to Hermano Mayor: The dialectics of Salvadoran transnationalism. *Ethnic and Racial Studies* 22 (2): 290-315.

Lee-Young, J. 2004. Victor victorious? *Report on Business* 20 (7): 50-56.

Leonard, K. 1997. *The South Asian Americans*. Westport, CN: Greenwood.

Lessinger, J. 2000. Indian immigrants in the United States: Transnationalism and the American dream. Paper presented at the conference "Culture and Economy in the Indian Diaspora," India International Centre, New Delhi, 8-10 April.

Leveridge, A. 1972. *Your loving Anna: Letters from the Ontario frontier, 1882-1891*. Ed. L. Tivy. Toronto: University of Toronto Press.

Levin, M.D. 2002. Flow and place: Transnationalism in four cases. *Anthropologica* 44 (1): 3-12.

Levitt, C., and W. Shaffir. 1990. *Aliya* and return migration of Canadian Jews: Personal accounts of incentives and disappointed hopes. *Jewish Journal of Sociology* 32 (2): 95-106.

Levitt, P. 2000. Migrants participate across borders: Towards an understanding of forms and consequences. In N. Foner, R.G. Rumbaut, and S.J. Gold, eds., *Immigration research for a new century: Multidisciplinary perspectives*, 459-79. New York: Russell Sage Foundation.

–. 2001a. Transnational migration: Taking stock and future directions. *Global Networks* 1 (3): 195-216.

–. 2001b. *The transnational villagers*. Los Angeles: University of California Press.

–. 2002. The ties that change: Relations to the ancestral home over the life cycle. In P. Levitt and M.C. Waters, eds., *The changing face of home: The transnational lives of the second generation*, 123-44. New York: Russell Sage Foundation.

–. 2003. Keeping feet in both worlds: Transnational practices and immigrant incorporation in the United States. In C. Joppke and E. Morawska, eds., *Toward assimilation and citizenship: Immigrants in liberal nation-states*, 177-94. London: Palgrave.

–, and R. de la Dehesa. 2003. Transnational migration and the redefinition of the state: Variations and explanations. *Ethnic and Racial Studies* 26 (4): 587-611.

–, J. DeWind, and S. Vertovec. 2003. International perspectives on transnational migration: An introduction. *International Migration Review* 37 (3): 565-75.

–, and N. Glick Schiller. 2004. Conceptualizing simultaneity: A transnational social field perspective on society. *International Migration Review* 38 (3): 1002-40.

–, and M.C. Waters, eds. 2002. *The changing face of home: The transnational lives of the second generation.* New York: Russell Sage Foundation.

Lewis, B. 1990. The roots of Muslim rage. *Atlantic Monthly* 266 (September): 47-60.

Ley, D. 1995. Between Europe and Asia: The case of the missing sequoias. *Ecumene* 2: 187-212.

–. 2003. Seeking homo economicus: The Canadian state and the strange story of the Business Immigration Program. *Annals of the Association of American Geographers* 93 (2): 426-41.

–, and J. Tutchener. 2001. Immigration, globalisation and house prices in Canada's gateway cities. *Housing Studies* 16 (12): 199-223.

–, and J. Waters. 2004. Transnational migration and the geographical imperative. In P. Jackson, P. Crang, and C. Dwyer, eds., *Transnational spaces*, 104-21. London: Routledge.

Li, P. 1990. The emergence of the new middle class among the Chinese in Canada. *Asian Culture* 14 (July): 187-94.

–. 1992a. The economics of brain drain: Recruitment of skilled labour to Canada. In V. Satzewich, ed., *Deconstructing a nation*, 145-62. Halifax: Fernwood.

–. 1992b. Ethnic enterprise in transition: Chinese business in Richmond, B.C., 1980-1990. *Canadian Ethnic Studies* 24 (1): 120-38.

–. 1993. Chinese investment and business in Canada: Ethnic entrepreneurship reconsidered. *Pacific Affairs* 66 (2): 219-43.

–. 1996. *The making of post-war Canada.* Toronto: Oxford University Press.

–. 1998. *Chinese in Canada.* 2nd ed. Toronto: Oxford University Press.

–. 2001a. Chinese Canadians in business. *Asian and Pacific Migration Journal* 10 (1): 99-121.

–. 2001b. Immigrants' propensity to self-employment: Evidence from Canada. *International Migration Review* 35 (4): 1106-28.

–. 2003a. Chinese diaspora in occidental societies: Canada and Europe. In D. Hoerder, C. Harzig, and A. Shubert, eds., *Historical practice of diversity: Transcultural interactions from the early modern Mediterranean to the postcolonial world*, 134-51. New York: Berghahn.

–. 2003b. *Destination Canada: Immigration debates and issues.* Toronto: Oxford University Press.

–. 2004. The limits of jurisprudence: The search for social justice in the Chinese Canadian redress case. Paper presented at the international conference "Mending the Past: Memory and the Politics of Forgiveness," Université du Québec à Montréal (UQAM), Montreal, 13-15 October.

Liodakis, N. 2002. The vertical mosaic within: Class, gender and nativity within ethnicity. PhD dissertation, McMaster University, Hamilton.

Lipietz, A. 1987. *Mirages and miracles.* London: Verso.

Lissak, R.S. 1989. *Pluralism and progressives: Hull House and the new immigrants, 1890-1919.* Chicago: University of Chicago Press.

Liu, X.F. 1996. A case study of the labour market status of recent mainland Chinese immigrants, Metropolitan Toronto. *International Migration* 34 (4): 583-605.

Lo, L., and S. Wang. 1997. Settlement patterns of Toronto's Chinese immigrants: Convergence or divergence? *Canadian Journal of Regional Science* 20 (1-2): 49-72.

Loaiza Cardenas, E. 1989. Socio-demographic characteristics and economic attainment of Latin American immigrants in Canada: A Census data assessment, 1981, 1986. PhD dissertation, University of Western Ontario, London.

Lochak, D. 2002. *Les droits de l'homme.* Paris: La Découverte.

Lyon, A.J., and E.M. Uçarer. 2001. Mobilizing ethnic conflict: Kurdish separatism in Germany and the PKK. *Ethnic and Racial Studies* 24 (6): 925-48.

Ma Mung, E. 1999. Dispersal as a resource. Paper presented at the international ISSCO conference "The Chinese Diaspora in Latin America and the Caribbean," University of Havana, Havana, Cuba, 10-12 December.

McAdam, D., J.D. McCarthy, and M. Zald. 1996. *Comparative perspectives on social movements: Political opportunities, mobilizing structures, and cultural framings*. Cambridge: Cambridge University Press.

–, S. Tarrow, and C. Tilly. 2001. *Dynamics of contention*. Cambridge: Cambridge University Press.

McAndrew, M., and M. Potvin, dir. 1996. *Le racisme au Québec: Élément d'un diagnostic*. Collection Études et recherches, No. 13. Montreal: Gouvernement du Québec, Ministère des Affaires internationales, de l'immigration et des communautés culturelles.

Macdonald, C.L., and C. Sirianni, eds. 1996. *Working in the service society*. Philadelphia: Temple University Press.

Mackey, E. 1999. *The house of difference: Cultural politics and national identity in Canada*. London: Routledge.

Macklin, A. 2001. Borderline security. In R.J. Daniels, P. Macklem, and K. Roach, eds., *The security of freedom: Essays on Canada's anti-terrorism bill*. Toronto: University of Toronto Press.

McLellan, J. 1999. *Many petals of the lotus*. Toronto: University of Toronto Press.

McMichael, P. 1996. *Development and social change: A global perspective*. Thousand Oaks: Pine Forge Press.

Magocsi, P.R., ed. 1999. *Encyclopedia of Canada's peoples*. Toronto: University of Toronto Press.

Mahler, S. 1998. Theoretical and empirical contributions toward a research agenda for transnationalism. In M.P. Smith and L.E. Guarnizo, eds., *Transnationalism from below*, 64-100. New Brunswick: Transaction.

–. 1999. Engendering transnational migration: A case study of Salvadorans. *American Behavioral Scientist* 42 (4): 690-719.

Man, G.C. 1997. Women's work is never done: Social organization of work and the experiences of middle-class Hong Kong Chinese immigrant families in Canada. *Advances in Gender Research* 2: 183-226.

Mandaville, P. 2001. *Transnational Muslim politics: Reimagining the umma*. London: Routledge.

Mankekar, P. 1994. Reflections on diasporic identities: A prolegomenon to an analysis of political bifocality. *Diaspora* 3 (3): 349-71.

Marsden, F. 1977. *Chilean refugee households in Canada: Final report of a two-stage survey, 1975-76*. Mimeo. Ottawa. Copy in personal files of Luin Goldring, Department of Sociology, York University, Toronto.

Marshall, D. 1982. Toward an understanding of Caribbean migration. In M. Kritz, ed., *U.S. immigration and refugee policy: Global and domestic issues*. Lexington: Lexington Books.

Massey, D., et al. 1987. *Return to Aztlán: The social process of international migration from western Mexico*. Berkeley: University of California Press.

Mata, F. 1985. Latin American immigration to Canada: Some reflections on the immigration statistics. *Canadian Journal of Latin American and Caribbean Studies* 10 (20): 35-40.

–. 1988. *Immigrants from the Hispanic world in Canada: Demographic profiles and social adaptation*. Toronto: Multicultural Sector, Secretary of State, Canada.

–. 2002. A look at life satisfaction and ethnicity in Canada. *Canadian Ethnic Studies* 34 (1): 51-64.

Matthews, F.H. 1977. *Quest for an American Sociology: Robert E. Park and the Chicago School*. Montreal and Kingston: McGill-Queen's University Press.

Maynard, F.B. 1964. Raisins and almonds. 1st ed. Reprint, Markham, ON: PaperJacks, 1973.

Medeiros, T. 2004. Educacao: O mundo da luso descendencia na tradicao e na inovacao. Paper presented at the conference "II Jornadas: Emigracao/Comunidades." Regional Government of the Azores, Ponta Delgada, Sao Miguel, Acores, 4-8 January.

Memorandum on Future Japanese Policy. 30 April to 14 May 1945. National Archives of Canada, Record Group 27, Department of Labour, Japanese Division, file 23-2-17-6.

Menyah, D. 2002. Immigrant entrepreneurship: A case study of Ghanaian small-scale businesses in the Greater Toronto area. Major research paper, Department of Geography, York University, Toronto.

Meyer, B., and P. Geschiere, eds. 1999. *Globalization and identity: Dialectics of flow and closure.* Oxford: Blackwell.

Migration Policy Institute. 2004a. *Canada: Stock of foreign-born population by country of birth, various years, 1991 to 2001.* Migration information source. http://www.migrationinformation.org/GlobalData/countrydata/data.cfm.

–. 2004b. *Comparing migrant stock: The foreign born in Australia, Canada, and the United States by region of origin.* Migration information source. http://www.migrationinformation.org/DataTools/migrant_stock_region.cfm.

–. 2004c. *United States: Stock of foreign-born population by country of birth as a percentage of total foreign born, 1995 to 2002.* Migration information source. http://www.migrationinformation.org/GlobalData/countrydata/data.cfm.

Miki, R., and C. Kobayashi. 1991. *Justice in our time: The Canadian redress settlement.* Vancouver and Winnipeg: Talonbooks and the National Association of Japanese Canadians.

Miles, A. 2004. *From Cuenca to Queens: An anthropological story of transnational migration.* 1st ed. Austin: University of Texas Press.

Mills, F. 1989. Determinants and consequences of the migration culture of St Kitts-Nevis. In P. Pessar, ed., *When borders don't divide: Labor migration and refugee movements in the Americas,* 42-95. New York: Center for Migration Studies.

Milner, B. 1992. *The hidden establishment: The inside story of Canada's international business elite.* Toronto: Penguin Books.

Miloslavich, C. 1999. *Needs assessment: Women's health in the Hispanic community.* Toronto: Hispanic Development Council.

Mintz, S. 1998. The localization of anthropological practice: From area studies to transnationalism. *Critique of Anthropology* 18 (2): 117-33.

Mitchell, Alanna. 2001. Canadian Muslims, Arabs anxious. *Globe and Mail,* 12 October, A13. http://www.arts.ualberta.ca/peace/articles/alanna_mitchell_oct_12.htm.

Mitchell, K. 1995. Flexible circulation in the Pacific Rim: Capitalisms in cultural context. *Economic Geography* 71 (4): 364-82.

–. 1997. Transnational discourse: Bringing geography back in. *Antipode* 29 (2): 101-14.

Mitra, A. 1997. Virtual commonality: Looking for India on the Internet. In S. Jones, ed., *Virtual culture: Identity and communication in cybersociety,* 55-79. London: Sage.

Mittleman, J.H. 1994. The global restructuring of production and migration. In Y. Sakamoto, ed., *Global transformation: Challenges to the state system,* 276-98. New York: United Nations University Press.

Moctezuma, M. 2000. La organización de los migrantes zacatecanos en Estados Unidos. *Cuadernos Agrarios* n.s. 19-20: 81-104.

Monzón, L., and E. Tudakovic. 2004. Remittances: A preliminary research. *Focal Point: Canadian Foundation for the Americas,* special edition, 5-7 March.

Moody, K. 1997. *Workers in a lean world.* London: Verso.

Morton, J. 1974. *In the sea of sterile mountains.* Vancouver: J.J. Douglas.

Motyl, A., et al. 1998. After empire: Competing discourses and inter-state conflict in post-imperial eastern Europe. In B.R. Rubin and J. Snyder, eds., *Post-Soviet political order: Conflict and state building,* 14-33. London: Routledge.

Mountz, A., and R. Wright. 1996. Daily life in the transnational migrant community of San Augustin, Oaxaca and Poughkeepsie, New York. *Diaspora* 5 (3): 403-28.

Munch, R. 2001. *Nation and citizenship in the global age.* London: Palgrave.

Murdie, R., and C. Teixeira. 2003. Towards a comfortable neighbourhood and appropriate housing: Immigrant experiences in Toronto. In P. Anisef and M. Lanphier, eds., *The world in a city,* 132-91. Toronto: University of Toronto Press.

Murray, M. 1995. Markham: Can good salesmanship turn into racism? *Toronto Star,* 27 August, F1.

Neuwirth, G. 1989. *The settlement of Salvadoran refugees in Ottawa and Toronto.* Ottawa: Employment and Immigration Canada.

Noivo, E. 1997. *Inside ethnic families: Three generations of Portuguese-Canadians.* Montreal and Kingston: McGill-Queen's University Press.

Nolin, C. 2001. Transnational ruptures: Political violence and refugee and immigrant experiences in Guatemala and Canada. PhD dissertation, Queen's University, Kingston.

–. 2004. Spatializing the immobility of Guatemalan transnationalism in Canada. *Canadian Journal of Latin American and Caribbean Studies* 29 (57-58): 267-88.

Nonini, D., and A. Ong. 1997. Chinese transnationalism as an alternative modernity. In A. Ong and D. Nonini, eds., *Ungrounded empires: The cultural politics of modern Chinese transnationalism*, 3-33. New York: Routledge.

Nurse, K. 1999. Globalization and Trinidad carnival: Diaspora, hybridity and identity in global culture. *Cultural Studies* 13 (4): 661-90.

Olds, K. 2001. *Globalization and urban change: Capital, culture and Pacific Rim mega-projects.* Oxford: Oxford University Press.

Ong, A. 1999. *Flexible citizenship: The cultural logic of transnationality.* Durham: Duke University Press.

–, and D. Nonini. 1997a. Toward a cultural politics of diaspora and transnationalism. In A. Ong and D. Nonini, eds., *Ungrounded empires: The cultural politics of Chinese transnationalism,* 323-32. New York: Routledge.

–, and D. Nonini, eds. 1997b. *Ungrounded empires: The cultural politics of Chinese transnationalism.* New York: Routledge.

Ontario Municipal Board. 1996. *Whitwell Developments Ltd. versus Richmond Hill (Town).* Mimeo. 12 April.

Opitz-Black, E.M. 2002. Searching for networks: German immigrants in today's Toronto, Canada. MA thesis, University of Bremen, Germany.

Orozco, M. 2003. *Hometown associations and their present and future partnerships: New development opportunities.* Washington, DC: Inter-American Dialogue.

Ortiz, F. 1940. Del fenómeno de la transculturación y su importancia en Cuba. *Revista Bimestre Cubana* 27: 273-78. Also in Fernando Ortiz, *Contrapunteo cubano del tabaco y el azúcar,* 1st ed., 1940; reprint, Havana: Editorial de Ciencias Sociales, 1983. First English edition, *Cuban Counterpoint: Tobacco and Sugar.* Trans. Harriet de Onís. New York: Knopf, 1947; reprint, Durham: Duke University Press, 1995.

Østergaard-Nielsen, E. 2001. Transnational political practices and the receiving state: Turks and Kurds in Germany and the Netherlands. *Global Networks* 1 (3): 261-81.

–. 2003. The politics of migrants' transnational political practices. *International Migration Review* 37 (3): 760-86.

Ouellette, D. 2004. *Is there a Muslim vote in Canada?* http://www.FrontpageMagazine.com.

Owusu, T. 1998. To buy or not to buy: Determinants of home ownership among Ghanaian immigrants in Toronto. *Canadian Geographer* 42 (1): 40-52.

Painchaud, C., and R. Poulin. 1988. *Les Italiens au Québec.* Hull, QC: Les Éditions Asticou.

Pal, L.A. 1993. *Interests of the state. The politics of language, multiculturalism and feminism in Canada.* Montreal and Kingston: McGill-Queen's University Press.

Panagako, A. 2000. Revisiting the immigrant family: The impact of transnational migration on family and marriage in the Greek diaspora. Paper presented at the 99th Annual American Anthropological Association (AAA) meeting, San Francisco Hilton, San Francisco, 15-19 November.

Parekh, B. 1994. Some reflections on the Hindu diaspora. *New Community* 20 (4): 603-20.

–. 2000. *Rethinking multiculturalism: Cultural diversity and political theory.* London: Macmillan.

Park, R. 1950. *Race and culture.* Glencoe, IL: Free Press.

Parrenas, R.S. 2001. *Servants of globalization. Women, migration, and domestic work.* Stanford: Stanford University Press.

Patel, D. 1980. *Inter-racial conflict: Policy alternatives.* Montreal: Institute for Research on Public Policy.

–. 2000a. Canada's emerging transnational communities: Policy issues. Paper presented at the 5th International Metropolis Conference, Vancouver, 13-17 November.

–. 2000b. Modern technology, identity and culture: The South Asian diasporas. Paper presented at the 36th International Congress of Asian and North African Studies, Montreal, 27 August to 2 September.

–. 2002. Cultural heritage, identity and belonging among transnational communities and globalization: Emerging issues and challenges. Paper presented at the conference "Cultural Citizenship: Challenges to Globalization," Deakin University, Melbourne, 5-8 December.

Patrias, C. 1994. *Patriots and proletarians: Politicizing Hungarian immigrants in interwar Canada.* Montreal and Kingston: McGill-Queen's University Press.

Penslar, D., M. Marrus, and J.G. Stein, eds. 2005. *Contemporary antisemitism: Canada and the world.* Toronto: University of Toronto Press.

Penta, M. 2000. Indian high-tech workers bring skills, culture to US. *Ottawa Citizen,* 7 August, D4.

Persons, S. 1987. *Ethnic studies at Chicago, 1905-45.* Urbana: University of Illinois Press.

Pessar, P., and S. Mahler. 2003. Transnational migration: Bringing gender in. *International Migration Review* 37 (3): 812-46.

Petrone, P. 1995. *Breaking the mould: A memoir.* Toronto: Guernica.

Pew Research Center for the People and the Press. 2002. *Survey results for Canada, from the 2002 Global Attitudes Survey.* http://www.globeandmail.com/serlet/ArticleNews/front/RTGAM/20021204/wsurvadd/Frony/homeBN/breakingnews.

Phillips, L. 1999. Ecuadorians. In P.R. Magocsi, ed., *Encyclopedia of Canada's peoples,* 451-53. Toronto: University of Toronto Press.

Plaza, D. 2000. Transnational grannies: The changing family responsibilities of elderly African Caribbean-born women resident in Britain. *Social Indicators Research* 1 (1): 75-105.

–. 2001. A socio-historic examination of Caribbean migration to Canada: Moving to the beat of changes in immigration policy. *Wabaggi Journal of Diaspora Studies* 4 (1): 39-80.

Popkin, E. 1999. Guatemalan Mayan migration to Los Angeles: Constructing transnational linkages in the context of the settlement process. *Ethnic and Racial Studies* 22 (2): 267-89.

Porter, J. 1965. The vertical mosaic. Toronto: University of Toronto Press.

Portes, A. 1999. Conclusion: Towards a new world: The origins and effects of transnational activities. *Ethnic and Racial Studies* 22 (2): 463-77.

–. 2001. Introduction: The debates and significance of immigrant transnationalism. *Global Networks* 1 (3): 181-93.

–. 2003. Conclusion: Theoretical convergencies and empirical evidence in the study of immigrant transnationalism. *International Migration Review* 37 (3): 874-92.

–, L.E. Guarnizo, and P. Landolt. 1999. The study of transnationalism: Pitfalls and promise of an emergent research field. *Ethnic and Racial Studies* 22 (2): 217-37.

–, W. Haller, and L. Guarnizo. 2002. Transnational entrepreneurs: An alternative form of immigrant economic adaptation. *American Sociological Review* 67 (April): 278-98.

–, and R.G. Rumbaut, eds. 2001. *Legacies. The story of the immigrant second generation.* Berkeley: University of California Press.

Poster, M. 1998. Virtual ethnicity: Tribal identity in an age of global communications. In S. Jones, ed., *Cybersociety 2.0,* 184-212. London: Sage.

Preibisch, K. 2004. Migrant agricultural workers and processes of social inclusion in rural Canada: Encuentros and desencuentros. *Canadian Journal of Latin American and Caribbean Studies* 29 (57-58): 203-39.

Preston, V. 2003. Does neighbourhood matter? A case study of immigrant women's employment in Toronto. Paper presented at the national meeting of the Canadian Association of Geographers, Victoria, BC, 26-30 May.

–, and W. Giles. 1997. Ethnicity, gender and labour markets in Canada: A case study of immigrant women in Toronto. *Canadian Journal of Urban Research* 6 (2): 135-56.

–, A. Kobayashi, and G. Man. Forthcoming. Transnationalism, gender, and civic participation: Canadian case studies of Hong Kong immigrants. *Environment and Planning A.*

–, and L. Lo. 2000. Asian theme malls in suburban Toronto: Land use conflict in Richmond Hill. *Canadian Geographer* 44 (2): 182-90.

–, L. Lo, and S. Wang. 2003. Immigrants' economic status in Toronto: Stories of triumph and disappointment. In P. Anisef and M. Lanphier, eds., *The world in a city,* 192-262. Toronto: University of Toronto Press.

Pries, L. 2001. The approach of transnational social spaces. In L. Pries, ed., *New transnational social spaces: International migration and transnational companies in the early 21st century,* 3-33. London: Routledge.

Pusić, V. 1997. Croatia's struggle for democracy. *Revija za Sociologiju* 28 (1-2): 95-110.

Qadeer, M. 1997. Pluralistic planning for multicultural cities. *Journal of the American Planning Association* 63 (4): 481-95.

RAC/Republicans Abroad Canada. 2003. *A report on the Republicans Abroad International Meeting.* http://www.republicansabroad.ca/rai_meeting2003.htm.

–. 2004. *History of the Republicans Abroad Canada, 1988-2001.* http://www.republicansabroad.ca/history01.htm.

Radhakrishnan, R. 1996. *Diasporic mediations: Between home and location.* Minneapolis: University of Minnesota Press.

Rai, A. 1995. India on-line: Electronic bulletin boards and the construction of a diasporic Hindu identity. *Diaspora* 4 (1): 31-58.

Ramet, S. 1996. *Balkan Babel: The disintegration from the death of Tito to ethnic war.* Boulder: Westview Press.

Rasporich, A.W. 1982. *For a better life: A history of the Croatians in Canada.* Toronto: McClelland and Stewart.

Ray, B. 2003. *The role of cities in immigrant integration.* Migration information source. http://www.migrationinformation.org.

Recalde, A. 2002. *Recent Latin Americans in Vancouver: Unyielding diverse needs versus insufficient services.* Vancouver: RIIM-Research, Vancouver Centre of Excellence Research on Immigration and Integration in the Metropolis.

Reitz, J. 2002. *Host societies and the reception of immigrants.* La Jolla, CA: Center for Comparative Immigration Studies.

–, and R. Breton. 1994. *The illusion of difference: Realities of ethnicity in Canada and the United States.* Toronto: C.D. Howe Institute.

Renaud, J., et al. 2002. *What a difference ten years can make: The settlement experience of immigrants admitted to Quebec in 1989.* Sainte-Foy, QC: Les Publications du Québec.

Rex, J. 1996. National identity in the democratic multi-cultural state. *Sociological Research Online* 1 (2). http://www.socresonline.org.uk/socresonline/1/2/1.html.

Richmond, A. 1993. Education and qualifications of Caribbean migrants in Metropolitan Toronto. *New Community* 19 (2): 263-80.

Robinson, William. 2004. *A theory of global capitalism: Production, class, and state in a transnational world.* Baltimore: John Hopkins University.

Rockhill, K., and P. Tomic. 1992. *Accessing ESL: An exploration into the effects of institutionalized racism and sexism in shaping the lives of Latin American immigrant and refugee women in Metropolitan Toronto.* Toronto: Ontario Ministry of Education.

Romero, J. 1985. Ecuador's soccer club in history of LEFA. *Bulletin of the Multicultural History Society of Ontario,* 7.

Rose, J. 2001. Contexts of interpretation: Assessing urban immigrant reception in Richmond, BC. *Canadian Geographer* 45 (4): 474-93.

Rosenberg, L. 1981. *The errand runner. Reflections of a rabbi's daughter.* Toronto: Wiley.

Rouse, R. 1991. Mexican migration and the social space of postmodernism. *Diaspora* 1 (1): 8-23.

–. 1992. Making sense of settlement: Class formation, cultural struggle and transnationalism among Mexican migrants in the United States. *Annals of the New York Academy of Sciences* 645: 25-52.

Roy, P.E. 2003. *The Oriental question: Consolidating a white man's province, 1914-41.* Vancouver: UBC Press.

Rumbaut, R. 2002. Severed or sustained attachments? Language, identity, and imagined communities in the post-immigrant generation. In P. Levitt and M.C. Waters, eds., *The changing face of home: The transnational lives of the second generation,* 43-95. New York: Russell Sage Foundation.

–, and A. Portes, eds. 2001. *Ethnicites: Children of immigrants in America.* Berkeley: University of California Press.

Safieddin, Hicham. 2003. One religion, 12 voices. Interviews. *Toronto Star,* 11 September, B01.

Said, E. 1998. *The myth of "The clash of civilizations."* Film. Media Education Foundation (MEF). http://www.mediaed.org/hanouts/pdfs/SAID_CLASH.pdf.

Saifullah Khan, V., ed. 1979. *Minority families in Britain: Support and stress.* London and Basingstoke: Macmillan.

Salverson, L.G. 1939. *Confessions of an immigrant's daughter.* 1st ed. Toronto: Ryerson; reprint, Toronto: University of Toronto Press, 1981.

Sartre, Jean-Paul. 1983. *Saint Genêt: Actor and martyr.* New York: Pantheon Books.

Sassen, S. 1996. *Losing control? Sovereignty in an age of globalization.* New York: Columbia University Press.

–. 1998. The de facto transnationalizing of immigration policy. In C. Joppke, ed., *Challenge to the nation-state: Immigration in western Europe and the United States.* Oxford: Oxford University Press.

–. 2001. *The global city.* Rev. ed. Princeton: Princeton University Press.

–. 2003. Spatialities and temporalities of the global: Elements for a theorization. In A. Appadurai, ed., *Globalization,* 260-78. Durham: Duke University Press.

Satzewich, V. 1988. The Canadian state and the racialization of Caribbean migrant farm labour, 1947-1966. *Ethnic and Racial Studies* 11 (3): 282-304.

–. 1989. Racism and Canadian immigration policy: The government's view of Caribbean migration, 1962-1966. *Canadian Ethnic Studies* 21 (1): 77-97.

–. 1998a. Race, racism and racialization: Contested concepts. In V. Satzewich, ed., *Racism and social inequality in Canada,* 25-45. Toronto: Thompson Educational Publishers.

–, ed. 1998b. *Racism and social inequality in Canada.* Toronto: Thompson Educational Publishers.

–. 2002. *The Ukrainian diaspora.* London: Routledge.

–, and L. Wong. 2003. Immigration, ethnicity, and race: The transformation of transnationalism, localism, and identities. In W. Clement and L. Vosko, eds., *Changing Canada: Political economy as transformation,* 363-90. Montreal and Kingston: McGill-Queen's University Press.

Saxenian, A.L. 1999. *Silicon Valley's new immigrant entrepreneurs.* San Francisco: Public Policy Institute of California.

–. 2002. *Local and global networks of immigrant professionals in Silicon Valley.* San Francisco: Public Policy Institute of California.

Schmitter-Heisler, B. 2000. The sociology of immigration. In C.B. Brettell and J.F. Hollifield, eds., *Migration theory: Talking across disciplines,* 77-95. New York: Routledge.

Schneider, A.G. 1986. *The Finnish baker's daughters.* Toronto: Multicultural History Society of Ontario (MHSO).

Schoenfeld, S. 1999. Reluctant cosmopolitans: The impact of continentalism, multiculturalism and globalization on Jewish identity in Canada. In Steven M. Cohen and Gaby Horenczyk, eds., *National variation in Jewish identity,* 137-55. New York: State University of New York Press.

–, J. Schoenfeld, and G. McCabe. 1999. From diaspora to diaspora: Jewish migrants from South Africa to Toronto. Paper presented at a meeting of the Society for the Scientific Study of Religion, Boston, 8 November.

Schuck, P.H. 1998. Plural citizenships. In N.M.J. Pickus, ed., *Immigration and citizenship in the 21st century,* 149-91. Lanham, MD: Rowman and Littlefield.

Schulte-Tenckhoff, I. 1997. *La question des peuples autochtones.* Bruxelles: Bruylant.

Segal, M. 1991. Indian video films and Asian-British identities. *Cultural Studies in Birmingham* 1: 52-87.

Shaffir, W. 2001. Canadian *aliya:* Some properties of acculturation. Paper presented at the 13th World Congress of Jewish Studies, Jerusalem, 13-16 August.

Shain, Y. 1999. *Marketing the American creed abroad: Diasporas in the U.S. and their homelands.* Cambridge: Cambridge University Press.

–. 2000. American Jews and the construction of Israel's Jewish identity. *Diaspora* 9 (2): 163-202.

Shankar, S. 1999/2000. Cultural politics amongst South Asians in North America. *Amerasia Journal* 5 (3): 151-61.

Sharma, N. 2001. On being not Canadian: The social organization of migrant workers in Canada. *Canadian Review of Sociology and Anthropology* 38 (4): 415-40.

Sheffer, G. 1986. A new field of study: Diasporas in international relations. In G. Sheffer, ed., *Modern diasporas in international politics*, 1-15. New York: St. Martin's.

–. 2003. *Diaspora politics: At home abroad*. Cambridge: Cambridge University Press.

Sherazee, A. 2002. Criminalization of dissent. *Fireweed* (77): 20-27.

–. 2004. Criminalizing dissent: Secret trials, racial profiling and the enemy within. Paper presented at the conference "Race, Racism and Empire: The Local and the Global, York University, Toronto, 30 April to 1 May.

Shohat, E. 1995. The struggle over representation: Casting, coalitions and the politics of identification. In R. de la Campa, E.A. Kaplan, and M. Sprinker, eds., *Late imperial culture*, 166-78. New York: Verso.

–. 2002. Dislocated identities: Reflections of an Arab Jew. In Inderpal Grewal and Caren Kaplan, eds., *An introduction to women's studies: Gender in a transnational world*. Montreal and Boston: McGraw-Hill.

Shukla, S. 1997. Building diaspora and nation: The 1991 cultural festival of India. *Cultural Studies* 11 (2): 296-315.

Siddiqui, H. 2003. Siding with the U.S. against Canada. *Toronto Star*, 6 April, F1.

Siemiatycki, M., and V. Preston. 2004. State and media construction of transnational communities: A case study of recent migration from Hong Kong to Canada. Paper presented at the conference "Politics of Transnational Ties: Implications for Research, Communities, and Policy," York University, Toronto, 8-9 March.

–, and A. Saloojee. 2002. Ethnoracial political representation in Toronto: Patterns and problems. *Journal of International Migration and Integration* 3 (2): 241-73.

Simalchik, J. 2004. Chilean refugees and Canada: Home reinvented. *Canadian Issues* (March): 52-53.

Simmons, A. 1997. Globalization and backlash racism in the 1990s: The case of Asian immigration to Canada. In E. Laquian et al., eds., *The silent debate: Asian immigration and racism in Canada*, 29-50. Vancouver: Institute of Asian Research, UBC Press.

–. 1998. Racism and immigration policy. In V. Satzewich, ed., *Racism and social inequality in Canada*, 87-114. Toronto: Thompson Educational Publishing.

–. 1999. Economic integration and designer immigrants: Canadian policy in the 1990s. In M. Castro, ed., *Free markets, open societies, closed borders? Trends in international migration and immigration policy in the Americas*, 53-69. Miami: North-South Press, University of Miami.

–, and J.P. Guengant. 1992. Caribbean exodus and the world system. In M. Kritz, L. Lim, and H. Zlotnik, eds., *International migration systems: A global approach*, 96-114. New York: Oxford University Press.

–, and D. Plaza. 1998. Breaking through the glass ceiling: The pursuit of university training among African-Caribbean migrants and their children in Toronto. *Canadian Ethnic Studies* 30 (3): 99-120.

Simpson, J. 2003. The American "dream palace." *Globe and Mail*, 4 March, A15.

Singer, A. 2004. *The rise of new immigrant gateways*. Living cities Census series. Washington, DC: Brookings Institution.

Singh, S. 1997. The social construction of a collective "Indian" ethno-religious identity in a context of ethnic diversity: A case study of an Indo-Caribbean Hindu temple in Toronto. PhD dissertation, Department of Sociology, University of Toronto.

Singhvi, L.M. 2000. *Report of the High Level Committee on the Indian diaspora*. India: Ministry of External Affairs, Foreign Secretary's Office, 18 August. http://www.indiaday.org/government_policy/singhvi.asp.

Skeldon, R. 1994. *Reluctant exiles? Migration from Hong Kong and the new overseas Chinese*. Armonk: M.E. Sharpe.

Sklair, L. 1991. *Sociology of the global system*. Baltimore: Johns Hopkins University Press.

–. 1998. The transnational capitalist class. In J. Carrier and D. Miller, eds., *Virtualism: A new political economy*, 135-59. Oxford: Berg.

–. 2001. *The transnational capitalist class*. London: Blackwell.

–. 2002. *Globalization: Capitalism and its alternatives*. Oxford: Oxford University Press.

Skrbiš, Z. 1995. Long distance nationalism? Second generation Croatians and Slovenians in Australia. In A. Pavkoviæ et al., eds., *Nationalism and postcommunism: A collection of essays*, 159-73. Sydney and Brookfield, VT: Dartmouth.

–. 1999. *Long distance nationalism: Diasporas, homelands and identities*. Sydney and Brookfield, VT: Dartmouth.

Small, P., and B. DeMara. 2001. Canadian Muslims feel under siege. *Toronto Star*, 14 September, A2.

Smart, A., and J. Smart. 2000. Failures and strategies of Hong Kong firms in China: An ethnographic perspective. In H. Wai-chung Yeung and K. Olds, eds., *Globalization of Chinese business firms*, 244-71. London: Macmillan.

Smith, C.D., and S. Hess. 1985. Trials and errors: The experience of Central American refugees in Montreal. *Refuge: Canada's Periodical on Refugees* 5 (4): 10-11.

Smith, M.P. 2000. *Transnational urbanism: Locating globalization*. Malden: Blackwell.

–. 2001. *Transnational urbanism: Locating globalization*. Oxford: Blackwell.

–, and L.E. Guarnizo, eds. 1998. *Transnationalism from below*. Vol. 6. New Brunswick: Transaction.

Smith, R.C. 1998. Politics of membership within the context of Mexico and US migration. In M.P. Smith and L.E. Guarnizo, eds., *Transnationalism from below*, vol. 6, 196-238. New Brunswick: Transaction.

–. 2003. Migrant membership as an instituted process: Transnationalization, the state and the extra-territorial conduct of Mexican politics. *International Migration Review* 37 (2): 297-343.

Sollors, W., ed. 1989. *The invention of ethnicity*. New York: Oxford University Press.

Sommier, I. 2001. *Les nouveaux mouvements contestataires*. Paris: Flammarion.

Sopta, M. 1994. Croatian Canadians and the new Croatia. In M. Sopta and G. Scardellato, eds., *Unknown journey: A history of Croatians in Canada*, 77-79. Polyphony, No. 14. Toronto: Multicultural History Society of Ontario.

–. 2001. Cemo svim mladim Hrvatima iz Dijaspora Platiti Dolazak u Hrvasktu. *Jutarnji List* 27: 8-9.

Sørensen, N., and K. Olwig, eds. 2002. *Work and migration: Life and livelihoods in a globalizing world*. London: Routledge.

Soysal, Y. 1994. *Limits of citizenship*. Chicago: University of Chicago Press.

Spears, J. 1995. Mad about malls. *Toronto Star*, 4 July, B1.

Spiro, P. 1999. *Embracing dual nationality*. Carnegie Endowment for International Peace, International Migration Policy. http://www.ceip.org/files/publications/Pub_by_author.asp#anchor.

Spivak, G. 2000. Thinking cultural questions in "pure" literary terms. In Paul Gilroy, L. Grossberg, and A. McRobbie, eds., *Without guarantees: In honour of Stuart Hall*, 335-57. New York: Verso.

Stainsby, M. 1989. The private world of Victor Li. *Vancouver Sun*, 25 February, B1.

Statistics Canada. 1991. *Canada's balance of international payments, first quarter 1991*. Ottawa.

–. 2001. *Census of population: Ethnocultural portrait of Canada: Ethnic origin*. Catalogue No. 97F0010XCB01001. Ottawa. http://www12.statcan.ca/english/census01/products.

–. 2003a. *Canada's ethnocultural portrait: The changing mosaic, 2001 Census*. Catalogue No. 96F0030X1E2001008. Ottawa.

–. 2003b. *Earnings of Canadians: Making a living in the new economy, 2001 Census*. Catalogue No. 96F0030. Ottawa.

–. 2003c. *Ethnic Diversity Survey, 2002: Portrait of a multicultural society*. http://www.statcan.ca/english/freepub/89-593-XIE/ pdf/89-593-XIE03001.pdf.

–. 2003d. *Immigrant population by place of birth and period of immigration*. http://www.statcan.ca/english/Pgdb/popula.htm#imm.

–. 2003e. *Immigrant status and period of immigration (10a) and place of birth of respondent (260) for immigrants and non-permanent residents, for Canada, provinces, territories, Census metropolitan areas and Census agglomerations, 2001 Census.* Catalogue No. 97F0009X CB01002. Ottawa.

–. 2003f. Longitudinal Survey of Immigrants to Canada. *Ottawa Daily,* 4 September, 1-17.

–. 2003g. *Microdata user guide: Longitudinal survey of immigrants to Canada: Wave 1.* Ottawa.

–. 2003h. *Special tabulations on LSIC data.* Ottawa.

–. 2003i. *2001 Census of Canada.* Ottawa.

–. 2004. *Special tabulations of the Longitudinal Survey of Immigrants to Canada.* Ottawa.

Stavenhagen, R. 2002. Reflections on racism and public policy. *United Nations Research Institute for Social Development Bulletin* 25: 43-44.

Stein, E. 2003. Construction of an enemy. *Monthly Review* 55 (3): 125-29.

Stonequist, E. 1961. *The marginal man: A study in personality and culture conflict.* New York: Russell and Russell.

Strauss, A. 1969. *Mirrors and masks: The search for identity.* San Francisco: Sociology Press.

Strauss, S. 2002. I feel an old evil stirring. *Globe and Mail,* 25 April, A26.

Stubbs, P. 1998. Conflict and cooperation in the virtual community: Email and the wars of Yugoslav succession. *Sociological Research Online* 3 (3). http://www.socresonline.org.uk/socresonline/3/3/7.html.

Subtelny, O. 1991. *Ukrainians in North America: An illustrated history.* Toronto: University of Toronto Press.

Sunahara, A. 1981. *The politics of racism. The uprooting of Japanese Canadians during the Second World War.* Toronto: James Lorimer.

Suro, R. 2003. *Remittance senders and receivers: Tracking the transnational channels.* Washington, DC: Multilateral Investment Fund, Inter-American Development Bank, Pew Hispanic Center and Bendixen and Associates.

Szonyi, M. 2002. Paper tigers. *National Post Business* (July): 34-44.

Tabory, E., and B. Lazerwitz. 1977. Motivation for migration: A comparative study of American and Soviet academic immigrants to Israel. *Ethnicity* 4 (2): 91-102.

Tahmasebi, V. 2004. Islamic identity and secular, progressive voices of Iranian women in the diaspora: Problems and dilemmas. Paper presented at the symposium "Women's Voices from the Middle East," York University, Toronto, 11 March.

Tambiah, S. 2000. Transnational movements, diaspora, and multiple modernities. *Daedalus* 129 (1): 163-94.

Tanner, M. 1996. *Croatia: A nation forged in war.* New Haven: Yale University Press.

Taras, D., and D. Goldberg. 1989. *The domestic battleground.* Montreal and Kingston: McGill-Queen's University Press.

–, and M. Weinfeld. 1993. Continuity and criticism: North American Jews and Israel. In Robert Brym, William Shaffir, and Morton Weinfeld, eds., *The Jews in Canada,* 293-310. Toronto: Oxford University Press.

Tarrow, S. 1998. *Power in movement: Social movements and contentious politics.* 2nd ed. Cambridge: Cambridge University Press.

–. 2000. La contestation transnationale. *Cultures et conflits* (38-39): 187-220.

Tatla, S.D. 1999. *The Sikh diaspora: The search for statehood.* London: University College London (UCL) Press.

Taylor, C. 1994. *Multiculturalism: Examining the politics of recognition.* Ed. A. Guttman. Princeton: Princeton University Press.

Teixeira, C. 1999. Portuguese. In P.R. Magocsi, ed., *Encyclopedia of Canada's peoples,* 1075-83. Toronto: University of Toronto Press.

–, and V. Pereira da Rosa. 2000a. Introduction: A historical and geographical perspective. In C. Teixeira and V. Pereira da Rosa, eds., *The Portuguese in Canada,* 3-14. Toronto: University of Toronto Press.

–, and V. Pereira da Rosa, eds. 2000b. *The Portuguese in Canada.* Toronto: University of Toronto Press.

Thobani, S. 2002. Racism and Canadian democracy in times of war. Paper presented at the conference "Racism and National Consciousness," University of Toronto, 26 October.

–. 2004a. Contesting empire: A case for anti-racist feminism. Paper presented at the conference "Race, Racism and Empire: The Local and the Global," York University, Toronto, 29 April to 1 May.

–. 2004b. Imperial longings, multicultural belongings. Paper presented at the conference "Race, Racism and Empire: The Local and the Global," York University, Toronto, 29 April to 1 May.

Thomas, W. 2004. *Developing ethnic markets critical to future of businesses*. http://www. weeklyvoice.com.

Tilly, L., and J. Scott. 1978. *Women, work and family*. New York: Holt, Rinehart and Winston.

Todorova, M. 1997. *Imagining the Balkans*. London: Oxford University Press.

Tölölyan, K. 2000. Elites and institutions in the Armenian transition. *Diaspora* 9 (1): 107-36.

Tomlinson, J. 1999. *Globalization and culture*. Chicago: University of Chicago Press.

Torczyner, J.L. 1997. *Diversity, mobility and change: The dynamics of black communities in Canada*. Montreal: McGill Consortium for Ethnicity and Strategic Social Planning.

Tossutti, L.S. 2002. How transnational factors influence the success of ethnic, religious and regional parties in 21 states. *Party Politics* 8 (1): 51-74.

Town of Markham. 1996. *Working together towards better understanding and harmony in the Town of Markham*. Markham, ON: Mayor's Advisory Committee, 25 June.

Troper, H. 2003. Becoming an immigrant city: A history of immigration into Toronto since the Second World War. In P. Anisef and M. Lanphier, eds., *The world in a city*, 19-62. Toronto: University of Toronto Press.

Turner, J., and A. Simmons. 1993. L'immigration antillaise au Canada, 1967-1987: Contraintes structurelles et expériences vécues. In D. Cordell et al., eds., *Population, reproduction, sociétés: Perspectives et enjeux de la démographie sociale*, 395-418. Montreal: Presses de l'Université de Montréal.

United States Congress. 1911. *Immigration Commission, reports of the Immigration Commission: Dillingham Commission*. 41 vols. Washington, DC: Government Printing Office.

van der Veer, P., ed. 1995. *Nation and migration: The politics of space in the South Asian diaspora*. Philadelphia: University of Philadelphia Press.

Van Hear, N. 1998. *New diasporas: The mass exodus, dispersal and regrouping of migrant communities*. Seattle: University of Washington Press.

Vecoli, R.J. 1964. The Contadini in Chicago: A critique of *The uprooted*. *Journal of American History* 51: 404-17.

Veronis, L. 2002. Beyond transnationalism: The contributions of Latin American migrants to the social and political landscape of Toronto. Paper presented at the national meeting of the Canadian Association of Geographers, Toronto, ON, University of Toronto, 29 May to 2 June.

Vertovec, S. 1999. Conceiving and researching transnationalism. *Ethnic and Racial Studies* 22 (2): 447-62.

–. 2000. *The Hindu diaspora: Comparative patterns*. London: Routledge.

–. 2001a. Transnationalism and identity. *Journal of Ethnic and Migration Studies* 27 (4): 573-82.

–. 2001b. *Transnational challenges to the new multiculturalism*. http://www.transcomm. ox.ac.uk/working_papers.htm.

–, and R. Cohen. 1999. *Migration, diasporas and transnationalism*. Cheltenham: Edward Elgar.

Voluntary Repatriation Survey among Japanese in Canada, 1945. National Archives of Canada, Record Group 27, Department of Labour, Japanese Division, vol. 1529, file 23-2-17-6.

Wahlbeck, O. 2002. The concept of diaspora as an analytic tool in the study of refugee communities. *Journal of Ethnic and Migration Studies* 28 (2): 221-38.

Walaszek, A. 2003. Labor diasporas in comparative perspective: Polish and Italian migrant workers in the Atlantic world between the 1870s and the 1920s. In D. Hoerder, C. Harzig, and A. Shubert, eds., *Historical practice of diversity: Transcultural interactions from the early modern Mediterranean to the postcolonial world*, 152-76. New York: Berghahn.

Waldinger, R., and D. Fitzgerald. 2004. Transnationalism in question. *American Journal of Sociology* 109 (5): 1177-95.

–, and M. Lichter. 2003. *How the other half works: Immigration and the social organization of labor.* Berkeley, CA: University of California Press.

Waller, Harold. 1981. A reexamination of Zionism in Canada. In M. Weinfeld, W. Shaffir, and I. Cotler, eds., *The Canadian Jewish mosaic*, 343-57. Toronto: John Wiley and Sons.

Wallerstein, I. 1974-88. *The modern world-system.* 3 vols. New York: Academic Press.

–. 1990. Culture as the ideological battleground of the modern world-system. *Theory, Culture and Society* 7 (2): 31-55.

Walton-Roberts, M. 2000. Indo-Canadian transnationalism: What does it mean for immigration policy and practice? Paper presented at the 5th International Metropolis Conference, Vancouver, 13-17 November.

–. 2003. Transnational geographies: Indian immigration to Canada. *Canadian Geographer* 47 (3): 235-50.

Wang, G. 2000. *The Chinese overseas.* Cambridge: Harvard University Press.

Wang, S. 1999. Chinese commercial activity in the Toronto CMA: New development patterns and impacts. *Canadian Geographer* 43 (1): 19-35.

Ward, W.P. 1978. *White Canada forever: Popular attitudes and public policy toward Orientals in British Columbia.* Montreal and Kingston: McGill-Queen's University Press.

Waters, J. 2001. *The flexible family? Recent immigration and astronaut households in Vancouver, British Columbia.* Working Paper No. 01-02. Vancouver: Research on Immigration and Integration in the Metropolis (RIIM).

–. 2002. Flexible families? Astronaut households and the experiences of lone mothers in Vancouver, British Columbia. *Social and Cultural Geography* 3 (2): 117-34.

–. 2003. Flexible citizens? Transnationalism and citizenship among economic immigrants in Vancouver. *Canadian Geographer* 47 (3): 219-34.

Waters, M.C. 1995. *Globalization.* London: Routledge.

Wayland, Sarah. 2003. Immigration and transnational political ties: Croatians and Sri Lankan Tamils in Canada, *Canadian Ethnic Studies* 35 (2): 61-85.

–. 2004. Ethnonationalist networks and transnational opportunities: The Sri Lankan Tamil diaspora. *Review of International Studies* 30 (3): 405-26.

Weinfeld, Morton. 2001. *Like everyone else but different: The paradoxical success of Canadian Jews.* Toronto: McClelland and Stewart.

Weinreich, P. 1979. Ethnicity and adolescent identity conflicts. In V. Saifullah Khan, ed., *Minority families in Britain: Support and stress*, 89-107. London and Basingstoke: Macmillan.

Wente, M. 2001. Why do they hate us so much? *Globe and Mail*, 22 September, A13.

Werbner, P. 1999. Global pathways: Working class cosmopolitans and the creation of transnational ethnic worlds. *Social Anthropology* 7 (1): 17-35.

–. 2000. Divided loyalties, empowered citizenship? Muslims in Britain. *Citizenship Studies* 4 (3): 307-24.

Westhead, R. 2003. Billionaire's son prepares for takeover; Li Ka-Shing 28th richest man in the world now, Victor Li will try to turn around Air Canada. *Toronto Star*, 10 November, A13.

White, P., and L. Hurdley. 2003. International migration and the housing market: Japanese corporate movers in London. *Urban Studies* 40 (4): 687-706.

Wieviorka, M. 1998. *Le racisme, une introduction.* Paris: La Découverte.

Wikipedia. 2005. http://www.en.wikipedia.org.mohamed_elmasry.

Wilhelm, K., and D. Biers. 2000. No place like home. *Far Eastern Economic Review,* 15 June, 72-75.

Williams, R. 1992. *A sacred thread: Modern transmission of Hindu traditions in India and abroad.* Chambersburg, PA: Anima Books.

Wimmer, A., and N. Glick Schiller. 2002. Methodological nationalism and beyond: Nation-state building, migration and the social sciences. *Global Networks* 2 (4): 301-30.

Winant, H. 1997. Behind blue eyes: Contemporary white racial politics. *New Left Review* 225 (September-October): 73-88.

Winland, D. 1998. Our home and native land: Canadian ethnic scholarship and the challenge of transnationalism. *Canadian Review of Sociology and Anthropology* 35 (4): 555-77.

–. 2002. The politics of desire and disdain: Croatian identity between home and homeland. *American Ethnologist* 29 (3): 693-718.

Wolpert, S. 1993. *A new history of India.* Oxford: Oxford University Press.

Wong, B. 1998. *Ethnicity and entrepreneurship: The new Chinese immigrants in the San Francisco Bay area.* Needham Heights, MA: Allyn and Bacon.

Wong, L. 1997. Globalization and transnational migration: A study of recent Chinese capitalist migration from the Asia Pacific to Canada. *International Sociology* 12 (3): 329-51.

–. 2002a. Home away from home: Transnationalism and the Canadian citizenship regime. In V. Roudometof and P. Kennedy, eds., *Communities across borders: New immigrants and transnational cultures,* 169-81. London: Routledge.

–. 2002b. Transnationalism, diasporic communities, and changing identity: Implications for Canadian citizenship policy. In D. Cameron and J. Stein, eds., *Street protests and fantasy parks: Globalization, culture, and the state,* 49-87. Vancouver: UBC Press.

–. 2003. Unpublished raw data from Vancouver and Calgary Chinese Business Survey.

–, and Michelle Ng. 1998. Chinese immigrant entrepreneurs in Vancouver: A case study of ethnic business development. *Canadian Ethnic Studies* 30 (1): 64-85.

–, and Michelle Ng. 2002. The emergence of small transnational enterprise in Vancouver: The case of Chinese entrepreneur immigrants. *International Journal of Urban and Regional Research* 26 (3): 508-30.

Wong, M. 2000. Ghanaian women in Toronto's labour market: Negotiating gendered roles and transnational household strategies. *Canadian Ethnic Studies* 32 (3): 45-74.

–. 2003. Borders that separate, blood that binds: Transnational activities of Ghanaian women in Toronto. PhD dissertation, York University, Toronto.

Wood, P. 2002. *Nationalism from the margins.* Montreal and Kingston: McGill-Queen's University Press.

Woodill, L.R.J. 2000. *A search for home: Refugee voices in the Romero House Community.* Toronto: City of Toronto.

Woodsworth, J.S. 1972. *Strangers within our gates.* Toronto: University of Toronto Press.

Woodward, S.L. 1995. *Balkan tragedy: Chaos and dissolution after the Cold War.* Washington, DC: Brookings Institution.

Wright, C. 2003. Moments of emergence: Organizing by and with undocumented and non-citizen people in Canada after September 11. *Refuge* 21 (3): 5-15.

–. 2004. The nationalization of Maher Arar. Paper presented at the symposium "Acts of Citizenship," York University, Toronto, 25-27 March.

Wu, W-P. 2000. Transaction cost, cultural values and Chinese business networks: An integrated approach. In K.B. Chan, ed., *Chinese business networks: State economy and culture,* 35-56. Singapore: Prentice Hall.

Yeoh, B.S.A., et al. 2003. Transnationalism and its edges. *Ethnic and Racial Studies* 26 (2): 207-17.

Yeung, H.W-C., and K. Olds. 2000. Globalizing Chinese business firms: Where are they coming from, where are they heading? In H.W-C. Yeung and K. Olds, eds., *Globalization of Chinese business firms,* 1-28. London: Macmillan.

Young, R. 1995. *Colonial desire.* New York: Routledge.

Zabin, C., and L. Escala. 1998. *Mexican hometown associations and Mexican immigrant political empowerment in Los Angeles.* Washington, DC: Aspen Institute.

Zhou, Y., and Y-F. Tseng. 2001. Regrounding the ungrounded empires: Localization as the geographical catalyst for transnationalism. *Global Networks* 1 (2): 131-53.

Zolberg, A.R. 1999. Matters of state: Theorizing immigration policy. In C. Hirschman, P. Kasinitz, and J. DeWind, eds., *The handbook of international migration,* 71-93. New York: Russell Sage Foundation.

Contributors

Luis L.M. Aguiar is an associate professor of sociology at the University of British Columbia, Okanagan Campus. He researches neoliberalism and its impact on immigrant and minority workers in the Canadian building-cleaning industry. He is coediting a book on janitors facing neoliberalism and the global economy. In addition, he has written on whiteness and growing up immigrant in Montreal. At the moment, he is engaged in studying the Okanagan Valley and its changing status as a hinterland in the global economy. A research project on former Canadian boxing champion Eddie Melo and pop diva Nelly Furtado is in development. He teaches urban sociology, race and ethnic relations in Canada, the sociology of tourism, cultural studies, qualitative methods, and globalization and labour.

Sedef Arat-Koc is an associate professor in the Department of Politics and Public Administration at Ryerson University in Toronto. Previously, she taught in the Women's Studies Program and the Department of Sociology at Trent University in Peterborough, Ontario. Most of her publications have been on issues of citizenship and immigration in Canada, especially as they concern immigrant women. Her latest book, *Caregivers Break the Silence* (2001), focuses on the policy impacts of the live-in caregiver program in Canada. Arat-Koc's current work is on racialization of Arabs and Muslims in Canada since 11 September 2001 and on "whiteness" in Turkey in relationship to globalization, neoliberalism, and imperialism.

Ann-Marie Field is a researcher at the Centre de recherche sur l'immigration, l'ethnicité et la citoyenneté (CRIEC) at the Université du Québec à Montréal (UQAM). She recently completed her PhD in political science at Carleton University. Her thesis, entitled "Counter-Hegemonic Citizenship, Hate Crimes, and the Safety of Lesbians, Gays, Bisexuals and Transgendered People in Canada, 1993-2003," focuses on hate crimes in the Canadian context and, more generally, on questions of citizenship and diversity.

Luin Goldring is an associate professor of sociology and a Fellow at the Centre for Research on Latin America and the Caribbean at York University in Toronto. She is presently involved in collaborative research projects on Latin Americans' transnational engagements and incorporation in Canada. Her earlier work on Mexico–United States migration led to publications on relations between the Mexican state and migrant organizations and society, gendered citizenship in transnational contexts, remittances and development, and transnational communities. Her current areas of interest include transnational families, legal status as a dimension of social exclusion, social citizenship and neoliberalism, and the politics of sending and receiving states vis-à-vis organized emigrants and immigrants.

Christiane Harzig teaches migration history at Arizona State University. She has published on German, American, and Canadian history, specializing in gender, migration, and policy issues. Among her latest publications is *Immigration and Politics: Historical Memory and Political Culture as Resources in Canada, Sweden and the Netherlands,* in German (2004). She recently received the John A. Diefenbaker Award, which enabled her to work at the University of Winnipeg studying global migration systems of domestic workers.

Daniel Hiebert is a geographer at the University of British Columbia and also codirector of the Vancouver Centre of Excellence for Research on Immigration and Integration in the Metropolis. His research focuses mainly on the impacts of immigration on Canadian cities, and he is also engaged in studying Canadian immigration policy more generally and comparing it with similar policies in other countries.

Connie Ho is a researcher with the Ethno-Cultural Council of Calgary and a graduate of Concordia University. Her research interests are voluntary associations, civic participation, ethnicity, and immigration. She recently completed a paper entitled "Is Canada 'Moving toward an Integrated and Transparent Approach to the Recognition of Foreign Credentials' As It Claims?" Currently, she is working on a project entitled "Claiming Citizenship: Building Civic Participation and Active Citizenship in Calgary's Ethno-Cultural Communities."

Dirk Hoerder teaches North American social history and history of migrations at Paris 8 (Université Vincennes–Saint-Denis) and at the University of Bremen in the Department of Social Sciences. He has been director of the Labor Migration Project. His areas of interest are the history of worldwide migration systems and the sociology of migrant acculturation. He has published *Creating Societies: Immigrant Lives in Canada* (1999), a study of immigrant acculturation as seen through letters, diaries, and autobiographies. His *Cultures in Contact: European and World Migrations, 11th Century to the 1990s* (2002) received the Social Science History Association's Sharlin Prize for best book in social history.

Audrey Kobayashi is a professor and Queen's Research Chair in the Department of Geography at Queen's University. She is the principal investigator (with David Ley, Valerie Preston, and Myer Siemiatycki) of a research project on Hong Kong immigration to Canada. She has published widely on immigration, racism, employment equity, and human rights; recently she coedited (with Philomena Essed and David Goldberg) the *Blackwell Companion to Gender Studies* (2005). She is editor of the *Annals of the Association of American Geographers: People, Place and Region.*

Micheline Labelle has a PhD in anthropology. She is a professor of sociology at the Université du Québec à Montréal (UQAM). She currently heads the Centre de recherche sur l'immigration, l'ethnicité et la citoyenneté (CRIEC) and the Observatoire international sur le racisme et les discriminations at UQAM. Between 1993 and 1996, she held the Concordia-UQAM Chair in Ethnic Studies. She has published numerous articles on ethnic relations, multiculturalism, and integration in the Canadian and Quebec contexts, nationalism, diversity and citizenship, ethnic mobilization, racism and racialization processes, and transnationalism and diversity. She recently coedited two books: *Le devoir de mémoire et les politiques du pardon* (2005) and *Contestation transnationale, diversité et citoyenneté dans l'espace québécois* (2004). She is a member of the administration of the Association internationale des études québécoises.

David Ley is Canada Research Chair of Geography at the University of British Columbia. His current research examines the social geographies of immigration and has appeared in recent issues of *Global Networks, Annals of the Association of American Geographers, Urban Studies, Die Erde,* and *Transactions of the Institute of British Geographers.* His books include *The New Middle Class and the Remaking of the Central City, Neighbourhood Organizations and the Welfare State,* with Shlomo Hasson (1994), and *Millionaire Migrants,* a forthcoming study of business immigrants to Canada from East Asia.

Kim Matthews is a PhD candidate in sociology at McMaster University in Hamilton, Ontario, where she holds a Social Sciences and Humanities Research Council of Canada Doctoral Fellowship. Her dissertation is a comparative study of Ismailis of Indian origin in Toronto and Montreal. Her article "Boundaries of Diaspora Identity: The Case of Central and East African-Asians in Canada" was published in *Communities across Borders: New Immigrants and Transnational Cultures,* edited by Paul Kennedy and Victor Roudometof (2002). Her research interests include transnationalism, diasporas, globalization, race and ethnic relations, identity, and multiculturalism.

Dhiru Patel is a senior policy officer in the federal Department of Canadian Heritage, addressing policy and research issues that relate to the growing diversity of Canadian society. His *Dealing with Interracial Conflict: Policy Alternatives* (1980) made a significant contribution to the development of the federal government's policy on racism, leading to changes in its policy of multiculturalism. Dr. Patel has presented papers at national and international forums on identity, belonging, globalization, citizenship, and transnationalism, particularly as they relate to the younger generations. He is currently working on a chapter on Canadian public policy on racism for a forthcoming edited volume on racism in Canada.

Dwaine E. Plaza is an associate professor at Oregon State University in the Department of Sociology. He completed a doctorate at York University in Toronto in 1996. He went on to do a postdoctoral fellowship at Oxford Brookes University in 1997. Since then he has lived in Oregon. He has written extensively on the topic of Caribbean migration within the international diaspora. His published articles include "In Pursuit of the Mobility Dream: Second Generation British/Caribbeans Returning to Jamaica and Barbados" (2002), "A Socio-historic Examination of Caribbean Migration to Canada: Moving to the Beat of Changes in Immigration Policy" (2001), and "Transnational Grannies: The Changing Family Responsibility of Elderly African Caribbean-Born Women Resident in Britain" (2000). He is a coeditor of the book *Returning to the Source: The Final Stage of the Caribbean Migration Circuit* (2006).

Valerie Preston is a professor of geography at York University. Her research and teaching interests include the impacts of immigration on contemporary Canadian cities, transnational migration and citizenship, gender and urban labour markets, feminist geography, and urban social geography. Her most recent articles include coauthored publications about the withdrawal of highly skilled immigrant women from Canadian labour markets, the effects of transnationalism on women's civic participation, and feminist views of urban geography. She is currently coediting a special issue of *Geojournal* about spatial aspects of gender-based planning and policy analysis.

François Rocher is a professor of political science at Carleton University. In 2001-02 he was president of the Société québécoise de science politique and from 2002 to 2005 director of the School of Canadian Studies at Carleton University. His research interests include constitutional politics in Canada, Canadian identity, Canadian federalism, and citizenship. He is the coeditor of *Contestation transnationale, diversité et citoyenneté dans l'espace québécois* (2004), *The Conditions of Diversity in Multinational Democracies* (2003), and *New Trends in Canadian Federalism* (2003).

Vic Satzewich is a professor of sociology at McMaster University and past president of the Canadian Sociology and Anthropology Association. His research interests are in the areas of immigration policy and immigrant settlement, racism, migrant farm workers, Aboriginal peoples, and Ukrainian communities. His books include *The Ukrainian Diaspora* (2002), *First Nations: Race, Class and Gender Relations*, with Terry Wotherspoon (2000), and *Racism and the Incorporation of Foreign Labour: Farm Labour Migration to Canada since 1945* (1991). He is also the editor of *Deconstructing a Nation: Immigration, Multiculturalism and Racism in '90s Canada* (1990) and *Racism and Social Inequality in Canada* (1998).

Stuart Schoenfeld is a professor of sociology at Glendon College, York University. He has written extensively on contemporary Judaism, with a particular emphasis on bar and bat mitzvah as folk rituals and on Jewish life in Canada. He is also a scholar of contemporary environmental issues, with a current project on environment and peace building in the Middle East.

William Shaffir is a professor in the Department of Sociology at McMaster University. He is the author of books and articles in the areas of Hassidic Jews, professional socialization, methods of field research, religious conversion and disaffiliation, and ethnic tensions and violence. His most recent study examines how incumbents who are not re-elected cope with defeat at the polls and how this experience is rationalized. Among his current research are two projects: the first examines how Hassidic communities contend with social change that impacts their religion and organization; and the second, how a metropolitan police service organizes its work and activities for policing an increasingly diversified ethnic and racial population. Finally, he is a coeditor of *Doing Ethnography: Researching Everyday Life* (2005).

Myer Siemiatycki is a professor in the Department of Politics and Public Administration at Ryerson University, where he is director of the Master's Program in Immigration and Settlement Studies. His research explores immigrant and minority community civic engagement. He has authored and coauthored studies of minority political representation, minority-religion claims on public space, urban citizenship in Toronto, and transnationalism among Hong Kong Canadians.

Alan B. Simmons is a sociologist at York University in Toronto. His research and teaching interests include globalization and international migration, transnational migrant communities in the Americas, and immigrant economic and cultural incorporation in Canada. His books include *Journeys of Fear: Refugee Return and National Transformation in Guatemala*, with Liisa North (1999), and *International Migration and Human Rights in North America: The Impact of Free Trade and Restructuring* (1996). Reports from his ongoing research on Central American immigrants in Toronto, Latin American youth in Canada, and remittance flows from Caribbean communities in Montreal and Toronto may be found at http://www.arts.yorku.ca/soci/asimmons/cv/cv.html.

Pamela Sugiman is an associate professor of sociology at Ryerson University. She received a PhD in sociology from the University of Toronto in 1991. She is the author of *Labour's Dilemma: The Gender Politics of Auto Workers in Canada, 1937-1979* (1994), in addition to a number of articles on the experiences of Japanese Canadians during the Second World War. She is currently writing about the relationship between personal memory and collective history and about the intergenerational transmission of memory. She is also completing a book about Japanese Canadian women's memories of war.

Sarah V. Wayland completed a PhD in political science at the University of Maryland in 1995. She has published scholarly articles on various aspects of immigration, citizenship, and diaspora politics, most recently in *Canadian Ethnic Studies* (2003) and *Review of International Studies* (2004). For 2005-06, she is the Community Scholar in Law Reform of the Law Commission of Canada and the Community Foundations of Canada, researching legal and policy barriers to the settlement of newcomers.

Morton Weinfeld is a professor of sociology at McGill University, where he holds the Chair in Canadian Ethnic Studies. He received his PhD from Harvard University in 1977, the year that he arrived at McGill. He has published widely on ethnicity and public policy and on the sociology of Jewish life. Among his most recent books are *Like Everyone Else but Different: The Paradoxical Success of Canadian Jews* (2001) and *Still Moving: Recent Jewish Migration in Comparative Perspective*, with Daniel Elazar (2000).

Daphne Winland is an associate professor of anthropology at York University. She is the author of numerous articles and book chapters on Ontario Mennonites, Laotian Hmong refugees, and most recently, transnational politics among diasporic and homeland Croats. These appear in such journals as *Diaspora, American Ethnologist, Ethnopolitics, Canadian Review of Sociology and Anthropology*, and the *Journal of Historical Sociology*. The results of her Croatian research are also contained in her forthcoming book, *The Politics of Desire and Disdain: Croats between "Home" and "Homeland."* Her current project investigates contemporary Croatians' struggles to reinvent themselves as Europeans in the changing political, social, and cultural landscape of postcommunist eastern Europe.

Lloyd Wong is an associate professor of sociology at the University of Calgary and the Social and Cultural Domain leader at the Prairie Centre of Excellence for Research on Immigration and Integration. His research interests include racism and ethnic discrimination, immigration, Chinese ethnic entrepreneurship, and transnationalism and citizenship. Recent articles on transnational social space, the global immigration marketplace, and transnational enterprises appear in *International Migration, Asian and Pacific Migration Journal*, and the *International Journal of Urban and Regional Research*. Recent book chapters appear in *Changing Canada: Political Economy as Transformation*, with V. Satzewich, edited by Wallace Clement and Leah Vosko (2003); and *Street Protests and Fantasy Parks: Globalization, Culture, and the State*, edited by Janice Stein and David Cameron (2002).

Index

Note: (t) denotes a table, (f) a figure

acculturation, 24, 37, 47, 84, 178. *See also* assimilation; integration
Adachi, Ken, 55
adaptation, theory of, 3-4
Africans, 117, 120, 134, 193, 288-90
Aiken, Sharryn, 235
Air Canada, 250-51, 251-52
Air India flight 182 bombing, 34, 232
Akenson, Donald, 2
Al-Ali, N., 189, 199
Aliweiwi, Jehad, 224
aliya, 278, 283-86, 289
Alliance Party, 175
American emigration to Canada, 164-79; background and context of, 165-67; citizenship, 167-70; and ties to US electoral politics, 174-77; US attitudes toward, 165; and war resisters, 170-73. *See also* United States
Amex (newspaper), 172, 173
Amnesty International, 125
Anthias, Floya, 2
anthropological studies, 73-74
anti-Semitism, 279, 290-93
Arab Canadians: and community of siege since 9/11, 216-17, 219-21, 222, 223; conflated with Muslims, 218-19; discrimination toward, 226-27, 233; and intensification of ethnic identity, 223-24; linked to anti-Semitism by Jews, 292, 293; and NGOs, 120, 121, 122, 125; politicization of, 224-25, 237; sense of belonging in Canada, 107, 122, 216-17, 221-22, 223, 231, 237, 238-39; ties to homeland, 225-26
Arar, Maher, 234
Argentines, 192, 195, 197

Asad, Talal, 227
assimilation: of immigrant groups, 23, 65, 67, 143, 158-59, 210, 294; as natural policy of nation-states, 48; studies of, 4, 35-36, 297-98. *See also* acculturation; integration
astronauts/astronaut families, 74, 97, 103, 247
Australia, 231, 266, 267, 274
Azores, 210, 211-12, 213

Ballard, R., 158
Barbados, 144-45. *See also* Caribbean community
Barbados Gays and Lesbians Against Discrimination (BGLAD), 144-45
Basch, Linda, 3
Bell, Carole, 107, 108
BGLAD (Barbados Gays and Lesbians Against Discrimination), 144-45
Bhatia, Sabeer, 153
Bilingualism and Biculturalism Royal Commission, 50
Bill C-36, 232-33
Black Youth in Action (BYIA), 120, 121, 125
Blanc, Cristina, 3
Bloemraad, I., 23
B'nai B'rith, 120, 124, 289, 290, 291
Bosnians, 263
Brah, Avtar, 239
British Columbia, Government of, 208
Bubrin, V., 273
Bush, Jeb, 175
business community: and discriminatory policies, 205, 226-27; family businesses, 42, 100, 102, 154; high-tech, 153, 154,

203; and integration with US after 9/11, 230, 235. *See also* capital flows of Chinese Canadians; entrepreneurship business immigration, 245, 248, 249, 254-57
BYIA (Black Youth in Action), 120, 121, 125

Cainkar, Louise, 226
Campani, G., 207
Canada, Government of: and Bill C-36, 232-33; and Chinese immigration, 243-44, 248; citizenship policy, 12, 49-50; immigrant surveys, 185-87, 252-59; immigration policy changes, 135-37, 147, 197, 206, 269; and Israel, 281, 282, 293; and Japanese Canadians in WWII, 52-53, 54-62, 63-64, 67; and Latin American immigration, 197; and multiculturalism, 1, 136; and NGOs, 123, 124; and policies concerning transnationals, 161, 162; and policies of integration with US, 226-27, 230-31, 234-36, 240n4, 293; policy of torture by proxy, 234; and political activism of immigrants, 176, 190-91, 264; racially motivated immigration, 205-6; reaction to 9/11, 221, 222, 232-35, 238; refugee policy, 192, 197; and transnational capitalism, 250, 251, 257; and US immigration, 166
Canadian Council for Refugees (CCR), 120
Canadian Federation of Nurses Unions, 239
Canadian Imperial Bank of Commerce (CIBC), 250, 251
Canadian Jewish Congress, 281
Canadian Multiculturalism Act (1988), 136
Canadian Togolese Community (CTC), 118, 121-22
capital flows of Chinese Canadians: after settling in Canada, 256-59; background of, 241; from capitalist class, 245-47, 248-52; in early years, 243-44; money brought into Canada, 252-56, 253(t), 255(t); from small and medium-sized business, 247-48. *See also* entrepreneurship
Carella, Tony, 214
Caribana parade, 145
Caribbean community, 130-48; background of, 130, 131, 134, 137, 146-47; and Canadian policy on, 135-37; and center of their culture, 138-39; and colonialism, 133-35; Indo-Caribbeans,

141-42, 143-44, 152, 159; links to other Caribbean communities, 82, 130-31; media of, 130, 149n2; political activism of, 191-92; racism toward, 132, 139-40, 147, 148; rate of arrival in Canada, 137-38; research literature on, 131-33, 182-83, 185; sources of tension inside, 140-46; in US, 134-35, 137-38, 147, 194
Castells, Manuel, 19, 115
Castles, S., 24, 162
CCJC (Co-operative Committee on Japanese Canadians), 57
CCR (Canadian Council for Refugees), 120
Centre for Research-Action on Race Relations (CRARR), 116, 117
Cesar, Carlos, 212
chain migration, 181, 189, 194, 197, 206-7
Chan, Kwok Bun, 246
Cheran, R., 29
Cheung Kong (Holdings) Ltd., 249-50
Chicago School of Sociology, 36
Chileans, 119, 190-91, 195
Chinese Canadians, 241-59; and citizenship, 101-2, 246, 250; discrimination toward, 105, 243; economic ties to homeland, 92, 105, 258; employment of, 96-97, 104-6, 242, 244-45; entrepreneurship of, 153, 243, 244-49, 256-58; and head tax, 123, 242, 243, 244; history of, 242-43, 244; immigration status, 95-96, 100, 244-45, 248, 254-56; links to family, 96, 97, 100, 102, 103-4, 243, 246-47, 248; money brought into Canada, 252-56, 253(t), 255(t), 256; money flow into Canada after settling, 256-59; national identity of, 100-101, 107-8, 109, 243, 259; and remittances, 100, 102, 186, 243, 258-59; V. Li's business empire, 249-52; in Vancouver, 82-84
Chrétien, Jean, 227, 251
CIBC, 250, 251
CIC (Citizenship and Immigration Canada), 252-56
CIEP (Comparative Immigrant Entrepreneurship Project), 74, 88-90
cities, 93-94, 245-46. *See also* suburbanization
citizenship: and Chinese, 101-2, 246, 250; effect of 9/11 on, 113, 169, 217; effect of globalism on, 111, 112, 116, 126-29, 161-62, 203, 283; effect of receiving states' policies on, 4, 12, 22-23, 49-50; effect of sending states' policies on, 21, 25-27, 101-2, 269; and Japanese

repatriation after WWII, 62-64, 65-66; link to travel to homeland, 82-84, 89; new conceptions of, 239, 283; and US immigrants to Canada, 167-70; in Vancouver survey, 84, 86, 87(t), 89. *See also* national identity and sense of belonging to Canada
Citizenship and Immigration Canada (CIC), 252-56, 253(t), 255(t)
civic participation, 100-101
civil-society, 126
civil-society organizations, 190, 191, 192. *See also* NGOs
"clash of civilizations" theory, 227-29, 236-37
class distinctions, 46, 78-81, 88. *See also* socio-economic status
Co-operative Committee on Japanese Canadians (CCJC), 57, 64
code-switching, 143, 158
Cohen, Rina, 5, 286-88
Cole, Sally, 210-11
Colombians, 192, 195, 197
colonialism, 133-35, 157
commercial investments, 106-8, 199
communications: of early immigrants, 39, 40-41, 42, 45; in the global age, 151, 203. *See also* cultural ties to homeland; family and transnational movement; Internet; travel to and from homeland
communities under siege, 216-17, 225-26
Comparative Immigrant Entrepreneurship Project (CIEP), 74, 88-90
CONACOH (Conseil national des citoyens et citoyennes d'origine haïtienne), 125
Concordia University riot, 291
configurations of transnational engagement, 182
Connor, W., 5
Conseil national des citoyens et citoyennes d'origine haïtienne (CONACOH), 125
consulates, 199
Cotler, Irwin, 291
CRARR (Centre for Research-Action on Race Relations), 116, 117
criminalization, 220, 233
Croatia, 26, 27, 264, 267, 271
Croatian Canadians, 261-77; background of, 261-62, 268-69; changing sense of their identity, 276-77; effect of war of independence on, 271-72, 274-76; ethnic pride of, 269-71, 274-75, 276; political activism in Canada, 268, 270-71, 272-74; political activism in homeland, 265-67; relations with Serbs, 273, 275-76; socio-

cultural ties to homeland, 269-70, 274-75
cross-cultural identification, 143
CTC (Canadian Togolese Community), 121-22
Cuba, 31, 36
cultural blending, 178
cultural pluralism. *See* multiculturalism
cultural ties to homeland: of Arabs/Muslims since 9/11, 225-26; of Caribbean immigrants, 130-31, 143; of Croatians, 269-70; of Hong Kong immigrants with homeland, 100; of Italians, 208; between migrant and homeland, 42, 43, 151; of South Asians, 158-59; of US immigrants in Canada, 167, 170
cultural transfer, 36
"cumulative causation," 194

DA (Democrats Abroad), 174-76
DAC (Democrats Abroad Canada), 174, 175, 176
Danforth, L., 264
Dashevsky, A, 165
de Kerckhove, D., 161, 162
democracies/democratic institutions, 21, 33, 51-52, 67, 162, 177
Democrats Abroad Canada (DAC), 174, 175, 176
Democrats Abroad (DA), 174-76
descendants of immigrants. *See* second generation immigrants
Deshpande, Desh, 153
deterritorialization, 11-12, 74
diasporas: concepts of, 2, 236, 294-95; defined, 5-6, 19, 294; networks of, 119-21, 121-22; studies of, 3
Diaz, H., 191
discrimination: and formation of transnational communities, 24, 48; in hiring Arabs/Muslims, 226-27, 233; toward Chinese, 105, 243; toward Croatians, 269, 271; toward gays and lesbians, 144-45; toward US in Canada, 169-70, 177-78. *See also* race/racism
domestic servants and caregivers: in the global labour market, 203; in Quebec, 116, 123; in Toronto, 94; in Vancouver survey, 80, 82, 88
Dominion Act of 1923, 65
Dua, Enakshi, 216
dual citizenship: Canada's policy on, 12; impact on immigrants, 4, 22-23, 84; impact on sending states, 26; of specific immigrant groups, 65, 101-2, 168, 169; of US immigrants, 169

duration of settlement and transnationalism, 80, 81(t), 86, 88
dynastic states, 38, 47-48, 49

East Asians, 82, 88-89. *See also* Chinese
  Canadians; Japanese Canadians; Koreans
economic ties to homeland: and Chinese
  immigrants, 92, 105, 258; of Jews, 281-82,
  285-86. *See also* capital flows of Chinese
  Canadians; entrepreneurship; remittances
Ecuadoreans, 191
EDS (Ethnic Diversity Survey), 163n10,
  185, 186-87, 188(t)
education, 78-80, 96, 136, 140, 142, 282
Efaw, Fritz, 172
El Salvador, 28, 189-90, 191
electoral policies, 26-27, 49, 174, 177,
  213, 282
Elliot, Fraser, 251
Elmasry, Mohamed, 225
"emergent transnationalism," 199
employment: of Chinese Canadians, 96-
  97, 104-6, 242, 244-45; and effect of 9/11
  on Muslims, 226-27; and flow of money
  into Canada from, 256-58; of Hong
  Kong immigrants in Toronto, 104-6; as
  spur to emigration, 142, 208; and transnationalism in Vancouver, 79(t), 80,
  81(t), 83, 84, 85(t), 87(t); and unfairness
  toward immigrants, 116, 140; of US
  immigrants to Canada, 166, 167, 170
entrepreneurship: Chinese, 153, 243, 244-
  49, 256-58, 258; CIEP study, 74, 88-90;
  for early Canadian immigrants, 42, 49;
  as escape from life of labour, 10; and
  immigrant ties to homeland, 77; impact
  on cities, 93, 97, 100; of Japanese
  Canadians, 56; of Jewish Canadians,
  282; of Latin Americans, 185, 186; link
  to citizenship, 89, 206; link to ethnicity,
  82-84; links with homeland, 74, 77, 151,
  248-52; South Asian, 153-54; and US
  immigration to Canada, 166, 178;
  Vancouver study, 72, 78-88. *See also*
  capital flows of Chinese Canadians
ethnic communities and associations: of
  Caribbeans, 135; for Chinese Canadians,
  100-101; of Croatians, 269-70, 271;
  defined and examples of, 43-44; Jewish,
  44, 279-81, 288; of Latin Americans, 189;
  and maintaining identity, 50; and politics,
  32, 270-71. *See also* social organizations
Ethnic Diversity Survey (EDS), 163n10,
  185, 186-87, 188(t)
ethnic economies, 105-6, 244-45, 247
ethnic enclaves, 37, 38, 105

ethnicity/ethnic-identities: of Arabs and
  Muslims after 9/11, 223-24; of Caribbean
  community, 141-42; of Croatians, 265-
  66, 269, 270, 272, 274-75, 276-77; effect
  of multiculturalism on, 276; falling
  between one and another, 142-43, 143-
  44, 276; importance of, in Vancouver
  survey, 82-84; importance of Internet in,
  274; of Japanese, 67, 68; of Jews, 280-82,
  284, 286, 287, 288; link to family transnationalism, 82-84, 185, 187, 188(t);
  link to travel to homeland, 82-84, 89;
  lumping together, 143, 150, 277; of
  South Asians, 158-59; theories of, 21,
  38-39. *See also* citizenship; national
  identity and sense of belonging to Canada
ethnographic studies, 6, 73
Europe, 38, 82, 193. *See also* southern
  Europeans and specific nations and
  nationalities
Exclusion Act (Chinese Immigration Act),
  242, 244
exile orientation, 172-73

Faist, Thomas, 24, 39, 112, 248
family and transnational movement: of
  Arabs/Muslims, 226; of Caribbean
  communities, 147; of Chinese, 96, 97,
  100, 103-4, 243, 246-47, 248; of
  Ghanaian women, 204; of Japanese, 53-
  54, 68; of Jews, 281, 282, 289; of Latin
  Americans, 185-86, 187, 188(t), 189; link
  to ethnicity, 82-84, 185, 187, 188(t); of
  South Asians, 82, 152-53, 154, 155, 156,
  160; of US immigrants, 172; in Vancouver,
  78, 79(t), 81(t), 82, 83(t), 84, 85(t), 87(t)
family economies/businesses, 42, 100,
  102, 154
family reunification: and Chinese
  Canadians, 244; as immigration policy,
  137-38, 197, 206; as source of contact
  with homeland, 185, 189; stories of, 207
federated communities, 281
Filipinos, 32, 94
food as cultural tie, 42, 103, 130
foreign exchange, 42
France, 23, 46, 297
Friedmann, John, 71
friendship ties to homeland, 97, 103, 104,
  246-47
Fung, Robert, 251

gender equality and transnationalism,
  9-10, 132, 142. *See also* women
Germany, 23, 24, 25, 30, 31, 210
Geschiere, P., 162

Ghanaians, 94, 204
Gillis, John, 270
Gilroy, P., 132-33
Glenny, Misha, 266
global economy: effect of globalization on, 10, 202-3; effect of South Asian immigration on, 153-54; examples of, as spur to migration, 39, 41, 52, 134, 135
globalization: and areas of national/regional jurisdiction, 116, 126, 177; effect on citizenship, 111, 112, 116, 126-29, 161-62, 203, 283; effect on social relations, 19-20; examples of, 39, 71; and multiple ethnic-identities, 144; and racism, 114, 203, 292; of the world economy, 10, 202-3, 248-49
Globe and Mail, 291
"glocal" economy, 160, 161-62
Gold, Gerald, 286-88
Goldring, L., 10, 132
Gordon, Milton, 36
Great Britain. *See* United Kingdom
Greeks, 33, 159, 208, 215n4, 264
guanxi, 246-47, 251
Guarnizo, L.E., 29, 112
Guatemalans, 187, 189, 191
Guyana, 134, 136, 138-39, 141. *See also* Caribbean community

Hagan, John, 170-72, 173
Hage, Ghassan, 231
Haitians, 118, 119, 131. *See also* Caribbean community
Handlin, Oscar, 36
Harney, Robert, 39, 208
HDZ (Hrvatska Demokratska Zajednica), 266, 267, 274
head tax on Chinese, 123, 242, 243, 244
Helweg, A.W., 157
Hiebert, D., 184-85, 186
high-tech business, 153, 154, 203
historic wrongdoing, 116, 118, 120, 123. *See also* head tax on Chinese
home states. *See* sending states
homeland-oriented political organizations, 24
homosexuality, 144-45
Hondagneu-Sotelo, P., 204
Hondurans, 195
Hong Kong immigrants: description of immigration to Toronto, 91-92, 94-97, 98-99(t); transnational links in Toronto, 102-9; types of ties to homeland, 97, 100, 101-2. *See also* Chinese Canadians
host states. *See* receiving states
housing. *See* residential choices

Hrvatska Demokratska Zajednica (HDZ), 266, 267, 274
Hughes, Everett, 36
Hughes, Helen M., 36
Huguenots, 47
Hungarians, 263
Huntington, Samuel, 228
Husky Energy Inc., 249, 250, 251
hybrid identities, 11-12, 143, 236-37. *See also* dual citizenship; multiple citizenship

Iacovetta, F., 206, 207
identity markers, 116-17
Illusion of Difference (Reitz and Breton), 297
IMF (International Monetary Fund), 258
Immigration and Refugee Protection Act, 236
immigration history: from 1899 to 1910, 41-42, 45-46; from 1914 to 1960s, 49, 205-6; schools of, 36-38, 39-40, 51; of special groups, 47-48
immigration status: and Canadian policy, 135-37, 197; of Chinese immigrants, 95-96, 100, 244-45, 248, 254-56; of southern Europeans, 206; ties to transnationalism, 88; of US immigrants, 166
India: and Air India bombing, 34, 232; citizenship laws, 26, 162; and family businesses, 154; immigrants from, in the Caribbean, 134, 141; immigrants from, in Vancouver, 90n5. *See also* South Asians
Indo-Caribbeans, 141-42, 143-44, 152, 159
information networks, 40-42, 274. *See also* Internet
integration, 89, 286-87. *See also* acculturation; assimilation
International Federation for Human Rights, 117, 124-25
international law, 123
International Monetary Fund (IMF), 258
Internet, 118, 274, 282, 288, 290, 292
internment camps, 53
"intersectionality," 116
Iraq war, 169, 176, 238
Ireland, 212-13
Islam, 225. *See also* Muslim Canadians
Islamists, militant, 292
Israel: citizenship laws, 25-26; electoral policies, 26-27; as focus of anti-Semitism, 290-93; as focus of Jewish immigrant dreams, 278-79, 283-86, 287, 289-90; and Jewish globalized identity,

282-83; ties to Canada, 281, 282, 286-88, 293. *See also* Jewish Canadians
Italian Canadians, 204-5, 206, 207-8, 214
Italy, 42, 213-14
Itzigsohn, J., 73

Jamaica, 131, 134, 136, 138, 144. *See also* Caribbean community
Japanese Canadian Committee for Democracy (JCCD), 57
Japanese Canadians, 52-68; in internment camps, 52-53; proof of loyalty, 64-66; repatriation negotiations, 57-64; repatriation survey, 54-57; repercussions of repatriation policy, 66-68
JCCD (Japanese Canadian Committee for Democracy), 57
Jewish Canadians, 278-98; and anti-Semitism, 290-93; desire to return to Israel, 278-79, 283-86, 287, 289-90; and ethno-cultural communities, 44, 279-81, 288; history of, 279-80, 281, 294; and NGOs, 120; from South Africa, 288-90; ties to Israel, 281-82, 287, 290; Toronto Israelis, 286-88
Jonas, George, 220-21
Jones-Correa, M., 161
Jusdanis, G., 262

Kabbani, Rana, 225-26
Khawaja, Dr., 234
Khouri, Raja, 222, 237
King, Mackenzie, 59, 64, 67
King government, 54-55
Kitigawa, M., 52
Klimt, A., 210
Kobayashi, C., 62
Koopmans, R., 24
Koreans, 94
Kotkin, J., 154, 155
Kowalchuk, L., 191
Kurds, 30

labour markets, 41-42, 105, 106, 116, 203. *See also* employment
labour migrants: between 1899 and 1910, 41-42; to Canada, 49, 195; from Caribbean, 134, 142; Chinese, 242-43; in global age, 203; Mexican, 194; from southern Europe, 204-5, 208; in Toronto, 94, 105. *See also* domestic servants and caregivers; employment
Laguerre, Michel, 112
Lal, V., 154
land-use disputes, 106-8, 109

Landolt, Patricia, 28, 189-90
landsmannschaften, 279-80
language: and Caribbean identity, 143; and ethnic-identity of Jews, 287; and Portuguese identity, 211; and race in Toronto, 105, 107, 108; and trans-nationalism in Vancouver, 82-84, 85(t), 89; and US immigrants, 178
Latin Americans, 180-200; comparison of US and Canadian experience of, 180-81, 184, 192, 193, 197-98; ideas for further research, 199-200; links to homeland of, 29, 82, 185, 189, 204; major Canadian studies on, 184-87; Mexican immigration to US and Canada, 193-95; and refugee solidarity organizations, 190-92; remittances of, 183, 185, 186, 199; seen as homogenous group, 116-17; social organizations of, 183, 189, 190-91, 194, 198; statistics on, in Canada, 187, 195-97, 196(t); survey of research literature on, 73, 181-84; two case studies of, 187-90; in US, 180-83, 189, 193-98
Latvia, 27
Lau, John, 249
"law of return," 25, 26
LDL (Ligue des droits et libertés), 117, 118-19, 120, 124-25
Leveridge family, 42
Levitt, Cyril, 283-86
Levitt, P., 33
Lewis, Bernard, 228
Ley, D., 184-85, 186
Li, Victor, 241, 249-52
Li Ka-Shing, 249, 250
Lichter, M., 205
life-worlds, new, 44-45
life writings of migrants, 38, 41
Liodakis, N., 208-9
Lithuania, 27
longitudinal research, 7
Longitudinal Survey of Immigrants in Canada (LSIC), 185-86, 252, 256-59
loyalty: of Japanese immigrants, 53, 54, 57, 60, 64-66; of Jewish Canadians, 291; questions of, since 9/11, 216, 224, 229-30, 273-74. *See also* national identity and sense of belonging to Canada
LSIC (Longitudinal Survey of Canada), 185-86, 252, 256-59

Macedonians, 264
Macklin, Audrey, 232, 233, 234
MacNamara, Arthur, 60, 61, 63-64
Mahler, S., 10

malls controversy in Toronto, 106-8
Mandaville, Peter, 225
Mankekar, P., 132
"marginal man" hypothesis, 142-43
marginalization of identity, 142-43, 143-44, 147
marriage, intragroup, 145, 280
Martin, Paul, 251
Mata, F., 195
McDonough, Alexa, 230
McLeod, Lyn, 273
media: Caribbean, 130, 149n2; and Chinese capitalist class, 248; and "clash of civili-zations," 227-28, 228-29; coverage of anti-Semitism, 291; coverage of Asian-mall controversy in Toronto, 108; Croatian, 265, 274; fomenting racism after 9/11, 220-21, 222; Jewish, 278, 282, 288; South Asian, 155-56; and support of "war on terrorism," 235; of US immigrants, 167
Mennonites, 51
Mexicans: in Canada, 194-95, 197; and solidarity organizations, 191-92; in US, 183, 193-95. *See also* Latin Americans
Meyer, B., 162
Miki, R., 62
Mills, F., 132
minoritization, 7, 23-25, 48
minority defense groups, 115-17, 117-19
Mitchell, Humphrey, 57, 58, 60, 64
mobility, 4, 74, 77, 105, 203
Motwani, R., 154
multiculturalism: Canadian government policy of, 1, 136; effect of 9/11 on, 216, 222, 231, 238; ideas for future research on, 297; impact of, on immigrants, 23-24, 50-51, 216-17, 269, 276; link to transnationalism, 4; of South Asia, 154-55; in Toronto, 92, 109
multidimensional transnational relationships, 153(f)
multiple citizenship, 4, 12, 26
multiply differentiated neighbourhoods, 51
Muslim associations, 124
Muslim Canadians: and community of siege since 9/11, 216-17, 219-21, 222, 223, 224-26, 237-38; conflated with Arabs, 218-19; discrimination toward, 226-27, 233; and intensification of ethnic-identity, 220, 223-24, 225; linked to anti-Semitism by Jews, 292, 293; politicization of, 224-25, 237; sense of belonging to Canada, 107, 216-17, 221-22, 223, 231, 237, 238-39; ties to homeland, 225-26

nation-states: effect of fighting terror on, 217, 231; effect of globalization on, 20, 127-29, 162; immigration policies of, 46-47, 48; and mass migration in 19th century, 38, 40; policy factors effecting immigrants, 12, 20-25, 147; and tensions caused by transnationalism, 133, 282-83, 298. *See also* Canada, Government of; United States
national identity and sense of belonging to Canada: of Arabs/Muslims before 9/11, 107, 122; of Caribbeans, 134, 135, 147; of Chinese Canadians, 100-101, 107-8, 109, 243, 259; and citizenship laws, 12, 49-50, 50-51; of Croatians, 268-69, 271-72, 274-75, 276-77; effect of 9/11 on Canada's identity, 113, 229-30, 232, 239-40, 273-74; effect of 9/11 on Muslims and Arabs, 216-17, 219-21, 222, 223, 224-26, 231, 238-39; effect of political events on, 122, 171, 271; of Jews and Israelis, 283, 284-85, 288; of Latin Americans, 189; link with transnationalism, 84, 86, 87(t), 89, 159; mistaken notions of, 66-67; of second generation immigrants, 276; of South Asians, 154-55, 156, 158-59; of US immigrants, 168-69, 171-72
Natives rights, 124-25
Netherlands, 23, 24
NGOs (nongovernmental organizations): claims against minority rights made in Quebec, 115-17; motivations of, 10, 121-22; participation in diasporic networks, 119-21; strategies used by, 117-19; transnationalism of their strategy, 123-24, 125; use of international standards, 122-26
Nicaraguans, 191
9/11 effect: on Arab/Muslim communities, 216-17, 219-21, 222, 223, 224-26, 231, 237-38; and Bill C-36, 232-33, 234; and Canada-US integration, 227, 229, 230-31, 234-36; on citizenship, 113, 169, 217; and "clash of civilizations" theory, 227-29; on minorities, 113, 125, 159-60, 273-74; and questions of loyalty to Canada, 216, 224, 229-30, 273-74; and security measures, 113, 217, 220, 234-36; on transethnic cooperation, 238-40; on transnationalism, 8, 162, 216-18, 219, 298
Nolin, Catherine, 187, 189
nongovernmental organizations. *see* NGOs
Nonini, D., 219, 246

Northern Passage: American Vietnam War Resisters in Canada (Hagan), 170-71

OAS (Organization of American States), 120
Ong, A., 217, 219, 246, 262
Organization of American States (OAS), 120
Ortiz, Fernando, 36
Østergaard-Nielsen, E., 24

Palestinians, 119-20
Parekh, B., 157, 161
passports, 102
perceived transnational communities, 53
Pessar, P., 10
Pickersgill, T.B., 54, 55, 60, 61
place-of-origin networks, 189, 198
Poland/Polish immigrants, 26, 27, 48
political activism: of Arabs and Muslims, 224-25, 229, 232, 237-39; of Azorean immigrants, 212; benefits and drawbacks of, 33, 132, 237-38; of Chinese Canadians, 100, 101(t); of Croatian Canadians, 265-68, 270-71, 272-74; of East Europeans, 262-63, 263-64; impact of receiving states' policies on, 20-25; impact of sending states' policies on, 21, 25-27, 190, 265-68; of Jews, 281; of Latin American refugees, 190-92; reaction of receiving states to, 30-31, 33, 173-74, 214; and solidarity organizations, 190-92, 263; of South Asians, 156, 160; studies and surveys of, 31-33, 74, 262; of US immigrants in Canada, 168-69, 172-73, 176-77. *See also* NGOs; protest politics
political repression, 28, 48
political transnationalism, 18-19, 151. *See also* political activism
politics/political activism: of immigrants, 30
Portes, Alejandro, 3-4, 10, 39, 73-74, 182, 297-98
Portugal, 213
Portuguese Canadians: immigration to Canada, 208-9; racism toward, 205, 215n2; ties to homeland, 210-11, 213
positionality, 223, 268-69, 271, 276-77
postnationalism, 127-29
Premji, Aziz, 153
Pries, L., 5
Progressive Conservative Party, 175
Project Thread, 234
property holding, 78-87, 82-84, 185
protest politics: actors in, 114-15; background to, 111-12, 112-14; claims made against Quebec society, 115-17; and diasporic networks, 119-21; motivations for, 121-22; strategies used in, 117-19; use of international standards in, 122-26. *See also* NGOs; political activism
Prussia, 48
psychological transnationalism, 187, 189

Quebec: actors in protest politics in, 114-15; background to protest politics in, 111-12; politics in, as spur to leave, 284; and sense of citizenship within, 127, 128; study on immigrants, 73

RA (Republicans Abroad), 174, 175, 176
RAC (Republicans Abroad Canada), 174, 175, 176
race/racism: anti-Semitism, 279, 290-93; and Asian retail development in Toronto, 107-8; in Canadian immigration policy, 45-46, 50, 133-34, 135, 136, 197, 205; and Caribbean communities, 132, 139-40, 147, 148; cause of transnationalism, 148, 225-26; and Chinese, 243; claims against, in Quebec, 114, 116-17, 123; and globalization, 114, 203, 292; international history of, 36, 113-14; and intragroup marriage, 280; and Japanese Canadians, 52-53, 55-56, 60, 66, 67; and Muslims since 9/11, 113, 216, 219-21, 222, 223-24, 233, 239; NGOs fight against, 117, 118, 124, 125; and Portuguese, 205, 215n2; and socioeconomic status, 105, 145; and South Asians, 143, 157-58; stereotyping people, 143, 205, 218, 221, 287
RCMP, 54, 55
receiving states: immigration process of, 28-29, 38; impact of political systems on immigrants, 21, 40, 48; policy factors affecting immigrants, 20-25, 31, 135-37, 166, 189, 194, 208; and political activism, 30-31, 33, 173-74, 214; repercussions of transnationalism for, 30-31, 33, 183, 298
refugees: acculturation process of, 47; in Canada, 51, 189, 197, 254-55, 263; NGOs and, 120, 123; political ties home of, 28, 189; seen as security threat, 235-36; and solidarity organizations, 190-92; studies on Latin American, 184, 189, 190; in Vancouver survey, 80, 88
religion/religious groups: and Arab/Muslim identity after 9/11, 220, 223-24, 225; and ethnic identity, 143, 279-80; and Jewish identity, 279-80, 282, 287, 289; research on, 4; in solidarity groups, 238

remittances: of Arabs/Muslims, 226; of Caribbeans, 130, 186; of Chinese, 100, 102, 186, 243, 258-59; of Ghanaian women, 204; of Hong Kong in Toronto, 102; of Latin Americans, 183, 185, 186, 199; link to ethnicity, 82-84, 185, 186; of Mexicans, 194; of southern Europeans, 211; of US immigrants, 178; in Vancouver survey, 77, 79-88
repatriation of Japanese: negotiations on, 57-64; and proof of loyalty, 64-66; repercussions of, 66-68; survey, 54-57
Republicans Abroad (RA), 174, 175, 176
Republicans Abroad Canada (RAC), 174, 175, 176
residential choices: of Caribbean community, 145-46; of Chinese, 103-4; of Jews, 280-81; of Latin Americans, 198-99
resistance identities, 115
retail development, 106-8
returnees: Croatian, 272, 275; Jewish, 278, 283-86, 287, 289; Portuguese, 210
reunification of families, 58-64, 66
Robinson, William, 249

St. Kitts, 132. *See also* Caribbean community
St. Laurent, Louis, 64, 67
Sandinista regime, 190, 191
Sassen, S., 5, 217
Saucedo, S.G., 73
Saxenian, A.L., 153
Schiller, Glick, 39
Schiller, Nina, 3
second generation immigrants: amount of political activity, 32-33, 101; cultural adaptation to new home, 43, 159; disputes with first-generation, 62, 117, 140, 146, 288; dropping politics of first-generation, 276, 288; losing touch with original culture, 186, 211, 214; and "marginal man" position, 142-43, 276; nisei Japanese, 52, 62-63, 66, 67; research on, 4, 297-98; southern European, 202, 209, 211
security measures after 9/11, 113, 217, 220, 234-36, 235-36
segmented identities, 143, 156, 158
segregation, 23, 24
selective engagement, 154-55
sending money home. *See* remittances
sending states: displaced as center of culture, 138-39; institutionalized associations with emigrants, 183, 189, 199, 211-13, 267, 272, 282; and political activism of nationals abroad, 156, 172-

73, 190-92, 266-67; prepares emigrants for departure, 41, 154, 210; repercussions of transnationalism for, 298. *See also* sending states' policies affecting emigrants
sending states' policies affecting emigrants: economics, 134-35, 197; freedom of expression and citizenship, 21, 25-27, 269; political instability, 190, 192, 195, 265-68; provoking discrimination toward, 169-70, 290-91, 293
Serbs, 263-64, 273, 275-76
sexual orientation, 144-45
Shaffir, William, 283-86
Shain, Y., 33
Sherazee, Amina, 232
Shohat, Ella, 237, 238
Siddiqui, Haroon, 230
Sifton, Clifford, 45-46
Simalchik, J., 190
Simpson, Jeffrey, 291
Sklair, L., 249
Slovaks, 43-44
Smith, M.P., 112
social fields. *See* social spaces, transnational
social organizations: of Chinese, 100, 101(t); created by immigrants, 93-94; of Croatians, 270-71, 272, 274-75; of Jews, 281; of Latin Americans, 183, 189, 190-91, 194, 198
social spaces, transnational: and acculturation, 24, 47; of Caribbeans, 138-39; and Chinese entrepreneurs, 247-48, 251; created by Hong Kong immigrants, 102-8; descriptions of, 5, 93, 151, 178, 203; different criteria for studying, 9, 74; Faist's theory of, 5, 39, 112, 248; as haven from oppression, 25, 68, 112, 204; of Jews, 294; of South Asians, 156; of US immigrants in Canada, 177, 178-79
socialism, 280
socialization, 37-38, 157, 276, 288
socio-economic status: of Caribbean community, 145-46; of Chinese Canadians, 97, 242, 254-56; of Portuguese Canadians, 208-9; and racism, 105, 145; of South Asians, 153-54; and transnationalism, 10-11; of US immigrants, 167
Šola, John, 273
solidarity organizations, 181, 190-92
Sopta, Marin, 273
Sopta, Mary, 273
South African Jews, 288-90
South Asians, 150-62; definition of, 150, 151-52; entrepreneurship of, 153-54;

further research needed on, 160-61; links to family and community, 82, 152-53, 154, 155, 156, 160; political activism of, 156, 160; and racism, 143, 157-58; socio-cultural values of, 156, 158-59
Southeast Asians, 82, 89
southern Europeans, 204-15; chain migration of, 206-7; links to homeland, 207-8, 210-14; Portuguese economic position in Canada, 208-9; and racist immigration policy, 205-6. *See also* specific nations and nationalities
Soviet Union, 263
"spatially immobile," 65
Spector, Norman, 291
Spiro, P., 12
Spivak, Gayatri, 219
Sri Lanka, 29, 30, 31. *See also* South Asians
Statham, P., 24
Stavenhagen, Rodolfo, 113-14
Stikeman Elliot, 251
Strauss, Stephen, 291
students, international, 258
suburbanization: of Caribbean community, 145-46; of Chinese Canadians, 103-4; of Mexicans in US, 194; in Vancouver and Toronto, 72, 97
Supreme Court of Canada, 64

Tambiah, S., 161
TCC (transnational capitalist class), 248-52
temporary migrants, 258
terrorism. *See* 9/11 effect
Thobani, Sunera, 229-30
Ting, James, 248
Togo/Togolese, 118, 119, 121-22
Tölölyan, K., 262
translocal cultures, 12, 38, 50, 151, 162
transnational capitalist class (TCC), 248-52
transnationalism: concepts of, 5-6, 18; defined, 151, 203; historical perspective on, 8-9; ideas for future research into, 110, 214-15, 296-98; methodology used for studying, 6-7; studies on, 3, 72-73, 112-14, 182-83, 204; theory first introduced, 3, 39-40. *See also* capital flows of Chinese Canadians; economic ties to homeland; entrepreneurship; ethnicity/ethnic-identities; family and transnational movement; national identity and sense of belonging to Canada; political activism; remittances; social spaces, transnational; travel to and from homeland and specific ethnic groups

transportation, 39
travel to and from homeland: of Arabs/ Muslims, 226-27; of Chinese, 100, 102, 243; of Jews, 282; of Latin Americans, 185, 189; link to citizenship and ethnicity, 82-84, 89; of South Asians, 155; of southern Europeans, 207, 210; of US immigrants, 167, 172; in Vancouver survey, 78-83, 85(t), 87(t), 88
Trinidad and Tobago, 134, 136, 138, 141, 144-45. *See also* Caribbean community
Trinity Time Investments Ltd., 250, 251
Troper, H., 206
Tudjman, Franjo, 266, 267, 273
Turkey, 30

Ukrainians, 45-46, 262-63
Uniformed and Overseas Citizens Absentee Voting Act (UOCAVA), 174
United Kingdom: and Canada's identity confusion with, 49-50; and Caribbean immigration, 134-35; emigration to Canada, 194, 297; multicultural policies of, 24; and South Asian immigration, 158, 159, 163n4
United Nations, 113, 120
United States: and Arab/Muslim reaction since 9/11, 226, 239; and Caribbean immigration, 134-35, 137-38, 147, 194; and Chinese immigration, 243, 246-47; and "clash of civilizations" policy, 227-28; closeness of Canada to, since 9/11, 226-27, 229, 230-31, 234-36, 240n4, 293; electoral policies of, 26, 49, 174, 177; foreign policies of, 31, 173, 176; and immigrant political activism, 31, 33, 173; immigration patterns compared to Canada, 1, 193-98, 296-97; institutionalized association with emigrants, 174-77; and Israel, 293; and Latin American immigration, 73, 180-83, 189, 193-98; and remittances, 258; schools of immigration study, 35-36, 74, 164; and South Asian immigration, 153, 160. *See also* American emigration to Canada
UOCAVA (Uniformed and Overseas Citizens Absentee Voting Act), 174
utopia, 44

van der Veer, P., 150
Van Hear, Nicholas, 5, 66
Vecoli, Rudolph J., 36
Vertovec, S., 4, 6, 112, 133, 151, 178, 212
village-level associations, 189, 198
visible minorities, 89, 219-21, 269
Volpe, Joe, 214

Waldinger, R., 205
Waller, Harold, 278-79
war, 44, 47
Waters, Malcolm C., 20
Weinreich, P., 158
Wente, Margaret, 229
Western Union, 258
women, 9-10, 132, 142, 204, 205-6
Wong, Bernard, 246-47
Wong, Madeleine, 204
World Conference against Racism
  (Durban), 118, 124, 125

yordim, 286-88
Yugoslavia, 27, 263-64, 264-65. *See also*
  Croatian Canadians; Serbs

Zionism: among Canadian Jews, 279, 280,
  290; among Israelis, 286; among South
  African Jews, 289; efforts to undermine,
  292-93

Printed and bound in Canada by Friesens
Set in Stone by Artegraphica Design Co. Ltd.
Copy editor: Robert Lewis
Proofreader: Deborah Kerr
Indexer: Adrian Mather

April 27/09